THE END
OF HISTORY
AND
THE
LAST
MAN

THE END OF HISTORY AND THE LAST MAN

Francis Fukuyama

HAMISH HAMILTON · LONDON

HAMISH HAMILTON LTD
Published by the Penguin Group
Penguin Books Ltd, 27 Wrights Lane, London W8 5TZ, England
Penguin Books USA Inc., 375 Hudson Street, New York, New York 10014, USA
Penguin Books Australia Ltd, Ringwood, Victoria, Australia
Penguin Books Canada Ltd, 10 Alcorn Avenue, Toronto, Ontario, Canada M4V 3B2
Penguin Books (NZ) Ltd, 182–190 Wairau Road, Auckland 10, New Zealand

Penguin Books Ltd, Registered Offices: Harmondsworth, Middlesex, England

First published in the United States of America by The Free Press 1992
First published in Great Britain by Hamish Hamilton Ltd 1992
3 5 7 9 10 8 6 4 2

Printed in England by Clays Ltd, St Ives plc

A CIP catalogue record for this book is available from the British Library

ISBN 0-241-13013-1

To Julia and David

CONTENTS

ACKNOWLEDGMENTS

The "End of History" would never have existed, either as an article or as this present book, without the invitation to deliver a lecture by that title during the 1988–89 academic year, extended by Professors Nathan Tarcov and Allan Bloom of the John M. Olin Center for Inquiry into the Theory and Practice of Democracy at the University of Chicago. Both have been long-time teachers and friends from whom I have learned an enormous amount over the years—starting with, but by no means limited to, political philosophy. That original lecture became a well-known article due, in no small measure, to the efforts of Owen Harries, editor of the journal *The National Interest,* and to the work of that journal's small staff. Erwin Glikes of the Free Press and Andrew Franklin of Hamish Hamilton provided crucial encouragement and advice in moving from the article to the book, and in the editing of the final manuscript.

The present volume has profited enormously from conversations and readings by any number of friends and colleagues. Most important of these has been Abram Shulsky, who will find many of his ideas and insights recorded here. I would like to pay special thanks to Irving Kristol, David Epstein, Alvin Bernstein, Henry Higuera, Yoshihisa Komori, Yoshio Fukuyama, and George Holmgren, all of whom took the time to read and comment on the manuscript. In addition, I would like to thank the many people— some of them known to me and many others not—who commented usefully on various aspects of the present thesis as it was presented in a variety of seminars and lectures in this country and abroad.

James Thomson, president of the RAND Corporation, was kind enough to provide me office space while drafting this book. Gary and Linda Armstrong took time out from writing their dissertations to help me in the collection of research materials, and provided valuable advice on a number of topics in the course of writing. Rosalie Fonoroff helped in the proofreading. In lieu of conventional thanks to a typist for helping to prepare the manuscript, I should perhaps acknowledge the work of the designers of the Intel 80386 microprocessor.

Last but most important, it was my wife, Laura, who encouraged me to write both the original article and the present book, and who has stood by me through all of the subsequent criticism and controversy. She has been a careful reader of the manuscript, and has contributed in innumerable ways to its final form and content. My daughter Julia and my son David, the latter of whom chose to be born as the book was being written, helped too, simply by being there.

By Way of an
Introduction

The distant origins of the present volume lie in an article entitled "The End of History?" which I wrote for the journal *The National Interest* in the summer of 1989.[1] In it, I argued that a remarkable consensus concerning the legitimacy of liberal democracy as a system of government had emerged throughout the world over the past few years, as it conquered rival ideologies like hereditary monarchy, fascism, and most recently communism. More than that, however, I argued that liberal democracy may constitute the "end point of mankind's ideological evolution" and the "final form of human government," and as such constituted the "end of history." That is, while earlier forms of government were characterized by grave defects and irrationalities that led to their eventual collapse, liberal democracy was arguably free from such fundamental internal contradictions. This was not to say that today's stable democracies, like the United States, France, or Switzerland, were not without injustice or serious social problems. But these problems were ones of incomplete implementation of the twin principles of liberty and equality on which modern democracy is founded, rather than of flaws in the principles themselves. While some present-day countries might fail to achieve stable liberal democracy, and others might lapse back into other, more primitive forms of rule like theocracy or military dictatorship, the *ideal* of liberal democracy could not be improved on.

The original article excited an extraordinary amount of commentary and controversy, first in the United States, and then in a series of countries as different as England, France, Italy, the Soviet Union, Brazil, South Africa, Japan, and South Korea. Criticism took every conceivable form, some of it based on simple misunderstanding of my original intent, and others penetrating more perceptively to the core of my argument.[2] Many people were confused in the first instance by my use of the word "history." Understanding history in a conventional sense as the occurrence of events, people pointed to the fall of the Berlin Wall, the Chinese communist crackdown in Tiananmen Square, and the Iraqi invasion of Kuwait as evidence that "history was continuing," and that I was *ipso facto* proven wrong.

And yet what I suggested had come to an end was not the occurrence of events, even large and grave events, but History: that is, history understood as a single, coherent, evolutionary process, when taking into account the experience of all peoples in all times. This understanding of History was most closely associated with the great German philosopher G. W. F. Hegel. It was made part of our daily intellectual atmosphere by Karl Marx, who borrowed this concept of History from Hegel, and is implicit in our use of words like "primitive" or "advanced," "traditional" or "modern," when referring to different types of human societies. For both of these thinkers, there was a coherent development of human societies from simple tribal ones based on slavery and subsistence agriculture, through various theocracies, monarchies, and feudal aristocracies, up through modern liberal democracy and technologically driven capitalism. This evolutionary process was neither random nor unintelligible, even if it did not proceed in a straight line, and even if it was possible to question whether man was happier or better off as a result of historical "progress."

Both Hegel and Marx believed that the evolution of human societies was not open-ended, but would end when mankind had achieved a form of society that satisfied its deepest and most fundamental longings. Both thinkers thus posited an "end of history": for Hegel this was the liberal state, while for Marx it was a communist society. This did not mean that the natural cycle of birth, life, and death would end, that important events would no longer happen, or that newspapers reporting them would cease to be published. It meant, rather, that there would be no further progress in the development of underlying principles and institutions, because all of the really big questions had been settled.

The present book is not a restatement of my original article, nor is it an effort to continue the discussion with that article's many critics and commentators. Least of all is it an account of the end of the Cold War, or any other pressing topic in contemporary politics. While this book is informed by recent world events, its subject returns to a very old question: Whether, at the end of the twentieth century, it makes sense for us once again to speak of a coherent and directional History of mankind that will eventually lead the greater part of humanity to liberal democracy? The answer I arrive at is yes, for two separate reasons. One has to do with economics, and the other has to do with what is termed the "struggle for recognition."

It is of course not sufficient to appeal to the authority of Hegel, Marx, or any of their contemporary followers to establish the validity of a directional History. In the century and a half since they wrote, their intellectual legacy has been relentlessly assaulted from all directions. The most profound thinkers of the twentieth century have directly attacked the idea that history is a coherent or intelligible process; indeed, they have denied the possibility that any aspect of human life is philosophically intelligible. We in the West have become thoroughly pessimistic with regard to the possibility of overall progress in democratic institutions. This profound pessimism is not accidental, but born of the truly terrible political events of the first half of the twentieth century—two destructive world wars, the rise of totalitarian ideologies, and the turning of science against man in the form of nuclear weapons and environmental damage. The life experiences of the victims of this past century's political violence—from the survivors of Hitlerism and Stalinism to the victims of Pol Pot—would deny that there has been such a thing as historical progress. Indeed, we have become so accustomed by now to expect that the future will contain bad news with respect to the health and security of decent, liberal, democratic political practices that we have problems recognizing good news when it comes.

And yet, good news has come. The most remarkable development of the last quarter of the twentieth century has been the revelation of enormous weaknesses at the core of the world's seemingly strong dictatorships, whether they be of the military-authoritarian Right, or the communist-totalitarian Left. From Latin America to Eastern Europe, from the Soviet Union to the Middle East and Asia, strong governments have been failing over the last two decades. And while they have not given way in all cases to stable liberal democracies, liberal democracy remains the only coherent political aspiration that spans different regions and cultures around the globe. In addition, liberal principles in economics—the "free market"—have spread, and have succeeded in producing unprecedented levels of material prosperity, both in industrially developed countries and in countries that had been, at the close of World War II, part of the impoverished Third World. A liberal revolution in economic thinking has sometimes preceded, sometimes followed, the move toward political freedom around the globe.

All of these developments, so much at odds with the terrible history of the first half of the century when totalitarian governments of the Right and Left were on the march, suggest the need to look again at the question of whether there is some deeper connecting thread underlying them, or whether they are merely accidental instances of good luck. By raising once again the question of whether there is such a thing as a Universal History of mankind, I am resuming a discussion that was begun in the early nineteenth century, but more or less abandoned in our time because of the enormity of events that mankind has experienced since then. While drawing on the ideas of philosophers like Kant and Hegel who have addressed this question before, I hope that the arguments presented here will stand on their own.

This volume immodestly presents not one but *two* separate efforts to outline such a Universal History. After establishing in Part I why we need to raise once again the possibility of Universal History, I propose an initial answer in Part II by attempting to use modern natural science as a regulator or mechanism to explain the directionality and coherence of History. Modern natural science is a useful starting point because it is the only important social activity that by common consensus is both cumulative and directional, even if its ultimate impact on human happiness is ambiguous. The progressive conquest of nature made possible with the development of the scientific method in the sixteenth and seventeenth centuries has proceeded according to certain definite rules laid down not by man, but by nature and nature's laws.

The unfolding of modern natural science has had a uniform effect on all societies that have experienced it, for two reasons. In the first place, technology confers decisive military advantages on those countries that possess it, and given the continuing possibility of war in the international system of states, no state that values its independence can ignore the need for defensive modernization. Second, modern natural science establishes a uniform horizon of economic production possibilities. Technology makes possible the limitless accumulation of wealth, and thus the satisfaction of an ever-expanding set of human desires. This process guarantees an increasing homogenization of all human societies, regardless of their historical origins or cultural inheritances. All countries undergoing economic modernization must increasingly resemble

one another: they must unify nationally on the basis of a centralized state, urbanize, replace traditional forms of social organization like tribe, sect, and family with economically rational ones
based on function and efficiency, and provide for the universal
education of their citizens. Such societies have become increasingly linked with one another through global markets and the
spread of a universal consumer culture. Moreover, the logic of
modern natural science would seem to dictate a universal evolution in the direction of capitalism. The experiences of the Soviet
Union, China, and other socialist countries indicate that while
highly centralized economies are sufficient to reach the level of
industrialization represented by Europe in the 1950s, they are
woefully inadequate in creating what have been termed complex
"post-industrial" economies in which information and technological innovation play a much larger role.

But while the historical mechanism represented by modern
natural science is sufficient to explain a great deal about the character of historical change and the growing uniformity of modern
societies, it is not sufficient to account for the phenomenon of
democracy. There is no question but that the world's most developed countries are also its most successful democracies. But while
modern natural science guides us to the gates of the Promised
Land of liberal democracy, it does not deliver us to the Promised
Land itself, for there is no economically necessary reason why
advanced industrialization should produce political liberty. Stable
democracy has at times emerged in pre-industrial societies, as it
did in the United States in 1776. On the other hand, there are
many historical and contemporary examples of technologically
advanced capitalism coexisting with political authoritarianism,
from Meiji Japan and Bismarckian Germany to present-day Singapore and Thailand. In many cases, authoritarian states are capable of producing rates of economic growth unachievable in
democratic societies.

Our first effort to establish the basis for a directional history is
thus only partly successful. What we have called the "logic of
modern natural science" is in effect an economic interpretation of
historical change, but one which (unlike its Marxist variant) leads
to capitalism rather than socialism as its final result. The logic of
modern science can explain a great deal about our world: why we
residents of developed democracies are office workers rather than
peasants eking out a living on the land, why we are members of

labor unions or professional organizations rather than tribes or clans, why we obey the authority of a bureaucratic superior rather than a priest, why we are literate and speak a common national language.

But economic interpretations of history are incomplete and unsatisfying, because man is not simply an economic animal. In particular, such interpretations cannot really explain why we are democrats, that is, proponents of the principle of popular sovereignty and the guarantee of basic rights under a rule of law. It is for this reason that the book turns to a second, parallel account of the historical process in Part III, an account that seeks to recover the whole of man and not just his economic side. To do this, we return to Hegel and Hegel's non-materialist account of History, based on the "struggle for recognition."

According to Hegel, human beings like animals have natural needs and desires for objects outside themselves such as food, drink, shelter, and above all the preservation of their own bodies. Man differs fundamentally from the animals, however, because in addition he desires the desire of other men, that is, he wants to be "recognized." In particular, he wants to be recognized as a *human being*, that is, as a being with a certain worth or dignity. This worth in the first instance is related to his willingness to risk his life in a struggle over pure prestige. For only man is able to overcome his most basic animal instincts—chief among them his instinct for self-preservation—for the sake of higher, abstract principles and goals. According to Hegel, the desire for recognition initially drives two primordial combatants to seek to make the other "recognize" their humanness by staking their lives in a mortal battle. When the natural fear of death leads one combatant to submit, the relationship of master and slave is born. The stakes in this bloody battle at the beginning of history are not food, shelter, or security, but pure prestige. And precisely because the goal of the battle is not determined by biology, Hegel sees in it the first glimmer of human freedom.

The desire for recognition may at first appear to be an unfamiliar concept, but it is as old as the tradition of Western political philosophy, and constitutes a thoroughly familiar part of the human personality. It was first described by Plato in the *Republic*, when he noted that there were three parts to the soul, a desiring part, a reasoning part, and a part that he called *thymos*, or "spiritedness." Much of human behavior can be explained as a com-

bination of the first two parts, desire and reason: desire induces
men to seek things outside themselves, while reason or calculation
shows them the best way to get them. But in addition, human
beings seek recognition of their own worth, or of the people,
things, or principles that they invest with worth. The propensity
to invest the self with a certain value, and to demand recognition
for that value, is what in today's popular language we would call
"self-esteem." The propensity to feel self-esteem arises out of the
part of the soul called *thymos*. It is like an innate human sense of
justice. People believe that they have a certain worth, and when
other people treat them as though they are worth less than that,
they experience the emotion of *anger*. Conversely, when people
fail to live up to their own sense of worth, they feel *shame,* and
when they are evaluated correctly in proportion to their worth,
they feel *pride*. The desire for recognition, and the accompanying
emotions of anger, shame, and pride, are parts of the human
personality critical to political life. According to Hegel, they are
what drives the whole historical process.

By Hegel's account, the desire to be recognized as a human
being with dignity drove man at the beginning of history into a
bloody battle to the death for prestige. The outcome of this battle
was a division of human society into a class of masters, who were
willing to risk their lives, and a class of slaves, who gave in to their
natural fear of death. But the relationship of lordship and bondage, which took a wide variety of forms in all of the unequal,
aristocratic societies that have characterized the greater part of
human history, failed ultimately to satisfy the desire for recognition of either the masters or the slaves. The slave, of course, was
not acknowledged as a human being in any way whatsoever. But
the recognition enjoyed by the master was deficient as well, because he was not recognized by other masters, but slaves whose
humanity was as yet incomplete. Dissatisfaction with the flawed
recognition available in aristocratic societies constituted a "contradiction" that engendered further stages of history.

Hegel believed that the "contradiction" inherent in the relationship of lordship and bondage was finally overcome as a result
of the French and, one would have to add, American revolutions.
These democratic revolutions abolished the distinction between
master and slave by making the former slaves their own masters
and by establishing the principles of popular sovereignty and the
rule of law. The inherently unequal recognition of masters and

slaves is replaced by universal and reciprocal recognition, where every citizen recognizes the dignity and humanity of every other citizen, and where that dignity is recognized in turn by the state through the granting of *rights*.

This Hegelian understanding of the meaning of contemporary liberal democracy differs in a significant way from the Anglo-Saxon understanding that was the theoretical basis of liberalism in countries like Britain and the United States. In that tradition, the prideful quest for recognition was to be subordinated to enlightened self-interest—desire combined with reason—and particularly the desire for self-preservation of the body. While Hobbes, Locke, and the American Founding Fathers like Jefferson and Madison believed that rights to a large extent existed as a means of preserving a private sphere where men can enrich themselves and satisfy the desiring parts of their souls,[3] Hegel saw rights as ends in themselves, because what truly satisfies human beings is not so much material prosperity as recognition of their status and dignity. With the American and French revolutions, Hegel asserted that history comes to an end because the longing that had driven the historical process—the struggle for recognition—has now been satisfied in a society characterized by universal and reciprocal recognition. No other arrangement of human social institutions is better able to satisfy this longing, and hence no further progressive historical change is possible.

The desire for recognition, then, can provide the missing link between liberal economics and liberal politics that was missing from the economic account of History in Part II. Desire and reason are together sufficient to explain the process of industrialization, and a large part of economic life more generally. But they cannot explain the striving for liberal democracy, which ultimately arises out of *thymos,* the part of the soul that demands recognition. The social changes that accompany advanced industrialization, in particular universal education, appear to liberate a certain demand for recognition that did not exist among poorer and less educated people. As standards of living increase, as populations become more cosmopolitan and better educated, and as society as a whole achieves a greater equality of condition, people begin to demand not simply more wealth but recognition of their status. If people were nothing more than desire and reason, they would be content to live in market-oriented authoritarian states like Franco's Spain, or a South Korea or Brazil under military rule. But they also have a thymotic pride in their own self-worth, and this leads them to demand democratic governments that treat them like adults rather than children, recognizing their autonomy as free individuals. Communism is being superseded by liberal democracy in our time because of the realization that the former provides a gravely defective form of recognition.

An understanding of the importance of the desire for recognition as the motor of history allows us to reinterpret many phenomena that are otherwise seemingly familiar to us, such as culture, religion, work, nationalism, and war. Part IV is an attempt to do precisely this, and to project into the future some of the different ways that the desire for recognition will be manifest. A religious believer, for example, seeks recognition for his particular gods or sacred practices, while a nationalist demands recognition for his particular linguistic, cultural, or ethnic group. Both of these forms of recognition are less rational than the universal recognition of the liberal state, because they are based on arbitrary distinctions between sacred and profane, or between human social groups. For this reason, religion, nationalism, and a people's complex of ethical habits and customs (more broadly "culture") have traditionally been interpreted as obstacles to the establishment of successful democratic political institutions and free-market economies.

But the truth is considerably more complicated, for the success of liberal politics and liberal economics frequently rests on irrational forms of recognition that liberalism was supposed to overcome. For democracy to work, citizens need to develop an irrational pride in their own democratic institutions, and must also develop what Tocqueville called the "art of associating," which rests on prideful attachment to small communities. These communities are frequently based on religion, ethnicity, or other forms of recognition that fall short of the universal recognition on which the liberal state is based. The same is true for liberal economics. Labor has traditionally been understood in the Western liberal economic tradition as an essentially unpleasant activity undertaken for the sake of the satisfaction of human desires and the relief of human pain. But in certain cultures with a strong work ethic, such as that of the Protestant entrepreneurs who created European capitalism, or of the elites who modernized Japan after the Meiji restoration, work was also undertaken for the sake of recognition. To this day, the work ethic in many

Asian countries is sustained not so much by material incentives, as by the recognition provided for work by overlapping social groups, from the family to the nation, on which these societies are based. This suggests that liberal economics succeeds not simply on the basis of liberal principles, but requires irrational forms of *thymos* as well.

The struggle for recognition provides us with insight into the nature of international politics. The desire for recognition that led to the original bloody battle for prestige between two individual combatants leads logically to imperialism and world empire. The relationship of lordship and bondage on a domestic level is naturally replicated on the level of states, where nations as a whole seek recognition and enter into bloody battles for supremacy. Nationalism, a modern yet not-fully-rational form of recognition, has been the vehicle for the struggle for recognition over the past hundred years, and the source of this century's most intense conflicts. This is the world of "power politics," described by such foreign policy "realists" as Henry Kissinger.

But if war is fundamentally driven by the desire for recognition, it stands to reason that the liberal revolution which abolishes the relationship of lordship and bondage by making former slaves their own masters should have a similar effect on the relationship between states. Liberal democracy replaces the irrational desire to be recognized as greater than others with a rational desire to be recognized as equal. A world made up of liberal democracies, then, should have much less incentive for war, since all nations would reciprocally recognize one another's legitimacy. And indeed, there is substantial empirical evidence from the past couple of hundred years that liberal democracies do not behave imperialistically toward one another, even if they are perfectly capable of going to war with states that are not democracies and do not share their fundamental values. Nationalism is currently on the rise in regions like Eastern Europe and the Soviet Union where peoples have long been denied their national identities, and yet within the world's oldest and most secure nationalities, nationalism is undergoing a process of change. The demand for national recognition in Western Europe has been domesticated and made compatible with universal recognition, much like religion three or four centuries before.

The fifth and final part of this book addresses the question of the "end of history," and the creature who emerges at the end, the "last man." In the course of the original debate over the *National Interest* article, many people assumed that the possibility of the end of history revolved around the question of whether there were viable alternatives to liberal democracy visible in the world today. There was a great deal of controversy over such questions as whether communism was truly dead, whether religion or ultranationalism might make a comeback, and the like. But the deeper and more profound question concerns the goodness of liberal democracy itself, and not only whether it will succeed against its present-day rivals. Assuming that liberal democracy is, for the moment, safe from external enemies, could we assume that successful democratic societies could remain that way indefinitely? Or is liberal democracy prey to serious internal contradictions, contradictions so serious that they will eventually undermine it as a political system? There is no doubt that contemporary democracies face any number of serious problems, from drugs, homelessness, and crime to environmental damage and the frivolity of consumerism. But these problems are not obviously insoluble on the basis of liberal principles, nor so serious that they would necessarily lead to the collapse of society as a whole, as communism collapsed in the 1980s.

Writing in the twentieth century, Hegel's great interpreter, Alexandre Kojève, asserted intransigently that history had ended because what he called the "universal and homogeneous state"— what we can understand as liberal democracy—definitely solved the question of recognition by replacing the relationship of lordship and bondage with universal and equal recognition. What man had been seeking throughout the course of history—what had driven the prior "stages of history"—was recognition. In the modern world, he finally found it, and was "completely satisfied." This claim was made seriously by Kojève, and it deserves to be taken seriously by us. For it is possible to understand *the* problem of politics over the millennia of human history as the effort to solve the problem of recognition. Recognition is the central problem of politics because it is the origin of tyranny, imperialism, and the desire to dominate. But while it has a dark side, it cannot simply be abolished from political life, because it is simultaneously the psychological ground for political virtues like courage, public-spiritedness, and justice. All political communities must make use of the desire for recognition, while at the same time protecting themselves from its destructive effects. If contemporary constitutional government has indeed found a formula whereby all are recognized in a way that nonetheless avoids the emergence of tyranny, then it would indeed have a special claim to stability and longevity among the regimes that have emerged on earth.

But is the recognition available to citizens of contemporary liberal democracies "completely satisfying?" The long-term future of liberal democracy, and the alternatives to it that may one day arise, depend above all on the answer to this question. In Part V we sketch two broad responses, from the Left and the Right, respectively. The Left would say that universal recognition in liberal democracy is necessarily incomplete because capitalism creates economic inequality and requires a division of labor that *ipso facto* implies unequal recognition. In this respect, a nation's absolute level of prosperity provides no solution, because there will continue to be those who are relatively poor and therefore invisible as human beings to their fellow citizens. Liberal democracy, in other words, continues to recognize equal people unequally.

The second, and in my view more powerful, criticism of universal recognition comes from the Right that was profoundly concerned with the leveling effects of the French Revolution's commitment to human equality. This Right found its most brilliant spokesman in the philosopher Friedrich Nietzsche, whose views were in some respects anticipated by that great observer of democratic societies, Alexis de Tocqueville. Nietzsche believed that modern democracy represented not the self-mastery of former slaves, but the unconditional victory of the slave and a kind of slavish morality. The typical citizen of a liberal democracy was a "last man" who, schooled by the founders of modern liberalism, gave up prideful belief in his or her own superior worth in favor of comfortable self-preservation. Liberal democracy produced "men without chests," composed of desire and reason but lacking *thymos,* clever at finding new ways to satisfy a host of petty wants through the calculation of long-term self-interest. The last man had no desire to be recognized as greater than others, and without such desire no excellence or achievement was possible. Content with his happiness and unable to feel any sense of shame for being unable to rise above those wants, the last man ceased to be human.

Following Nietzsche's line of thought, we are compelled to ask the following questions: Is not the man who is completely satisfied by nothing more than universal and equal recognition something less than a full human being, indeed, an object of contempt, a "last man" with neither striving nor aspiration? Is there not a side of the human personality that deliberately seeks out struggle, danger, risk, and daring, and will this side not remain unfulfilled by the "peace and prosperity" of contemporary liberal democracy? Does not the satisfaction of certain human beings depend on recognition that is inherently unequal? Indeed, does not the desire for unequal recognition constitute the basis of a livable life, not just for bygone aristocratic societies, but also in modern liberal democracies? Will not their future survival depend, to some extent, on the degree to which their citizens seek to be recognized not just as equal, but as superior to others? And might not the fear of becoming contemptible "last men" not lead men to assert themselves in new and unforeseen ways, even to the point of becoming once again bestial "first men" engaged in bloody prestige battles, this time with modern weapons?

This books seeks to address these questions. They arise naturally once we ask whether there is such a thing as progress, and whether we can construct a coherent and directional Universal History of mankind. Totalitarianisms of the Right and Left have kept us too busy to consider the latter question seriously for the better part of this century. But the fading of these totalitarianisms, as the century comes to an end, invites us to raise this old question one more time.

Part I

AN OLD QUESTION
ASKED ANEW

I

Our Pessimism

As decent and sober a thinker as Immanuel Kant could still seriously believe that war served the purposes of Providence. After Hiroshima, all war is known to be at best a necessary evil. As saintly a theologian as St. Thomas Aquinas could in all seriousness argue that tyrants serve providential ends, for if it were not for tyrants there would be no opportunity for martyrdom. After Auschwitz, anyone using this argument would be guilty of blasphemy. . . . After these dread events, occurring in the heart of the modern, enlightened, technological world, can one still believe in the God who is necessary Progress any more than in the God who manifests His Power in the form of super-intending Providence?

—Emile Fackenheim, God's Presence in History[1]

The twentieth century, it is safe to say, has made all of us into deep historical pessimists.

As individuals, we can of course be optimistic concerning our personal prospects for health and happiness. By long-standing tradition, Americans as a people are said to be continually hopeful about the future. But when we come to larger questions, such as whether there has been or will be progress in history, the verdict is decidedly different. The soberest and most thoughtful minds of this century have seen no reason to think that the world is moving toward what we in the West consider decent and humane political institutions—that is, liberal democracy. Our deepest thinkers have concluded that there is no such thing as History—that is, a meaningful order to the broad sweep of human events. Our own experience has taught us, seemingly, that the future is more likely than not to contain new and unimagined evils, from fanatical

3

dictatorships and bloody genocides to the banalization of life through modern consumerism, and that unprecedented disasters await us from nuclear winter to global warming.

The pessimism of the twentieth century stands in sharp contrast to the optimism of the previous one. Though Europe began the nineteenth century convulsed by war and revolution, it was by and large a century of peace and unprecedented increases in material well-being. There were two broad grounds for optimism. The first was the belief that modern science would improve human life by conquering disease and poverty. Nature, long man's adversary, would be mastered by modern technology and made to serve the end of human happiness. Second, free democratic governments would continue to spread to more and more countries around the world. The "Spirit of 1776," or the ideals of the French Revolution, would vanquish the world's tyrants, autocrats, and superstitious priests. Blind obedience to authority would be replaced by rational self-government, in which all men, free and equal, would have to obey no masters but themselves. In light of the broad movement of civilization, even bloody wars like those of Napoleon could be interpreted by philosophers as socially progressive in their results, because they fostered the spread of republican government. A number of theories, some serious and the others less so, were put forward to explain how human history constituted a coherent whole, whose twists and turns could be understood as leading to the good things of the modern era. In 1880 a certain Robert Mackenzie was able to write:

> Human history is a record of progress—a record of accumulating knowledge and increasing wisdom, of continual advancement from a lower to a higher platform of intelligence and well-being. Each generation passes on to the next the treasures which it inherited, beneficially modified by its own experience, enlarged by the fruits of all the victories which itself has gained. . . . The growth of man's well-being, rescued from the mischievous tampering of self-willed princes, is left now to the beneficent regulation of great providential laws.[2]

Under the heading of "torture," the famous eleventh edition of the *Encyclopaedia Britannica* published in 1910–11 explained that "the whole subject is one of only historical interest as far as Europe is concerned."[3] On the very eve of World War I, the journalist Norman Angell published his book *The Great Illusion,* in which he argued that free trade had rendered territorial aggrandizement obsolete, and that war had become economically irrational.[4]

The extreme pessimism of our own century is due at least in part to the cruelty with which these earlier expectations were shattered. The First World War was a critical event in the undermining of Europe's self-confidence. The war of course brought down the old political order represented by the German, Austrian, and Russian monarchies, but its deeper impact was psychological. Four years of indescribably horrible trench warfare, in which tens of thousands died in a single day over a few yards of devastated territory, was, in the words of Paul Fussell, "a hideous embarrassment to the prevailing Meliorist myth which had dominated public consciousness for a century," reversing "the idea of Progress."[5] The virtues of loyalty, hard work, perseverance, and patriotism were brought to bear in the systematic and pointless slaughter of other men, thereby discrediting the entire bourgeois world which had created these values.[6] As Paul, the young soldier hero of Erich Maria Remarque's *All Quiet on the Western Front,* explains, "For us lads of eighteen [our teachers at school] ought to have been mediators and guides to the world of maturity, the world of work, of duty, of culture, of progress—to the future. . . . But the first death we saw shattered this belief." In words echoed by young Americans during the Vietnam War, he concluded that "our generation was more to be trusted than theirs."[7] The notion that the industrial progress of Europe could be turned to war without moral redemption or meaning led to bitter denunciations of all attempts to find larger patterns or meaning in history. Thus, the renowned British historian H. A. L. Fisher could write in 1934 that "Men wiser and more learned than I have discerned in history a plot, a rhythm, a predetermined pattern. These harmonies are concealed from me. I can see only one emergency following upon another as wave follows upon wave."[8]

The First World War was, as it turned out, only a foretaste of the new forms of evil that were soon to emerge. If modern science made possible weapons of unprecedented destructiveness like the machine gun and the bomber, modern politics created a state of unprecedented power, for which a new word, *totalitarianism,* had to be coined. Backed by efficient police power, mass political parties, and radical ideologies that sought to control all aspects of human life, this new type of state embarked on a project no less ambitious than world domination. The genocides perpetrated by the totalitarian regimes of Hitler's Germany and Stalin's Russia were without precedent in human history, and in many respects were made possible by modernity itself.[9] There have of course been many bloody tyrannies before the twentieth century, but Hitler and Stalin put both modern technology and modern political organization in the service of evil. It had previously been beyond the technical ability of "traditional" tyrannies to contemplate something so ambitious as the elimination of an entire *class* of people like the Jews of Europe or the kulaks in the Soviet Union. Yet this was precisely the task made possible by the technical and social advances of the previous century. The wars unleashed by these totalitarian ideologies were also of a new sort, involving the mass destruction of civilian populations and economic resources—hence the term, "total war." To defend themselves from this threat, liberal democracies were led to adopt military strategies like the bombing of Dresden or Hiroshima that in earlier ages would have been called genocidal.

Nineteenth-century theories of progress associated human evil with a backward state of social development. While Stalinism did arise in a backward, semi-European country known for its despotic government, the Holocaust emerged in a country with the most advanced industrial economy and one of the most cultured and well-educated populations in Europe. If such events could happen in Germany, why then could they not happen in any other advanced country? And if economic development, education, and culture were not a guarantee against a phenomenon like nazism, what was the point of historical progress?[10]

The experience of the twentieth century made highly problematic the claims of progress on the basis of science and technology. For the ability of technology to better human life is critically dependent on a parallel moral progress in man. Without the latter, the power of technology will simply be turned to evil purposes, and mankind will be *worse* off than it was previously. The total wars of the twentieth century would not have been possible without the basic advances of the Industrial Revolution: iron, steel, the internal combustion engine, and the airplane. And since Hiroshima, mankind has lived under the shadow of the most terrible technological advance of all, that of nuclear weapons. The fantastic economic growth made possible by modern science had a dark side, for it has led to severe environmental damage to many parts of the planet, and raised the possibility of an eventual global ecological catastrophe. It is frequently asserted that global information technology and instant communications have promoted democratic ideals, as in the case of CNN's worldwide broadcasting of the occupation of Tienanmen Square in 1989, or of the revolutions in Eastern Europe later that year. But communications technology itself is value-neutral. Ayatollah Khomeini's reactionary ideas were imported into Iran prior to the 1978 revolution on cassette tape recorders that the Shah's economic modernization of the country had made widely available. If television and instant global communications had existed in the 1930s, they would have been used to great effect by Nazi propagandists like Leni Riefenstahl and Joseph Goebbels to promote fascist rather than democratic ideas.

The traumatic events of the twentieth century formed the backdrop to a profound intellectual crisis as well. It is possible to speak of historical progress only if one knows where mankind is going. Most nineteenth-century Europeans thought that progress meant progress toward democracy. But for most of this century, there has been no consensus on this question. Liberal democracy was challenged by two major rival ideologies—fascism and communism—which offered radically different visions of a good society. People in the West themselves came to question whether liberal democracy was in fact a general aspiration of all mankind, and whether their earlier confidence that it was did not reflect a narrow ethnocentrism on their part. As Europeans were forced to confront the non-European world, first as colonial masters, then as patrons during the Cold War and theoretical equals in a world of sovereign nation states, they came to question the universality of their own ideals. The suicidal self-destructiveness of the European state system in two world wars gave lie to the notion of superior Western rationality, while the distinction between civilized and barbarian that was instinctive to Europeans in the nineteenth century was much harder to make after the Nazi death camps. Instead of human history leading in a single direction, there seemed to be as many goals as there were peoples or civilizations, with liberal democracy having no particular privilege among them.

In our own time, one of the clearest manifestations of our pessimism was the almost universal belief in the permanence of a vigorous, communist-totalitarian alternative to Western liberal democracy. When he was secretary of state in the 1970s, Henry Kissinger warned his countrymen that "today, for the first time in our history, we face the stark reality that the [communist] challenge is *unending*. . . . We must learn to conduct foreign policy as other nations have had to conduct it for so many centuries—without escape and without respite. . . . *This condition will not go away*."[11] According to Kissinger, it was utopian to try to reform the fundamental political and social structures of hostile powers like the USSR. Political maturity meant acceptance of the world as it was and not the way we wanted it to be, which meant coming to terms with Brezhnev's Soviet Union. And while the conflict between communism and democracy could be moderated, it and the possibility of apocalyptic war could never be overcome completely.

Kissinger's view was by no means unique. Virtually everyone professionally engaged in the study of politics and foreign policy believed in the permanence of communism; its worldwide collapse in the late 1980s was therefore almost totally unanticipated. This failure was not simply a matter of ideological dogma interfering with a "dispassionate" view of events. It affected people across the political spectrum, right, left, and center, journalists as well as scholars, and politicians both East and West.[12] The roots of a blindness so pervasive were much more profound than mere partisanship, and lay in the extraordinary historical pessimism engendered by the events of this century.

As recently as 1983, Jean-François Revel declared that "democracy may, after all, turn out to have been a historical accident, a brief parenthesis that is closing before our eyes . . ."[13] The Right, of course, had never believed that communism had achieved any degree of legitimacy in the eyes of the populations it controlled, and saw quite clearly the economic failings of socialist societies. But much of the Right believed that a "failed society" like the Soviet Union had nonetheless found the key to power through the invention of Leninist totalitarianism, by which a small band of "bureaucrat-dictators" could bring to bear the power of modern organization and technology and rule over large populations more or less indefinitely. Totalitarianism had succeeded not just in intimidating subject populations, but in forcing them to internalize the values of their communist masters. This was one of the distinctions that Jeanne Kirkpatrick, in a famous 1979 article, drew between traditional authoritarian regimes of the Right and radical totalitarianisms of the Left. While the former "leave in place existing allocations of wealth, power, status" and "worship traditional gods and observe traditional taboos," radical totalitarianisms of the Left seek to "claim jurisdiction over the whole of the society" and violate "internalized values and habits." A totalitarian state, in contrast to a merely authoritarian one, was able to control its underlying society so ruthlessly that it was fundamentally invulnerable to change or reform: thus "the history of this century provides no grounds for expecting that radical totalitarian regimes will transform themselves."[14]

Underlying this belief in the dynamism of totalitarian states was a profound lack of confidence in democracy. This lack of confidence was manifested in Kirkpatrick's view that few of the currently non-democratic countries in the Third World would be able to democratize successfully (the possibility of a communist regime democratizing being discounted entirely), and in Revel's belief that the strong and established democracies of Europe and North America lacked the inner conviction to defend themselves. Citing the numerous economic, social, and cultural requirements for successful democratization, Kirkpatrick criticized as typically American the idea that it was possible to democratize governments anytime and anywhere. The idea that there could be a democratic center in the Third World was a trap and an illusion; experience taught us that the world was divided between authoritarianisms of the Right and totalitarianisms of the Left. Revel, for his part, repeated in a much more extreme form the criticism originally made by Tocqueville that democracies have great difficulties sustaining serious and long-term foreign policies.[15] They are hamstrung by their very democratic nature: by the plurality of the voices, the self-doubt and self-criticism that characterize democratic debate. Hence, "As things stand, relatively minor causes of discontent corrode, disturb, unsettle, paralyze, the democracies faster and more deeply than horrendous famine and constant poverty do the Communist regimes, whose subject peoples have no real rights or means of redressing their wrongs. Societies of which permanent criticism is an integral feature are the only livable ones, but they are also the most fragile."[16]

The Left came to a similar conclusion by a different route. By the 1980s, most "progressives" in Europe and America no longer believed that Soviet communism represented their future, as did many such thinkers through the end of World War II. Yet there persisted a belief on the Left in the legitimacy of Marxism-Leninism for *other* people, a legitimacy which usually increased in proportion to geographical and cultural distance. Thus, while Soviet-style communism was not necessarily a realistic choice for people in the United States or Britain, it was held to be an authentic alternative for the Russians, with their traditions of autocracy and central control, not to mention the Chinese, who allegedly turned to it to overcome a legacy of foreign domination, backwardness, and humiliation. The same was said to be true for the Cubans and Nicaraguans, who had been victimized by American imperialism, and for the Vietnamese, for whom communism was regarded as a virtual national tradition. Many on the Left shared the view that a radical socialist regime in the Third World could legitimate itself, even in the absence of free elections and open discussion, by engaging in land reform, providing free health care, and raising literacy levels. Given these views, it is not surprising that there were few people on the Left who predicted revolutionary instability in the Soviet bloc or in China.

Indeed, the belief in the legitimacy and permanence of communism took on a number of bizarre forms in the waning days of the Cold War. One prominent student of the Soviet Union maintained that the Soviet system had, under Brezhnev, achieved what he called "institutional pluralism," and that "the Soviet leadership almost seems to have made the Soviet Union closer to the spirit of the pluralist model of American political science than is the United States. . . ."[17] Soviet society, pre-Gorbachev, was "not inert and passive but participatory in almost all sense of the term," with a greater proportion of Soviet citizens "participating" in politics than in the United States.[18] The same kind of thinking characterized some scholarship on Eastern Europe, where, despite the obviously imposed nature of communism, many scholars saw a tremendous social stability. One specialist asserted in 1987 that "if we were now to compare [the states of Eastern Europe] to many countries in the world—for example to a number of Latin American cases—they would seem to be epitomes of stability," and criticized the traditional image of "an 'illegitimate' party . . . counterpoised against a necessarily hostile and unbelieving populace."[19]

While some of these views simply represented projection of the recent past into the future, many of them rested on a judgment concerning the *legitimacy* of communism in the East. That is, for all of the undeniable problems of their societies, communist rulers had worked out a "social contract" with their peoples, of the sort satirized in the Soviet saying that "they pretend to pay us and we pretend to work."[20] These regimes were neither productive nor dynamic, but were said to govern with a certain degree of consent from their populations because they provided security and stability.[21] As the political scientist Samuel Huntington wrote in 1968:

> The United States, Great Britain, and the Soviet Union have different forms of government, but in all three systems the government governs. Each country is a political community with an overwhelming consensus among the people on the legitimacy of the political system. In each country the citizens and their leaders share a vision of the public interest of the society and of the traditions and principles upon which the political community is based.[22]

Huntington had no particular sympathy for communism, but believed that the weight of evidence forced us to conclude that it had managed to earn a degree of popular approval over the years.

The pessimism of the present with regard to the possibility of progress in history was born out of two separate but parallel crises: the crisis of twentieth-century politics, and the intellectual crisis of Western rationalism. The former killed tens of millions of people and forced hundreds of millions to live under new and more brutal forms of slavery; the latter left liberal democracy without the intellectual resources with which to defend itself. The two were interrelated and cannot be understood separately from one another. On the one hand, the lack of intellectual consensus made the wars and revolutions of this century more ideological and therefore more extreme than they would otherwise have been. The Russian and Chinese revolutions and the Nazi conquests during the Second World War saw the return, in a magnified form, of the kind of brutality that characterized the religious wars of the sixteenth century, for what was at stake was not just territory and resources, but the value systems and ways of life of entire populations. On the other hand, the violence of those ideologically driven conflicts and their terrible outcomes had a devastating effect on the self-confidence of liberal democracies, whose isolation in a world of totalitarian and authoritarian regimes led to serious doubts about the universality of liberal notions of right.

And yet, despite the powerful reasons for pessimism given us by our experience in the first half of this century, events in its second half have been pointing in a very different and unexpected direction. As we reach the 1990s, the world as a whole has not revealed new evils, but has gotten *better* in certain distinct ways. Chief among the surprises that have occurred in the recent past was the totally unexpected collapse of communism throughout much of the world in the late 1980s. But this development, striking as it was, was only part of a larger pattern of events that had been taking shape since World War II. Authoritarian dictatorships of all kinds, both on the Right and on the Left, have been collapsing.[23] In some cases, the collapse has led to the establishment of prosperous and stable liberal democracies. In others, authoritarianism has been followed by instability, or by yet another form of dictatorship. But whether successful democracy eventually emerged, authoritarians of all stripes have been undergoing a severe crisis in virtually every part of the globe. If the early twentieth century's major political innovation was the invention of the strong states of totalitarian Germany or Russia, then the past few decades have revealed a tremendous weakness at their core. And this weakness, so massive and unexpected, suggests that the pessimistic lessons about history that our century supposedly taught us need to be rethought from the beginning.

2

The Weakness of Strong States I

The current crisis of authoritarianism did not begin with Gorbachev's *perestroika* or the fall of the Berlin Wall. It started over one and a half decades earlier, with the fall of a series of right-wing authoritarian governments in Southern Europe. In 1974 the Caetano regime in Portugal was ousted in an army coup. After a period of instability verging on civil war, the socialist Mario Soares was elected prime minister in April 1976, and the country has seen peaceful democratic rule ever since. The colonels who had been ruling Greece since 1967 were ousted also in 1974, giving way to the popularly elected Karamanlis regime. And in 1975, General Francisco Franco died in Spain, paving the way for a remarkably peaceful transition to democracy two years later. In addition, the Turkish military took over the country in September 1980 as a result of the terrorism engulfing its society, but returned the country to civilian rule by 1983. Since then, all of these countries have held regular, free, multi-party elections.

The transformation that occurred in Southern Europe in less than a decade was remarkable. These countries had earlier been seen as the black sheep of Europe, condemned by their religious and authoritarian traditions to reside outside the mainstream of democratic Western European development. And yet by the 1980s each country had made a successful transition to functioning and stable democracy, so stable in fact that (with the possible exception of Turkey) the people living in them could hardly imagine the situation being otherwise.

A similar set of democratic transitions took place in Latin

America in the 1980s. This began in 1980 with the restoration of a democratically elected government in Peru after twelve years of military rule. The 1982 Falklands/Malvinas War precipitated the downfall of the military junta in Argentina, and the rise of the democratically elected Alfonsin government. The Argentine transition was quickly followed by others throughout Latin America, with military regimes stepping down in Uruguay and Brazil in 1983 and 1984, respectively. By the end of the decade the dictatorships of Stroessner in Paraguay and Pinochet in Chile had given way to popularly elected governments, and in early 1990 even Nicaragua's Sandinista government had fallen to a coalition led by Violetta Chamorro in a free election. Many observers felt less confident about the permanence of the new Latin American democracies than they did about those in Southern Europe. Democracies have come and gone in this region, and virtually all of the new democracies were in a state of acute economic crisis whose most visible manifestation was the debt crisis. Countries like Peru and Colombia, moreover, faced severe internal challenge from insurgency and drugs. Nonetheless, these new democracies proved remarkably resilient, as if their earlier experience of authoritarianism had inoculated them against too easy a return to military rule. The fact remained that, from a low point in the early 1970s when only a handful of Latin American countries were democratic, by the beginning of the 1990s Cuba and Guyana were the only countries in the Western Hemisphere not permitting reasonably free elections.

There were comparable developments in East Asia. In 1986 the Marcos dictatorship was overthrown in the Philippines, and replaced by President Corazon Aquino who was brought into office on a tide of popular support. The following year, General Chun stepped down in South Korea and permitted the election of Roh Tae Woo as president. While the Taiwanese political system was not reformed in such a dramatic way, there was considerable democratic ferment below the surface after the death of Chiang Ching-kuo in January 1988. With the passing of much of the old guard in the ruling Guomindang party, there has been growing participation by other sectors of Taiwanese society in the Nationalist Parliament, including many native Taiwanese. And finally, the authoritarian government of Burma has been rocked by pro-democracy ferment.

In February 1990, the Afrikaner-dominated government of

F. W. de Klerk in South Africa announced the freeing of Nelson Mandela and the unbanning of the African National Congress and the South African Communist party. He thereby inaugurated a period of negotiations on a transition to power sharing between blacks and whites, and eventual majority rule.

In retrospect, we have had difficulty perceiving the depths of the crisis in which dictatorships found themselves due to a mistaken belief in the ability of authoritarian systems to perpetuate themselves, or more broadly, in the viability of strong states. The state in a liberal democracy is by definition weak: preservation of a sphere of individual rights means a sharp delimitation of its power. Authoritarian regimes on the Right and Left, by contrast, have sought to use the power of the state to encroach on the private sphere and to control it for various purposes—whether to build military strength, to promote an egalitarian social order, or to bring about rapid economic growth. What was lost in the realm of individual liberty was to be regained at the level of national purpose.

The critical weakness that eventually toppled these strong states was in the last analysis a failure of legitimacy—that is, a crisis on the level of ideas. Legitimacy is not justice or right in an absolute sense; it is a relative concept that exists in people's subjective perceptions. All regimes capable of effective action must be based on some principle of legitimacy.[1] There is no such thing as a dictator who rules purely "by force," as is commonly said, for instance, of Hitler. A tyrant can rule his children, old men, or perhaps his wife by force, if he is physically stronger than they are, but he is not likely to be able to rule more than two or three people in this fashion and certainly not a nation of millions.[2] When we say that a dictator like Hitler ruled "by force," what we mean is that Hitler's supporters, including the Nazi Party, the Gestapo, and the Wehrmacht, were able to physically intimidate the larger population. But what made these supporters loyal to Hitler? Certainly not his ability to intimidate them physically: ultimately it rested upon their belief in his legitimate authority. Security apparatuses can themselves be controlled by intimidation, but at *some* point in the system, the dictator must have loyal subordinates who believe in his legitimate authority. Similarly for the most lowly and corrupt mafia chieftain: he would not be a *capo* if his "family" did not accept, on some grounds, his "legitimacy." As Socrates explains in Plato's *Republic*, even among a band of

robbers there must be some principle of justice that permits them
to divide their spoils. Legitimacy is thus crucial to even the most
unjust and bloody-minded dictatorship.

It is clearly not the case that a regime needs to establish legitimate authority for the greater part of its population in order to
survive. There are numerous contemporary examples of minority
dictatorships that are actively hated by large parts of their populations, but have succeeded in staying in power for decades. Such
is the case of the *Alawi*-dominated regime in Syria, or Saddam
Hussein's Ba'athist faction in Iraq. It goes without saying that
Latin America's various military juntas and oligarchies have ruled
without broad popular support. A lack of legitimacy among the
population as a whole does not spell a crisis of legitimacy for the
regime unless it begins to infect the elites tied to the regime itself,
and particularly those that hold the monopoly of coercive power,
such as the ruling party, the armed forces, and the police. When
we speak of a crisis of legitimacy in an authoritarian system, then,
we speak of a crisis within those elites whose cohesion is essential
for the regime to act effectively.

A dictator's legitimacy can spring from a variety of sources:
from personal loyalty on the part of a pampered army, to an
elaborate ideology that justifies his right to rule. In this century,
the most important systematic attempt to establish a coherent,
right-wing, non-democratic, non-egalitarian principle of legitimacy was fascism. Fascism was not a "universal" doctrine like
liberalism or communism, insofar as it denied the existence of a
common humanity or equality of human rights. Fascist ultranationalism maintained that the ultimate source of legitimacy was
race or nation, specifically, the right of "master races" like the
Germans to rule other people. Power and will were extolled over
reason or equality, and were considered titles to rule in themselves. Nazism's assertion of German racial superiority had to be
actively proven through conflict with other cultures. War was
therefore a normal rather than a pathological condition.

Fascism was not around long enough to suffer an internal
crisis of legitimacy, but was defeated by force of arms. Hitler and
his remaining followers went to their deaths in their Berlin bun-
ker believing to the last in the rightness of the Nazi cause and in
Hitler's legitimate authority. The appeal of fascism was undermined in most people's eyes retrospectively, as a consequence of
that defeat.[3] That is, Hitler had based his claim to legitimacy on

the promise of world domination; what the Germans got instead was horrifying devastation and occupation by supposedly inferior races. Fascism was highly appealing not only to Germans but to many people around the world when it was mainly a matter of torchlight parades and bloodless victories, but made much less sense when its inherent militarism was carried to its logical conclusion. Fascism suffered, one might say, from an internal contradiction: its very emphasis on militarism and war led it inevitably into a self-destructive conflict with the international system. As a result, it has not been a serious ideological competitor to liberal democracy since the end of the Second World War.

Of course, we could ask how legitimate fascism would be today if Hitler had not been defeated. But fascism's internal contradiction went deeper than the likelihood that it would be defeated militarily by the international system. If Hitler had emerged victorious, fascism would nonetheless have lost its inner *raison d'être* in the peace of a universal empire where German nationhood could no longer be asserted through war and conquest.

After Hitler's defeat, what remained as an alternative to liberal democracy on the Right was a group of persistent but in the end unsystematic military dictatorships. Most of these regimes had no grander vision than the preservation of a traditional social order, and their chief weakness was the lack of a plausible long-term basis of legitimacy. None was able to formulate, as Hitler did, a coherent doctrine of nation that could justify perpetual authoritarian rule. All of them had to accept the *principle* of democracy and popular sovereignty, and argue that for various reasons their countries were not ready for democracy, either because of a threat from communism, terrorism, or the economic mismanagement of the previous democratic regime. Each had to justify itself as transitional, pending the ultimate return of democracy.[4]

The weakness implied by the lack of a coherent source of legitimacy did not, however, spell the quick or inevitable collapse of right-wing authoritarian governments. Democratic regimes in Latin America and Southern Europe had serious weaknesses as well, in terms of their ability to deal with a variety of serious social and economic problems.[5] Few had been able to generate rapid economic growth, and many were plagued by terrorism. But the lack of legitimacy became a crucial source of weakness for right-wing authoritarianism when, as was almost always inevitably the case, these regimes faced a crisis or failure in some area of policy.

Legitimate regimes have a fund of goodwill that excuses them from short-term mistakes, even serious ones, and failure can be expiated by the removal of a prime minister or cabinet. In illegitimate regimes, on the other hand, failure frequently precipitates an overturning of the regime itself.

An example of this was Portugal. The dictatorship of Antonio de Oliveira Salazar and his successor, Marcello Caetano, had a superficial stability that prompted some observers to describe the Portuguese people as "passive, fatalistic and endlessly melancholy."[6] Just like the Germans and the Japanese before them, the Portuguese people proved wrong those outside Western observers who earlier deemed them unready for democracy. The Caetano dictatorship collapsed in April 1974 when its own military turned against it and formed the *Movimento das Forcas Armadas* (MFA).[7] Their immediate motive was Portugal's deepening and unwinnable colonial war in Africa, which consumed a quarter of the Portuguese budget and the energies of a large part of the Portuguese military. The transition to democracy was not a smooth one because the MFA was by no means uniformly suffused with democratic ideas. A significant part of the officer corps was influenced by the strict Stalinist Portuguese Communist party of Álvaro Cunhal. But in contrast to the 1930s, the center and democratic right proved unexpectedly resilient: after a stormy period of political and social turmoil, Mario Soares' moderate Socialist party won a plurality of votes in April 1976. This occurred to no small degree as a result of assistance from outside organizations, ranging from the German Social Democratic party to the American CIA. But outside help would have proved feckless had Portugal not possessed a surprisingly strong civil society— political parties, unions, the Church—which were able to mobilize and control broad popular support for democracy. The allure of modern West European consumer civilization also played a role; in the words of one observer, "Workers . . . [who] might have marched in demonstrations and chanted slogans of Socialist revolution . . . spent their money on the clothes, appliances, and artifacts of West European consumer societies to whose standard of living they aspired."[8]

The Spanish transition to democracy the following year was perhaps the purest recent case of the failure of authoritarian legitimacy. General Francisco Franco was, in many ways, the last exponent of the nineteenth-century European conservatism that based itself on throne and altar, the same conservatism that went down to defeat in the French Revolution. But Catholic consciousness in Spain was in the process of changing dramatically from the 1930s: the church as a whole had liberalized after Vatican II in the 1960s, and important parts of Spanish Catholicism adopted the Christian democracy of Western Europe. Not only did the Spanish church discover that there was no necessary conflict between Christianity and democracy, it increasingly took on the role of human rights advocate and critic of the Francoist dictatorship.[9] This new consciousness was reflected in the *Opus Dei* movement of Catholic lay technocrats, many of whom entered the administration after 1957 and had been intimately involved with the subsequent economic liberalization. Thus, when Franco died in November 1975, important parts of his regime were prepared to accept the legitimacy of a series of negotiated "pacts" that peacefully dissolved all important Francoist institutions, legalized an opposition that included the Spanish Communist party, and permitted elections for a constituent assembly that would write a fully democratic constitution. This could not have happened if important elements of the old regime (most importantly, King Juan Carlos) had not believed that Francoism was an anachronism in a democratic Europe, a Europe that Spain had come to resemble increasingly on a social and economic plane.[10] The last Francoist Cortes did a remarkable thing: it overwhelmingly passed a law in November 1976 that in effect constituted its own suicide by stipulating that the next Cortes be democratically elected. As in Portugal, the Spanish population as a whole provided the ultimate ground for democracy by supporting a democratic center, first by giving strong support to the December 1976 referendum approving democratic elections, and then by calmly voting Suarez's center-right party into office in June 1977.[11]

In the cases of the Greek and Argentine turns to democracy in 1974 and 1983, respectively, the military in both countries was not forcibly ousted from power. They gave way to civilian authority instead through inner divisions within their ranks, reflecting a loss of belief in their right to rule. As in Portugal, external failure was the proximate cause. The Greek colonels who came to power in 1967 had never sought legitimation on grounds other than democracy, arguing only that they were preparing the way for the restoration of a "healthy" and "regenerated" political system.[12] The military regime was thus vulnerable when it discredited itself by supporting a Greek Cypriot bid for unity with the mainland, leading to the occupation of Cyprus by Turkey and the possibility of full-scale war.[13] The major aim of the military junta that took over power in Argentina from President Isabella Perón in 1976 was to rid Argentine society of terrorism; it accomplished this in a brutal war and thereby undercut its chief *raison d'être*. The military junta's decision to invade the Falklands/Malvinas was subsequently sufficient to discredit it by provoking an unnecessary war which it could not subsequently win.[14]

In other cases, strong military governments proved ineffective in dealing with the economic and social problems that had delegitimized their democratic predecessors. The Peruvian military turned over power to a civilian government in 1980 in the face of a rapidly accelerating economic crisis, in which the government of General Francisco Morales Bermudez found it could not cope with a series of strikes and intractable social problems.[15] The Brazilian military presided over a period of remarkable economic growth from 1968 to 1973, but in the face of a world oil crisis and slowdown, Brazil's military rulers found they had no particular gift for economic management. By the time the last military president, João Figueiredo, stepped down in favor of an elected civilian president, many in the military were relieved, and even ashamed of the mistakes they had made.[16] The Uruguayan military initially took power to wage a "dirty war" against the Tupemaros insurgency in 1973–74. Uruguay had a relatively strong democratic tradition, however, which is perhaps what persuaded the Uruguayan military to put the institutionalization of its rule to the test through a plebiscite in 1980. It lost, and by 1983 had voluntarily stepped aside.[17]

Architects of the apartheid system in South Africa, like former Prime Minister H. F. Verwoerd, denied the liberal premise of universal human equality, and believed that there was a natural division and hierarchy between mankind's races.[18] Apartheid was an effort to permit the industrial development of South Africa based on the use of black labor, while at the same time seeking to reverse and prevent the urbanization of South Africa's blacks that is the natural concomitant of any process of industrialization. Such an effort at social engineering was both monumental in its ambition and, in retrospect, monumentally foolish in its ultimate aim: by 1981, almost eighteen million blacks were arrested under the so-called "pass-laws" for the crime of wanting to live near their places of employment. The impossibility of defying the laws of modern economics had, by the late 1980s, led to a revolution in Afrikaner thinking that caused F. W. de Klerk, well before he became state president, to assert that "the economy demands the permanent presence of millions of blacks in urban areas" and that "it does not help to bluff ourselves about this."[19] The apartheid system's loss of legitimacy among whites was thus ultimately based on its ineffectiveness, and has led to an acceptance on the part of a majority of Afrikaners of a new system of power sharing with blacks.[20]

While recognizing the real differences that exist between these cases, there was a remarkable consistency in the democratic transitions in Southern Europe, Latin America, and South Africa. Apart from Somoza in Nicaragua, there was not one single instance in which the old regime was forced from power through violent upheaval or revolution.[21] What permitted regime change was the *voluntary* decision on the part of at least certain members of the old regime to give up power in favor of a democratically elected government. While this willing retreat from power was always provoked by some immediate crisis, it was ultimately made possible by a growing belief that democracy was the only legitimate source of authority in the modern world. Once they accomplished the limited aims they set for themselves—eliminating terrorism, restoring social order, ending economic chaos, and so forth—authoritarians of the Right in Latin America and Europe found themselves unable to justify their continuation in power, and lost confidence in themselves. It is difficult to kill people in the name of throne and altar if the king himself seeks to be no more than the titular monarch of a democratic country, or if the Church is in the forefront of the struggle for human rights. So much, then, for that bit of conventional wisdom that maintains that "nobody gives up power voluntarily."

It goes without saying that many of the old authoritarians were not converted to democracy overnight, and that they were frequently victims of their own incompetence and miscalculation. Neither General Pinochet in Chile nor the Sandinistas in Nicaragua expected to lose the elections to which they submitted themselves. But the fact is that even the most die-hard dictators believed they had to endow themselves with at least a patina of democratic legitimacy by staging an election. And in many cases, the relinquishing of power by strong men in uniform was done at

considerable personal risk, since they thereby lost their chief protection against the vengeance of those whom they had mistreated.

It is perhaps not surprising that right-wing authoritarians
were swept from power by the idea of democracy. The power of
most strong states on the Right was actually relatively limited when
it came to the economy or society as a whole. Their leaders represented traditional social groups who were becoming increasingly marginal to their societies, and the generals and colonels
who ruled were generally bereft of ideas and intellect. But what
about those communist totalitarian powers of the Left? Had they
not redefined the very meaning of the term "strong state," and
discovered a formula for self-perpetuating power?

3

The Weakness of Strong States II, or, Eating Pineapples on the Moon

All right, then, here are some excerpts from a Kuybyshev ninth-grader, written as recently as the 1960s: "It is 1981. Communism: Communism is the abundance of material and cultural blessings. . . . All of the city transportation is electrified, and harmful enterprises are removed beyond the city limits. . . . We are on the Moon, we are walking by flower bushes and fruit trees . . ."

So how many years does that make it that we have been eating pineapples on the Moon? If only we could someday eat our fill of tomatoes here on earth!

—Andrey Nuikin, "The Bee and the Communist Ideal"[1]

Totalitarianism was a concept developed in the West after World War II to describe the Soviet Union and Nazi Germany, which were tyrannies of a very different character from the traditional authoritarianisms of the nineteenth century.[2] Hitler and Stalin redefined the meaning of a strong state by the very audacity of their social and political agendas. Traditional despotisms like Franco's Spain or the various military dictatorships of Latin America never sought to crush "civil society"—that is, society's sphere of private interests—but only to control it. Franco's Falangist party or the Peronist movement in Argentina failed to develop systematic ideologies and made only half-hearted efforts to change popular values and attitudes.

The totalitarian state, by contrast, was based on an explicit

23

ideology that provided a comprehensive view of human life. Totalitarianism sought to destroy civil society in its entirety, in its search for "total" control over the lives of its citizens. From the moment the Bolsheviks seized power in 1917, the Soviet state systematically attacked all potential competing sources of authority in Russian society, including opposition political parties, the press, trade unions, private enterprises, and the Church. While institutions remained at the end of the 1930s bearing some of those names, all were ghostly shadows of their former selves, organized and completely controlled by the regime. What was left was a society whose members were reduced to "atoms," unconnected to any "mediating institutions" short of an all-powerful government.

The totalitarian state hoped to remake Soviet man himself by changing the very structure of his beliefs and values through control of the press, education, and propaganda. This extended down to a human being's most personal and intimate relations, those of the family. The young Pavel Morozov, who denounced his parents to Stalin's police, was for many years held up by the regime as a model Soviet child. In Mikhail Heller's words, "The human relations that make up the society's fabric—the family, religion, historical memory, language—become targets, as society is systematically and methodically atomized, and the individual's close relationships are supplanted by others chosen for him, and approved by the state."[3]

Ken Kesey's 1962 novel, *One Flew Over the Cuckoo's Nest,* provides an illustration of the totalitarian aspiration. The book centers around the inmates of an insane asylum who lead lives of childish inanity under the eyes of a tyrannical Big Nurse. The novel's hero, McMurphy, tries to liberate them by breaking the asylum's rules and eventually leading the inmates to freedom. But he discovers in the process that none of the inmates is being kept there against his will; in the end, all are afraid of the world outside and remain voluntarily incarcerated, in a relationship of secure dependence on Big Nurse. This then was the ultimate goal of totalitarianism: not simply to deprive the new Soviet man of his freedom, but to make him fear freedom in favor of security, and to affirm the goodness of his chains even in the absence of coercion.

Many people believed that the efficacy of Soviet totalitarianism would be buttressed by the authoritarian traditions of the

Russian people pre-dating Bolshevism. A European view of the Russians popular in the nineteenth century was exemplified by the French traveler Custine, who characterized them as a race "broken to slavery, [who] have . . . taken seriously only terror and ambition."[4] Western confidence in the stability of Soviet communism rested on a belief, conscious or not, that the Russian people were not interested in or ready for democracy. Soviet rule, after all, was not imposed on the Russians by an external power in 1917, as it was in Eastern Europe after World War II, and it had survived for six or seven decades after the Bolshevik Revolution, weathering famine, upheaval, and invasion. This suggested that the system had won a certain degree of legitimacy among the broader population, and certainly within ruling elites, reflecting that society's own natural inclinations toward authoritarianism. Thus, while Western observers were perfectly ready to credit the Polish people with a desire to overturn communism if given the chance, the same was not held to be true of the Russians. They were, in other words, contented inmates of the asylum, held there not by bars and straightjackets but by their own craving for security, order, authority, and some extra benefits that the Soviet regime had managed to throw in like imperial grandeur and superpower status. The strong Soviet state looked very strong indeed, nowhere more so than in the global strategic competition with the United States.

The totalitarian state, it was believed, could not only perpetuate itself indefinitely, it could replicate itself throughout the world like a virus. When communism was exported to East Germany, Cuba, Vietnam, or Ethiopia, it came complete with a vanguard party, centralized ministries, a police apparatus, and an ideology to govern all aspects of life. These institutions appeared to be effective, regardless of the national or cultural traditions of the countries in question.

What happened to this self-perpetuating mechanism of power?

The year 1989—the two hundredth anniversary of the French Revolution, and of the ratification of the U.S. Constitution—marked the decisive collapse of communism as a factor in world history.

Since the early 1980s, so rapid and continuous has the pace of change been in the communist world that at times we tend to take change for granted, and forget the magnitude of what has happened. It would, therefore, be useful to review the major milestones of this period:

- In the early 1980s, the Chinese communist leadership began permitting peasants, who constituted 80 percent of China's population, to grow and sell their own food. Agriculture was in effect de-collectivized, and capitalist market relationships began reappearing not only throughout the countryside, but in urban industry as well.
- In 1986, the Soviet press began to publish articles critical of the crimes of the Stalin era, a subject which had not been broached since Khrushchev's ouster in the early 1960s. Press freedom expanded rapidly thereafter, as one taboo after another was broken. By 1989, Gorbachev and the rest of the Soviet leadership could be attacked openly in the press, and in 1990 and 1991 large demonstrations occurred across the Soviet Union calling for his resignation.
- In March 1989, elections were held for a newly restructured Congress of People's Deputies and Supreme Soviet. Further elections took place the next year in each of the USSR's fifteen constituent republics, and on a local level. The Communist party tried to rig these elections in its favor, but even so did not manage to prevent any number of local parliaments from coming under the control of non-communist deputies.
- In the spring of 1989, Beijing was temporarily taken over by tens of thousands of students calling for an end to corruption and for the establishment of democracy in China. They were eventually crushed ruthlessly by the Chinese army in June, but not before they were able to publicly call into question the legitimacy of the Chinese Communist party.
- In February 1989, the Red Army withdrew from Afghanistan. This, as it turned out, was only the first of a series of withdrawals.
- In early 1989, reformers in the Hungarian Socialist Workers party announced plans for free, multi-party elections the following year. In April 1989, a round table agreement led to a power-sharing agreement between the

Polish Workers party and the Solidarity trade union. As a result of elections—which the Polish communists also tried unsuccessfully to rig—a Solidarity government came to power in July.

- In July and August 1989, tens and then hundreds of thousands of East Germans began fleeing into West Germany, leading to a crisis that rapidly led to the tearing down of the Berlin Wall and the collapse of the East German state.

- The East German collapse then triggered the fall of communist governments in Czechoslovakia, Bulgaria, and Romania. By early 1991, all formerly communist states in Eastern Europe, including Albania and the major republics of Yugoslavia, had held reasonably free, multiparty elections. Communists were initially turned out of office everywhere except in Romania, Bulgaria, Serbia, and Albania, while in Bulgaria, the elected Communist government was soon forced to step down.[5] The political basis for the Warsaw Pact disappeared, and Soviet forces began to withdraw from Eastern Europe.

- In January 1990, Article Six of the Soviet Constitution, guaranteeing the Communist party a "leading role," was revoked.

- In the wake of the abolition of Article Six, a number of non-communist political parties were established in the Soviet Union, and came to power in a number of Soviet Republics. Most striking was the election of Boris Yeltsin as president of the Russian Republic in the spring of 1990, who with many of his supporters in the Russian Parliament subsequently left the Communist party. This same group then began advocating the restoration of private property and markets.

- Freely elected parliaments in every constituent republic, including Russia and the Ukraine, declared their "sovereignty" in the course of 1990. The parliaments in the Baltic states went well beyond this to declare their complete independence from the Soviet Union in March 1990. This did not lead to an immediate crackdown, as many had anticipated, but to a power struggle within Russia over whether or not to preserve the old Union.

- In June 1991, Russia held its first completely free

popular election, and elected Yeltsin president of the
Russian Federation. This reflected the rapidly
accelerating devolution of power from Moscow to the
periphery.

• In August 1991, a coup against Gorbachev by a group of
communist hardliners collapsed. This occurred partly as
a result of the plotters' incompetence and lack of resolve,
but also because of a remarkable outpouring of support,
led by Boris Yeltsin, for democratic institutions on the
part of the allegedly passive and authority-craving Soviet
people.

A sober student of communist affairs back in 1980 would have
said that none of these events was likely or even possible in the
coming decade. This judgment would have been based on the
view that any one of the above developments would have undermined a key element of communist totalitarian power, thereby
dealing a mortal blow to the system as a whole. And, indeed, the
final curtain came down when the old USSR dissolved itself and
the communist party was banned in Russia following the failure of
the August 1991 coup. How, then, were earlier expectations belied, and what accounts for the extraordinary weaknesses of this
strong state, revealed to us since the onset of *perestroika*?

The most basic weakness whose full gravity escaped the attention of Western observers was economic. It was much more difficult to tolerate economic failure in the Soviet system because the
regime itself had explicitly based its claims to legitimacy on its
ability to deliver its people a high material standard of living.
Hard as it is to recall now, economic growth had actually been
considered a strength of the Soviet state up through the early
1970s: between 1928 and 1955, Soviet GNP had increased at a
yearly rate of 4.4 to 6.3 percent, and had grown half again as fast
as U.S. GNP in the two decades thereafter, giving real credence to
Khrushchev's threat to overtake and then bury the United States.[6]
But by the mid-1970s, this rate of growth had slowed to a range
estimated by the CIA at 2.0 to 2.3 percent per annum between
1975 and 1985. There is increasing evidence that these figures
overstate growth considerably by not taking hidden inflation into
account; various reformist Soviet economists have asserted that
growth in this period was 0.6 to 1.0 percent, or even zero.[7] Flat
overall GNP growth, coupled with yearly increases in defense

spending through the early 1980s of 2 to 3 percent, meant that the civilian economy was actually shrinking at an appreciable rate for the decade before Gorbachev came to power.[8] Anyone who has stayed in a Soviet hotel, shopped in a Soviet department store, or traveled in the countryside where one can find the most abject poverty, should have realized that there were very serious problems with the Soviet economy not entirely reflected in official statistics.

As important was the way the economic crisis was interpreted. By the late 1980s, a remarkable intellectual revolution had occurred within the Soviet economic establishment. The old guard from the Brezhnev days was replaced within three or four years of Gorbachev's rise by reformist economists like Abel Aganbegyan, Nikolay Petrakov, Stanislav Shatalin, Oleg Bogomolov, Leonid Abalkin, Grigory Yavlinsky, and Nikolay Shmelev. All of these men understood—albeit imperfectly, in some cases—the basic principles of liberal economic theory, and were convinced that the centralized Soviet administrative-command system was at the root of the USSR's economic decline.[9]

It would be a mistake, however, to interpret the subsequent course of *perestroika* simply in terms of economic imperatives.[10] As Gorbachev himself pointed out, the Soviet Union in 1985 was not in a crisis situation, but one of "pre-crisis." Other states have weathered far more serious economic difficulties. During the Great Depression, for example, real U.S. GNP fell by nearly a third, but this did not lead to a general discrediting of the American system. The grave weaknesses of the Soviet economy had been recognized for some time, and there was a panoply of traditional reforms that could have been attempted to stem the decline.[11]

To understand the true weaknesses of the Soviet state, then, the economic problem has to be put in the context of a much larger crisis, that of the legitimacy of the system as a whole. Economic failure was only one of a number of failures in the Soviet system, that had the effect of catalyzing rejection of the belief system and exposing the weakness of the underlying structure. The most fundamental failure of totalitarianism was its failure to control thought. Soviet citizens, as it turned out, had all along retained an ability to think for themselves. Many understood, despite years of government propaganda, that their government was lying to them. People remained enormously angry at the personal sufferings they had endured under Stalinism. Virtually every family had lost members or friends during collectivization, or the Great Terror of the 1930s, or during the war, whose costs had been made much greater by Stalin's foreign policy mistakes. They knew that these victims had been unjustly persecuted, and that the Soviet regime had never owned up to its responsibility for such horrendous crimes. People understood as well that a new kind of class system had arisen in this supposedly classless society, a class of party functionaries who were as corrupt and privileged as anyone under the old regime, but far more hypocritical.

As evidence for this, consider the use of words in Gorbachev's Soviet Union, such as "democratization" *(demokratizatsiya)*, used incessantly by Gorbachev to define his own aims. Lenin, of course, maintained that the Soviet Union had achieved a truer form of democracy through the dictatorship of the party than the "formal" democracies of the West. Yet nobody in the contemporary Soviet Union who uses the term "democratization" has any illusions that it means anything other than Western democracy, and not Leninist centralism. Similarly for Soviets the term "economic" (as in "economic considerations" or "economically optimal") today means "efficient" as defined by *capitalist* laws of supply and demand. And any number of Soviet young people, despairing of the deteriorating quality of life in the USSR, will tell you that their only desire is to live in a "normal" country, that is to say, a liberal democracy undistorted by the ideology of Marxism-Leninism. As one Soviet friend told me in 1988, she has had a hard time getting her children to do their homework since "everybody knows" that democracy means "you can do whatever you wish."

More importantly, the people who felt anger were not just the system's victims, but its beneficiaries as well. Aleksandr Yakovlev, the Politburo member from 1986 to 1990 who was the architect of the policy of *glasnost'*, Eduard Shevardnadze, the foreign minister who articulated the policy of "new thinking," and Boris Yeltsin, the president of Russia, all spent their careers in the heart of the Communist party's apparatus. Like the members of the Francoist Cortes, or the Argentine and Greek generals who voluntarily gave up power, these individuals knew that there was a very deep sickness at the heart of the Soviet system, and were put in positions of major responsibility where they could do something about it. The reform efforts of the late 1980s were not imposed on the Soviet Union from the outside, though competition with the United States underlined the need for reform. Instead, they came about as a result of an internal crisis of confidence that had infected a broad segment of the Soviet elite over the preceding generation.

The undermining of the system's legitimacy was not planned ahead of time, nor did it occur overnight. Gorbachev initially used *glasnost'* and democratization as tools to consolidate his own leadership position, and later to mobilize popular opposition to the entrenched economic bureaucracy. In doing so he was not deviating from the tactics that Khrushchev had used in the 1950s.[12] But these initial acts of largely symbolic political liberalization soon took on a life of their own and became changes sought for their own sake. Gorbachev's initial call for *glasnost'* and *perestroika* struck an immediate responsive chord among the host of intellectuals, who did not need to be convinced of the system's defects. And it turned out that there was only one consistent set of standards by which the old system was measured and found a failure: those of liberal democracy, that is, the productivity of market-oriented economics and the freedom of democratic politics.[13]

The Soviet people, humiliated by their rulers and despised not only by the rest of Europe but by their own intellectuals as passive accomplices of authoritarianism, proved everyone wrong. After 1989, civil society began reconstituting itself from the clear-cut ground of totalitarianism, through the formation of tens of thousands of new associations—political parties, labor unions, new journals and newspapers, ecology clubs, literary societies, churches, nationalist groups, and the like. The Soviet people's supposed acceptance of the legitimacy of the old authoritarian social contract was belied by the enormous majorities that voted against representatives of the old communist apparatus at every available opportunity. The political maturity of the Russian people, in particular, was nowhere more evident than in their selection of a Boris Yeltsin as their first popularly elected president, rather than a semi-fascist demagogue like Serbia's Milosevic, or a half-hearted democrat like Gorbachev. This maturity was further demonstrated when the Russian people rose to Yeltsin's call to defend their new democratic institutions against the conservative coup launched in August 1981. Like the Eastern Europeans before them, they proved not inert and atomized, but spontaneously ready to defend their dignity and rights.[14]

So massive a disillusionment with the Soviet Union's underlying belief structure could not have occurred overnight, suggesting that totalitarianism as a system had failed well before the 1980s. And indeed, the beginning of the end of totalitarianism can probably be traced all the way back to the period following the death of Stalin in 1953, when the regime ended the use of indiscriminate terror.[15] After Khrushchev's so-called "secret speech" in 1956 and the closing of Stalin's Gulag, the regime could no longer rely on pure coercion to enforce its policies, and increasingly had to resort to cajolery, cooptation, and bribery to get people to go along with its goals. The transition away from pure terror was in some sense inevitable, because under the Stalinist system, no one in the leadership itself could ever feel secure—not Stalin's police chiefs Yezhov and Beria, who were both executed, not his foreign minister Molotov, whose wife was sent to the Gulag, not his successor Khrushchev, who vividly described how an odd glance from Stalin could make a member of the Politburo fear for his life—not Stalin himself, who was constantly fearful of plots. The dismantling of a system of terror so deadly to its practitioners therefore became almost mandatory once Stalin's death made it possible for the top leadership to do so.

The Soviet regime's decision not to kill people indiscriminately changed the balance of power between state and society in favor of the latter, and meant that henceforth the Soviet state would not remain in control of all aspects of Soviet life. Consumer demand, or the black market, or local political machines, could no longer be simply crushed or manipulated. Intimidation by the police remained an important weapon of the state, but it was often held in the background and had to be supplemented by other policy instruments like the promise of more consumer goods. Prior to Gorbachev, as much as 20 percent of Soviet GNP was produced in or filtered through the black market, totally outside the control of central planners.

An example of the center's weakening control was the emergence of a number of "mafias" in the non-Russian republics of the USSR during the 1960s and 70s, such as the infamous "cotton mafia" that prospered in Uzbekistan under the leadership of Communist party first secretary Rashidov. Protected by his personal relationship with Soviet president Brezhnev, Brezhnev's daughter Galina, and her husband Churbanov (a police official in Moscow), Rashidov was able to preside over a corrupt bureaucratic empire for many years. This group of officials succeeded in cooking the books on cotton production in the republic, funneling vast amounts of resources into personal bank accounts, and running the local party organization with virtually no oversight from Moscow. Mafias of varying sorts proliferated throughout Soviet society in this period, primarily in the non-Russian republics, but also in places like Moscow and Leningrad as well.

Such a system cannot be described as totalitarian; nor is it just another form of authoritarianism like the dictatorships of Latin America. Perhaps the best label to describe the Soviet Union and Eastern Europe of the Brezhnev era is that used by Václav Havel, who called these regimes "post-totalitarian," indicating that while they were no longer bloody police states of the 1930s and 40s, they still lived under the shadow of earlier totalitarian practice.[16] Totalitarianism was not sufficient to kill the democratic idea in these societies, but its legacy constrained their ability to democratize subsequently.

Totalitarianism failed as well in the People's Republic of China and the countries of Eastern Europe. Central government control over the Chinese economy even at the height of the PRC's "Stalinist" period had never been as complete as in the Soviet Union, with perhaps a quarter of the economy never having come under the purview of the national plan. When Deng Xiaoping set the country on the course of economic reform in 1978, many Chinese still had a vivid memory of markets and entrepreneurship from the 1950s, so it is perhaps not surprising that they were able to take advantage of economic liberalization in the following decade. While continuing to pay lip service to Mao and Marxism-Leninism, Deng effectively restored private property in the countryside and opened up the country to the global capitalist economy. Initiation of the economic reform constituted an early and clear-sighted recognition by the communist leadership of the failure of socialist central planning.

A totalitarian state that permits an extensive private sector is by definition no longer totalitarian. Civil society—in the form of spontaneous business organizations, entrepreneurs, informal societies, and so on—regenerated itself very quickly in China in the atmosphere of relative freedom that prevailed between 1978 and the 1989 crackdown. The Chinese leadership calculated that it could guarantee its own legitimacy by taking on the role of agent of China's modernization and reform, rather than by dogged defense of Marxist orthodoxies.

But legitimacy was as difficult to achieve as in the Soviet case. Economic modernization required an opening of Chinese society to foreign ideas and influences; it devolved power from the state to civil society; it offered opportunities for corruption and other social abuses that are difficult to correct in one-party political systems; and it created an increasingly well-educated and cosmopolitan elite in the large cities that served as the functional equivalent of a middle class. It was the latter whose children organized the protests that began in Tienanmen Square in April 1989 on the anniversary of Hu Yaobang's death.[17] These students, some of whom had studied in the West and who were familiar with political practices outside of China, were no longer satisfied with the Chinese Communist party's lopsided reform that permitted considerable economic freedom but no political freedom whatsoever.

There are those who have suggested that the student protests in Tienanmen Square were less the expression of a spontaneous demand for political participation than the reflection of a power struggle taking place for Deng's mantle between Zhao Ziyang and Li Peng.[18] This might well be so: Zhao was clearly more sympathetic to the student protesters than the rest of the leadership, and he made a desperate bid to save himself by appealing to them prior to the June 4 crackdown.[19] But the fact that the protests were the product of political manipulation from above does not mean that they were not the expression of a more fundamental dissatisfaction in Chinese society with the existing political system. Moreover, succession is a vulnerability of all would-be totalitarianisms. With no commonly accepted constitutional mechanism for succession to power, contenders for leadership are constantly tempted to play the reform card as a means of getting the better of their rivals. But playing this card almost inevitably unleashes new forces and attitudes in society that then escape the control of the manipulator.

After the events of 1989, China has become just another Asian authoritarian state. It lacks internal legitimacy for a broad sector of its own elite, particularly among the young who will someday inherit the country, and is not guided by a coherent ideology. The PRC will no longer serve as a model for revolutionaries around the world, as it once did under Mao, all the more so when it is compared to the fast-growing capitalist states of the region.

As late as the summer of 1989, when the East German refugee crisis was just beginning, many people in the West speculated that socialism had taken root in East Germany and other parts of Eastern Europe, and that given their freedom, the peoples of these countries would choose a "humane" left-wing alternative that was neither communism nor capitalist democracy. This proved to be a total illusion. The failure of totalitarianism in Eastern Europe, where Soviet institutions were forcibly imposed on unwilling populations, came much more quickly than it did in either the Soviet Union or China. This perhaps should not have been surprising. Civil society had been destroyed in a less thoroughgoing way, depending on the specific country in question: in Poland, for example, agriculture had not been collectivized as it had in neighboring Ukraine and Belorussia, and the Church was left more or less independent. In addition to all of the reasons that the Soviet population had for resisting communist values, the force of local nationalism served to keep alive the memory of pre-communist society, and permitted its rapid regeneration after the upheavals of late 1989. Once the Soviets indicated they would not intervene to prop up local allies in Eastern Europe, the only surprising outcome was the totality of the demoralization of the communist apparatuses in all of the Eastern European countries, and the fact that hardly anyone in the old guard was willing to lift a finger in self-defense.

In sub-Saharan Africa, African socialism and the post-colonial tradition of strong one-party states had become almost totally discredited by the end of the 1980s, as much of the region experienced economic collapse and civil war. Most disastrous was the experience of rigidly Marxist states like Ethiopia, Angola, and Mozambique. Functioning democracies emerged in Botswana, Gambia, Senegal, Mauritius, and Namibia, while authoritarian rulers were compelled to promise free elections in a host of other African countries.

China, of course, continues to be ruled by a communist government, as do Cuba, North Korea, and Vietnam. But a very great change took place in the perception of communism after the sudden collapse of six communist regimes in Eastern Europe between July and December 1989. Communism, which had once portrayed itself as a higher and more advanced form of civilization than liberal democracy, would henceforth be associated with a high degree of political and economic backwardness. While communist power persists in the world, it has ceased to reflect a dynamic and appealing idea. Those who call themselves communists now find themselves fighting continuous rearguard actions to preserve something of their former position and power. Communists now find themselves in the unenviable position of defending an old and reactionary social order whose time has long since passed, like the monarchists who managed to survive into the twentieth century. The ideological threat they once posed to liberal democracy is finished, and with the withdrawal of the Red Army from Eastern Europe, much of the military threat will be gone as well.

While democratic ideas undermined the legitimacy of communist regimes around the world, democracy itself has had tremendous difficulties in establishing itself. The student protests in China were crushed by the party and army, and some of Deng's earlier economic reforms were subsequently rescinded. The future of democracy is far from secure in the Soviet Union's fifteen republics. Bulgaria and Romania have seen continuous political turmoil since their former communist rulers were turned out of office. The Yugoslav state has experienced civil war and disintegration. Only Hungary, Czechoslovakia, Poland, and the former East Germany appear poised to make a transition to stable democracy and market economies in the next decade, though even in these cases the economic problems they face are proving much larger than previously expected.

The argument has been made that even though communism is dead, it is rapidly being replaced by an intolerant and aggressive nationalism. It is premature to commemorate the passing of the strong state—so the argument goes—for where communist totalitarianism fails to survive, it will simply be replaced by nationalist authoritarianism, or perhaps even by fascism of a Russian or Serbian variety. This part of the world will be neither peaceful nor democratic any time in the near future, and according to this school of thought will turn out to be just as dangerous to existing Western democracies as the old Soviet Union was.

But we should not be surprised if all of the formerly communist countries do not make a rapid and smooth transition to stable democracy; in fact, it would be very surprising if this did happen. There are enormous obstacles that need to be overcome before successful democracies can arise. For example, the old Soviet Union was simply incapable of democratizing. A USSR free enough to be considered a genuine democracy would immediately split up along national and ethnic lines into a series of smaller states. This does not mean, however, that individual parts of the USSR, including the Russian Federation or the Ukraine, could not democratize. But democratization will have to be preceded by a painful process of national separation, one that will not be accomplished quickly or without bloodshed. This process began with the renegotiation of the Union Treaty among nine of the USSR's fifteen republics in April 1991, and accelerated rapidly after the failed August coup.

Moreover, there is no inherent contradiction between democracy and at least some of the newly emerging nationalisms. While stable liberal democracy is highly unlikely to be established in Uzbekistan or Tadjkistan anytime soon, there is no reason to think that Lithuania or Estonia will be less liberal than Sweden or Finland once given their national independence. Nor is it the case that the new nationalisms being unleashed are necessarily expansionist or aggressive. One of the most remarkable developments of the late 1980s to early 1990s has been the evolution of the mainstream of Russian nationalism in the direction of a "small Russia" concept, evident not just in the thinking of liberals like Boris Yeltsin, but among conservative nationalists like Eduard Volodin and Victor Astaf'yev.

We should be careful to distinguish transitional conditions from permanent ones. In parts of the Soviet Union and Eastern Europe, we are likely to see Marxist-Leninists replaced by a variety of dictators, nationalists, and colonels; even communists may stage comebacks in certain areas. But the authoritarianism they represent will remain localized and unsystematic. Like the various military dictators in Latin America, they will eventually have to confront the fact that they have no long-term source of legitimacy, and no good formula for solving the long-term economic and political problems they will face. The only coherent ideology that enjoys widespread legitimacy in this part of the world remains liberal democracy. While many of the peoples of this region may not make the transition to democracy in this generation, they may well do so in the next. Western Europe's transition to liberal democracy was long and hard as well, a fact that did not prevent every country in that region from eventually completing the journey.

Communist totalitarianism was supposed to be a formula for halting the natural and organic processes of social evolution and replacing them with a series of forced revolutions from above: the destruction of old social classes, rapid industrialization, and the collectivization of agriculture. This type of large-scale social engineering was supposed to have set communist societies apart from non-totalitarian ones, because social change originated in the state rather than in society. The normal rules of economic and political modernization, held by social scientists to be virtually universal in "normal" societies, were suspended.[20] The reform processes of the 1980s in the Soviet Union and China will have revealed something very important about human social evolution, even if they do not succeed in the near term. For while totalitarianism managed to destroy the visible institutions of pre-revolutionary Russian and Chinese society, it was utterly ineffective in its aspirations to create a new man of either the Soviet or Maoist variety. Elites in both countries emerged from the Brezhnev and Mao eras looking far more like their Western counterparts at a comparable level of economic development than anyone had anticipated. Their most advanced elites were able to appreciate, if not exactly able to share, the common consumer culture of Western Europe, America, and Japan, and many of their political ideas as well. While retaining numerous uniquely "post-totalitarian" traits, people in the Soviet Union and PRC turned out not to be the atomized, dependent, authority-craving children that earlier Western theories projected them to be. They proved instead to be adults who could tell truth from falsehood, right from wrong, and who sought, like other adults in the old age of mankind, recognition of their adulthood and autonomy.

4

The Worldwide Liberal Revolution

*We stand at the gates of an important epoch, a time of ferment, when spirit
moves forward in a leap, transcends its previous shape and takes on a new
one. All the mass of previous representations, concepts, and bonds linking our
world together are dissolving and collapsing like a dream picture. A new phase
of the spirit is preparing itself. Philosophy especially has to welcome its
appearance and acknowledge it, while others, who oppose it impotently, cling to
the past.*

—G. W. F. Hegel, in a lecture on September 18, 1806[1]

On both the communist Left and the authoritarian Right there
has been a bankruptcy of serious ideas capable of sustaining the
internal political cohesion of strong governments, whether based
on "monolithic" parties, military juntas, or personalistic dictatorships. The absence of legitimate authority has meant that when an
authoritarian government met with failure in some area of policy,
there was no higher principle to which the regime could appeal.
Some have compared legitimacy to a kind of cash reserve. All
governments, democratic and authoritarian, have their ups and
downs; but only legitimate governments have this reserve to draw
on in times of crisis.

The weakness of authoritarian states of the Right lay in their
failure to control civil society. Coming to power with a certain
mandate to restore order or to impose "economic discipline,"
many found themselves no more successful than their democratic
predecessors in stimulating steady economic growth or in creating
a sense of social order. And those that were successful were
hoisted on their own petard. For the societies on top of which they

39

sat began to outgrow them as they became better educated, more prosperous, and middle class. As memory of the specific emergency that had justified strong government faded, those societies became less and less ready to tolerate military rule.

Totalitarian governments of the Left sought to avoid these problems by subordinating the whole of civil society to their control, including what their citizens were allowed to think. But such a system in its pure form could be maintained only through a terror that threatened the system's own rulers. Once that terror was relaxed, a long process of degeneration set in, during which the state lost control of certain key aspects of civil society. Most important was its loss of control over the belief system. And since the socialist formula for economic growth was defective, the state could not prevent its citizens from taking note of this fact and drawing their own conclusions.

Moreover, few totalitarian regimes could replicate themselves through one or more succession crises. In the absence of commonly accepted rules of succession, it would always be a temptation for some ambitious contender for power to throw the whole system into question by calls for fundamental reform in the struggle against his rivals. The reform card is a powerful trump because dissatisfaction with Stalinist systems is high everywhere. Thus Khrushchev used anti-Stalinism against Beria and Malenkov, Gorbachev used it against his Brezhnev-era competitors, and Zhao Ziyang used it against the hard-line Li Peng. The question of whether the individuals or groups contending for power were real democrats was in a sense irrelevant, since the succession process tended to undermine the old regime's credibility by exposing its inevitable abuses. New social and political forces, more sincerely committed to liberal ideas, were unleashed and soon escaped the control of those who planned the first limited reforms.

The weakness of strong states has meant that many former authoritarianisms have now given way to democracy, while the former post-totalitarian states have become simple authoritarianisms, if not democracies. The Soviet Union has devolved power to its constituent republics, and while China continues to be a dictatorship, the regime has lost control of significant parts of society. Neither country possesses any longer the ideological coherence once given them by Marxism-Leninism: the conservatives opposed to reform in the Soviet Union are as likely to place an Orthodox icon on their wall as a picture of Lenin. The would-be makers of the August 1991 coup resembled a Latin American military junta, with army officers and police officials playing a major role.

In addition to the crisis of political authoritarianism, there has been a quieter but no less significant revolution going on in the field of economics. The development that was both manifestation and cause of this revolution was the phenomenal economic growth of East Asia since World War II. This success story was not limited to early modernizers like Japan, but eventually came to include virtually all countries in Asia willing to adopt market principles and integrate themselves fully into the global, capitalist economic system. Their performance suggested that poor countries without resources other than their own hardworking populations could take advantage of the openness of the international economic system and create unimagined amounts of new wealth, rapidly closing the gap with the more established capitalist powers of Europe and North America.

The East Asian economic miracle was carefully observed around the world, nowhere more than in the communist bloc. Communism's terminal crisis began in some sense when the Chinese leadership recognized that they were being left behind by the rest of capitalist Asia, and saw that socialist central planning had condemned China to backwardness and poverty. The ensuing Chinese liberalizing reforms led to a doubling of grain production in five years and provided a new demonstration of the power of market principles. The Asian lesson was later absorbed by economists in the Soviet Union, who knew the terrible waste and inefficiency that central planning had brought about in their own country. The Eastern Europeans had less need to be taught; they understood better than other communists that their failure to reach the living standards of their fellow Europeans in the West was due to the socialist system imposed on them after the war by the Soviets.

But students of the East Asian economic miracle were not restricted to the communist bloc. A remarkable transformation has taken place in the economic thinking of Latin Americans as well.[2] In the 1950s, when the Argentine economist Raul Prebisch headed the United Nations Economic Committee for Latin America, it was fashionable to attribute the underdevelopment not only of Latin America but of the Third World more generally to the global capitalist system. It was argued that early developers in Europe and America had in effect structured the world economy in their favor and condemned those who came later to dependent positions as providers of raw materials. By the early 1990s, that understanding had changed entirely: President Carlos Salinas de Gortari in Mexico, President Carlos Menem in Argentina, and President Fernando Collor de Mello in Brazil, all sought to implement far-reaching programs of economic liberalization after coming to power, accepting the need for market competition and openness to the world economy. Chile put liberal economic principles into practice earlier in the 1980s under Pinochet, with the result that its economy was the healthiest of any in the Southern Cone as it emerged from dictatorship under the leadership of President Patricio Alwyn. These new, democratically elected leaders started from the premise that underdevelopment was not due to the inherent inequities of capitalism, but rather to the insufficient degree of capitalism that had been practiced in their countries in the past. Privatization and free trade have become the new watchwords in place of nationalization and import substitution. The Marxist orthodoxy of Latin American intellectuals has come under increasing challenge from writers like Hernando de Soto, Mario Vargas Llosa, and Carlos Rangel, who have begun to find a significant audience for liberal, market-oriented economic ideas.

As mankind approaches the end of the millennium, the twin crises of authoritarianism and socialist central planning have left only one competitor standing in the ring as an ideology of potentially universal validity: liberal democracy, the doctrine of individual freedom and popular sovereignty. Two hundred years after they first animated the French and American revolutions, the principles of liberty and equality have proven not just durable but resurgent.[3]

Liberalism and democracy, while closely related, are separate concepts. Political liberalism can be defined simply as a rule of law that recognizes certain individual rights or freedoms from government control. While there can be a wide variety of definitions of fundamental rights, we will use the one contained in Lord Bryce's classic work on democracy, which limits them to three: civil rights, "the exemption from control of the citizen in respect of his person and property"; religious rights, "exemption from control in the expression of religious opinions and the practice of worship"; and what he calls political rights, "exemption from control in matters which do not so plainly affect the welfare of the whole community as to render control necessary," including the fundamental right of press freedom.[4] It has been a common practice for socialist countries to press for the recognition of various second- and third-generation economic rights, such as the right to employment, housing, or health care. The problem with such an expanded list is that the achievement of these rights is not clearly compatible with other rights like those of property or free economic exchange. In our definition we will stick to Bryce's shorter and more traditional list of rights, which is compatible with those contained in the American Bill of Rights.

Democracy, on the other hand, is the right held universally by all citizens to have a share of political power, that is, the right of all citizens to vote and participate in politics. The right to participate in political power can be thought of as yet another liberal right—indeed, the most important one—and it is for this reason that liberalism has been closely associated historically with democracy.

In judging which countries are democratic, we will use a strictly formal definition of democracy. A country is democratic if it grants its people the right to choose their own government through periodic, secret-ballot, multi-party elections,[5] on the basis of universal and equal adult suffrage.[6] It is true that formal democracy alone does not always guarantee equal participation and rights. Democratic procedures can be manipulated by elites, and do not always accurately reflect the will or true self-interests of the people. But once we move away from a formal definition, we open up the possibility of infinite abuse of the democratic principle. In this century, the greatest enemies of democracy have attacked "formal" democracy in the name of "substantive" democracy. This was the justification used by Lenin and the Bolshevik party to close down the Russian Constituent Assembly and proclaim a party dictatorship, which was to achieve substantive democracy "in the name of the people." Formal democracy, on the other hand, provides real institutional safeguards against dictatorship, and is much more likely to produce "substantive" democracy in the end.

While liberalism and democracy usually go together, they can be separated in theory. It is possible for a country to be liberal without being particularly democratic, as was eighteenth-century Britain. A broad list of rights, including the franchise, was fully protected for a narrow social elite, but denied to others. It is also possible for a country to be democratic without being liberal, that is, without protecting the rights of individuals and minorities. A good example of this is the contemporary Islamic Republic of Iran, which has held regular elections that were reasonably fair by Third World standards, making the country more democratic than it was in the time of the Shah. Islamic Iran, however, is not a liberal state; there are no guarantees of free speech, assembly, and, above all, of religion. The most elementary rights of Iranian citizens are not protected by the rule of law, a situation that is worse for Iran's ethnic and religious minorities.

In its economic manifestation, liberalism is the recognition of the right of free economic activity and economic exchange based on private property and markets. Since the term "capitalism" has acquired so many pejorative connotations over the years, it has recently become a fashion to speak of "free-market economics" instead; both are acceptable alternative terms for economic liberalism. It is evident that there are many possible interpretations of this rather broad definition of economic liberalism, ranging from the United States of Ronald Reagan and the Britain of Margaret Thatcher to the social democracies of Scandinavia and the relatively statist regimes in Mexico and India. All contemporary capitalist states have large public sectors, while most socialist states have permitted a degree of private economic activity. There has been considerable controversy over the point at which the public sector becomes large enough to disqualify a state as liberal. Rather than try to set a precise percentage, it is probably more useful to look at what attitude the state takes *in principle* to the legitimacy of private property and enterprise. Those that protect such economic rights we will consider liberal; those that are opposed or base themselves on other principles (such as "economic justice") will not qualify.

The present crisis of authoritarianism has not necessarily led to the emergence of liberal democratic regimes, nor are all the new democracies which have emerged secure. The newly democratic countries of Eastern Europe face wrenching transformations of their economies, while the new democracies in Latin America are hobbled by a terrible legacy of prior economic mismanagement. Many of the fast developers in East Asia, while economically liberal, have not accepted the challenge of political liberalization. The liberal revolution has left certain areas like the Middle East relatively untouched.[7] It is altogether possible to imagine states like Peru or the Philippines relapsing into some kind of dictatorship under the weight of the crushing problems they face.

But the fact that there will be setbacks and disappointments in the process of democratization, or that not every market economy will prosper, should not distract us from the larger pattern that is emerging in world history. The apparent number of choices that countries face in determining how they will organize themselves politically and economically has been *diminishing* over time. Of the different types of regimes that have emerged in the course of human history, from monarchies and aristocracies, to religious theocracies, to the fascist and communist dictatorships of this century, the only form of government that has survived intact to the end of the twentieth century has been liberal democracy.

What is emerging victorious, in other words, is not so much liberal practice, as the liberal *idea*. That is to say, for a very large part of the world, there is now no ideology with pretensions to universality that is in a position to challenge liberal democracy, and no universal principle of legitimacy other than the sovereignty of the people. Monarchism in its various forms had been largely defeated by the beginning of this century. Fascism and communism, liberal democracy's main competitors up till now, have both discredited themselves. If the Soviet Union (or its successor states) fails to democratize, if Peru or the Philippines relapse into some form of authoritarianism, democracy will most likely have yielded to a colonel or bureaucrat who claims to speak in the name of the Russian, Peruvian, or Philippine people alone. Even non-democrats will have to speak the language of democracy in order to justify their deviation from the single universal standard.

It is true that Islam constitutes a systematic and coherent ideology, just like liberalism and communism, with its own code of morality and doctrine of political and social justice. The appeal of Islam is potentially universal, reaching out to all men as men, and not just to members of a particular ethnic or national group. And Islam has indeed defeated liberal democracy in many parts of the Islamic world, posing a grave threat to liberal practices even in countries where it has not achieved political power directly. The end of the Cold War in Europe was followed immediately by a challenge to the West from Iraq, in which Islam was arguably a factor.[8]

Despite the power demonstrated by Islam in its current revival, however, it remains the case that this religion has virtually no appeal outside those areas that were culturally Islamic to begin with. The days of Islam's cultural conquests, it would seem, are over: it can win back lapsed adherents, but has no resonance for young people in Berlin, Tokyo, or Moscow. And while nearly a billion people are culturally Islamic—one-fifth of the world's population—they cannot challenge liberal democracy on its own territory on the level of ideas.[9] Indeed, the Islamic world would seem more vulnerable to liberal ideas in the long run than the reverse, since such liberalism has attracted numerous and powerful Muslim adherents over the past century and a half. Part of the reason for the current, fundamentalist revival is the strength of the perceived threat from liberal, Western values to traditional Islamic societies.

We who live in stable, long-standing liberal democracies face an unusual situation. In our grandparents' time, many reasonable people could foresee a radiant socialist future in which private property and capitalism had been abolished, and in which politics itself was somehow overcome. Today, by contrast, we have trouble imagining a world that is radically better than our own, or a future that is not essentially democratic and capitalist. Within that framework, of course, many things could be improved: we could house the homeless, guarantee opportunity for minorities and women, improve competitiveness, and create new jobs. We can also imagine future worlds that are significantly worse than what we know now, in which national, racial, or religious intolerance makes a comeback, or in which we are overwhelmed by war or environmental collapse. But we cannot picture to ourselves a world that is *essentially* different from the present one, and at the same time better. Other, less reflective ages also thought of themselves as the best, but we arrive at this conclusion exhausted, as it were, from the pursuit of alternatives we felt *had* to be better than liberal democracy.[10]

The fact that this is so, and the breadth of the current worldwide liberal revolution, invites us to raise the following question: Are we simply witnessing a momentary upturn in the fortunes of liberal democracy, or is there some longer-term pattern of development at work that will eventually lead all countries in the direction of liberal democracy?

It is possible, after all, that the present trend toward democracy is a cyclical phenomenon. One need only look back to the late 1960s and early 70s, when the United States was undergoing a crisis of self-confidence brought on by its involvement in the Vietnam War and the Watergate scandal. The West as a whole was thrown into economic crisis as a result of the OPEC oil embargo; most of Latin America's democracies were overthrown in a series of military coups; and un- or anti-democratic regimes seemed to be prospering around the world, from the Soviet Union, Cuba, and Vietnam to Saudi Arabia, Iran, and South Africa. What reason, then, do we have to expect that the situation of the 1970s will not recur, or worse yet, that the 1930s, with its clash of virulent anti-democratic ideologies, can not return?

Can it not be argued, moreover, that the current crisis of authoritarianism is a fluke, a rare convergence of political planets that will not recur for the next hundred years? For careful study of the different transitions away from authoritarianism in the 1970s and 80s will yield a plethora of lessons concerning the accidental nature of these events. The more one knows about a particular country, the more one is aware of the "maelstrom of external contingency" that differentiated that country from its neighbors, and the seemingly fortuitous circumstances that led to a democratic outcome.[11] Things could have worked out very differently: the Portuguese Communist party could have emerged victorious in 1975, or the Spanish transition might not have resulted in democracy had King Juan Carlos not played so skillful and moderating a role. Liberal ideas have no force independent of the human actors who put them into effect, and if Andropov or Chernenko had lived longer, or if Gorbachev himself had a different personality, the course of events in the Soviet Union and Eastern Europe between 1985 and 1991 would have been quite different. Following the current fashion in the social sciences, one is tempted to say that unpredictable political factors like leadership and public opinion dominate the democratization process and ensure that every case will be unique both in process and outcome.

But it is precisely if we look not just at the past fifteen years, but at the *whole scope of history,* that liberal democracy begins to occupy a special kind of place. While there have been cycles in the worldwide fortunes of democracy, there has also been a pronounced secular trend in a democratic direction. The table on pages 49–50 illustrates this pattern over time. It indicates that the growth of democracy has not been continuous or unidirectional; Latin America had fewer democracies in 1975 than it did in 1955, and the world as a whole was less democratic in 1940 than it was in 1919. Periods of democratic upsurge are interrupted by radical discontinuities and setbacks, such as those represented by nazism and Stalinism. On the other hand, all of these reverses tended to be themselves reversed eventually, leading over time to an impressive overall growth in the number of democracies around the world. The percentage of the world's population living under democratic government would grow dramatically, moreover, should the Soviet Union or China democratize in the next generation, in whole or in part. Indeed, the growth of liberal democracy, together with its companion, economic liberalism, has been the most remarkable macropolitical phenomenon of the last four hundred years.

It is true that democracies have been relatively rare in human history, so rare that before 1776 there was not a single one in existence anywhere in the world. (The democracy of Periclean Athens does not qualify, because it did not systematically protect individual rights.)[13] Counted in the number of years they have existed, factory production and automobiles and cities with multiple millions of inhabitants have been equally rare, while practices like slavery, hereditary monarchies, and dynastic marriages have persisted for enormous periods of time. What is significant, however, is not the frequency or length of occurrence, but the trend: in the developed world, we would as little expect to see the disappearance of cities or cars in the near future as we would the re-emergence of slavery.

It is against this background that the remarkable worldwide character of the current liberal revolution takes on special significance. For it constitutes further evidence that there is a fundamental process at work that dictates a common evolutionary pattern for *all* human societies—in short, something like a Universal History of mankind in the direction of liberal democracy. The existence of peaks and troughs in this development is undeniable. But to cite the failure of liberal democracy in any given country, or even in an entire region of the world, as evidence of

Liberal Democracies Worldwide[12]

	1790	1848	1900	1919	1940	1960	1975	1990
United States	x	x	x	x	x	x	x	x
Canada			x	x	x	x	x	x
Switzerland	x	x	x	x	x	x	x	x
Great Britain		x	x	x	x	x	x	x
France	x		x	x		x	x	x
Belgium		x	x	x		x	x	x
Netherlands		x	x	x		x	x	x
Denmark			x	x		x	x	x
Piedmont/Italy			x	x		x	x	x
Spain								x
Portugal								x
Sweden			x	x	x	x	x	x
Norway				x		x	x	x
Greece			x			x		x
Austria				x		x	x	x
Germany, West				x		x	x	x
Germany, East				x				x
Poland				x				x
Czechoslovakia				x				x
Hungary								x
Bulgaria								x
Romania								x
Turkey						x	x	x
Latvia								x
Lithuania								x
Estonia				x				x
Finland				x	x	x	x	x
Ireland					x	x	x	x
Australia				x	x	x	x	x
New Zealand				x	x	x	x	x
Chile			x	x		x		x
Argentina			x	x				x
Brazil						x		x
Uruguay				x	x	x		x
Paraguay								x
Mexico					x	x	x	x
Colombia				x	x	x	x	x
Costa Rica				x	x	x	x	x
Bolivia						x		x
Venezuela						x	x	x
Peru						x		x

continued

Liberal Democracies Worldwide[12] (*continued*)

	1790	1848	1900	1919	1940	1960	1975	1990
Ecuador						x		x
El Salvador						x		x
Nicaragua								x
Honduras								x
Jamaica							x	x
Dominican Republic								x
Trinidad							x	x
Japan						x	x	x
India						x	x	x
Sri Lanka						x	x	x
Singapore							x	x
South Korea								x
Thailand								x
Philippines						x		x
Mauritius								x
Senegal							x	x
Botswana								x
Namibia								x
Papua New Guinea								x
Israel						x	x	x
Lebanon						x		
Totals	3	5	13	25	13	36	30	61

democracy's overall weakness, reveals a striking narrowness of view. Cycles and discontinuities in themselves are not incompatible with a history that is directional and universal, just as the existence of business cycles does not negate the possibility of long-term economic growth.

Just as impressive as the growth in the number of democracies is the fact that democratic government has broken out of its original beachhead in Western Europe and North America, and has made significant inroads in other parts of the world that do not share the political, religious, and cultural traditions of those areas. The argument was once made that there was a distinct Iberian tradition that was "authoritarian, patrimonial, Catholic, stratified, corporate and semi-feudal to the core."[14] To hold Spain, Portugal, or the countries of Latin America to the standards of the liberal democracy of Western Europe or the United States was to be guilty of "ethnocentrism."[15] Yet those universal standards of rights were those to which people in the Iberian tradition held *themselves,* and since the mid-1970s Spain and Portugal have graduated to the ranks of stable democracies, tied ever more tightly to an economically integrating Europe. These same standards have had meaning for peoples in Latin America, Eastern Europe, Asia, and many other parts of the world as well. The success of democracy in a wide variety of places and among many different peoples would suggest that the principles of liberty and equality on which they are based are not accidents or the results of ethnocentric prejudice, but are in fact discoveries about the nature of man as man, whose truth does not diminish but grows more evident as one's point of view becomes more cosmopolitan.

The question of whether there is such a thing as a Universal History of mankind that takes into account the experiences of all times and all peoples is not new; it is in fact a very old one which recent events compel us to raise anew. From the beginning, the most serious and systematic attempts to write Universal Histories saw the central issue in history as the development of Freedom. History was not a blind concatenation of events, but a meaningful whole in which human ideas concerning the nature of a just political and social order developed and played themselves out. And if we are now at a point where we cannot imagine a world substantially different from our own, in which there is no apparent or obvious way in which the future will represent a fundamental improvement over our current order, then we must also take into consideration the possibility that History itself might be at an end.

Part Two, then, will take up the question of whether, at the end of the twentieth century, it makes sense for us to shake off our acquired pessimism and reconsider once again whether it is possible to write a Universal History of mankind.

Part II

THE OLD AGE OF MANKIND

5

An Idea for a Universal History

The historical imagination has never flown so far, even in a dream; for now the history of man is merely the continuation of that of animals and plants; the universal historian finds traces of himself even in the utter depths of the sea, in the living slime. He stands astounded in the face of the enormous way that man has run, and his gaze quivers before the mightier wonder, the modern man who can see all the way! He stands proudly on the pyramid of the world-process; and while he lays the final stone of his knowledge, he seems to cry aloud to listening Nature: "We are at the top, we are at the top; we are the completion of Nature!"

—*Nietzsche,* The Use and Abuse of History[1]

A Universal History of mankind is not the same thing as a history of the universe. That is, it is not an encyclopaedic catalogue of everything that is known about humanity, but rather an attempt to find a meaningful pattern in the overall development of human societies generally.[2] The effort to write a Universal History is itself not universal to all peoples and cultures. Despite the fact that the Western philosophical and historical tradition started in Greece, the writers of Greek antiquity never undertook such a project. Plato in the *Republic* spoke about a certain natural cycle of regimes, while Aristotle's *Politics* discussed the causes of revolution and how one type of regime yields to another.[3] Aristotle believed that no regime could satisfy man completely, and that the dissatisfaction would lead men to replace one regime with another in an endless cycle. Democracy did not occupy a special place in this sequence, either with respect to goodness or stability; in fact, both writers suggested that democracy had a tendency to give way to tyranny. Moreover, Aristotle did not assume the continuity of history. That is, he believed that the cycle of regimes was embedded in a larger natural cycle, whereby cataclysms like floods would periodically eliminate not only existing human societies, but all memory of them as well, forcing men to start the historical process over again from the beginning.[4] In the Greek view, history thus is not secular but cyclical.

The first truly Universal Histories in the Western tradition were Christian.[5] While there were Greek and Roman efforts to write histories of the known world, it was Christianity that first introduced the concept of the equality of all men in the sight of God, and thereby conceived of a shared destiny for all the peoples of the world. A Christian historian such as Saint Augustine had no interest in the particular histories of the Greeks or the Jews as such; what mattered was the redemption of man as man, an event that would constitute the working out of God's will on earth. All nations were but branches of a more general humanity, whose fate could be understood in terms of God's plan for mankind. Christianity moreover introduced the concept of a history that was finite in time, beginning with God's creation of man and ending with his final salvation.[6] For Christians, the end of earthly history would be marked by the day of judgment that would usher in the kingdom of heaven, at which point the earth and earthly events would literally cease to exist. As the Christian account of history makes clear, an "end of history" is implicit in the writing of all Universal Histories. The particular events of history can become meaningful only with respect to some larger end or goal, the achievement of which necessarily brings the historical process to a close. This final end of man is what makes all particular events potentially intelligible.

The revival of interest in the ancients that took place in the Renaissance provided an historical horizon to thought that the ancients themselves lacked. The metaphor comparing human history to the life of a single man, and the idea that modern man, building on the accomplishments of the ancients, lived in the "old age of mankind," was suggested by several writers in this period, including Pascal.[7] The most important early attempts to write secular versions of a Universal History, however, were undertaken in conjunction with the establishment of the scientific method in the sixteenth century. The method that we associate with Galileo, Bacon, and Descartes assumed the possibility of a knowledge and therefore a mastery of nature, which was in turn subject to a set of coherent and universal laws. Knowledge of these laws was not only accessible to man as man, but was cumulative, such that successive generations could be spared the efforts and mistakes of earlier ones. Thus the modern notion of progress had its origins in the success of modern natural science, and allowed Francis Bacon to assert the superiority of modernity to antiquity on the basis of inventions like the compass, printing press, and gunpowder. This concept of progress as the cumulative and endless acquisition of knowledge was stated most clearly by Bernard Le Bovier de Fontenelle in 1688:

> A good cultivated mind contains, so to speak, all minds of preceding centuries; it is but a single identical mind which has been developing and improving itself all the time . . . but I am obliged to confess that the man in question will have no old age; he will always be equally capable of those things for which his youth is suited, and he will be ever more and more capable of those things which are suited to his prime; that is to say, to abandon the allegory, men will never degenerate, and there will be no end to the growth and development of human wisdom.[8]

The progress envisioned by Fontenelle was primarily in the domain of scientific knowledge; he did not develop a corresponding theory of social or political progress. The father of the modern notion of social progress was Machiavelli, for it was he who proposed that politics be liberated from the moral constraints of classical philosophy, and that man conquer *fortuna*. Other theories of progress were advanced by Enlightenment writers such as Voltaire, the French encyclopaedists, the economist Turgot, and his friend and biographer Condorcet. Condorcet's *Progress of the Human Mind* contained a ten-stage Universal History of man, the last era of which—yet to be achieved—was characterized by equality of opportunity, liberty, rationality, democracy, and universal education.[9] Like Fontenelle, Condorcet postulated no term to human perfectibility, implying the possibility of an eleventh stage of history unknown to man at the present.

The most serious efforts at writing Universal Histories were undertaken, however, in the German idealist tradition. The idea was proposed by the great Immanuel Kant in a 1784 essay, *An Idea for a Universal History from a Cosmopolitan Point of View*. This work, though only sixteen pages long, defined the essential terms of reference for all subsequent efforts to write a Universal History.[10]

Kant was fully aware that "this idiotic course of things human" seemed to show no particular pattern on its surface, and that human history appeared to be one of constant warfare and cruelty. He nonetheless wondered whether there was not a regular movement to human history such that what seemed chaotic from the standpoint of a single individual might not reveal a slow and progressive evolution over a long period of time. This was particularly true in the development of man's reason. No one individual, for example, could expect to discover the whole of mathematics, but the cumulative character of mathematical knowledge allowed each generation to build on the accomplishments of preceding ones.[11]

Kant suggested that history would have an end point, that is to say, a final purpose that was implied in man's current potentialities and which made the whole of history intelligible. This end point was the realization of human freedom, for "a society in which freedom under external laws is associated in the highest degree with irresistible power, i.e., a perfectly just civic constitution, is the highest problem Nature assigns to the human race." The achievement of such a just civic constitution and its universalization throughout the world would then be the criterion by which one could understand progress in history. It also provided a standard by which one could undertake the tremendous effort of abstraction required to separate what was essential in this evolution from the great mass of facts about events that constitute the raw material of history. The question to be answered by a Universal History then was whether, when taking all societies and all times into account, there was overall reason to expect general human progress in the direction of republican government, that is, what we today understand as liberal democracy.[12]

Kant also outlined in general terms the mechanism that would propel mankind to the higher level of rationality represented by liberal institutions. This mechanism was not reason, but rather reason's opposite: the selfish antagonism created by man's "asocial sociability," which leads men to leave the war of all against all and join together in civil societies, and then encourage the arts and sciences so that those societies can remain competitive with one another. It was precisely man's competitiveness and vanity, his desire to dominate and rule, which was the wellspring of social creativity, ensuring the realization of potentials "unborn in an Arcadian shepherd's life."

Kant's essay did not itself constitute a Universal History. Written when the philosopher was sixty years of age, his *Idea* merely pointed to the need for a new Kepler or Newton who could explain the universal laws of human historical evolution. Kant noted that the genius who undertook such a history would have to be qualified both as a philosopher, so as to understand what was important in human affairs, and as an historian who could assimilate the history of all times and all peoples into a meaningful whole. He would follow "the influence of Greek history on the construction and misconstruction of the Roman state which swallowed up the Greek, then the Roman influence on the barbarians who in turn destroyed it, and so on down to our times; if one adds episodes from the national histories of the enlightened nations, one will discover a regular progress in the constitution of states on our continent (which will probably give law, eventually, to all the others.)" The story was one of the successive destruction of civilizations, but each overthrow preserved something from the earlier period and thereby prepared the way for a higher level of life. The task of writing this history, he concluded modestly, was beyond his abilities, but if successfully carried out could contribute to the achievement of universal republican government by giving man a clear view of his future.[13]

Kant's project of writing a Universal History that was at once philosophically serious and grounded in a mastery of empirical history was left to his successor, Georg Wilhelm Friedrich Hegel, to complete in the generation following Kant's death. Hegel has never had a good reputation in the Anglo-Saxon world, where he has been accused of being a reactionary apologist for the Prussian monarchy, a forerunner of twentieth-century totalitarianism, and, worst of all from an English perspective, a difficult-to-read metaphysician.[14] This prejudice against Hegel has blinded people to his importance as one of the constitutive philosophers of modernity. Whether or not we acknowledge our debt to him, we owe to Hegel the most fundamental aspects of our present-day consciousness.

It is remarkable the extent to which Hegel's system fulfilled all the particulars of Kant's proposal for a Universal History, both in form and substance.[15] Hegel, like Kant, defined his project as the

writing of a Universal History which would provide "the exhibi-
tion of Spirit [i.e., collective human consciousness] in the process
of working out the knowledge of that which it is potentially."[16]
Hegel sought to explain the "good" contained in the various real
states and civilizations of history, the reasons why they were ultimately overthrown, and the "germ of enlightenment" that survived from each and thereby paved the way for higher levels of
development. As in Kant's view of man's "asocial sociability," Hegel saw progress in history arising *not* from the steady development of reason, but through the blind interplay of the passions
that led men to conflict, revolution, and war—his famous "cunning of reason." History proceeds through a continual process of
conflict, wherein systems of thought as well as political systems
collide and fall apart from their own internal contradictions. They
are then replaced by less contradictory and therefore higher ones,
which give rise to new and different contradictions—the so-called
dialectic. Hegel was one of the first European philosophers to take
seriously the "national histories of other peoples" outside of Europe like those of India and China, and to incorporate them into
his overall scheme. And as Kant postulated, there was an end
point to the process of history, which is the realization of freedom
here on earth: "The History of the world is none other than the
progress of the consciousness of Freedom." The unfolding of
Universal History could be understood as the growth of the equality of human freedom, summed up in Hegel's epigram that "the
Eastern nations knew that *one* was free; the Greek and Roman
world only that *some* are free; while *we* know that all men absolutely (man as *man*) are free."[17] For Hegel, the embodiment of
human freedom was the modern constitutional state, or again,
what we have called liberal democracy. The Universal History of
mankind was nothing other than man's progressive rise to full
rationality, and to a self-conscious awareness of how that rationality expresses itself in liberal self-government.

Hegel has frequently been accused of worshipping the state
and its authority, and therefore of being an enemy of liberalism
and democracy. A fuller consideration of this charge is beyond
the scope of the present work.[18] Suffice it to say that by his own
account, Hegel was *the* philosopher of freedom, who saw the entire historical process culminating in the realization of freedom in
concrete political and social institutions. Rather than being known
as the champion of the state, Hegel could equally well be under-

stood as the defender of civil society, that is, the philosopher who justified preservation of a large realm of private economic and political activity independent of the control of the state. This is certainly the way that Marx understood him, and why he attacked Hegel as an apologist for the bourgeoisie.

There has been considerable mystification concerning the Hegelian dialectic. This began with Marx's collaborator Friedrich Engels, who believed that the dialectic was a "method" that could be appropriated from Hegel separately from the content of his system. Others have asserted that for Hegel, the dialectic was a metaphysical device that allowed one to deduce the whole of human history from *a priori* or logical first principles, independently of empirical data and knowledge of real historical events. This view of the dialectic is untenable; a reading of Hegel's historical works will reveal that historical accident and contingency play a large role in them.[19] The Hegelian dialectic is similar to its Platonic predecessor, the Socratic dialogue, that is, a conversation between two human beings on some important subject like the nature of the good or the meaning of justice. Such discussions are resolved on the basis of the principle of contradiction: that is, the less self-contradictory side wins, or, if both are found in the course of the conversation to be self-contradictory, then a third position emerges free of the contradictions of the initial two. But this third position may itself contain new, unforeseen contradictions, thereby giving rise to yet another conversation and another resolution. For Hegel, the dialectic takes place not only on the level of philosophical discussions, but between societies, or, as contemporary social scientists would say, between socio-economic systems. One might describe history as a dialogue between societies, in which those with grave internal contradictions fail and are succeeded by others that manage to overcome those contradictions. Thus for Hegel the Roman Empire ultimately collapsed because it established the universal legal equality of all men, but without recognizing their rights and inner human dignity. This recognition could only be found in the Judeo-Christian tradition, that established the universal equality of man on the basis of his moral freedom.[20] The Christian world was in turn subject to other contradictions. The classical example was the medieval city, which protected within it merchants and traders who constituted the germs of a capitalist economic order. Their superior economic efficiency eventually exposed the irrationality of moral constraints on economic productivity, and thereby abolished the very city that gave them birth.

Where Hegel differed most substantially from earlier writers of Universal Histories like Fontenelle or Condorcet was in his vastly more profound philosophical grounding for concepts such as nature, freedom, history, truth, and reason. While Hegel may not have been the first philosopher to write about history, he was the first *historicist* philosopher—that is, a philosopher who believed in the essential historical relativity of truth.[21] Hegel maintained that all human consciousness was limited by the particular social and cultural conditions of man's surrounding environment—or as we say, by "the times." Past thought, whether of ordinary people or great philosophers and scientists, was not true absolutely or "objectively," but only relative to the historical or cultural horizon within which that person lived. Human history must therefore be seen not only as a succession of different civilizations and levels of material accomplishment, but more importantly as a succession of different forms of consciousness. Consciousness—the way in which human beings think about fundamental questions of right and wrong, the activities they find satisfying, their beliefs about the gods, even the way in which they perceive the world—has changed fundamentally over time. And since these perspectives were mutually contradictory, it follows that the vast majority of them were wrong, or forms of "false consciousness" to be unmasked by subsequent history. The world's great religions, according to Hegel, were not true in themselves, but were *ideologies* which arose out of the particular historical needs of the people who believed in them. Christianity, in particular, was an ideology that grew out of slavery, and whose proclamation of universal equality served the interests of slaves in their own liberation.

The radical nature of Hegelian historicism is hard to perceive today because it is so much a part of our own intellectual horizon. We assume that there is an historical "perspectivism" to thought and share a general prejudice against ways of thinking that are not "up to date." Historicism is implicit in the position of the contemporary feminist who regards her mother's or grandmother's devotion to family and home as a quaint holdover from an earlier age. Much as that progenitor's voluntary submission to a male-dominated culture might have been right "for her time" and may even have made her happy, it is no longer acceptable and constitutes a form of "false consciousness." Historicism is also implicit in the attitude of a black who denies that it is possible for a white person to ever understand what it means to *be* black. For though the consciousness of blacks and whites is not necessarily separated by historical time, they are held to be separated by the horizon of culture and experience within which each was nurtured, and across which there is only the most limited of communication.

The radicalness of Hegel's historicism is evident in his very concept of man. With one important exception, virtually every philosopher writing before Hegel believed that there was such a thing as "human nature," that is, a more or less permanent set of traits—passions, desires, abilities, virtues, and so forth—that characterized man as man.[22] While individual men could obviously vary, the essential nature of man did not change over time, whether he or she was a Chinese peasant or a modern European trade unionist. This philosophical view is reflected in the common cliché that "human nature never changes," used most often in the context of one of the less attractive human characteristics like greed, lust, or cruelty. Hegel, by contrast, did not deny that man had a natural side arising from needs of the body like food or sleep, but believed that in his most essential characteristics man was *undetermined* and therefore free to create his own nature.[23]

Thus the nature of human desire, according to Hegel, is not given for all time, but changes between historical periods and cultures.[24] To take one example, an inhabitant of contemporary America or France or Japan spends the greater part of his or her energies in pursuit of things—a certain type of car or athletic shoes or designer gown—or of status—the right neighborhood or school or job. Most of these objects of desire did not even exist and therefore could not have been desired in earlier times, and would probably not be desired by a present-day resident of an impoverished Third World country, whose time would be spent in search of more basic needs like security or food. Consumerism and the science of marketing that caters to it refer to desires that have literally been *created* by man himself, and which will give way to others in the future.[25] Our present desires are conditioned by our social milieu, which in turn is the product of the entirety of our historical past. And the specific objects of desire are only one of the aspects of "human nature" that have changed over time; the importance of desire in relation to the other elements of human character has also evolved. Hegel's Universal History therefore gives an account not only of the progress of knowledge and institutions, but of the changing nature of man himself. For it is human nature to have no fixed nature, not to *be* but to *become* something other than it once was.

Where Hegel differed from Fontenelle and from the more radical historicists who came after him was that he did not believe that the historical process would continue indefinitely, but would come to an end with an achievement of free societies in the real world. There would, in other words, be an *end of history*. This did not mean that there would be an end to events arising out of the births, deaths, and social interactions of humankind, or that there would be a cap on factual knowledge about the world. Hegel, however, had defined history as the progress of man to higher levels of rationality and freedom, and this process had a logical terminal point in the achievement of absolute self-consciousness. This self-consciousness, he believed, was embodied in his own philosophical system, just as human freedom was embodied in the modern liberal state that emerged in Europe after the French Revolution and in North America after the American Revolution. When Hegel declared that history had ended after the Battle of Jena in 1806, he was obviously not making the claim that the liberal state was victorious throughout the world; its victory was not even certain in his little corner of Germany at the time. What he was saying was that the principles of liberty and equality underlying the modern liberal state had been discovered and implemented in the most advanced countries, and that there were no alternative principles or forms of social and political organization that were superior to liberalism. Liberal societies were, in other words, free from the "contradictions" that characterized earlier forms of social organization and would therefore bring the historical dialectic to a close.

From the moment Hegel formulated his system, people were not inclined to take seriously his claim that history ended with the modern liberal state. Almost immediately, Hegel came under attack from the other great nineteenth-century writer of a Universal History, Karl Marx. Indeed, we are unaware of our intellectual debt to Hegel in large part because his legacy has passed to us via Marx, who appropriated large parts of the Hegelian system for his own purposes. Marx accepted from Hegel a view of the fundamental historicity of human affairs, the notion that human society has evolved over the course of time from primitive social structures to more complex and highly developed ones. He agreed as well that the historical process is fundamentally dialectical, that is, that earlier forms of political and social organization contained internal "contradictions" that became evident over time and led to their downfall and replacement by something higher. And Marx shared Hegel's belief in the possibility of an end of history. That is, he foresaw a final form of society that was free from contradictions, and whose achievement would terminate the historical process.

Where Marx differed from Hegel was over just what kind of society emerged at the end of history. Marx believed that the liberal state failed to resolve one fundamental contradiction, that of class conflict, the struggle between the bourgeoisie and proletariat. Marx turned Hegel's historicism against him, arguing that the liberal state did not represent the universalization of freedom, but only the victory of freedom for a certain class, the bourgeoisie. Hegel believed that alienation—the division of man against himself and his subsequent loss of control over his destiny—had been adequately resolved at the end of history through the philosophical recognition of the freedom possible in the liberal state. Marx, on the other hand, observed that in liberal societies man remains alienated from himself because capital, a human creation, has turned into man's lord and master and controls him.[26] The bureaucracy of the liberal state, which Hegel called the "universal class" because it represented the interests of the people as a whole, for Marx represented only particular interests within civil society, those of the capitalists who dominated it. Hegel the philosopher did not achieve "absolute self-consciousness," but was himself a product of his times, an apologist for the bourgeoisie. The Marxist end of history would come only with victory of the true "universal class," the proletariat, and the subsequent achievement of a global communist utopia that would end class struggle once and for all.[27]

The Marxist critique of Hegel and of liberal society is by now so familiar that it scarcely bears repeating. Yet the monumental failure of Marxism as a basis for real-world societies—plainly evident 140 years after the *Communist Manifesto*—raises the question of whether Hegel's Universal History was not in the end the more prophetic one. This possibility was put forward in the middle of this century by Alexandre Kojève, the French-Russian philosopher who taught a highly influential series of seminars at Paris's

École Pratique des Hautes Études in the 1930s.[28] If Marx was Hegel's greatest nineteenth-century interpreter, then Kojève was surely his greatest interpreter in the twentieth century. Like Marx, Kojève did not feel bound merely to explicate the thought of Hegel, but used it creatively instead to build his own understanding of modernity. Raymond Aron gives us a glimpse of Kojève's brilliance and originality:

> [Kojève] fascinated an audience of superintellectuals inclined toward doubt or criticism. Why? His talent, his dialectical virtuosity had something to do with it. . . . [His speaker's art] was intimately connected with his subject and his personality. The subject was both world history and [Hegel's] *Phenomenology*. The latter shed light on the former. Everything took on meaning. Even those who were suspicious of historical providence, who suspected the artifice behind the art, did not resist the magician; at the moment, the intelligibility he conferred on the time and on events was enough of a proof.[29]

At the center of Kojève's teaching was the startling assertion that Hegel had been essentially right, and that world history, for all the twists and turns it had taken in subsequent years, had effectively ended in the year 1806. It is difficult to read through the layers of irony in Kojève's work to uncover his true intent, but behind this seemingly odd conclusion is the thought that the principles of liberty and equality that emerged from the French Revolution, embodied in what Kojève called the modern "universal and homogeneous state," represented the end point of human ideological evolution beyond which it was impossible to progress further. Kojève was of course aware that there had been many bloody wars and revolutions in the years since 1806, but these he regarded as essentially an "alignment of the provinces."[30] In other words, communism did not represent a *higher* stage than liberal democracy, it was part of the *same* stage of history that would eventually universalize the spread of liberty and equality to all parts of the world. Though the Bolshevik and Chinese revolutions seemed like monumental events at the time, their only lasting effect would be to spread the already established principles of liberty and equality to formerly backward and oppressed peoples, and to force those countries of the developed world already living in accordance with such principles to implement them more completely.

One can get a glimpse of Kojève's brilliance, as well as his peculiarity, from the following passage:

> Observing what was taking place around me and reflecting on what had taken place in the world since the Battle of Jena, I understood that Hegel was right to see in this battle the end of History properly so-called. In and by this battle the vanguard of humanity virtually attained the limit and the aim, that is, the end, of Man's historical evolution. What has happened since then was but an extension in space of the universal revolutionary force actualized in France by Robespierre-Napoleon. From the authentically historical point of view, the two world wars with their retinue of large and small revolutions had only the effect of bringing the backward civilizations of the peripheral provinces into line with the most advanced (real or virtual) European historical positions. If the sovietization of Russia and the communization of China are anything more than or different from the democratization of imperial Germany (by way of Hitlerism) or the accession of Togoland to independence, nay, the self-determination of the Papuans, it is only because the Sino-Soviet actualization of Robespierrian Bonapartism obliges post-Napoleonic Europe to speed up the elimination of the numerous more or less anachronistic sequels to its pre-revolutionary past.[31]

The fullest embodiment of the principles of the French Revolution were for Kojève the countries of postwar Western Europe, that is, those capitalist democracies that had achieved a high degree of material abundance and political stability.[32] For these were societies with no fundamental "contradictions" remaining: self-satisfied and self-sustaining, they had no further great political goals to struggle for and could preoccupy themselves with economic activity alone. Kojève gave up teaching in the latter part of his life to work as a bureaucrat for the European Community. The end of history, he believed, meant the end not only of large political struggles and conflicts, but the end of philosophy as well; the European Community was therefore an appropriate institutional embodiment of the end of history.

The Universal Histories represented by the monumental works of Hegel and Marx were followed by other, less impressive ones. The second half of the nineteenth century saw a number of relatively optimistic theories about progressive social evolution,

such as those of the positivist Auguste Comte and the social Dar-
winist Herbert Spencer. The latter saw social evolution as part of
a larger process of biological evolution, subject to laws similar to
those of the survival of the fittest.

The twentieth century also saw several attempts at Universal
Histories—though of a decidedly darker character—including Os-
wald Spengler's *Decline of the West,* and Arnold Toynbee's *The
Study of History,* which drew its inspiration from the former work.[33]
Both Spengler and Toynbee divide history into the histories of
distinct peoples—"cultures" in the former case and "societies" in
the latter—each of which was said to be subject to certain uniform
laws of growth and decay. They thus broke with the tradition that
began with the Christian historians and culminated in Hegel and
Marx of a unitary and progressive history of mankind. Spengler
and Toynbee return, in a certain sense, to the cyclical histories of
individual peoples that characterized Greek and Roman histori-
ography. Though both works were widely read at the time, they
both suffer from a similar organicist flaw by drawing a questionable analogy between a culture or society and a biological organ-
ism. Spengler remains popular because of his pessimism and
seems to have had some influence on statesmen like Henry Kissinger, but neither writer achieved the degree of seriousness of
their German predecessors.

The last significant Universal History to be written in the twentieth century was not the work of a single individual, but rather a
collective effort on the part of a group of social scientists—mostly
American—writing after World War II, under the general rubric
of "modernization theory."[34] Karl Marx, in the preface to the
English edition of *Das Kapital,* had stated that "The country that
is more developed industrially only shows, to the less developed,
the image of its own future." This was, consciously or not, the
beginning premise of modernization theory. Drawing heavily on
the work of Marx and of the sociologists Weber and Durkheim,
modernization theory posited that industrial development followed a coherent pattern of growth, and would in time produce
certain uniform social and political structures across different
countries and cultures.[35] By studying countries like Britain or the
United States that industrialized and democratized first, one could
unlock a universal pattern that all countries would eventually follow.[36] While Max Weber took a despairing and pessimistic view of
the increasing rationalism and secularism of mankind's historical

"progress," postwar modernization theory gave his ideas a decidedly optimistic and, one is tempted to say, typically American cast. While there was disagreement among modernization theorists as to how unilinear historical evolution would be, and whether there were alternative paths to modernity, none doubted that history was directional or that the liberal democracy of the advanced industrial nations lay at its end. In the 1950s and 60s they worked, with great enthusiasm, to harness their new social science to the task of helping the newly independent countries of the Third World develop economically and politically.[37]

Modernization theory eventually fell victim to the accusation that it was *ethnocentric,* that is, that it elevated the Western European and North American development experience to the level of universal truth, without recognizing its own "culture-boundness."[38] "As a result of Western political and cultural hegemony," one critic charged, "the ethnocentric notion has been encouraged that only the West's political development represents a valid model."[39] This critique was deeper than the simple charge that there were many other paths to modernity than those specific ones followed by countries like Britain and America. It questioned the very concept of modernity itself, in particular whether all nations really wanted to adopt the West's liberal democratic principles, and whether there were not equally valid cultural starting and end points.[40]

The charge of ethnocentrism spelled the death knell for modernization theory. For the social scientists who formulated this theory shared the relativistic assumptions of their critics: they believed they had no scientific or empirical grounds on which they could defend the values of liberal democracy, and could only emphasize that they had no intention of being ethnocentric themselves.[41]

It is safe to say that the enormous historical pessimism engendered by the twentieth century has discredited most Universal Histories. The use of Marx's concept of "History" to justify terror in the Soviet Union, China, and other communist countries has given that word a particularly sinister connotation in the eyes of many. The notion that history is directional, meaningful, progressive, or even comprehensible is very foreign to the main currents of thought of our time. To speak as Hegel did of World History is to invite sneers and bemused condescension from intellectuals who believe they grasp the world in all its complexity and tragedy.

It is no accident that the only writers of Universal Histories who have achieved any degree of popular success in this century were those like Spengler and Toynbee who described the decline and decay of Western values and institutions.

But while our pessimism is understandable, it is contradicted by the empirical flow of events in the second half of the century. We need to ask whether our pessimism is not becoming something of a pose, adopted as lightly as was the optimism of the nineteenth century. For a naive optimist whose expectations are belied appears foolish, while a pessimist proven wrong maintains an aura of profundity and seriousness. It is therefore safer to follow the second course. But the appearance of democratic forces in parts of the world where they were never expected to exist, the instability of authoritarian forms of government, and the complete absence of coherent *theoretical* alternatives to liberal democracy force us to raise Kant's old question anew: Is there such a thing as a Universal History of mankind, taken from a point of view far more cosmopolitan than was possible in Kant's day?

6

The Mechanism of Desire

Let us go back to the beginning, so to speak, and look at the question without appeal to the authority of earlier theories of history: Is history directional, and is there reason to think that there will be a universal evolution in the direction of liberal democracy?

Let us consider at the outset only the question of directionality, leaving aside for the moment the question of whether that directionality implies progress in terms of either morality or human happiness. Do all or most societies evolve in a certain uniform direction, or do their histories follow either a cyclical or simply random path?[1] If the latter, then it is possible that mankind can simply repeat any social or political practice of the past: slavery may recur, Europeans may crown themselves princes and emperors, and American women can lose the right to vote. A directional history, by contrast, implies that no form of social organization, once superseded, is ever repeated by the same society (though different societies at different stages of development can, naturally, repeat a similar evolutionary pattern).

But if history is never to repeat itself, there must be a constant and uniform Mechanism or set of historical first causes that dictates evolution in a single direction, and that somehow preserves the memory of earlier periods into the present. Cyclical or random views of history do not exclude the possibility of social change and limited regularities in development, but they do not require a single source of historical causation. They must also encompass a process of *de*-generation as well, by which consciousness of earlier achievements is completely wiped out. For without the possibility of a total historical *forgetting*, each successive cycle would build, if only in small ways, on the experiences of earlier ones.

As a first cut at understanding the Mechanism that gives history its directionality, let us take our cue from Fontenelle and Bacon, and posit knowledge as the key to the directionality of history—in particular, knowledge about the natural universe that we can obtain through science. For if we look around at the entire range of human social endeavor, the only one that is by common consensus unequivocally cumulative and directional is modern natural science. The same cannot be said for activities like painting, poetry, music, or architecture: it is not clear that Rauschenberg is a better painter than Michelangelo or Schoenberg superior to Bach, simply because they lived in the twentieth century; Shakespeare and the Parthenon represent a certain kind of perfection and it makes no sense to speak of "advancing" beyond them. Natural science, on the other hand, builds upon itself: there are certain "facts" about nature that were hidden from the great Sir Isaac Newton, that are accessible to any undergraduate physics student today simply because he or she was born later. The scientific understanding of nature is neither cyclical nor random; mankind does not return periodically to the same state of ignorance, nor are the results of modern natural science subject to human caprice. Human beings are free to pursue certain branches of science rather than others, and they can obviously apply the results as they please, but neither dictators nor parliaments can repeal the laws of nature, much as they are tempted to do so.[2]

Scientific knowledge has been accumulating for a very long period, and has had a consistent if frequently unperceived effect in shaping the fundamental character of human societies. Those that possess ferrous metallurgy and agriculture were quite different from ones that only knew stone tools or hunting and gathering. But a qualitative change occurred in the relationship of scientific knowledge to the historical process with the rise of *modern* natural science, that is, from the discovery of the scientific method by men like Descartes, Bacon, and Spinoza in the sixteenth and seventeenth centuries. The possibility of mastering nature opened up by modern natural science was not a universal feature of all societies, but had to be invented at a certain point in history by certain Europeans. However, once having been invented, the scientific method became a universal possession of rational man, potentially accessible to everyone regardless of differences in culture or nationality. Discovery of the scientific method created a fundamental, non-cyclical division of historical time into periods before and after. And once discovered, the progressive and continuous unfolding of modern natural science has provided a directional Mechanism for explaining many aspects of subsequent historical development.

The first way in which modern natural science produces historical change that is both directional and universal is through military competition. The universality of science provides the basis for the global unification of mankind in the first instance because of the prevalence of war and conflict in the international system. Modern natural science confers a decisive military advantage on those societies that can develop, produce, and deploy technology the most effectively, and the relative advantage conferred by technology increases as the rate of technological change accelerates.[3] Zulu spears were no match for British rifles, no matter how brave individual warriors were: mastery of science was the reason why Europe could conquer most of what is now the Third World in the eighteenth and nineteenth centuries, and diffusion of that science from Europe is now permitting the Third World to regain some of its sovereignty in the twentieth.

The possibility of war is a great force for the rationalization of societies, and for the creation of uniform social structures across cultures. Any state that hopes to maintain its political autonomy is forced to adopt the technology of its enemies and rivals. More than that, however, the threat of war forces states to restructure their social systems along lines most conducive to producing and deploying technology. For example, states must be of a certain size in order to compete with their neighbors, which creates powerful incentives for national unity; they must be able to mobilize resources on a national level, which requires the creation of a strong centralized state authority with the power of taxation and regulation; they must break down various forms of regional, religious, and kinship ties which potentially obstruct national unity; they must increase educational levels in order to produce an elite capable of disposing of technology; they must maintain contact with and awareness of developments taking place beyond their borders; and, with the introduction of mass armies during the Napoleonic Wars, they must at least open the door to the enfranchisement of the poorer classes of their societies if they are to be capable of total mobilization. All of these developments could occur for other motives—for example, economic ones—but war frames the need for social modernization in a particularly acute way and provides an unambiguous test of its success.

There are numerous historical examples of so-called "defensive modernizations," in which countries were forced to reform as a result of military threat.[4] The great centralizing monarchies of the sixteenth and seventeenth centuries, like those of Louis XIII in France or Philip II in Spain, sought to consolidate power over their territories in large measure in order to guarantee the revenues required to wage war with their neighbors. In the seventeenth century, these monarchies were at peace for only three out of the hundred years; the enormous economic requirements for raising armies provided the chief incentive for central governments to break the power of feudal and regional institutions and create what we recognize as "modern" state structures.[5] The rise of monarchical absolutism in turn had a leveling effect on French society by reducing aristocratic privileges, and opening the way for new social groups that would become crucial during the Revolution.

A similar process occurred in the Ottoman Empire and in Japan. The incursion of a French army into Egypt under Napoleon in 1798 shook Egyptian society and led to a major reform of the Egyptian military under its Ottoman pasha, Mohammed Ali. This new army, trained with European help, was so successful that it challenged Ottoman control of much of the Middle East, and prompted the Ottoman sultan Mahmud II to undertake a far-reaching set of reforms that duplicated those of the European monarchs from the previous two centuries. Mahmud broke the old feudal order by massacring the Janissaries (an elite corps of palace guards) in 1826 opened up a series of secular schools, and dramatically increased the power of the central Ottoman bureaucracy. Similarly, the superiority of Commodore Perry's naval guns was decisive in persuading the *daimyos* in Japan that they had no choice but to open their country up and accept the challenge of foreign competition. (This did not happen without resistance; as late as the 1850s a gunnery specialist, Takashima Shuhan, was jailed for advocating the adoption of Western military technology.) Under the slogan "Rich Country, Strong Army," the new leadership of Japan replaced old temple schools with a system of compulsory education administered by the state, recruited a mass peasant army in place of the samurai warriors, and established national taxation, banking, and currency systems. The wholesale transformation of Japanese society brought about during the Meiji restoration and the re-centralization of the Japanese state was motivated by an urgent sense that Japan had to learn to absorb Western technology if it was not to lose its national independence to European colonialism, as China had done.[6]

In other cases, ignominious defeat in war has been the spur to the adoption of rationalizing social reform. The reforms of vom Stein, Scharnhorst, and Gneisenau in Prussia were motivated by a recognition that Napoleon had been able to defeat their country at Jena-Auerstadt so easily because of the backwardness of the Prussian state and its total alienation from society. Military reforms such as the introduction of universal conscription were accompanied by introduction of the Napoleonic Code into Prussia, an event that for Hegel signaled the arrival of modernity in Germany.[7] Russia is an example of a country whose modernization and reform process over the past 350 years has been driven primarily by its military ambitions and setbacks.[8] Military modernization lay at the root of Peter the Great's efforts to turn Russia into a modern European monarchy; the city of St. Petersburg was originally conceived of as a naval base at the head of the Neva River. Russia's defeat in the Crimean War led directly to the reforms of Alexander II, including the abolition of serfdom, while its defeat in the Russo-Japanese War made possible the liberal reforms of Stolypin and the period of economic growth from 1905 to 1914.[9]

Perhaps the most recent example of defensive modernization was the initial phase of Mikhail Gorbachev's own *perestroika*. It is quite clear from his speeches and those of other senior Soviet officials that one of the chief reasons that they initially considered undertaking a fundamental reform of the Soviet economy was their realization that an unreformed Soviet Union was going to have serious problems remaining competitive, economically and militarily, into the twenty-first century. In particular, President Reagan's Strategic Defense Initiative (SDI) posed a severe challenge because it threatened to make obsolete an entire generation of Soviet nuclear weapons, and shifted the superpower competition into areas like microelectronics and other innovative technologies where the Soviet Union had serious disadvantages. Soviet leaders, including many in the military, understood that the corrupt economic system inherited from Brezhnev would be unable to keep up in an SDI-dominated world, and were willing to accept short-run retrenchment for the sake of long-run survival.[10]

The persistence of war and military competition among nations is thus, paradoxically, a great unifier of nations. Even as war leads to their destruction, it forces states to accept modern technological civilization and the social structures that support it. Modern natural science forces itself on man, whether he cares for it or not: most nations do not have the option of rejecting the technological rationalism of modernity if they want to preserve their national autonomy. We see here a demonstration of the truth of Kant's observation that historical change comes about as a result of man's "asocial sociability": it is conflict rather than cooperation that first induces men to live in societies and then develop the potential of those societies more fully.

It is possible to evade the requirement of technological rationalization for a certain length of time, if one lives in an isolated or undesirable territory. Alternatively, countries can get lucky. Islamic "science" was incapable of producing the F-4 fighter-bombers and Chieftain tanks required to defend Khomeini's Iran from ambitious neighbors like Iraq. Islamic Iran could attack the Western rationalism that did produce such weapons only because it could buy them with income from its oil resources. The fact that the mullahs who ruled Iran could simply watch a valuable resource gush out of the ground permitted them to indulge themselves in certain projects like worldwide Islamic revolution that other countries, not similarly blessed, could not pursue.[11]

The second way in which modern natural science can be expected to produce directional historical change is through the progressive conquest of nature for the purpose of satisfying human desires, a project that we otherwise call economic development. Industrialization is not simply the intensive application of technology to the manufacturing process and the creation of new machines. It is also the bringing to bear of human reason to the problem of social organization and the creation of a rational division of labor. These parallel uses of reason, for the creation of new machines and the organization of the production process, have succeeded beyond the wildest expectations of the early proponents of the scientific method. In Western Europe, per capita income grew more than tenfold from the mid-1700s to the present, starting from a base that was already higher than that of many present-day Third World countries.[12] Economic growth produced certain uniform social transformations in all societies, regardless of their prior social structure.

Modern natural science regulates the direction of economic development by establishing a constantly changing horizon of production possibilities.[13] The direction in which this technological horizon unfolds is very closely intertwined with the development of an increasingly rational organization of labor.[14] For example, technological improvements in communications and transportation—the building of roads, the development of ships and ports, the invention of railroads and the like—make possible an expansion in the size of markets, which in turn facilitate the realization of economies of scale through rationalization of the organization of labor. Specialized tasks which were unprofitable when a factory was selling to a couple of local villages suddenly become worthwhile when one sells to an entire nation, or to an even broader international market.[15] The increased productivity resulting from these changes then enlarges the internal market and creates new demands for an even greater division of labor.

The requirements of the rational organization of labor dictate certain consistent, large-scale changes in social structure. Industrial societies must be predominantly urban, because it is only in cities that one finds an adequate supply of skilled labor required to run modern industries, and because cities have the infrastructure and services to support large, highly specialized enterprises. Apartheid in South Africa ultimately broke down because it was built on the belief that black industrial labor could somehow be kept permanently in the countryside. For labor markets to function efficiently, labor has to become increasingly mobile: workers cannot remain permanently tied to a particular job, locale, or set of social relationships, but must become free to move about, learn new tasks and technologies, and sell their labor to the highest bidder. This has a powerful effect in undermining traditional social groups like tribes, clans, extended families, religious sects, and so on. The latter may in certain respects be more humanly satisfying to live in, but since they are not organized according to the rational principles of economic efficiency, they tend to lose out to those that are.

What replaces them are "modern" bureaucratic forms of organization. Workers are supposed to be accepted into these organizations on the basis of their training and ability, not as a result of family ties or status; and their performance is measured according to established, universal rules. Modern bureaucracies institutionalize the rational organization of labor by taking complex tasks and dividing them into a hierarchical structure of simpler ones, many of which can be performed as a matter of routine. Rational bureaucratic organization is likely in the long run to pervade every aspect of society in an industrialized country, regardless of whether the organization in question is a government agency, labor union, corporation, political party, newspaper, charitable trust, university, or professional association. In contrast to the nineteenth century, when four out of five Americans were self-employed and therefore not part of a bureaucratic organization, only one in ten falls into this category now. This "unplanned revolution" has replicated itself in all industrialized countries, regardless of whether that country was capitalist or socialist, and in spite of differences in the religious and cultural backgrounds of the pre-industrial societies out of which they emerged.[16]

It has proven not to be the case that industrial development necessarily implies bureaucracies of ever-increasing size, or gigantic industrial combines. Past a certain point, large bureaucracies become increasingly less efficient—being afflicted by what economists call diseconomies of scale—and are therefore less efficient than a larger number of smaller organizations. Nor do certain modern industries, like software engineering, need to be located in big cities. Nonetheless, these smaller units still need to be organized according to rational principles, and need the support of an urban society.

The rational organization of labor should not be regarded as a phenomenon separate in essence from technological innovation; both are aspects of the rationalization of economic life, the first in the sphere of social organization and the latter in the sphere of machine production. Karl Marx believed that the productivity of modern capitalism was based primarily on machine-production (that is, the application of technology) rather than the division of labor, and hoped that the latter could one day be abolished.[17] Technology would make it possible to eliminate the distinctions between town and country, oil baron and roughneck, investment banker and garbage collector, and create a society in which one could "hunt in the morning, fish in the afternoon, rear cattle in the evening, criticize after dinner."[18] Nothing that has occurred in the subsequent history of world economic development suggests that this is true: the rational organization of labor remains essential to modern economic productivity, even as the mind-numbing effects of detail-labor have been mitigated by advances in technology. Attempts by communist regimes to abolish the division of labor and to end the slavery of specialization have only led to a tyranny more monstrous than that of the Manchester workshops condemned by Marx.[19] Mao endeavored to abolish the distinctions between town and country and between mental and physical labor at several points, notably during the Great Leap Forward of the late 1950s and during the Cultural Revolution a decade later. Both of these efforts led to unimaginable human suffering, dwarfed only by the Khmer Rouge's attempt to merge town and country in Cambodia after 1975.

Neither the organization of labor[20] nor bureaucracies[21] were new at the time of the Industrial Revolution; what was new was their thoroughgoing rationalization according to the principles of economic efficiency. It is the demand for rationality that imposes uniformity on the social development of industrializing societies. Men may pursue a thousand and one goals in pre-industrial societies: religion or tradition may dictate that the life of an aristocratic warrior is superior to that of a city merchant; a priest may prescribe the "just price" for a certain commodity. But a society that lives by such rules will not allocate its resources efficiently, and will therefore not develop economically as fast as one that lives by rational rules.

To illustrate the homogenizing power of the division of labor, let us consider its effect on social relations in concrete cases. At the time of General Franco's victory over Republican forces in the Spanish civil war, Spain was a predominantly agricultural country. The social base of the Spanish Right rested on local notables and landowners in the countryside, who were able to mobilize masses of peasant supporters on the basis of tradition and personal loyalty. The Mafia, whether operating out of New Jersey or Palermo, owes its cohesion to similar sorts of personal and family ties, as do the local warlords who continue to dominate rural politics in Third World countries like El Salvador and the Philippines. Spain's economic development in the 1950s and 60s introduced modern market relationships into the countryside, and thereby brought about an unplanned social revolution that destroyed these traditional patron-client relationships.[22] Masses of peasants were drawn off the land into cities, depriving local no-

tables of supporters; the bosses themselves evolved into more efficient agricultural producers who were oriented outwards to
national and international markets; and the peasants who remained on the land become contractual employees selling their
labor.[23] A modern-day, would-be Franco would lack the social
basis on which to recruit any army. The pressure of economic
rationalization also explains why the Mafia persists in the relatively underdeveloped south of Italy rather than in its industrialized north. Patron-client relationships based on non-economic ties
obviously persist in modern societies—everyone knows of a boss'
son who was promoted ahead of his colleagues, or old-boy networks used in hiring—but they are usually declared illegal and
have to be carried out *sub rosa*.

In this chapter, we have sought to pose the question: Is history
directional? We have done this in a deliberately naive form, since
there are so many pessimists among us who would deny that
history exhibits any directionality whatsoever. We have selected
modern natural science as a possible underlying "mechanism" of
directional historical change, because it is the only large-scale social activity that is by consensus cumulative and therefore directional. The progressive unfolding of modern natural science
permits one to understand many of the specific details of historical evolution, for example, why men moved by horse-drawn car-
riage and railroad before they went by automobile and airplane,
or why later societies are more urbanized than earlier ones, or
why the modern political party, labor union, or nation-state has
replaced the tribe or clan as the primary axis of group loyalty in
industrialized societies.

But while modern natural science can explain some phenomena quite readily, there are many others—starting with the form
of government chosen by a particular society—which it can explain
only with great difficulty. Moreover, although modern natural
science may be regarded as a possible "regulator" of directional
historical change, it should in no way be regarded as the ultimate
cause of change. For one would immediately be driven to ask, *why
modern natural science?* While the internal logic of science may
explain why it unfolds as it does, science itself does not tell us why
men pursue science. Science as a social phenomenon unfolds not
simply because men are curious about the universe, but because
science permits them to gratify their desire for security, and for
the limitless acquisition of material goods. Modern corporations

do not maintain research and development staffs out of an abstract love of knowledge, but to make money. The desire for economic growth seems to be a universal characteristic of virtually all present-day societies, but if man is not simply an economic animal we would expect the explanation given above to be an incomplete one. This is a question to which we will return shortly.

We are not, for the time being, placing any moral or ethical valuation on the historical directionality implied by modern natural science. It should be taken for granted that phenomena like the division of labor and growing bureaucratization are profoundly ambiguous in their implications for human happiness, as has been underlined by Adam Smith, Marx, Weber, Durkheim, and other social scientists who first pointed to them as central characteristics of modern life. We are under no obligation at present to assume that the ability of modern science to raise economic productivity makes men more moral, happier, or otherwise better off than they were before. As the starting point of our analysis, we want to demonstrate provisionally that there are good reasons for thinking that the history produced as a consequence of the unfolding of modern natural science moves in a single coherent direction, and to examine further the consequences that flow from that conclusion.

If the discovery of modern natural science produces directional history, the question naturally arises, Can it be un-invented? Can the scientific method cease to dominate our lives, and is it possible for industrialized societies to return to pre-modern, pre-scientific ones? Is the directionality of history, in short, reversible?

7

No Barbarians at the Gates

In the Australian filmmaker George Miller's movie *The Road Warrior,* our present-day, oil-based civilization is portrayed as having collapsed as a result of an apocalyptic war. Science has been lost; latter-day Visigoths and Vandals ride around in the outback on Harley-Davidsons and dune buggies, trying to steal gasoline and bullets from one another because the production technology has been lost.

The possibility of the cataclysmic destruction of our modern, technological civilization and its sudden return to barbarism has been a constant subject of science fiction, particularly in the postwar period when the invention of nuclear weapons made this seem like a real possibility. Frequently, the kind of barbarism to which mankind descends is not a pure resurrection of earlier forms of social organization, but a curious mixture of old social forms and modern technology, as when emperors and dukes fly between solar systems in space ships. If, however, our assumptions about the interrelationships between modern natural science and modern social organization are correct, then such "mixed" outcomes would not be viable for long: for without the destruction or rejection of the scientific method itself, modern natural science would eventually reproduce itself and force the re-creation of many aspects of the modern, rational social world as well.

So let us consider the question: Is it possible for mankind as a whole to reverse the directionality of history through the rejection or loss of the scientific method? This problem can be broken down into two parts: first, can modern natural science be deliberately rejected by existing societies; and second, can a global cataclysm result in the involuntary loss of modern natural science?

The deliberate rejection of technology and a rationalized society has been suggested by any number of groups in modern times, from the Romantics of the early nineteenth century, to the hippie movement of the 1960s, to Ayatollah Khomeini and Islamic fundamentalism. At the moment, the most coherent and articulate source of opposition to technological civilization comes from the environmental movement. Contemporary environmentalism comprises many different groups and strands of thought, but the most radical among them have attacked the entire modern project of mastering nature through science, and have suggested that man might be happier if nature were not manipulated but returned to something more closely approximating its original, pre-industrial state.

Almost all of these anti-technological doctrines have a common ancestry in the thought of Jean-Jacques Rousseau, the first modern philosopher to question the goodness of historical "progress." Rousseau understood before Hegel the essential historicity of human experience, and how human nature itself had been modified over time. But unlike Hegel, he believed that historical change had served to make men profoundly unhappy. Take the ability of modern economies to satisfy human needs. Rousseau in the *Second Discourse* points out that true human needs are actually very few in number: man needs shelter from the elements and food to eat; even security is not necessarily a basic requirement because it presupposes that men living in contiguity with other men would naturally want to threaten each other.[1] All other human wants are not essential to happiness, but arise out of man's ability to compare himself to his neighbors and feel himself deprived if he does not have what they have. The wants created by modern consumerism arise, in other words, from man's vanity, or what Rousseau calls his *amour-propre*. The problem is that these new wants, created by man himself in historical time, are infinitely elastic and incapable of being fundamentally satisfied. Modern economies, for all of their enormous efficiency and innovation, create a new need for every want they satisfy. Men are made unhappy not because they fail to gratify some fixed set of desires, but by the gap that continually arises between new wants and their fulfillment.

Rousseau gives an example of this phenomenon in the collector who is more unhappy about the gaps in his collection than he is satisfied by those objects he owns. One might find a more contemporary illustration in the highly innovative modern consumer electronics industry. In the 1920s and 30s, it was the height of consumerist aspiration for a family to own a radio. Today in contemporary America there is hardly a teenager alive who does not own several, and who yet is extremely dissatisfied for not owning a Nintendo, or a portable compact disc player, or a beeper. It is obvious, moreover, that his acquisition of these items will not serve to make him any more satisfied, since by that time the Japanese will have invented some other new electronic gadget which he can aspire to own.

What could potentially make man happy, according to Rousseau, would be to get off the treadmill of modern technology and the endless cycle of wants it creates, and to recover some of the wholeness of natural man. Natural man did not live in society, did not compare himself to others, or live in the artificial world of fears, hopes, and expectations created by society. Rather, he was made happy by experiencing the sentiment of his own existence, of being a natural man in a natural world. He did not seek to use his reason to master nature; there was no need, for nature was essentially beneficent, nor was reason natural to him as a solitary individual.[2]

Rousseau's attack upon civilized man raised the first and most fundamental question mark over the entire project of conquering nature, the perspective that sees trees and mountains as raw materials rather than as places of rest and contemplation. His criticism of the Economic Man envisioned by John Locke and Adam Smith remains the basis of most present-day attacks on unlimited economic growth, and is the (oftentimes unconscious) intellectual basis for most contemporary environmentalism.[3] As industrialization and economic development continue, and as the consequent degradation of the natural environment becomes more and more obvious, Rousseau's critique of economic modernization has had greater appeal. Is it possible to imagine the emergence of a highly radicalized environmentalism that would seek to reject, on the basis of an updated Rousseauism, the entire modern project of the conquest of nature, as well as the technological civilization that rests on it? The answer, for a variety of reasons, would appear to be no.

   The first reason has to do with the expectations created by current economic growth. While individuals and small communities can "return to nature," quitting their jobs as investment bankers or real estate developers in order to live by a lake in the Adirondacks, a society-wide rejection of technology would mean the wholesale de-industrialization of a nation in Europe, America, or Japan, and its transformation, in effect, into an impoverished Third World country. There would perhaps be less air pollution and toxic waste, but also less modern medicine and communications, less birth control and therefore less sexual liberation. Rather than freeing man from the cycle of new wants, most people would become reacquainted with the life of a poor peasant tied to the land in an unending cycle of back-breaking labor. Many countries have, of course, existed at the level of subsistence agriculture for generations, and the people living in them have doubtless achieved considerable happiness; but the likelihood that they could do so having once experienced the consumerism of a technological society is doubtful, and that they could be persuaded as a society to exchange one for the other even more so. Moreover, if there were other countries that chose not to de-industrialize, the citizens of the ones that did would have a constant standard of comparison against which to judge themselves. Burma's decision after World War II to reject the goal of economic development common elsewhere in the Third World and to remain internationally isolated might have worked in a pre-industrial world, but proved very difficult to sustain in a region full of booming Singapores and Thailands.

   Only slightly less unrealistic is the alternative of breaking selectively with technology by seeking to somehow freeze technological development at its current level, or to permit technological innovation only on a highly selective basis. While this might better preserve current living standards, at least in the short run, it is not clear why life at an arbitrarily selected level of technology would seem particularly satisfying. It would offer neither the glitter of a dynamic and growing economy, nor a genuine return to nature. The effort to freeze technology has worked for small religious communities like the Amish or Mennonites, but would be much more difficult to realize in a large and stratified society. The social and economic inequalities that exist today in developed societies are much less disruptive politically if there is a growing economic pie to share; they would become much more serious if the United

States came to resemble a giant, stagnant East Germany. Further-more, freezing technology at the already high level of today's advanced countries is not likely to be an adequate solution for an impending ecological crisis, and fails to answer the question of whether the global ecosystem can tolerate the Third World catch-ing up. Selective innovation raises difficult questions as to what authority decides which technologies are acceptable. The politiciza-tion of innovation will inevitably have a chilling effect on eco-nomic growth as a whole.

Moreover, defense of the environment, far from *requiring* a break with modern technology and the economic world created by it, may in the long run require that world as its precondition. Indeed, apart from the *Fundi* wing of the Green movement in Germany and certain other extremists, the mainstream of the environmental movement recognizes that the most realistic solu-tions to environmental problems are likely to lie in the creation of alternative technologies, or technologies to actively protect the environment. A healthy environment is a luxury best afforded by those with wealth and economic dynamism; the worst environ-mental offenders, whether in the disposal of toxic wastes or de-forestation of tropical rain forests, are developing countries that feel their relative poverty does not give them any option but to exploit their own natural resources, or that do not have the social discipline to enforce environmental laws. Despite the depreda-tions of acid rain, the northeastern United States and many other parts of northern Europe are more heavily forested now than they were a hundred or even two hundred years ago.

For all of these reasons, then, it seems highly unlikely that our civilization will voluntarily choose the Rousseauian option and reject the role that modern natural science has come to play in our contemporary economic life. But let us also examine the more extreme case, where the choice is not voluntary but forced upon us by some cataclysm, either a global nuclear war or an environ-mental collapse which, despite our best efforts, attacks the phys-ical basis for contemporary human life. It is clearly possible to destroy the fruits of modern natural science; indeed, modern technology has given us the means to do so in a matter of minutes. But is it possible to destroy modern natural science itself, to re-lease us from the grip that the scientific method has held over our lives, and return mankind as a whole permanently to a pre-scientific level of civilization?[4]

Let us take the case of a global war involving weapons of mass destruction. Since Hiroshima we have envisioned this as a nuclear war, but it could now be the result of some new and terrible biological or chemical agent. Assuming that such a war does not trigger nuclear winter or some other natural process that makes the earth completely uninhabitable by man, we must assume that the conflict will destroy much of the population, power, and wealth of the belligerents, and perhaps of their major allies, with devastating consequences for neutral onlookers as well. There may be major environmental consequences that would make the military catastrophe merge with an ecological one. There will also likely be major changes in the configuration of world politics: the belligerents may be finished as great powers, their territory fragmented and occupied by countries that managed to stay out of the conflict, or else so poisoned that no one would want to live there. The war might come to envelop all of the technologically advanced countries capable of producing weapons of mass destruction, demolishing their factories, laboratories, libraries, and universities, eliminating knowledge of how to fabricate weapons of such enormous destructiveness. And as for the rest of the world that escaped the war's direct consequences, there might emerge such a great aversion to war and the technological civilization that made it possible that a number of states would voluntarily renounce advanced weaponry and the science that produced it. The survivors might decide, more forthrightly than now, to reject policies of deterrence that manifestly failed to protect mankind from destruction and, wiser and more moderate, seek to control new technologies in a far more thoroughgoing way than is the practice in our contemporary world. (An ecological catastrophe such as the melting of the ice caps or the desertification of North America and Europe through global warming could lead to a similar effort to control the scientific inventions that led to the disaster.) The horrors inflicted by science may lead to the revival of anti-modern and anti-technological religions, whose effect would be to erect moral and emotional barriers to the creation of new and potentially deadly technologies.

Yet even these extreme circumstances would appear unlikely to break the grip of technology over human civilization, and science's ability to replicate itself. The reasons for this again have to do with the relationship between science and war. For even if one could destroy modern weapons and the specific knowledge of how to produce them, one could not eliminate the memory of the method that made their production possible. The unification of human civilization through modern communications and transportation means that there is no part of mankind that is not aware of the scientific method and its potential, even if that part is currently incapable of generating technology or applying it successfully. There are, in other words, no true barbarians at the gates, unaware of the power of modern natural science. And as long as this is true, the ability to use modern natural science for military purposes will continue to give such states advantages over states that do not. The pointless destructiveness of the war just past will not necessarily teach men that no military technology can be used for rational purposes; there may be yet newer ones which men can convince themselves will give them decisive advantages. The good states, that had drawn moderating lessons from disaster and sought to control the technologies that caused it, would still have to live in a world with bad states that saw the disaster as an opportunity for their own ambitions. And, as Machiavelli taught at the beginning of the modern era, the good states will have to take their cue from the bad ones if they are to survive and remain states at all.[5] They will need to maintain a certain level of technology, if only to defend themselves, and indeed will have to encourage technological innovation in the military sphere if their enemies are also innovators. Even if in hesitant and controlled ways, good states that sought to control the creation of new technologies would slowly have to let the technological genie back out of the bottle.[6] Man's post-cataclysmic dependence on modern natural science would be even greater if it were ecological in nature, since technology might be the only way of making the earth habitable once again.

A truly cyclical history is conceivable only if we posit the possibility that a given civilization can vanish entirely without leaving any imprint on those that follow. This, in fact, occurred prior to the invention of modern natural science. Modern natural science, however, is so powerful, both for good and for evil, that it is very doubtful whether it can ever be forgotten or "un-invented" under conditions other than the physical annihilation of the human race. And if the grip of a progressive modern natural science is irreversible, then a directional history and all of the other variegated economic, social, and political consequences that flow from it are also not reversible in any fundamental sense.

8

Accumulation without End

Our country has not been lucky. Indeed, it was decided to carry out this Marxist experiment on us—fate pushed us in precisely this direction. Instead of some country in Africa, they began this experiment with us. In the end we proved that there is no place for this idea. It has simply pushed us off the path the world's civilized countries have taken. This is reflected today, when 40 percent of the people are living below the poverty level and, moreover, in constant humiliation when they receive produce upon presentation of ration cards. This is a constant humiliation, a reminder every hour that you are a slave in this country.

Boris Yeltsin, in a speech to a meeting of
Democratic Russia, Moscow, June 1, 1991.

All we have demonstrated up to this point is that the progressive unfolding of modern natural science produces a directional history and certain uniform social changes across different nations and cultures. Technology and the rational organization of labor are the preconditions for industrialization, which in turn engenders such social phenomena as urbanization, bureaucratization, the breakdown of extended family and tribal ties, and increasing levels of education. We have also shown how the dominance of modern natural science over human life is not likely to be reversed under any foreseeable circumstances, even under the most extreme circumstances. We have not, however, demonstrated that science leads in any necessary way either to capitalism in the economic sphere, or to liberal democracy in the political.

And indeed, there are examples of countries that have gone through the first stages of industrialization, that are economically

developed, urbanized, and secular, possessing a strong and coherent state structure and a relatively well-educated population,
but that are neither capitalist nor democratic. The chief example
of this for many years was Stalin's Soviet Union, which between
1928 and the late 1930s had accomplished a fantastic social transformation from a largely peasant agricultural country to an industrial powerhouse, without permitting its citizens either
economic or political freedom. Indeed, the speed with which this
transformation occurred seemed to demonstrate to many people
that centralized planning under a police-state tyranny was in fact
a *more* effective means of achieving rapid industrialization than
free people operating in free markets. Isaac Deutscher, writing in
the 1950s, could still maintain that centrally planned economies
were more efficient than the anarchical workings of market economies, and that nationalized industries were better able to modernize plant and equipment than those in the private sector.[1] The
existence, through 1989, of countries in Eastern Europe which
were both socialist and economically developed, appeared to indicate that centralized planning was not incompatible with economic modernity.

These examples from the communist world suggested at one
time that the progressive unfolding of modern natural science
could just as well lead us to Max Weber's nightmare of a rational
and bureaucratized tyranny, rather than to an open, creative,
and liberal society. Our Mechanism, then, needs to be extended.
In addition to explaining why economically developed countries
have urbanized societies and rational bureaucracies, the Mechanism should further demonstrate why we should expect
an eventual evolution in the direction of both economic and
political liberalism. In this and the following chapter, we will
investigate the Mechanism's relationship to capitalism in two
distinct cases: for advanced industrial societies, and for underdeveloped ones. Having established that the Mechanism in
some way makes capitalism inevitable, we will then return to the
question of whether it can be expected to produce democracy as
well.

Despite the bad moral odor that capitalism has had for both
the traditionalist-religious Right and the socialist-Marxist Left, its
ultimate victory as the world's only viable economic system is easier to explain in terms of the Mechanism than is the victory of

liberal democracy in the political sphere. For capitalism has proven far more efficient than centrally planned economic systems in developing and utilizing technology, and in adapting to the rapidly changing conditions of a global division of labor, *under the conditions of a mature industrial economy.*

Industrialization, we now know, is not a one-shot affair whereby countries are suddenly propelled into economic modernity, but rather a continuously evolving process without a clear end point, where today's modernity quickly becomes tomorrow's antiquity. The means of satisfying what Hegel called the "system of needs" has changed steadily as those needs themselves have changed. Industrialization for early social theorists like Marx and Engels consisted of light industries like textile manufacturing in England or the porcelain industry in France. This quickly gave way to developments like the propagation of railroads, the creation of the iron, steel, and chemical industries, shipbuilding and other forms of heavy manufacturing, and the growth of unified national markets, which constituted industrial modernity for Lenin, Stalin, and their Soviet followers. Britain, France, the United States, and Germany reached this level of development approximately by the First World War, Japan and the rest of Western Europe by World War II, and the Soviet Union and Eastern Europe in the 1950s. Today, they are hallmarks of an intermediate and, for the most advanced countries, long-since-bypassed phase of industrial development. What has replaced it has been given a variety of titles: a "mature industrial society," the stage of "high mass consumption," the "technetronic era," the "information age," or a "post-industrial society."[2] While specific formulations differ, all stress the vastly increased role of information, technical knowledge, and services at the expense of heavy manufacturing.

Modern natural science—in the familiar forms of technological innovation and the rational organization of labor—continues to dictate the character of "post-industrial" societies, much as it did that of societies entering the first stages of industrialization. Writing in 1967, Daniel Bell pointed out that the average time span between the initial discovery of a new technological innovation and recognition of its commercial possibilities fell from 30 years between 1880 and 1919, to 16 between 1919 and 1945, to 9 years from 1945 to 1967.[3] This figure has since decreased even further, with product cycles in the most advanced technologies like computers and software now measured in months rather than years. Figures like this do not begin to suggest the incredible diversity of products and services that have been created since 1945, many of them entirely *de novo*; nor do they suggest the complexity of such economies and the new forms of technical knowledge—not just in science and engineering, but in marketing, finance, distribution, and the like—required to keep them operating.

At the same time, the global division of labor, predicted but only very incompletely realized in Marx's time, has become a reality. International trade has grown at a compound annual rate of 13 percent over the last generation, with even higher rates of growth in specific sectors like international banking. In the decades before that it had seldom increased at a rate of more than 3 percent.[4] The continuing decrease in transportation and communications costs has resulted in the realization of economies of scale greater than were possible in even the largest national markets, such as those of the United States, Japan, or the individual countries of Western Europe. The result has been another of those unplanned and gradual revolutions: the unification of a very large part of mankind (outside the communist world) in a single market for German cars, Malaysian semiconductors, Argentine beef, Japanese fax machines, Canadian wheat, and American airplanes.

Technological innovation and the highly complex division of labor has created a tremendous increase in the demand for technical knowledge at all levels in the economy, and consequently for people who—to put it crudely—think rather than do. This includes not only scientists and engineers, but all of the structures that support them, like public schools, universities, and the communications industry. The higher "information" content of modern economic production is reflected in the rise of the service sector—professionals, managers, office workers, people involved in trade, marketing, and finance, as well as government workers and health care providers—at the expense of "traditional" manufacturing occupations.

Evolution in the direction of decentralized decision making and markets becomes a virtual inevitability for all industrial economies that hope to become "post-industrial." While

centrally planned economies could follow their capitalist counterparts into the age of coal, steel, and heavy manufacturing,[5] they were much less able to cope with the requirements
of the information age. One might say in fact that it was
in the highly complex and dynamic "post-industrial" economic
world that Marxism-Leninism as an economic system met its
Waterloo.

The failure of central planning in the final analysis is related
to the problem of technological innovation. Scientific inquiry
proceeds best in an atmosphere of freedom, where people are
permitted to think and communicate freely, and more importantly where they are rewarded for innovation. The Soviet
Union and China both promoted scientific inquiry, particularly
in "safe" areas of basic or theoretical research, and created material incentives to stimulate innovation in certain sectors like
aerospace and weapons design. But modern economies must in-
novate across the board, not only in hi-tech fields but in more
prosaic areas like the marketing of hamburgers and the creation
of new types of insurance. While the Soviet state could pamper
its nuclear physicists, it didn't have much left over for the designers of television sets, which exploded with some regularity,
or for those who might aspire to market new products to new
consumers, a completely non-existent field in the USSR and
China.

Centralized economies have not succeeded in making rational
investment decisions, or in effectively incorporating new technologies into the production process. This can occur only when managers receive adequate information on the effects of their
decisions, in the form of market-determined prices. And ultimately, it was competition that ensured that the feedback received
through the pricing system was accurate. Early reforms in Hungary and Yugoslavia, and to a lesser extent in the Soviet Union,
sought to give managers somewhat greater autonomy, but in the
absence of a rational pricing system, managerial autonomy had
little effect.

The complexity of modern economies proved to be simply
beyond the capabilities of centralized bureaucracies to manage,
no matter how advanced their technical capabilities. In place of
a demand-driven price system, Soviet planners have tried to de-
cree a "socially just" allocation of resources from above. For

many years, they believed that bigger computers and better linear programming would make possible an efficient centralized allocation of resources. This proved to be an illusion. *Goskomtsen*, the former Soviet state committee on prices, had to review some 200,000 prices every year, or three or four prices per day for every official working in that bureaucracy. This represented only 42 percent of the total number of price decisions made by Soviet officials every year,[6] which in turn was only a fraction of the number of pricing decisions that would have to have been made were the Soviet economy able to offer the same diversity of products and services as a Western capitalist economy. Bureaucrats sitting in Moscow or Beijing might have had a chance of setting a semblance of efficient prices when they had to supervise economies producing commodities numbering in the hundreds or low thousands; the task becomes impossible in an age when a single airplane can consist of hundreds of thousands of separate parts. In modern economies, moreover, pricing increasingly reflects differences in quality: a Chrysler Le Baron and a BMW are equally cars in terms of their overall technical specifications, and yet consumers have assigned a substantial premium to the latter based on a certain "feel" about it. The ability of bureaucrats to make distinctions reliably is, to say the least, problematic.

The need for central planners to maintain control over prices and allocations of goods prohibits them from participating in the international division of labor, and thereby from realizing the economies of scale it makes possible. Communist East Germany, with a population of seventeen million, tried valiantly to duplicate the world economy within its own borders, and in fact managed to make bad versions of a great many products that it could have purchased from the outside much more cheaply, from the pollution-producing Trabant car to Erich Honecker's prized memory chips.

Finally, central planning undermines an all-important aspect of human capital, the work ethic. Even a strong work ethic can be destroyed through social and economic policies that deny people personal incentives to work, and re-creating it can be extremely difficult. As we will see in Part Four below, there is good reason to believe that the strong work ethic of many societies is not the result of the modernization process, but rather is a holdover from that society's pre-modern culture and traditions. Having a strong work ethic may not be an absolute condition for a successful "post-industrial" economy, but it certainly helps, and may become a critical counterweight to the tendency of such economies to emphasize consumption over production.

It has been a common expectation that the technocratic imperatives of industrial maturity would eventually lead to a softening of communist central control, and its replacement by more liberal, market-oriented practices. The judgment of Raymond Aron that "technological complexity will strengthen the managerial class at the expense of the ideologists and militants" echoed an earlier one that technocrats would be the "gravediggers of communism."[7] These predictions in the end proved to be quite correct; what people in the West could not anticipate was how long it would take for them to be borne out. The Soviet and Chinese states proved themselves perfectly capable of bringing their societies up to the coal and steel age: the technology involved was not highly complex, and could be mastered by largely illiterate peasants forcibly pulled off the farm and put into simplified assembly lines. Specialists with the technical expertise required to run such an economy proved to be docile and easy to control politically.[8] Stalin once put the noted aircraft designer Tupolev in the Gulag, where he designed one of his best airplanes. Stalin's successors managed to co-opt managers and technocrats by offering them status and rewards in return for loyalty to the system.[9] Mao in China took a different course: seeking to avoid creation of a privileged technical intelligentsia as in the Soviet Union, he declared an all-out war against them, first during the Great Leap Forward in the late 1950s, and then again during the Cultural Revolution in the late 1960s. Engineers and scientists were forced to harvest crops and engage in other forms of back-breaking labor, while positions requiring technical competence went to politically correct ideologues.

This experience should teach us not to underestimate the ability of totalitarian or authoritarian states to resist the imperatives of economic rationality for a considerable length of time—in the cases of the Soviet Union and China, for a generation or more. But this resistance came, eventually, at the price of economic stagnation. The total failure of centrally planned economies in coun-

tries like the Soviet Union and China to move beyond a 1950s
level of industrialization undercut their ability to play important
roles on the international stage, or even to safeguard their own
national security. Mao's persecution of competent technocrats
during the Cultural Revolution proved to be an economic disaster
of the first order that set China back a generation. One of Deng
Xiaoping's first acts when coming to power in the mid-1970s was
therefore to restore prestige and dignity to the technical intelligentsia and to protect them from the vagaries of ideological politics, choosing the path of co-optation adopted by the Soviets a
generation earlier. But the efforts to co-opt technological elites in
the service of ideology eventually worked the other way as well:
that elite, given a relatively greater degree of freedom to think
and study the outside world, became familiar with and began to
adopt many of the ideas current in that world. As Mao feared, the
technological intelligentsia became the principal bearer of "bourgeois liberalism," and played a key role in the subsequent economic reform process.

By the end of the 1980s, then, China, the Soviet Union, and
the countries of Eastern Europe can be seen as having succumbed
to the economic logic of advanced industrialization.[10] Despite the
political crackdown ordered after Tiananmen Square, the Chinese leadership has accepted the need for markets and decentralized economic decision making, as well as close integration into
the global capitalist division of labor, and has shown itself willing
to accept greater social stratification accompanying the rise of a
technocratic elite. The countries of Eastern Europe all opted for
a return to market economic systems after their democratic revolutions in 1989, even though they differed amongst themselves
on the timing and pace of marketization. The Soviet leadership
was more reluctant to take the plunge into full-scale marketization, but after the political transformation brought about by the
failure of the August 1991 coup, moved toward implementing
far-reaching liberal economic reform.

Societies have a degree of freedom in the extent to which they
regulate and plan capitalist economies. The logic of our Mechanism does not dictate this degree in any rigid way. Nonetheless, the unfolding of technologically driven economic modernization creates strong incentives for developed countries to accept
the basic terms of the universal capitalist economic culture, by

permitting a substantial degree of economic competition and letting prices be determined by market mechanisms. No other path toward full economic modernity has been proven to be viable.

9

The Victory of the VCR

Not a single country in the world, no matter what its political system, has ever modernized with a closed-door policy.

—*Deng Xiaoping, in a 1982 speech*[1]

The fact that capitalism was in some sense inevitable for advanced countries, and that Marxist-Leninist socialism was a serious obstacle to the creation of wealth and a modern technological civilization, may have seemed like commonplace knowledge by the last decade of the twentieth century. What was less obvious were the relative merits of socialism versus capitalism for less developed countries that had not yet reached the level of industrialization represented by Europe in the 1950s. For impoverished countries for whom the coal and steel age was no more than a dream, the fact that the Soviet Union was not at the leading edge of information-age technologies was much less impressive than the fact that it had created an urban, industrial society in a single generation. Socialist central planning continued to be appealing because it offered a quick route to capital accumulation and the "rational" redirection of national resources into "balanced" industrial development. The Soviet Union had done this by squeezing its agricultural sector through outright terror in the 1920s and 30s, a process that had taken early industrializers like the United States and England a couple of centuries to accomplish by non-coercive means.

The argument in favor of socialism as the development strategy of choice for Third World countries was considerably strengthened by the apparently persistent failure of capitalism to produce sustained economic growth in regions like Latin America. Indeed, it is safe to say that were it not for the Third World, Marxism would have died a much quicker death in this century. But the continuing poverty of the underdeveloped world breathed new life into the doctrine by permitting the Left to attribute that poverty first to colonialism, and then, when there was no more colonialism, to "neo-colonialism," and finally to the behavior of multinational corporations. The most recent attempt to keep a form of Marxism alive in the Third World was so-called *dependencia* ("dependency") theory. Developed primarily in Latin America, it gave intellectual coherence to the self-assertion of the impoverished South as a whole against the wealthy, industrialized North in the 1960s and 70s. Allied to Southern nationalism, dependency theory took on a power greater than that justified by its intellectual underpinnings, and had a corrosive effect on prospects for economic development in many parts of the Third World for the better part of a generation.

The real father of dependency theory was Lenin himself. In his well-known 1914 pamphlet, *Imperialism: The Highest Stage of Capitalism* he sought to account for the fact that European capitalism had not led to the steady impoverishment of the working class, but had in fact permitted a rise in their living standards and the development of a reasonably self-satisfied, trade-union mentality among workers in Europe.[2] Capitalism had bought time for itself, he argued, by in effect exporting exploitation to the colonies, where native labor and raw materials could absorb European "surplus capital." Competition among "monopoly capitalists" led to the political division of the underdeveloped world and, ultimately, to conflict, war, and revolution among them. Lenin argued, in contrast to Marx, that the final contradiction which would bring down capitalism was not class struggle *within* the developed world, but between the developed North and the "global proletariat" in the underdeveloped world.

While several different schools of dependency theory eventually emerged in the 1960s,[3] they had their origin in the work of the Argentine economist Raul Prebisch. Prebisch, who headed the United Nation's Economic Committee for Latin America (ECLA) in the 1950s[4] and later the United Nations Conference on Trade and Development (UNCTAD), noted that the terms of trade for the world's "periphery" were declining relative to its "center." He argued that the sluggish growth of Third World regions like Latin America was a result of the global capitalist economic order, which kept them in a state of perpetual "dependent development."[5] The wealth of the North was therefore directly linked to the poverty of the South.[6]

According to classical liberal trade theory, participation in an open system of world trade should maximize the advantage of all, even if one country sold coffee beans and another computers. Economically backward latecomers to this system should in fact have certain advantages in economic development, since they could simply import technology from the earlier developers rather than having to create it themselves.[7] Dependency theory, by contrast, held that late development doomed a country to perpetual backwardness. The advanced countries controlled the world terms of trade and, through their multinational corporations, forced Third World countries into what was called "unbalanced development"—that is, the export of raw materials and other commodities with low processing content. The developed North had locked up the world market for sophisticated manufactured goods like automobiles and airplanes, leaving the Third World to be, in effect, global "hewers of wood and drawers of water."[8] Many *dependencistas* linked the international economic order to the authoritarian regimes that had recently come to power in Latin America in the wake of the Cuban Revolution.[9]

The policies that emerged from dependency theory were decidedly illiberal. The more moderate *dependencistas* sought to bypass Western multinational corporations and to encourage local industry by erecting high tariff walls against imports, a practice known as import substitution. The solutions recommended by the more radical dependency theorists sought to undermine the global economic order altogether by fostering revolution, withdrawal from the capitalist trading system, and integration into the Soviet bloc on the model of Cuba.[10] Thus, at the beginning of the 1970s when Marxist ideas were being recognized as a dismal basis for real societies in places like China and the Soviet Union, they were being revived by intellectuals in the Third World and in American and European universities as a formula for the underdeveloped world's future.

But while dependency theory lives on among left-wing intellectuals, it has by now been exploded as a theoretical model by one large phenomenon it cannot possibly explain: that is, the economic development of East Asia in the postwar period. Asian

economic success, apart from whatever material benefits it be-
stowed on the countries of Asia, has had the salutary effect of
finally laying to rest self-defeating ideas like *dependencia* theory
that were becoming in themselves an obstacle to growth by preventing clear thinking about the sources of economic development. For if, as dependency theory claimed, Third World
underdevelopment was due to the participation of less developed
countries in the global capitalist order, how could one possibly
explain the phenomenal economic growth that had occurred in
countries like South Korea, Taiwan, Hong Kong, Singapore, Malaysia, and Thailand? For after the war, almost all of these countries had deliberately eschewed policies of economic autarky and
import substitution that were then sweeping Latin America, and
instead pursued export-led growth with great single-mindedness,
deliberately tying themselves to foreign markets and capital
through links with multinational corporations.[11] One could not
argue, moreover, that these countries started with unfair advantages because they were endowed with natural resources or accumulated capital from the past; unlike the oil-rich countries of the
Middle East or certain mineral-rich countries in Latin America,
they entered the race with nothing more than the human capital
of their populations.

Postwar Asian experience demonstrated that late modernizers
were actually *advantaged* relative to more established industrial
powers, just as earlier liberal trade theories had predicted. The
late modernizers in Asia, beginning with Japan, were able to pur-
chase the most up-to-date technologies from the United States
and Europe and, unburdened by an aging and inefficient infrastructure, were able to become competitive (many Americans
would say too competitive) in hi-tech areas within a generation or
two. This proved to be true not only for Asia relative to Europe
and North America, but within Asia as well, where those countries
like Thailand and Malaysia that started their development process
later than Japan and South Korea have experienced no relative
disadvantage. Western multinational corporations behaved as liberal economic textbooks claimed they should: while "exploiting"
cheap labor in Asia, they provided markets, capital, and technology in return, and were the vehicles for the diffusion of technology that eventually allowed self-sustaining growth in the local
economies. This is perhaps the reason why one high Singaporean
official remarked that the three abominations his country would

not tolerate were "hippies, long-haired boys, and critics of multi-national corporations."[12]

The growth record compiled by these late modernizers was truly astounding. Japan grew at an annual rate of 9.8 percent in the 1960s and 6 percent in the 1970s; the "four tigers" (Hong Kong, Taiwan, Singapore, and South Korea) grew at 9.3 percent in the same period; and ASEAN as a whole saw growth of over 8 percent.[13] In Asia one could make direct comparisons of the relative performance of alternative economic systems. Taiwan and the People's Republic of China both started their separate existence in 1949 with roughly equal standards of living. Under a market system, Taiwan's real GNP grew at 8.7 percent per year, leading to a GNP per capita of $7,500 by 1989. The comparable figure for the PRC was approximately $350, much of which was itself due to nearly a decade of market-oriented reforms. In 1960 North and South Korea had roughly equal levels of GNP per capita. In 1961, South Korea dropped an import-substitution policy and brought domestic and international prices into line. The South Korean economy subsequently grew at a rate of 8.4 percent per year, leading to a 1989 per capita GNP of $4,550, more than four times that of the North.[14]

Nor has economic success come at the expense of social justice at home. It has been argued that wages were exploitatively low in Asia, and governments there have engaged in draconian policies to suppress consumer demand and enforce a very high rate of savings. But income distribution began to equalize rapidly in one country after another once they reached a certain level of prosperity.[15] Taiwan and South Korea have steadily decreased income inequality over the last generation: while Taiwan's top 20 percent made 15 times the income of the lowest 20 percent in 1952, the multiple fell to 4.5 times by 1980.[16] If growth continues at anything near its present rate, there is no reason to think that the rest of ASEAN will not continue to follow suit in the next generation.

In a last-ditch effort to save dependency theory, some of its proponents have tried to argue that the economic success of the Asian newly industrialized economies (NIEs) was due to planning, and that industrial policies and not capitalism lay at the root of their success.[17] But while economic planning does play a relatively greater role in Asia than in the United States, the most successful sectors within Asian economies have tended to be those permitting the greatest degree of competition in domestic markets and integration into international ones.[18] Most of those on the Left, moreover, who cite Asia as a positive example of state intervention in the economy, would not be able to stomach the semi-authoritarian Asian style of planning, with its quashing of labor and welfare demands. The Left's preferred kind of planning, with its intervention on behalf of the victims of capitalism, has historically had much more ambiguous economic results.

What Asia's postwar economic miracle demonstrates is that capitalism is a path toward economic development that is potentially available to all countries. No underdeveloped country in the Third World is disadvantaged simply because it began the growth process later than Europe, nor are the established industrial powers capable of blocking the development of a latecomer, provided that country plays by the rules of economic liberalism.

But if the capitalist "world system" is not an obstacle to economic development in the Third World, why have other market-oriented economies outside of Asia not grown as fast? For the phenomenon of economic stagnation in Latin America and other parts of the Third World is every bit as real as Asian economic success, and was what gave rise to dependency theory in the first place. If we reject neo-Marxist explanations like dependency theory, there are two broad categories of possible answers.

The first is a cultural explanation: that is, that the habits, customs, religions, and social structure of the peoples of regions like Latin America somehow obstruct the achievement of high levels of economic growth in a way that those of the peoples of Asia or Europe do not.[19] The cultural argument is a serious one to which we will return in Part Four. If there are significant cultural obstacles to making markets work in certain societies, then the universality of capitalism as a route to economic modernization would be thrown into question.

The second explanation is one of policy: capitalism has never worked in Latin America and other parts of the Third World because it has never been seriously tried. That is, most of the ostensibly "capitalist" economies of Latin America are seriously crippled by their mercantilist traditions and the all-pervasive state sectors established in the name of economic justice. This argument has a good deal of power, and since policies are much more readily changeable than cultures, it behooves us to explore this argument first.

While North America inherited the philosophy, traditions,

and culture of liberal England as it emerged out of the Glorious Revolution, Latin America inherited many of the feudal institutions of seventeenth- and eighteenth-century Spain and Portugal. Among these were the Spanish and Portuguese crowns' strong disposition to control economic activity for their own greater glory, a practice known as mercantilism. According to one specialist, "From colonial times to the present, the [Brazilian] government has never been removed from the economic sphere to the extent it has been in post-mercantilist Europe. . . . The crown was the supreme economic patron, and all commercial and productive activities depended on special licenses, grants of monopoly, and trade privileges."[20] It became common practice in Latin America to use state power to advance the economic interests of the upper classes, which took their cue from the old leisured and landed upper classes of Europe, rather than of the more entrepreneurial middle class that had emerged in England and France subsequent to the Spanish conquest of Latin America. These elites were protected by their own governments from international competition through import-substitution policies adopted by many Latin American governments from the 1930s through the 1960s. Import substitution limited local producers to small domestic markets where they could not realize potential economies of scale; the cost of producing an automobile in Brazil, Argentina, or Mexico, for example, ran from 60 to 150 percent higher than in the United States.[21]

The long-standing historical predisposition toward mercantilism was combined, in the twentieth century, with the desire of progressive forces in Latin America to use the state as a means of redistributing wealth from rich to poor in the interests of "social justice."[22] This took a variety of forms, including the labor legislation introduced in countries like Argentina, Brazil, and Chile in the 1930s and 40s, which discouraged the development of labor-intensive industries that had been crucial for Asian economic growth. The Left and the Right thus converged in their belief in the need for extensive government intervention in economic affairs. The result of this convergence is that many Latin American economies are dominated by bloated and inefficient state sectors that either attempt to manage economic activity directly or burden it with a tremendous regulatory overhead. In Brazil, the state not only runs posts and communications, but manufactures steel, mines iron ore and potash, prospects for oil, runs commercial and investment banks, generates electric power, and builds airplanes. These public-sector companies cannot go bankrupt, and use employment as a form of political patronage. Prices throughout the Brazilian economy, and particularly within the public sector, are set less by the market than by a process of political negotiation with powerful unions.[23]

Or take the case of Peru. Hernando de Soto in his book *The Other Path* documents how his institute in Lima attempted to set up a fictitious factory according to the formal legal rules established by the Peruvian government. Going through eleven bureaucratic procedures required took 289 days and a total cost of $1,231 in fees and lost wages (including the payment of two bribes), or thirty-two times the minimum monthly wage.[24] According to de Soto, regulatory barriers to the formation of new businesses constitute a major obstacle to entrepreneurship in Peru, particularly on the part of poor people, and explains the burgeoning of a huge "informal" (that is, illegal or extra-legal) economy of people unwilling and unable to cope with state-imposed barriers to trade. All of the major Latin American economies have large "informal" sectors, which produce as much as a quarter to a third of total GNP. Needless to say, forcing economic activity into illegal channels is hardly conducive to economic efficiency. In the words of novelist Mario Vargas Llosa, "One of the most widely believed myths about Latin America is that its backwardness results from the erroneous philosophy of economic liberalism . . ." In fact, Vargas Llosa argues, such liberalism has never existed; what existed in its place was a form of mercantilism, that is, "a bureaucratized and law-ridden state that regards the redistribution of national wealth as more important than the production of wealth," with redistribution taking the form of "the concession of monopolies or favored status to a small elite that depends on the state and on which the state itself is dependent."[25]

The cases of disastrous state intervention in economic affairs are legion in Latin America. The most notorious is that of Argentina, which in 1913 had a per capita GDP comparable to that of Switzerland, twice as large as Italy's, and half of Canada's. Today, the comparable figures are less than a sixth, a third, and a fifth, respectively. Argentina's long decline from development back into underdevelopment can be traced directly to its adoption of import-substitution policies in response to the worldwide economic crisis of the 1930s. These policies were reinforced and institutionalized under the leadership of Juan Perón in the 1950s, who also used the power of the state to redistribute wealth to the working class as a means of cementing his personal power base. The ability of political leaders to stubbornly reject the imperatives of economic reality is perhaps nowhere better demonstrated than in a letter Perón wrote in 1953 to Carlos Ibañez, president of Chile, in which he advised:

> Give to the people, especially the workers, all that is possible. When it seems to you that already you are giving them too much, give them more. You will see the results. Everyone will try to scare you with the specter of an economic collapse. But all of this is a lie. There is nothing more elastic than the economy which everyone fears so much because no one understands it.[26]

It is fair to say that Argentine technocrats now understand the nature of their country's economy better than Juan Perón did. Argentina now faces the daunting problem of undoing that statist economic legacy, a task which ironically enough fell to one of Perón's followers, President Carlos Menem.

More boldly than Menem's Argentina, Mexico under President Carlos Salinas de Gortari undertook a broad-ranging set of liberalizing economic reforms, including the reduction of tax rates and budget deficits, privatization (selling 875 of 1155 government-owned companies between 1982 and 1991), cracking down on tax evasion and other forms of corruption on the part of corporations, bureaucrats, and labor unions, and opening talks with the United States on a free-trade pact. The result, at the end of the 1980s, was three years of 3–4 percent real GNP growth and an inflation rate of less than 20 percent—very low by historic and regional standards.[27]

Socialism, then, is no more appealing as an economic model for developing countries than it is for advanced industrial societies. Thirty or forty years ago, the socialist alternative seemed much more plausible. Leaders of Third World countries, in the cases where they were honest enough to admit the enormous human cost of Soviet or Chinese-style modernization, could still argue that they were justified by the objective of industrialization. Their own societies were ignorant, violent, backward, and poverty-ridden. They argued that economic modernization under capitalist conditions was not a cost-free process, either, and in

any case their societies could not wait the decades that it took
Europe and North America to accomplish this process.

Today, this argument looks less and less tenable. The Asian
NIEs, repeating the experiences of Germany and Japan in the late
nineteenth and early twentieth centuries, have proven that economic liberalism allows late modernizers to catch up with and
even overtake the early ones, and that this goal can be accomplished within the space of a generation or two. And while this
was not exactly a cost-free process, the kinds of privations and
hardships suffered by the working classes in countries like Japan,
South Korea, Taiwan, and Hong Kong looked positively benign
when compared to the wholesale social terror unleashed on the
populations of the Soviet Union and China.

The recent experiences of the Soviet Union, China, and the
states of Eastern Europe in converting their command economies
back into market systems suggests a whole new category of considerations that should deter developing nations from choosing
the socialist path to development. Let us imagine that one is a
guerrilla leader in the jungles of Peru or a township in South
Africa, plotting a Marxist-Leninist or Maoist revolution against
the governments of those countries. As in 1917 or 1949, one
would have to anticipate the need to seize power and use the
coercive machinery of the state to break the old social order, and
to create new, centralized economic institutions. But in addition,
one would now have to anticipate (again, provided one is an in-
tellectually honest guerrilla) that the fruits of this first revolution
would be necessarily limited; that one could perhaps hope that in
a generation your country would reach the economic level of East
Germany in the 1960s or 70s. This would be no mean achievement, but one would have to anticipate further being stuck there
for a good long time. And if this guerrilla leader wanted to move
beyond an East German level of development, with all of its de-
moralizing social and environmental costs, one would have to further anticipate a second revolution, whereby the socialist central
planning mechanism was in turn smashed and capitalist institutions were restored. But this would not be an easy task either,
since by that time one's society would have acquired a totally irrational pricing system, one's managers would have lost touch
with the most up-to-date practices in the outside world, and one's
working class would have lost whatever work ethic they once possessed. In light of these problems, all of which one could foresee

in advance, it would seem to be much easier to be a free-market guerrilla instead and proceed directly to that second, capitalist revolution without passing through the socialist stage. That is, tear down the old state structures of regulation and bureaucracy, undermine the wealth, privileges, and status of the old social classes by exposing them to international competition, and free the creative energies of one's own civil society.

The logic of a progressive modern natural science predisposes human societies toward capitalism only to the extent that men can see their own economic self-interest clearly. Mercantilism, *dependencia* theory, and a host of other intellectual mirages have prevented people from achieving this clarity of vision. But the experiences of Asia and of Eastern Europe now provide important empirical test beds against which the claims of competing economic systems can be measured.

Our Mechanism can now explain the creation of a universal consumer culture based on liberal economic principles, for the Third World as well as the First and Second. The enormously productive and dynamic economic world created by advancing technology and the rational organization of labor has a tremendous homogenizing power. It is capable of linking different societies around the world to one another physically through the creation of global markets, and of creating parallel economic aspirations and practices in a host of diverse societies. The attractive power of this world creates a very strong *predisposition* for all human societies to participate in it, while success in this participation requires the adoption of the principles of economic liberalism. This is the ultimate victory of the VCR.

10

In the Land of Education

Thus I came to you, O men of today, and into the land of education. . . . But what happened to me? For all my anxiety I had to laugh. Never had my eyes beheld anything so dappled and motley. I laughed and laughed while my foot was still trembling, and my heart no less. "This is clearly the home of all paint pots," I said . . .

—*Nietzsche,* Thus Spoke Zarathustra[1]

We now come to the most difficult part of our argument: Does the Mechanism of modern natural science lead to liberal democracy? If the logic of advanced industrialization, determined by modern natural science, creates a strong predisposition in favor of capitalism and market economics, does it also produce free government and democratic participation? In a landmark article written in 1959, the sociologist Seymour Martin Lipset demonstrated that there was an extremely high degree of empirical correlation between stable democracy, on the one hand, and a country's level of economic development on the other, as well as with other indices related to economic development such as urbanization, education, and so forth.[2] Is there a necessary connection between advanced industrialization and political liberalism that accounts for this high degree of correlation? Or is it possible that political liberalism is simply a cultural artifact of European civilization and its various offshoots, which for independent reasons happen to have produced the most notable cases of successful industrialization?

As we will see, the relationship between economic development and democracy is far from accidental, but the motives be-

hind the choice of democracy are not fundamentally economic.
They have *another* source, and are facilitated, but not made necessary, by industrialization.

The tight relationship that exists between economic development, educational levels, and democracy is illustrated quite clearly
in Southern Europe. In 1958, Spain embarked on a program of
economic liberalization in which the mercantilist policies of the
Francoist state were replaced by liberal ones linking the Spanish
economy to that of the outside world. This led to a period of very
rapid economic growth: in the decade before Franco's death,
Spain's economy grew 7.1 percent per year. It was followed closely
by those of Portugal and Greece, which achieved growth rates of
6.2 and 6.4 percent per year, respectively.[3] The social transformations brought about by industrialization were dramatic: in
Spain, only 18 percent of the population lived in cities of over
100,000 population in 1950; by 1970, this figure had increased to
34 percent.[4] In 1950 half the populations of Spain, Portugal, and
Greece were engaged in agriculture, compared to an average of
24 percent for Western Europe as a whole; by 1970 only Greece
remained above that latter figure, while in Spain the percentage
had dropped to 21.[5] With urbanization came higher degrees of
education and personal income, and an appreciation of the consumer culture that was being created within the European Community. While these economic and social changes did not in
themselves bring about greater political pluralism, they created
the social milieu under which pluralism could flourish once political conditions became ripe. The Francoist commissar of the
Plan for Economic Development who oversaw much of Spain's
technocratic revolution, Laureano Lopez Rodo, was reported to
have said that Spain would be ready for democracy when per
capita income reached $2000. This proved quite prophetic: in
1974, on the eve of Franco's death, per capita GDP stood at
$2,446.[6]

A similar linkage between economic development and liberal
democracy can be seen in Asia. Japan, the first East Asian state
to modernize, was the first to achieve a stable liberal democracy.
(Japan's democratization was accomplished at the point of a
gun, so to speak, but the result proved durable long past the
point where democracy could be said to have been imposed co-
ercively.) Taiwan and South Korea, with the second- and third-

highest levels of education and per capita GNP, have
experienced the greatest change in their political systems.[7] In
Taiwan, for example, 45 percent of the ruling Guomindang
party's Central Committee have higher educational degrees,
many of them earned in the United States.[8] Forty-five percent
of Taiwanese and 37 percent of South Koreans receive some
higher education, compared with 60 percent of Americans and
22 percent of Britons. And indeed, it is the younger, better educated members of Taiwan's Parliament that have pushed the
most strongly to make it a more representative institution. Australia and New Zealand, those lands of European settlement in
Asia, had of course modernized economically and democratized
well before World War II.

    In South Africa, the apartheid system was codified following
the victory of D. F. Malan's National party in 1948. The Afrikaner
community that it represented was singularly backward in socio-
economic terms, particularly when compared to contemporane-
ous European societies. The Afrikaners in this period were largely
poor, uneducated farmers who had recently been driven to the
cities by drought and hardship.[9] The Afrikaners used their capture of state power to advance themselves socially and economically, primarily through public-sector employment. Between 1948
and 1988 they underwent a dramatic transformation into an urban, educated, and increasingly entrepreneurial white-collar society.[10] With that education came contact with the political norms
and trends of the outside world, from which they could not isolate
themselves. The liberalization of South African society had already started in the late 1970s with the re-legalization of black
trade unions and the relaxation of censorship laws. By the time of
F. W. de Klerk's opening to the African National Congress in
February 1990, the government was in many ways simply following the opinion of its white electorate, now little different in educational and occupational achievement from its counterparts in
Europe and America.

    The Soviet Union as well has been undergoing a comparable
social transformation, though at a slower pace than the countries
of Asia. It too has changed from an agricultural to an urban
society, with increasing levels of mass and specialized education.[11]
These sociological changes, going on in the background while the
Cold War was being fought out in Berlin and Cuba, were condi-

tions that encouraged the steps subsequently undertaken toward democratization.

Looking around the world, there remains a very strong overall correlation between advancing socio-economic modernization and the emergence of new democracies. Traditionally the most economically advanced regions, Western Europe and North America, have also hosted the world's oldest and most stable liberal democracies. Southern Europe has followed closely behind, and achieved stable democracy in the 1970s. Within Southern Europe, Portugal had the rockiest transition to democracy in the mid-1970s because it started from a lower socio-economic base; a great deal of social mobilization had to occur after rather than before the passing of the old regime. Right behind Europe economically is Asia, whose nations have democratized (or are in the process of doing so) in strict proportion to their degree of development. Of the formerly communist states in Eastern Europe, the most economically advanced among them—East Germany, Hungary, and Czechoslovakia, followed by Poland—also made the most rapid transitions to full democracy, while less developed Bulgaria, Romania, Serbia, and Albania all elected reform communists in 1990–91. The Soviet Union is at a roughly comparable level of development to the larger states of Latin America like Argentina, Brazil, Chile, and Mexico, and like them has failed to achieve a fully stable democratic order. Africa, the least developed region of the world, possesses only a handful of recent democracies, of uncertain stability.[12]

The only apparent regional anomaly is the Middle East, which possesses no stable democracies, and yet contains a number of states with per capita incomes on a European or Asian level. But this is easily explained by oil: income from petroleum has permitted states like Saudi Arabia, Iraq, Iran, and the UAE to acquire the trappings of modernity—automobiles, VCRs, Mirage fighter-bombers, and the like—without having had their societies go through the social transformations that come when such wealth is generated by the labor of their populations.

To explain why advancing industrialization should produce liberal democracy, three types of argument have been put forward. Each one is flawed to a certain degree. The first is a functional argument, to the effect that only democracy is capable of mediating the complex web of conflicting interests that are created by a modern economy. This view was argued most strongly by Talcott Parsons, who believed that democracy was an "evolutionary universal" of all societies:

> The basic argument for considering democratic association a universal . . . is that, the larger and more complex a society becomes, the more important is effective political organization, not only in its administrative capacity, but also, and not least, in its support of a universalistic legal order. . . . No institutional form basically different from the democratic association can . . . *mediate consensus in [the] exercise [of power and authority]* by particular persons and groups, and in the formation of particular binding policy decisions.[13]

To restate Parsons' point somewhat, democracies are best equipped to deal with the rapidly proliferating number of interest groups created by the industrialization process. Consider the completely new social actors that emerge in the course of industrialization: a working class, which becomes increasingly differentiated according to industrial and craft specialties, new layers of managerial personnel whose interests do not necessarily coincide with those of top management, government bureaucrats at a national, regional, and local level, and waves of immigrants from abroad, legal and illegal, who seek to take advantage of the open labor markets in developed countries. Democracy, the argument goes, is more functional in such a setting because it is more adaptable. Establishing universal and open criteria for participation in the political system allows new social groups and interests to express themselves and join in the general political consensus. Dictatorships can adapt to change as well, and in some cases can act more rapidly than democracies, as did the obligarchs ruling Meiji Japan after 1868. But history abounds with as many other cases of narrow ruling elites out of touch with the social changes that were occurring under their noses as a result of economic development, like the Prussian Junkers or the landowning elites in Argentina.

Democracy, according to this line of argument, is more functional than dictatorship because many of the conflicts that develop between these emerging social groups have to be adjudicated either in the legal system or, ultimately, in the political system.[14] The market alone cannot determine the appropriate level and location of public infrastructure investment, or rules for the settlement of labor disputes, or the degree of airline and trucking regulation, or occupational health and safety standards. Each one of these questions is "value-laden" to some extent, and must be referred to the political system. And if that system is going to adjudicate these conflicting interests fairly and in a way that receives the consent of all of the major actors within the economy, it must be democratic. A dictatorship could resolve such conflicts in the name of economic efficiency, but the smooth functioning of a modern economy depends on the willingness of its many interdependent social components to work together. If they do not believe in the legitimacy of the adjudicator, if there is no *trust* in the system, there will be no active and enthusiastic cooperation of the sort required to make the system as a whole function smoothly.[15]

An example of the way in which democracy could arguably be said to be more functional for developed countries is with respect to a central issue of our time, the environment. Among the most notable products of advanced industrialization are significant levels of pollution and environmental damage. These constitute what economists call externalities, that is, costs imposed on third parties which do not directly affect the enterprises doing the damage. Despite various theories blaming ecological damage either on capitalism or socialism, experience has shown that neither economic system is particularly good for the environment. Both private corporations as well as socialist enterprises and ministries will focus on growth or output and will seek to avoid paying for externalities wherever they can.[16] But since people want not only economic growth but a safe environment for themselves and their children, it becomes a function of the state to find a fair trade-off between the two, and to spread the costs of ecological protection around so that no one sector will bear them unduly.

And in this respect, the communist world's truly abysmal environmental record suggests that what is most effective in protecting the environment is neither capitalism nor socialism, but democracy. As a whole, democratic political systems reacted much more quickly to the growth of ecological consciousness in the 1960s and 70s than did the world's dictatorships. For without a political system that permits local communities to protest the siting of a highly toxic chemical plant in the middle of their communities, without freedom for watchdog organizations to monitor the behavior of companies and enterprises, without a national political leadership sufficiently sensitized that it is willing to devote substantial resources to protect the environment, a nation ends up with disasters like Chernobyl, or the desiccation of the Aral Sea, or an infant mortality rate in Krakow that is four times the already high Polish national average, or a 70 percent rate of miscarriages in Western Bohemia.[17] Democracies permit participation and therefore feedback, and without feedback, governments will always tend to favor the large enterprise that adds significantly to national wealth, over the long-term interests of dispersed groups of private citizens.

A second line of argument explaining why economic development should produce democracy has to do with the tendency of dictatorships or one-party rule to degenerate over time, and to degenerate more quickly when faced with the task of running an advanced technological society. Revolutionary regimes may govern effectively in their early years by virtue of what Max Weber called charismatic authority. But once the regime's founders have passed on, there is no guarantee that their successors will enjoy a comparable degree of authority, or even that they will be minimally competent at running the country. Long-standing dictatorships are capable of producing grotesque personalistic excesses like former Romanian ruler Nicolae Ceaucescu's 40,000-watt chandelier, built at a time when the state was declaring regular electricity blackouts. Self-destructive power struggles develop among followers of those who founded the regime, who succeed in checking one another but not in governing the country effectively. The alternative to ceaseless power struggle and arbitrary dictatorship is increasingly routinized and institutionalized procedures for selecting new leaders and vetting policies. If such procedures for changing leaders exist, the authors of bad policies can be replaced without bringing down the entire system.[18]

There is also a version of this thesis that applies to right-wing authoritarian transitions to democracy. Democracy emerges as the result of a pact or compromise between elite groups—the army, technocrats, industrial bourgeoisie—which, exhausted, frustrated, or mutually checked in their ambitions, accept pacts or power-sharing arrangements as a second-best outcome.[19] Under either the left-wing communist or right-wing authoritarian versions of this argument, democracy does not arise because anybody necessarily wants it, but rather as a byproduct of elite struggle.

The final and most powerful line of argument linking economic development with liberal democracy is that successful industrialization produces middle-class societies, and that middle-class societies demand political participation and equality of rights. Despite the disparities in income distribution that frequently arise in the early phases of industrialization, economic development ultimately tends to promote the broad equality of condition because it creates enormous demand for a large, educated work force. And such a broad equality of condition arguably predisposes people to oppose political systems that do not respect that equality or permit people to participate on an equal basis.

Middle-class societies arise as a result of universal education. The link between education and liberal democracy has been frequently noted, and would seem to be an all-important one.[20] Industrial societies require large numbers of highly skilled and educated workers, managers, technicians, and intellectuals; hence even the most dictatorial state cannot avoid the need for both mass education and open access to higher and specialized education if it wants to be economically advanced. Such societies cannot exist without a large and specialized educational establishment. Indeed, in the developed world social status is determined to a very large degree by one's level of educational achievement.[21] The class differences that exist in the contemporary United States, for example, are due primarily to differences in education. There are few obstacles to the advancement of a person with the proper educational credentials. Inequality creeps into the system as a result of unequal access to education; lack of education is the surest condemnation to second-class citizenship.

The effect of education on political attitudes is complicated, but there are reasons for thinking it at least creates the conditions for democratic society. The self-professed aim of modern education is to "liberate" people from prejudices and traditional forms of authority. Educated people are said not to obey authority blindly, but rather learn to think for themselves. Even if this doesn't happen on a mass basis, people can be taught to see their own self-interest more clearly, and over a longer time horizon. Education also makes people demand more of themselves and for themselves; in other words, they acquire a certain sense of dignity which they want to have respected by their fellow citizens and by the state. In a traditional peasant society, it is possible for a local landlord (or, for that matter, a communist commissar) to recruit peasants to kill other peasants and dispossess them of their land. They do so not because it is in their interest, but because they are used to obeying authority. Urban professionals in developed countries, on the other hand, can be recruited to a lot of nutty causes like liquid diets and marathon running, but they tend not to volunteer for private armies or death squads simply because someone in a uniform tells them to do so.

A variation of this argument would maintain that the scientific-technical elite required to run modern industrial economies would eventually demand greater political liberalization, because scientific inquiry can only proceed in an atmosphere of freedom and the open exchange of ideas. We saw earlier how the emergence of a large technocratic elite in the USSR and China created a certain bias in favor of markets and economic liberalization, since these were more in accord with the criteria of economic rationality. Here the argument is extended into the political realm: that scientific advance depends not only on freedom for scientific inquiry, but on a society and political system that are as a whole open to free debate and participation.[22]

These, then, are the arguments that can be made linking high levels of economic development with liberal democracy. The existence of an *empirical* connection between the two is undeniable. But none of these theories is, in the end, adequate to establish a necessary causal connection.

The argument we associated with Talcott Parsons, to the effect that liberal democracy is the system most capable of resolving conflicts on the basis of consent in a complex modern society, is true only up to a point. The universalism and formality that characterizes the rule of law in liberal democracies does provide a level playing field on which people can compete, form coalitions, and ultimately make compromises. But it is not necessarily the case that liberal democracy is the political system best suited to resolving social conflicts *per se*. A democracy's ability to peacefully resolve conflicts is greatest when those conflicts arise between so-called "interest groups" that share a larger, pre-existing consensus on the basic values or rules of the game, and when the conflicts are primarily economic in nature. But there are other kinds of non-economic conflicts that are far more intractable, having to do with issues like inherited social status and nationality, that democracy is not particularly good at resolving.

The success of American democracy at resolving conflicts between the various interest groups within its heterogeneous and dynamic population does not imply that democracy will similarly be able to resolve the conflicts that arise in other societies. The

American experience is quite unique insofar as Americans were, in Tocqueville's phrase, "born equal."[23] Despite the diversity of backgrounds, lands, and races to which Americans traced their ancestry, on coming to America they abandoned those identities by and large and assimilated into a new society without sharply defined social classes or long-standing ethnic and national divisions. America's social and ethnic structure has been sufficiently fluid to prevent the emergence of rigid social classes, significant subnationalisms, or linguistic minorities.[24] American democracy has therefore rarely faced some of the more intractable social conflicts of other, older societies.

Moreover, even American democracy has not been particularly successful in solving its most persistent ethnic problem, that of American blacks. Black slavery constituted the major exception to the generalization that Americans were "born equal," and American democracy could not in fact settle the question of slavery through democratic means. Long after the abolition of slavery, long, indeed after the achievement of full legal equality by American blacks, many remain profoundly alienated from the mainstream of American culture. Given the profoundly cultural nature of the problem, on the side both of blacks and whites, it is not clear that American democracy is really capable of doing what would be necessary to assimilate blacks fully, and to move from formal equality of opportunity to a broader equality of condition.

Liberal democracy may be more functional for a society that has already achieved a high degree of social equality and consensus concerning certain basic values. But for societies that are highly polarized along lines of social class, nationality, or religion, democracy can be a formula for stalemate and stagnation. The most typical form of polarization is that of class conflict in countries with highly stratified and inegalitarian class structures left over from a feudal social order. Such was the situation in France at the time of the Revolution, and such continues to be the case in Third World countries like the Philippines and Peru. Society is dominated by a traditional elite, most often of large landowners, who are neither tolerant of other classes nor efficient entrepreneurs. The establishment of formal democracy in such a country masks enormous disparities in wealth, prestige, status, and power, which these elites can use to control the democratic process. A familiar social pathology ensues: the dominance of old social classes generates an equally intransigent leftist opposition that believes that the democratic system itself is corrupt and needs to be smashed, along with the social groups protected by it. A democracy that protects the interests of a class of inefficient, leisured landowners and engenders a social civil war cannot be said to be "functional" in economic terms.[25]

Democracy is also not particularly good at resolving disputes between different ethnic or national groups. The question of national sovereignty is inherently uncompromisable: it either belongs to one people or another—Armenians or Azerbaijanis, Lithuanians or Russians—and when different groups come into conflict there is seldom a way of splitting the difference through peaceful democratic compromise, as there is in the case of economic disputes. The Soviet Union could not become democratic and at the same time remain unitary, for there was no consensus among the Soviet Union's nationalities that they shared a common citizenship and identity. Democracy would only emerge on the basis of the country's breakup into smaller national entities. American democracy has done surprisingly well dealing with ethnic diversity, but that diversity has been contained within certain bounds: none of America's ethnic groups constitutes historical communities living on their traditional lands and speaking their own language, with a memory of past nationhood and sovereignty.

A modernizing dictatorship can in principle be far more effective than a democracy in creating the social conditions that would permit both capitalist economic growth and, over time, the emergence of a stable democracy. Take, for example, the case of the Philippines. Filipino society to this day continues to be characterized by a highly inegalitarian social order in the countryside, where a small number of traditional landowning families control a very large proportion of the country's agricultural land. Like other landowning upper classes, the Philippine version is not characterized by a lot of dynamism and efficiency. Nonetheless, through their social position they have managed to dominate much of post-independence Filipino politics. The continued dominance of this social group has in turn bred one of Southeast Asia's few remaining Maoist guerrilla movements, that of the Communist party of the Philippines and its military wing, the New People's Army. The fall of the Marcos dictatorship and his replacement by Corazon Aquino

in 1986 did nothing to remedy either the problem of land distribution or the insurgency, not least because Mrs. Aquino's family
was among the largest landowners in the Philippines. Since her
election, efforts to implement a serious land reform program have
foundered on the opposition of a legislature largely controlled by
the very people who would be its targets. Democracy in this instance is constrained in bringing about the kind of egalitarian social
order that would be necessary either as the ground for capitalist
growth or for the long-term stability of democracy itself.[26] In such
circumstances, dictatorship could potentially be much more functional in bringing about a modern society, as it was when dictatorial
power was used to bring about land reform during the American
occupation of Japan.

A similar kind of reform effort was undertaken by the left-
wing military officers who ruled Peru between 1968 and 1980.
Before the military takeover, 50 percent of Peru's land was held
by seven hundred hacienda owners who also controlled much of
Peruvian politics. The military enacted the most sweeping land
reform in Latin America after Cuba's, replacing the old agrarian
obligarchs with a new, more modern elite of industrialists and
technobureaucats, and facilitating the dramatic growth of a middle class through improvements in education.[27] This dictatorial
interlude saddled Peru with an even larger and more inefficient
state sector,[28] but it did eliminate some of the most glaring social
inequalities and thereby improved somewhat the long-term prospects for the emergence of an economically modern sector after
the military returned to their barracks in 1980.

The use of dictatorial state power to break the grip of established social groups is not unique to the Leninist Left; its use by
right-wing regimes can pave the way toward market economics
and therefore the achievement of the most advanced levels of
industrialization. For capitalism flourishes best in a mobile and
egalitarian society where an entrepreneurial middle class has
pushed aside traditional landowners and other privileged but economically inefficient social groups. If a modernizing dictatorship
uses coercion to speed up this process, and at the same time avoids
the temptation to transfer resources and power from an inefficient traditional landowning class to an equally inefficient state
sector, then there is no reason why it should be economically
incompatible with the most modern forms of "post-industrial"
economic organization. It is this kind of logic that has led An-

dranik Migranian and other Soviet intellectuals to call for an "authoritarian transition" to a market economy in the USSR through
the creation of a national presidency with dictatorial powers.[29]

Sharp social cleavages along class, national, ethnic, or religious
lines can be mitigated by the process of capitalist economic development itself, improving the prospects for the emergence of a
democratic consensus over time. But there is no guarantee that
these differences will not persist as a country grows economically,
or indeed, that they will not come back in a more virulent form.
Economic development has not weakened the sense of national
identity among French Canadians in Quebec; indeed, their fear
of homogenization into the dominant Anglophone culture has
sharpened their desire to preserve their distinctiveness. To say
that democracy is more functional for societies "born equal"
like the United States begs the question of how a nation gets there
in the first place. Democracy, then, does not necessarily become
more functional as societies become more complex and diverse.
In fact, it fails precisely when the diversity of a society passes a
certain limit.

The second of the arguments presented above, that democracy eventually emerges as the by-product of a power struggle
among non-democratic elites on either the Left or the Right, is
also not satisfying as an explanation for why there should be a
universal evolution in the direction of liberal democracy. For by
this account, democracy is not the *preferred outcome* of any of the
groups struggling for leadership in the country. Democracy becomes instead a kind of truce between warring factions, and is
vulnerable to a shift in the balance of power between them that
would allow one particular group or elite to re-emerge triumphant. In other words, if democracy arises in the Soviet Union
only because ambitious figures like Gorbachev and Yeltsin need a
demagogic stick with which to beat the established party apparatus, it follows that the victory of one or the other would lead to a
rescinding of democratic gains. Similarly, this argument presumes
that democracy in Latin America is little more than a compromise
between the authoritarian Right and authoritarian Left, or between powerful groups on the Right, each of which has its own
preferred vision of society that it will impose when it is in a position to attain power. This may be an accurate way of describing
the process leading to democracy in certain specific countries, but
if democracy is nobody's first choice it will hardly be stable. Such

an explanation cannot be grounds for expecting a universal evolution in that direction.[30]

The final argument, that advancing industrialization produces
educated, middle-class societies that naturally prefer liberal rights
and democratic participation, is correct only up to a point. It is
reasonably clear that education is, if not an absolutely necessary
precondition, then at least a highly desirable adjunct to democracy. It is hard to imagine democracy working properly in a
largely illiterate society where the people cannot take advantage
of information about the choices open to them. But it is a rather
different matter to say that education *necessarily* leads to belief in
democratic norms. It is the case that rising educational levels in
countries from the Soviet Union and China to South Korea, Taiwan, and Brazil have been closely associated with the spread of
democratic norms. But fashionable ideas in the world's educational centers happen to be democratic at the present moment: it
is not surprising that a Taiwanese student receiving an engineering degree at UCLA should return home believing that liberal
democracy represents the highest form of political organization
for modern countries. But this is very different from arguing that
there is any *necessary* connection between his engineering training,
which is what will be economically important to Taiwan, and his
newfound belief in liberal democracy. Indeed, to think that education leads naturally to democratic values reflects considerable
presumption on the part of democratic man. In other periods,
when democratic ideas were not as broadly accepted, young people studying in the West just as frequently went home believing
that communism or fascism was the wave of the future for modern societies. Higher education in the United States and other
Western countries today generally inculcates in young people the
historicist and relativist perspective of twentieth-century thought.
This prepares them for citizenship in liberal democracies by encouraging a kind of tolerance for differing points of view, but it
also teaches them that there is no final ground for belief in the
superiority of liberal democracy to other forms of government.

The fact that educated, middle-class people in the most advanced, industrialized countries by and large prefer liberal democracy over various forms of authoritarianism begs the question
of why they show this preference. It seems fairly clear that the
preference for democracy is *not* dictated by the logic of the industrialization process itself. Indeed, the logic of that process

would seem to point in quite the opposite direction. For if a country's goal is economic growth above all other considerations, the truly winning combination would appear to be neither liberal democracy nor socialism of either a Leninist or democratic variety, but the combination of liberal economics and authoritarian politics that some observers have labeled the "bureaucratic-authoritarian state," or what we might term a "market-oriented authoritarianism."

There is considerable empirical evidence to indicate that market-oriented authoritarian modernizers do better economically than their democratic counterparts. Historically, some of the most impressive economic growth records have been compiled by this type of state, including Imperial Germany, Meiji Japan, the Russia of Witte and Stolypin, and, more recently, Brazil after the military takeover in 1964, Chile under Pinochet, and, of course, the NIEs of Asia.[31] Between 1961 and 1968, for example, the average annual growth rate of the developing world's democracies, including India, Ceylon, the Philippines, Chile, and Costa Rica, was only 2.1 percent, whereas the group of conservative authoritarian regimes (Spain, Portugal, Iran, Taiwan, South Korea, Thailand, and Pakistan) had an average growth rate of 5.2 percent.[32]

The reasons why a market-oriented authoritarian state should do better economically than a democratic one are reasonably straightforward, and were described by the economist Joseph Schumpeter in his book *Capitalism, Socialism, and Democracy*. While voters in democratic countries may affirm free-market principles in the abstract, they are all too ready to abandon them when their own short-term, economic self-interest is at stake. There is no presumption, in other words, that democratic publics will make economically rational choices, or that economic losers will not use their political power to protect their positions. Democratic regimes, reflecting the demands of the various interest groups in their societies, tend as a whole to spend more on welfare, to create disincentives to production through wage-leveling tax policies, to protect failing and non-competitive industries, and therefore to have larger budget deficits and higher rates of inflation. To take one example close to home, during the 1980s the United States spent much more than it produced through a series of mounting budget deficits, constraining future economic growth and the choices of future generations in order to maintain a high level of present consumption. Despite a widespread concern that this kind of improvidence would be damaging in the long term both economically and politically, the American democratic system was unable to deal seriously with the problem because it could not decide on how to fairly allocate the resulting pain of budget cuts and tax increases. Democracy in America has therefore not demonstrated a high degree of economic functionality in recent years.

Authoritarian regimes, on the other hand, are in principle better able to follow truly liberal economic policies undistorted by redistributive goals that constrain growth. They do not have to be accountable to workers in declining industries, or subsidize inefficient sectors simply because the latter have political clout. They can actually use the power of the state to hold down consumption in the interests of long-term growth. During its period of high growth in the 1960s, the South Korean government was able to suppress wage demands by banning strikes and forbidding talk of greater worker consumption and welfare. By contrast, South Korea's transition to democracy in 1987 led to an enormous proliferation of strikes and long-suppressed wage demands that the new, democratically elected regime had to meet. The result was significantly higher Korean labor costs and diminished competitiveness. Of course, communist regimes have been able to achieve extremely high rates of savings and investment by ruthlessly squeezing consumers, but their long-run growth and ability to modernize were hobbled by the absence of competition. Market-oriented authoritarians, on the other hand, have the best of both worlds: they are able to enforce a relatively high degree of social discipline on their populations, while permitting a sufficient degree of freedom to encourage innovation and the employment of the most up-to-date technologies.

If one argument against the economic efficiency of democracies is that they tamper too much with the market in the interests of redistribution and current consumption, another argument is that they do not tamper with it enough. Market-oriented authoritarian regimes are in many ways more statist in their economic policies than the developed democracies of North America and Western Europe. But this statism is single-mindedly directed toward promoting high economic growth rather than to goals like redistribution and social justice. It is not clear whether so-called "industrial policies," in which the state subsidizes or supports certain economic sectors at the expense of others have been more of a hindrance than a help to the economies of Japan and other Asian NIEs in the long run. But state intervention in the market, competently executed and remaining within the broad parameters of a competitive market, has quite evidently been fully compatible with very high levels of growth. Taiwanese planners in the late 1970s to early 1980s were able to shift investment resources from light industries like textiles to more advanced ones like electronics and semiconductors, despite the considerable pain and unemployment this created in the former sector. An industrial policy worked in Taiwan only because the state was able to shield its planning technocrats from political pressures so that they could reinforce the market and make decisions according to criteria of efficiency—in other words, it worked because Taiwan was *not* governed democratically. An American industrial policy is much less likely to improve its economic competitiveness, precisely because America is more democratic than Taiwan or the Asian NIEs. The planning process would quickly fall prey to pressures from Congress either to protect inefficient industries or to promote ones favored by special interests.

There is an unquestionable relationship between economic development and liberal democracy, which one can observe simply by looking around the world. But the exact nature of that relationship is more complicated than it first appeared, and is not adequately explained by any of the theories presented up to this point. The logic of modern natural science and the industrialization process it fosters does not point in a single direction in the sphere of politics, as it does in the sphere of economics. Liberal democracy is compatible with industrial maturity, and is preferred by the citizens of many industrially advanced states, but there does not appear to be a *necessary* connection between the two. The Mechanism underlying our directional history leads equally well to a bureaucratic-authoritarian future as to a liberal one. We will therefore have to look elsewhere in trying to understand the current crisis of authoritarianism and the worldwide democratic revolution.

II

The Former Question Answered

To Kant's question, Is it possible to write a Universal History from a cosmopolitan point of view? our provisional answer is yes.

Modern natural science has provided us with a Mechanism whose progressive unfolding gives both a directionality and a coherence to human history over the past several centuries. In an age when we can no longer identify the experiences of Europe and North America with those of humanity as a whole, the Mechanism is truly universal. Apart from fast-disappearing tribes in the jungles of Brazil or Papua New Guinea, there is not a single branch of mankind that has not been touched by the Mechanism, and which has not become linked to the rest of mankind through the universal economic nexus of modern consumerism. It is not the mark of provincialism but of cosmopolitanism to recognize that there has emerged in the last few centuries something like a true global culture, centering around technologically driven economic growth and the capitalist social relations necessary to produce and sustain it. Societies which have sought to resist this unification, from Tokugawa Japan and the Sublime Porte, to the Soviet Union, the People's Republic of China, Burma, and Iran, have managed to fight rearguard actions that have lasted only for a generation or two. Those that were not defeated by superior military technology were seduced by the glittering material world that modern natural science has created. While not every country is capable of becoming a consumer society in the near future, there is hardly a society in the world that does not embrace the goal itself.

Given the grip of modern natural science, it is difficult to sustain the idea that history is cyclical. This is not to say that there is no repetition in history. Those who have read Thucydides can note the parallels between the rivalry of Athens and Sparta and the Cold War conflict between the United States and the Soviet Union. Those who have watched the periodic rise and fall of certain great powers in antiquity and compared them to those of contemporary times, are not wrong in seeing similarities. But recurrence of certain long-standing historical patterns is compatible with a directional, dialectical history, as long as we understand that there is memory and movement between repetitions. Athenian democracy is not modern democracy, nor does Sparta find any contemporary counterpart, despite certain resemblances it might bear to Stalin's Soviet Union. A truly cyclical history like that envisioned by Plato or Aristotle would require a global cataclysm of such magnitude that all memory of earlier times would be lost. Even in an age of nuclear weapons and global warming, it is difficult to conceive of a cataclysm with the power to destroy the idea of modern natural science. And as long as a stake is not driven through that vampire's heart, it will reconstitute itself—with all of its social, economic, and political concomitants—within the space of a few generations. Reversing course in any fundamental way would mean a total break with modern natural science and the economic world created by it. There seems to be little prospect that any contemporary society will chose to do so, and military competition will in any case make membership in that world self-enforcing.

At the end of the twentieth century, Hitler and Stalin appear to be bypaths of history that led to dead ends, rather than real alternatives for human social organization. While their human costs were incalculable, these totalitarianisms in their purest form burned themselves out within a lifetime—Hitlerism in 1945, and Stalinism by 1956. Many other countries have tried to duplicate totalitarianism in some form, from the Chinese Revolution in 1949 to the genocidal Khmer Rouge in Cambodia in the mid-1970s, with a myriad of small ugly dictatorships in between, stretching from North Korea, South Yemen, Ethiopia, Cuba, and Afghanistan on the Left to Iran, Iraq, and Syria on the Right.[1] But the common characteristic of all of these latter-day, would-be totalitarianisms is that they have occurred in relatively backward and impoverished Third World countries.[2] The persistent failure of communism to make headway in the developed world, and its prevalence among countries that are just entering the first stages of industrialization, suggest that the "totalitarian temptation" has been, as Walt Rostow put it, primarily a "disease of the transition," a pathological condition arising out of the special political and social requirements of countries at a certain stage of socio-economic development.[3]

But what then about fascism, which did arise in a highly developed country? How is it possible to relegate German National Socialism to a "stage of history," rather than seeing it as a specific invention of modernity itself? And if the generation that lived through the 1930s was shocked out of its complacency by the explosion of hatreds supposedly "overcome" by the progress of civilization, who can guarantee that we will not be surprised by a new eruption coming from another source heretofore unrecognized?

The answer is, of course, that we have no guarantee and cannot assure future generations that there will be no future Hitlers or Pol Pots. A modern-day, would-be Hegelian who maintained that Hitler was *necessary* to bring democracy to Germany after 1945 would deserve ridicule. On the other hand, a Universal History need not justify every tyrannical regime and every war to expose a meaningful larger pattern in human evolution. The power and long-term regularity of that evolutionary process is not diminished if we admit that it was subject to large and apparently unexplainable discontinuities, any more than the biological theory of evolution is undermined by the fact of the sudden extinction of the dinosaurs.

It is not sufficient to simply cite the Holocaust and expect discourse on the question of progress or rationality in human history to end, much as the horror of this event should make us pause and contemplate. There is an inclination not to want to discuss the Holocaust's historical causes rationally, similar in many respects to the opposition of anti-nuclear activists to rational discourse about deterrence or the strategic employment of nuclear weapons. In both cases there is an underlying concern that "rationalization" will domesticate genocide. It is common among writers who see the Holocaust as in some way the cardinal event of modernity to maintain that it is both historically unique in its evil, and at the same time a manifestation of a potentially universal evil that lies below the surface of all societies. But one cannot have it both ways: if it is a uniquely evil event, one without historical precedent, then it must have had equally unique causes, causes that we would not expect to see easily duplicated in other countries at different times.[4] It therefore cannot be taken as in any way a necessary aspect of modernity. On the other hand, if it is a manifestation of a universal evil, then it becomes just an extreme version of a terrible but very familiar phenomenon of nationalist excess, which can slow down but not derail the locomotive of History.

I am inclined toward the view that the Holocaust was both a unique evil and the product of historically unique circumstances that converged in Germany during the 1920s and 30s. These conditions are not only not latent in most developed societies, but would be very hard (though not impossible) to duplicate in other societies in the future. Many of these circumstances, such as defeat in a long and brutal war and economic depression, are well known and potentially replicable in other countries. But others have to do with the special intellectual and cultural traditions of Germany at the time, its anti-materialism and emphasis on struggle and sacrifice, that made it very distinct from liberal France and England. These traditions, which were in no way "modern," were tested by the wrenching social disruptions caused by Imperial Germany's hothouse industrialization before and after the Franco-Prussian War. It is possible to understand nazism as another, albeit extreme, variant of the "disease of the transition," a byproduct of the modernization process that was by no means a necessary component of modernity itself.[5] None of this implies that a phenomenon like nazism is now impossible because we have advanced socially beyond such a stage. It does suggest, however, that fascism is a pathological and extreme condition, by which one cannot judge modernity as a whole.

To say that Stalinism or nazism are diseases of social development is not to be blind to their monstrosity or to lack sympathy for their victims. As Jean-François Revel has pointed out, the fact that liberal democracy is victorious in some countries in the 1980s does nothing for the majority of humanity in the past hundred years whose lives have been consumed by totalitarianism.[6]

On the other hand, the fact that *their* lives have been wasted and their pain unredeemed should not leave us speechless in trying to address the question of whether there is a rational pattern to history. There is a widespread expectation that a Universal

History, if one can be discerned, must function as a kind of secular theodicy, that is, a justification of all that exists in terms of history's final end. This no Universal History can reasonably be expected to do. From the beginning, such an intellectual construct represents an enormous abstraction from the detail and texture of history, and almost necessarily ends up ignoring entire peoples and ages that constitute "pre-history." Any Universal History we can construct will inevitably give no reasonable account of many occurrences which are all too real to the people who experience them. A Universal History is simply an intellectual tool; it cannot take the place of God in bringing personal redemption to every one of history's victims.

Nor does the existence of discontinuities in historical development like the Holocaust—horrifying as they may be—nullify the obvious fact that modernity is a coherent and extremely powerful whole. The existence of discontinuities does not make any less real the remarkable similarities in the experiences of people living through the process of modernization. No person could deny that twentieth-century life is different in fundamental ways from life in all previous ages, and few of those comfortable residents of developed democracies who scoff at the idea of historical progress in the abstract would be willing to make their lives in a backward, Third World country that represents, in effect, an earlier age of mankind. One can recognize the fact that modernity has permitted new scope for human evil, even question the fact of human *moral* progress, and yet continue to believe in the existence of a directional and coherent historical process.

12

No Democracy without Democrats

It should be evident by now that the Mechanism we have laid out is essentially an economic interpretation of history. The "logic of modern natural science" has no force of its own, apart from the human beings who want to make use of science to conquer nature so as to satisfy their needs, or to secure themselves against dangers. In itself, science (whether in the form of machine production or the rational organization of labor) dictates only a horizon of technological possibilities determined by the basic laws of nature. It is human desire that pushes men to exploit these possibilities: not the desire to satisfy a limited set of "natural" needs, but a highly elastic desire whose own horizon of possibilities is constantly being pushed back.

The Mechanism is, in other words, a kind of Marxist interpretation of history that leads to a completely non-Marxist conclusion. It is the desire of "man the species-being" to produce and consume that leads him to leave the countryside for the city, to work in large factories or large bureaucracies rather than on the land, to sell his labor to the highest bidder instead of working in the occupation of his ancestors, to acquire an education and to submit to the discipline of the clock.

But, contrary to Marx, the kind of society that permits people to produce and consume the largest quantity of products on the most equal basis is not a communist one, but a capitalist society. In volume 3 of *Capital*, Marx describes the realm of freedom that will emerge under communism in the following terms:

In fact, the realm of freedom actually begins only where la-
bour which is determined by necessity and mundane considerations ceases; thus in the very nature of things it lies beyond
the sphere of actual material production. Just as the savage
must wrestle with Nature to satisfy his wants, to maintain and
reproduce life, so must civilized man, and he must do so in all
social formations and under all possible modes of production.
With his development this realm of physical necessity expands
as a result of his wants; but, at the same time, the forces of
production which satisfy these wants also increase. Freedom
in this field can only consist in interchange with Nature, bringing it under their common control, instead of being ruled by
it as by the blind forces of Nature; and achieving this with the
least expenditure of energy and under conditions most fa-
vourable to, and worthy of, their human nature. But it nonetheless still remains a realm of necessity. Beyond it begins that
development of human energy which is an end in itself, the
true realm of freedom, which, however, can blossom forth
only with the realm of necessity as its basis. The shortening of
the working day is its basic prerequisite.[1]

The Marxist realm of freedom is, in effect, the four-hour working
day: that is, a society so productive that man's labor in the morning can satisfy all of his natural needs and those of his family and
fellows, leaving him the afternoon and evening to be a hunter, or
a poet, or a critic. In a way, real-world communist societies like the
Soviet Union or the former German Democratic Republic
achieved this realm of freedom, since few people put in more
than four hours of honest work a day. But the remainder of their
time was seldom spent writing poems or criticism, since this could
promptly land them in jail; it was spent waiting on line, drinking,
or scheming for the opportunity to take a vacation in a crowded
sanitarium on a polluted beach. But if the "necessary labor time"
required to satisfy basic physical needs was four hours on average
for workers in socialist societies, it was on the order of an hour or
two for corresponding capitalist societies, and the six or seven
hours of "surplus labor" time that rounded out the working day
did not go only into the pockets of capitalists, but allowed workers
to buy cars and washing machines, barbecues and campers.
Whether this constituted a "realm of freedom" in any meaningful
sense was another matter, but an American worker was far more
fully liberated from the "realm of necessity" than his Soviet counterpart.

Of course, statistics on productivity per worker bear no necessary relationship to happiness. As Marx explained, physical
needs increase along with productivity, and one would need to
know which type of society kept needs in better balance with
productive capabilities in order to know which one produced
more satisfied workers. The irony is that communist societies came
to acquire the ever-expanding horizon of wants generated by
Western consumerist societies without acquiring the means of satisfying them. Erich Honecker used to say that the standard of
living in the German Democratic Republic was "much higher than
in the Kaiser's time"; indeed, it was much higher than for most
societies in human history, and satisfied man's "natural" wants
many times over. But this was scarcely relevant. East Germans
compared themselves not to people of the Kaiser's time, but to
contemporary West Germans, and found their society lacking.

If man is primarily an economic animal driven by his desire
and reason, then the dialectical process of historical evolution
should be reasonably similar for different human societies and
cultures. This was the conclusion of "modernization theory,"
which borrowed from Marxism an essentially economic view of
the underlying forces of historical change. Modernization theory
looks much more persuasive in 1990 than it did fifteen or
twenty years earlier when it came under heavy attack in academic circles. Almost all countries that have succeeded in
achieving a high level of economic development have in fact
come to look increasingly similar to one another, rather than
less. While there are a variety of routes that countries can take
to get to the end of history, there are few versions of modernity
other than the capitalist liberal-democratic one that look like
they are going concerns.[2] Modernizing countries, from Spain
and Portugal to the Soviet Union and China to Taiwan and
South Korea, have all moved in this direction.

But like all economic theories of history, modernization theory is somehow not satisfying. It is a theory that works to the
extent that man is an economic creature, to the extent that he is
driven by the imperatives of economic growth and industrial rationality. Its undeniable power derives from the fact that human
beings, particularly in the aggregate, do in fact act out of such
motives for much of their lives. But there are other aspects of
human motivation that have nothing to do with economics, and it
is here that the discontinuities in history—the majority of man's

wars, the sudden eruptions of religious or ideological or nationalist passion that lead to phenomena like Hitler and Khomeini—find their origin. A true Universal History of mankind would have to be able to explain not only the broad and incremental evolutionary trends, but the discontinuous and unexpected ones as well.

From the preceding discussion it should be clear that we cannot explain the phenomenon of democracy adequately if we try to understand it solely in economic terms. An economic account of history gets us to the gates of the Promised Land of liberal democracy, but it does not quite deliver us to the other side. The process of economic modernization may bring about certain large-scale social changes like the transformation of tribal and agricultural societies into urban, educated, middle-class ones that in some way create the material conditions for democracy. But this process does not explain democracy itself, for if we look more deeply into the process, we find that democracy is almost never chosen for economic reasons. The first major democratic revolutions, those of the United States and France, both took place just as the Industrial Revolution was getting under way in England and before either country had "modernized" economically as we understand the term today. Their opting for the rights of man could therefore not have been conditioned by the industrialization process. The American Founding Fathers may have been angered over the attempts of the British Crown to tax them without representation in Parliament, but their decision to declare independence and fight Britain in order to establish a new democratic order can hardly be explained as a matter of economic efficiency. Then, as at many subsequent points in world history, the option of prosperity without liberty existed—from the Tory planters who opposed the Declaration of Independence in the United States, to the nineteenth-century authoritarian modernizers of Germany and Japan, to contemporaries like Deng Xiaoping, who offered his country economic liberalization and modernization under the continued tutelage of a dictatorial Communist party, and Lee Kuan Yew of Singapore, who has argued that democracy would be an obstacle to Singapore's spectacular economic success. And yet, people in all ages have taken the non-economic step of risking their lives and their livelihoods to fight for democratic rights. There is no democracy without democrats, that is, without a specifically Democratic Man that desires and shapes democracy even as he is shaped by it.

A Universal History based on the progressive unfolding of modern natural science can, moreover, make sense only of the past four hundred or so years of human history, dating from the discovery of the scientific method in the sixteenth and seventeenth centuries. Yet neither the scientific method nor the liberation of human desire that drove subsequent efforts to conquer nature and bend it to human purposes sprang *ex nihilo* from the pens of Descartes or Bacon. A fuller Universal History, even one that based itself in large measure on modern natural science, would have to understand the pre-modern origins of science, and of the desire that lay behind the desire of Economic Man.

Such considerations suggest that we have not come very far yet in our attempt to understand the basis either of the current worldwide liberal revolution, or of any Universal History that may underlie it. The modern economic world is a massive and imposing structure that holds much of our lives in an iron grip, but the process by which it came to be is not coterminous with history itself and not sufficient to tell us whether we have reached the end of history. For that, we would do better to rely, not on Marx and the social science tradition that sprang from his economically based view of history, but on Hegel, his "idealist" predecessor who was the first philosopher to answer Kant's challenge of writing a Universal History. For Hegel's understanding of the Mechanism that underlies the historical process is incomparably deeper than that of Marx or of any contemporary social scientist. For Hegel, the primary motor of human history is not modern natural science or the ever expanding horizon of desire that powers it, but rather a totally non-economic drive, the *struggle for recognition*. Hegel's Universal History complements the Mechanism we have just outlined, but gives us a broader understanding of man—"man as *man*"— that allows us to understand the discontinuities, the wars and sudden eruptions of irrationality out of the calm of economic development, that have characterized actual human history.

Returning to Hegel is important also because it provides us with a framework for understanding whether the human historical process can be expected to continue indefinitely, or whether we have in fact reached the end of history. As a beginning point for this analysis, let us accept the Hegelian-Marxist thesis that past history has proceeded *dialectically,* or through a process of contradiction, leaving aside for the time being the question of whether the dialectic has an ideal or material basis. That is, a certain form of socio-political organization arises in some part of the world, but contains an internal contradiction which over time leads to its own undermining and replacement by a different and more successful one. The problem of the end of history can be put in the following way: Are there any "contradictions" in our contemporary liberal democratic social order that would lead us to expect that the historical process will continue, and produce a new, higher order? We could recognize a "contradiction" if we saw a source of social discontent sufficiently radical to eventually cause the downfall of liberal democratic societies—the "system," in the language of the 1960s—as a whole. It is not sufficient to point to "problems" in contemporary liberal democracies, even if they are serious ones like budget deficits, inflation, crime, or drugs. A "problem" does not become a "contradiction" unless it is so serious that it not only cannot be solved within the system, but corrodes the legitimacy of the system itself such that the latter collapses under its own weight. For example, the steady impoverishment of the proletariat in capitalist societies was for Marx not just a "problem," but a "contradiction" because it would lead to a revolutionary situation that would bring down the entire structure of capitalist society and replace it with a different one. Conversely, we can argue that history has come to an end if the present form of social and political organization is *completely satisfying* to human beings in their most essential characteristics.

But how would we know if there are any remaining contradictions in our present order? There are essentially two approaches to this problem. In the first, we would observe the actual course of historical development to see whether there is a demonstrable pattern to history that indicates the superiority of one particular form of society. Just as a modern economist does not try to define a product's "utility" or "value" in itself, but rather accepts the marketplace's valuation of it as expressed in a price, so one would accept the judgment of the "marketplace" of world history. We can think of human history as a dialogue or competition between different regimes or forms of social organization. Societies "refute" one another in this dialogue by triumphing over them or by outlasting them—in some cases through military conquest, in others through the superiority of their economic system, in others because of their greater internal political cohesion.[3] If human societies over the centuries evolve toward or converge on a single form of socio-political organization like liberal democracy, if there do not appear to be viable alternatives to liberal democracy, and if people living in liberal democracies express no radical discontent with their lives, we can say that the dialogue has reached a final and definitive conclusion. The historicist philosopher would be compelled to accept liberal democracy's own claims to superiority and finality. *Die Weltgeschichte ist das Weltgericht:* world history is the final arbiter of right.[4]

This is not to say that those who take this approach must simply worship power and success under the dictum that "might makes right." One does not have to endorse every tyrant and would-be empire builder who struts on the stage of world history for a brief moment, but only that one regime or system which survives the *entire* process of world history. This implies an ability to solve the problem of human satisfaction that had been present in human history from the beginning, as well as an ability to survive and adapt to mankind's changing environment.[5]

Such an "historicist" approach, no matter how sophisticated, nonetheless suffers from the following problem: How do we know that an apparent lack of "contradictions" in the apparently victorious social system—here, liberal democracy—is not illusory, and that the progress of time will not reveal new contradictions requiring a further stage of human historical evolution? Without an underlying concept of human nature that posited a hierarchy of essential and non-essential human characteristics, it would be impossible to know whether an apparent social peace represented true satisfaction of human longings, rather than the work of a particularly efficient police apparatus, or merely the calm before a revolutionary storm. We should keep in mind that Europe on the eve of the French Revolution looked to many observers like a successful and satisfying social order, as did that in Iran in the 1970s or the countries of Eastern Europe in the 1980s. Or to take another example: some contemporary feminists assert that most prior history was the history of conflicts among "patriarchal" societies, but that "matriarchal" societies, more consensual, nurturing, and prone to peace, constitute a viable alternative. This cannot be demonstrated on the basis of empirical fact, since there are no existing examples of matriarchal societies.[6] And yet, the possibility of their *future* existence cannot be ruled out, if the feminist understanding of the possibilities for the liberation of the female side of the human personality proves to be correct. And if it is so, then we clearly have not reached the end of history.

An alternative approach to determining whether we have reached the end of history might be termed a "trans-historical" one, or an approach based on a concept of nature. That is, we would judge the adequacy of existing liberal democracies from the standpoint of a trans-historical concept of man. We would look not simply at *empirical* evidence of popular discontent in the real-world societies of, let us say, Britain or America. Rather, we would appeal to an understanding of human nature, those permanent though not consistently visible attributes of man as *man*, and measure the adequacy of contemporary democracies against this standard. This approach would free us from the tyranny of the present, that is, from the standards and expectations set by the very society we are trying to judge.[7]

The mere fact that human nature is not created "once and for all" but creates itself "in the course of *historical* time" does not spare us the need to talk about human nature, either as a structure within which man's self-creation occurs, or as an end point or *telos* toward which human historical development appears to be moving.[8] For example, if as Kant suggests man's reason cannot be fully developed except as the result of a long and cumulative social process, this does not therefore make reason any less "natural" an aspect of man.[9]

In the end, it would appear impossible to talk about "history," much less a "Universal History," without reference to a permanent, trans-historical standard, i.e., without reference to nature. For "history" is not a given, not merely a catalogue of everything that happened in the past, but a deliberate effort of abstraction in which we separate out important from unimportant events. The standards on which this abstraction are based are variable. In the past couple of generations, for example, there has been a movement away from diplomatic and military history toward social history, the history of women and minority groups, or the history of "everyday life." The fact that the objects of historical attention have shifted from the rich and powerful to those lower down the social scale does not imply the abandoning of standards of historical selection, but merely the changing of standards to fit a newer and more egalitarian consciousness. But neither the diplomatic historian nor the social historian can evade the choice between important and unimportant, and hence reference to a standard that exists somewhere "outside" of history (and, incidentally, outside of the sphere of competence of professional historians *qua* historians). This is all the more true of a Universal History, which raises the level of abstraction to an even higher degree. The Universal Historian must be ready to discard entire peoples and times as essentially pre- or non-historical, because they do not bear on the central "plot" of his or her story.

It seems inevitable, then, that we must move from a discussion of history to a discussion of nature if we are to address seriously the question of the end of history. We cannot discuss the long-term prospects for liberal democracy—its appeal to people who haven't experienced it, and its staying power for others long used to living by its rules—by focusing only on the "empirical" evidence presented to us by the contemporary world. We must instead raise directly and explicitly the nature of the trans-historical standards by which we evaluate the goodness or badness of any regime or social system. Kojève claims that we have reached the end of history because life in the universal and homogenous state is *completely satisfying* to its citizens. The modern liberal democratic world, in other words, is free of contradictions. In evaluating this claim, we do not want to be sidetracked by objections that misunderstand the point of Kojève's contention—for example, by pointing to this or that social group or individual which is demonstrably dissatisfied by being denied equal access to the good things of society due to poverty, racism, and so forth. The deeper question is one of first principles—that is, whether the "good things" of our society are truly good and satisfying to "man as *man*," or whether there is in principle a higher form of satisfaction that some other type of regime or social organization could provide. To answer this question, to understand whether in fact our age is the "old age of mankind," we must go back and look at natural man as he existed before the start of the historical process, in other words, at the "first man."

Part III
THE STRUGGLE FOR RECOGNITION

13

In the Beginning, a Battle to the Death for Pure Prestige

And it is solely by risking life that freedom is obtained; only thus is it tried and proved that the essential nature of self-consciousness is not bare existence, is not the merely immediate form in which it at first makes its appearance. . . . The individual, who has not staked his life, may, no doubt, be recognized as a person; but he has not attained the truth of this recognition as an independent self-consciousness.

—*G. W. F. Hegel,* The Phenomenology of Mind[1]

All human, anthropogenetic desire—the desire that generates self-consciousness, the human reality—is, finally, a function of the desire for "recognition." And the risk of life by which the human reality "comes to light" is a risk for the sake of such a desire. Therefore, to speak of the "origin" of self-consciousness is necessarily to speak of a fight to the death for "recognition."

—*Alexandre Kojève,* Introduction to the Reading of Hegel[2]

What is at stake for people around the world, from Spain and Argentina to Hungary and Poland, when they throw off dictatorship and establish a liberal democracy? To some extent, the answer is a purely negative one based on the mistakes and injustices of the preceding political order: they want to get rid of the hated colonels or party bosses who oppressed them, or to live without fear of arbitrary arrest. Those living in Eastern Europe and the Soviet Union think or hope that they are getting capitalist prosperity, since capitalism and democracy are closely intertwined in the minds of many. But as we have seen, it is perfectly possible to

143

have prosperity without freedom, as Spain, or South Korea, or Taiwan did under autocratic rule. And yet in each of these countries prosperity was not enough. Any attempt to portray the basic human impulse driving the liberal revolutions of the late twentieth century, or indeed of any liberal revolution since those of America and France in the eighteenth century, as merely an economic one, would be radically incomplete. The Mechanism created by modern natural science remains a partial and ultimately unsatisfying account of the historical process. Free government exercises a positive pull of its own: When the president of the United States or the president of France praises liberty and democracy, they are praised as good things in themselves, and this praise seems to have resonance for people around the world.

To understand this resonance, we need to return to Hegel, the philosopher who first answered Kant's call and wrote what remains in many ways the most serious Universal History. As interpreted by Alexandre Kojève, Hegel provides us with an alternative "mechanism" by which to understand the historical process, one based on the "struggle for recognition." While we need not abandon our economic account of history, "recognition" allows us to recover a totally non-materialist historical dialectic that is much richer in its understanding of human motivation than the Marxist version, or than the sociological tradition stemming from Marx.

There is, of course, a legitimate question as to whether Kojève's interpretation of Hegel, presented here, is really Hegel as he understood himself, or whether it contains an admixture of ideas that are properly "Kojèvian." Kojève does take certain elements of Hegel's teaching, such as the struggle for recognition and the end of history, and make them the centerpiece of that teaching in a way that Hegel himself may not have done. While uncovering the original Hegel is an important task for the purposes of the "present argument," we are interested not in Hegel *per se* but in Hegel-as-interpreted-by-Kojève, or perhaps a new, synthetic philosopher named Hegel-Kojève. In subsequent references to Hegel, we will actually be referring to Hegel-Kojève, and we will be more interested in the ideas themselves than in the philosophers who originally articulated them.[3]

One might think that to uncover the real meaning of liberalism, one would want to go even further back in time to the thought of those philosophers who were the original source of liberalism,

Hobbes and Locke. For the oldest and most durable liberal societies—those in the Anglo-Saxon tradition, like England, the United States, and Canada—have typically understood themselves in Lockean terms. We will in fact return to Hobbes and Locke, but Hegel is of particular interest to us for two reasons. In the first place, he provides us with an understanding of liberalism that is nobler than that of Hobbes and Locke. For virtually coeval with the enunciation of Lockean liberalism has been a persistent unease with the society thereby produced, and with the prototypic product of that society, the *bourgeois*. That unease is ultimately traceable to a single moral fact, that the *bourgeois* is primarily preoccupied with his own material well-being, and is neither public-spirited, nor virtuous, nor dedicated to the larger community around him or her. In short, the *bourgeois* is selfish; and the selfishness of the private individual has been at the core of critiques of liberal society both on the part of the Marxist Left and the aristocratic-republican Right. Hegel, in contrast to Hobbes and Locke, provides us with a self-understanding of liberal society which is based on the non-selfish part of the human personality, and seeks to preserve that part as the core of the modern political project. Whether he ultimately succeeds in this remains to be seen: the latter question will be the subject of the final part of this book.

The second reason for returning to Hegel is that the understanding of history as a "struggle for recognition" is actually a very useful and illuminating way of seeing the contemporary world. We inhabitants of liberal democratic countries are by now so used to accounts of current events that reduce motivation to economic causes, so thoroughly *bourgeois* in our own perceptions, that we are frequently surprised to discover how totally non-economic most political life is. Indeed, we do not even have a common vocabulary for talking about the prideful and assertive side of human nature that is responsible for driving most wars and political conflicts. The "struggle for recognition" is a concept as old as political philosophy, and refers to a phenomenon coterminous with political life itself. If it seems to us today a somewhat strange and unfamiliar term, it is only because of the successful "economization" of our thinking that has occurred in the past four hundred years. Yet the "struggle for recognition" is evident everywhere around us and underlies contemporary movements for liberal rights, whether in the Soviet Union, Eastern Europe, Southern Africa, Asia, Latin America, or in the United States itself.

To uncover the meaning of the "struggle for recognition," we need to understand Hegel's concept of man, or of human nature.[4] For those early modern theorists of liberalism who preceded Hegel, the discussion of human nature was presented as a portrayal of the First Man, that is, man in the "state of nature." Hobbes, Locke, and Rousseau never intended the state of nature to be understood as an empirical or historical account of primitive man, but rather a kind of experiment in thought to strip away those aspects of human personality that were simply the product of convention—such as the fact that one was Italian or an aristocrat or a Buddhist—and to uncover those characteristics that were common to man as man.

Hegel denied that he had a state of nature doctrine and in fact would have rejected the concept of a human nature, permanent and unchanging. Man, for him, was free and *un*-determined, and therefore capable of creating his own nature in the course of historical time. And yet, this process of historical self-creation had a starting point that looked for all intents and purposes like a state of nature teaching.[5] Hegel in the *Phenomenology of Mind* described a primitive "first man" living at the beginning of history whose philosophical function was indistinguishable from the "man in the state of nature" of Hobbes, Locke, and Rousseau. That is, this "first man" was a prototypic human being, possessing those fundamental human attributes that existed prior to the creation of civil society and the historical process.

Hegel's "first man" shares with the animals certain basic natural desires, such as the desire for food, for sleep, for shelter, and above all for the preservation of his own life. He is, to this extent, part of the natural or physical world. But Hegel's "first man" is radically different from the animals in that he desires not only real, "positive" objects—a steak, or fur jacket with which to keep warm, or a shelter in which to live—but also objects that are totally non-material. Above all, he desires the desire of other men, that is, to be wanted by others or to be *recognized*. Indeed, for Hegel, an individual could not become self-conscious, that is, become aware of himself as a separate human being, without being recognized by other human beings. Man, in other words, was from the start a *social* being: his own sense of self-worth and identity is intimately connected with the value that other people place on him. He is, in David Riesman's phrase, fundamentally "other directed."[6] While animals exhibit social behavior, this behavior is instinctual and is based on the mutual satisfaction of natural needs. A dolphin or a monkey desires a fish or banana, not the desire of another dolphin or monkey. As Kojève explains, only a man can desire "an object perfectly useless from the biological point of view (such as a medal, or the enemy's flag)"; he desires such objects not for themselves but because they are desired by other human beings.

But Hegel's "first man" differs from the animals in a second and much more fundamental way. This man wants not only to be recognized by other men, but to be recognized as a *man*. And what constitutes man's identity as man, the most fundamental and uniquely human characteristic, is man's ability to risk his own life. Thus the "first man" 's encounter with other men leads to a violent struggle in which each contestant seeks to make the other "recognize" him by risking his own life. Man is a fundamentally other-directed and social animal, but his sociability leads him not into a peaceful civil society, but into a violent struggle to the death for pure prestige. This "bloody battle" can have one of three results. It can lead to the death of both combatants, in which case life itself, human and natural, ends. It can lead to the death of one of the contestants, in which case the survivor remains unsatisfied because there is no longer another human consciousness to recognize him. Or, finally, the battle can terminate in the relationship of lordship and bondage, in which one of the contestants decides to submit to a life of slavery rather than face the risk of violent death. The master is then satisfied because he has risked his life and received recognition for having done so from another human being. The initial encounter between "first men" in Hegel's state of nature is every bit as violent as Hobbes's state of nature or Locke's state of war, but issues not in a social contract or other form of peaceful civil society, but in a highly unequal relationship of lordship and bondage.[7]

For Hegel just as for Marx, primitive society was divided into social classes. But unlike Marx, Hegel believed that the most important class differences were not based on economic function, such as whether one was a landlord or a peasant, but on one's attitude toward violent death. Society was divided between masters who were willing to risk their lives, and slaves who were not. The Hegelian understanding of early class stratification is probably historically more accurate than that of Marx. Many traditional aristocratic societies initially arose out of the "warrior ethos" of nomadic tribes who conquered more sedentary peoples through superior ruthlessness, cruelty, and bravery. After the initial conquest, the masters in subsequent generations settled down on estates and assumed an economic relationship as landlords exacting taxes or tribute from the vast mass of peasant "slaves" over whom they ruled. But the warrior ethos—the sense of innate superiority based on the willingness to risk death— remained the essential core of the culture of aristocratic societies the world over, long after years of peace and leisure allowed these same aristocrats to degenerate into pampered and effeminate courtiers.

Much of this Hegelian account of early man will sound very strange to modern ears, particularly his identification of the willingness to risk one's life in a battle for pure prestige as the most basic human trait. For isn't the willingness to risk one's life simply a primitive social custom that has long since passed out of the world, along with dueling and revenge murders?[8] In our world, there are still people who run around risking their lives in bloody battles over a name, or a flag, or a piece of clothing; but they tend to belong to gangs with names like the Bloods or the Crips, and make their living dealing drugs, or else live in countries like Afghanistan. In what sense can a man who is willing to kill and be killed over something of purely symbolic value, over prestige or recognition, be said to be more deeply human than someone who more sensibly backs down at a challenge, and submits his claim to peaceful arbitration or to the courts?

The importance of the willingness to risk's one's life in a battle for prestige can only be understood if we contemplate more deeply Hegel's view of the meaning of human freedom. In the Anglo-Saxon liberal tradition familiar to us, there is a commonsense understanding of freedom as something like the simple absence of restraint. Thus, according to Thomas Hobbes, "LIBERTY, or FREEDOM, signifies properly the absence of opposition—by opposition I mean external impediments of motion—and may be applied no less to irrational and inanimate creatures than to rational."[9] By this definition, a rock rolling down a hill and a hungry bear wandering around in the woods without constraint would both be said to be "free." But in fact, we know that the tumbling of the rock is determined by gravity and the slope of the hill, just as

the behavior of the bear is determined through the complex interaction of a variety of natural desires, instincts, and needs. A hungry bear foraging for food in the forest is "free" only in a formal
sense. It has no choice but to respond to its hunger and instincts.
Bears typically do not stage hunger strikes on behalf of higher
causes. The behaviors of the rock and the bear are determined by
their own physical natures and by the natural environment around
them. In that sense they are like machines programmed to operate
by a certain set of rules, the ultimate rules being the fundamental
laws of physics.

By Hobbes's definition, any human being not physically constrained from doing something would be considered "free." But
to the extent that a human being has a physical or animal nature, he or she can also be thought of as nothing more than a
finite collection of needs, instincts, wants, and passions, which
interact in a complicated but ultimately mechanical way that determine that person's behavior. Thus, a hungry and cold man
seeking to satisfy his natural needs for food and shelter is no
more free than the bear, or even the rock: he is simply a more
complicated machine operating according to a more complicated
set of rules. The fact that he faces no physical constraint in his
search for food and shelter creates only the appearance, but not
the reality, of freedom.

Hobbes's great political work, *Leviathan*, begins with just such a
portrayal of man as a highly complicated machine. He breaks human nature down into a series of basic passions like joy, pain, fear,
hope, indignation, and ambition, that in different combinations he
believes are sufficient to determine and explain the whole of human behavior. Thus Hobbes does not in the end believe that man
is free in the sense of having a capacity for moral choice. He can be
more or less rational in his behavior, but that rationality simply
serves ends like self-preservation that are given by nature. And nature, in turn, can be fully explained by the laws of matter-in-
motion, laws that had been recently explicated by Sir Isaac Newton.

Hegel, by contrast, starts with a completely different understanding of man. Not only is man not determined by his physical
or animal nature, but his very humanity consists in his ability to
overcome or negate that animal nature. He is free not just in
Hobbes's formal sense of being physically unconstrained, but free
in the metaphysical sense of being radically *un*-determined by
nature. This includes his own nature, the natural environment

around him, and nature's laws. He is, in short, capable of true *moral* choice, that is, choice between two courses of action not simply on the basis of the greater utility of one over another, not simply as the result of the victory of one set of passions and instincts over another, but because of an inherent freedom to make and adhere to his own rules. And man's specific *dignity* lies not in a superior calculating ability that makes him a cleverer machine than the lower animals, but precisely in this capacity for free moral choice.

But how do we know that man is free in this more profound sense? Certainly, many instances of human choice are in fact merely calculations of self-interest that serve nothing more than the satisfaction of animal desires or passions. For example, a man may forebear from stealing an apple from his neighbor's orchard not out of any moral sense, but because he fears that retribution will be more severe than his present hunger, or because he knows his neighbor will be going away on a trip and that the apples will soon be his for the taking. That he can calculate in this fashion does not make him any less determined by his natural instincts—in this case, hunger—than an animal who simply grabs for the apple.

Hegel would not deny that man has an animal side or a finite and determined nature: he must eat and sleep. But he is also demonstrably capable of acting in ways that totally contravene his natural instincts, and contravene them not for the sake of satisfying a higher or more powerful instinct, but, in a way, purely for the sake of the contravention. This is why the willingness to risk one's life in a battle for pure prestige plays such an important role in Hegel's account of history. For by risking his life, man proves that he can act contrary to his most powerful and basic instinct, the instinct for self-preservation. As Kojève puts it, man's human desire must win out over his animal desire for self-preservation. And that is why it is important that the primeval battle at the beginning of history be over prestige alone, or an apparent trifle like a medal or a flag that signifies recognition. The reason that I fight is to get another human being to recognize the fact that I am willing to risk my life, and that I am therefore free and authentically human. If the bloody battle were fought for some purpose (or as we modern bourgeois, schooled by Hobbes and Locke, would say, some "rational" purpose) such as the protection of our family or the acquisition of our opponent's land and possessions, then the battle itself would simply have been fought for the satisfaction of some other animal need. In fact, many lower animals are capable of risking their life in battle for the sake of, say, protecting their young, or staking out territory in which to forage. In each case, this behavior is instinctually determined and exists for the evolutionary purpose of assuring the survival of the species. Only man is capable of engaging in a bloody battle for the sole purpose of demonstrating that he has contempt for his own life, that he is something more than a complicated machine or a "slave to his passions,"[10] in short, that he has a specifically human dignity because he is free.

One might argue that "counterinstinctual" behavior such as the willingness to risk one's life in a prestige battle is simply determined by yet another deeper and more atavistic instinct, of which Hegel was not aware. Indeed, modern biology suggests that animals as well as men engage in prestige battles, though no one would assert the latter are moral agents. If we take the teaching of modern natural science seriously, the human realm is entirely subordinate to the realm of nature, and is equally determined by nature's laws. All human behavior can ultimately be explained by the sub-human, by psychology and anthropology, which in turn rest on biology and chemistry, and ultimately on the workings of the fundamental forces of nature. Hegel and his predecessor Immanuel Kant were aware of the threat that the materialistic foundations of modern natural science posed to the possibility of human free choice. The ultimate purpose of Kant's great *Critique of Pure Reason* was to fence off an "island" in the midst of the sea of mechanical natural causation that would, in a philosophically rigorous way, permit truly free, human moral choice to coexist with modern physics. Hegel accepted the existence of this "island," indeed, an island much larger and capacious than Kant envisioned. Both philosophers believed that in certain respects human beings were quite literally not subject to the laws of physics. This was not to say that human beings could move faster than the speed of light or repeal the action of gravity, but rather that moral phenomena could not simply be reduced to the mechanics of matter-in-motion.

It is beyond our present capacity or intention to analyze the adequacy of the "island" created by German idealism; the metaphysical question of the possibility of human free choice is, as Rousseau said, "l'abyme de la philosophie."[11] But if we put aside this tortured question for the moment, we can still note that as a *psychological* phenomenon, Hegel's emphasis on the importance of the risk of death points to something very real and important. Whether or not true free will exists, virtually all human beings act *as if* it does, and evaluate each other on the basis of their ability to make what they believe to be genuine moral choices. While much human activity is directed toward fulfilling natural needs, a significant amount of time is spent in pursuit of goals more evanescent. Men seek not just material comfort, but respect or recognition, and they believe that they are worthy of respect because they possess a certain value or dignity. A psychology, or a political science, that did not take into account man's desire for recognition, and his infrequent but very pronounced willingness to act at times contrary to even the strongest natural instinct, would misunderstand something very important about human behavior.

For Hegel, freedom was not just a psychological phenomenon, but the essence of what was distinctively human. In this sense, freedom and nature are diametrically opposed. Freedom does not mean the freedom to live in nature or according to nature; rather, freedom begins only where nature ends. Human freedom emerges only when man is able to transcend his natural, animal existence, and to create a new self *for himself*. The emblematic starting point for this process of self-creation is the struggle to the death for pure prestige.

But while this struggle for recognition is the first authentically human act, it is far from the last. The bloody battle between Hegel's "first men" is only the beginning point of the Hegelian dialectic, and leaves us still a very long way from modern liberal democracy. The problem of human history can be seen, in a certain sense, as the search for a way to satisfy the desire of *both* masters and slaves for recognition on a mutual and equal basis; history ends with the victory of a social order that accomplishes this goal.

Before describing the further stages in the evolution of the dialectic, however, it would be useful to contrast Hegel's account of the "first man" in the state of nature with those of the traditional founders of modern liberalism, Hobbes and Locke. For while Hegel's beginning and ending points are quite similar to those of the English thinkers, his concept of man is radically different, and provides us with a very different way of seeing contemporary liberal democracy.

14

The First Man

For every man looks that his companion should value him at the same rate he sets upon himself; and upon all signs of contempt or undervaluing naturally endeavors, as far as he dares . . . to extort a greater value from his contemners by damage and from others by example.

—*Thomas Hobbes*, Leviathan[1]

Contemporary liberal democracies did not emerge out of the shadowy mists of tradition. Like communist societies, they were deliberately created by human beings at a definite point in time, on the basis of a certain theoretical understanding of man and of the appropriate political institutions that should govern human society. While liberal democracy cannot trace its theoretical origins to a single author like Karl Marx, it does claim to be based on specific rational principles whose rich intellectual ancestry we can readily trace. The principles underlying American democracy, codified in the Declaration of Independence and the Constitution, were based on the writings of Jefferson, Madison, Hamilton, and the other American Founding Fathers, who in turn derived many of their ideas from the English liberal tradition of Thomas Hobbes and John Locke. If we are to uncover the self-understanding of the world's oldest liberal democracy—a self-understanding that has been adopted by many democratic societies outside North America—we need to look back to the political writings of Hobbes and Locke. For while these authors anticipate many of Hegel's assumptions concerning the nature of the "first man," they and the Anglo-Saxon liberal tradition that flows from them take a decidedly different attitude toward the desire for recognition.

Thomas Hobbes is today primarily known for two things: his characterization of the state of nature as "solitary, poor, nasty, brutish and short," and his doctrine of absolute monarchical sovereignty, which is frequently compared unfavorably to the more "liberal" Locke's assertion of a right of revolution against tyranny. But while Hobbes was by no means a democrat in the contemporary sense of the term, he was most definitely a liberal, and his philosophy was the fountainhead from which modern liberalism sprang. For it was Hobbes who first established the principle that the legitimacy of government stems from the rights of those governed, rather than from the divine right of kings, or from the natural superiority of those who rule. In this respect, the differences between him on the one hand, and Locke or the author of the American Declaration of Independence on the other, are trivial when compared with the gulf that separates Hobbes from writers closer to him in time like Filmer and Hooker.

Hobbes derives his principles of right and justice from his characterization of man in the state of nature. Hobbes's state of nature is an "inference from the Passions" that may never have existed as a general stage of human history, but which is everywhere latent when civil society breaks down—coming into the open, for example, in places like Lebanon after that country's descent into civil war in the mid-1970s. Just like Hegel's bloody battle, Hobbes's state of nature is meant to illuminate the human condition as it arises out of the interaction of most permanent and fundamental human passions.[2]

The similarities between Hobbes's "state of nature" and Hegel's bloody battle are striking. In the first place, both are characterized by extreme violence: the primary social reality is not love or concord, but a war of "every man against every man." And, although Hobbes does not use the term "struggle for recognition," the stakes in his original war of all against all are essentially the same as for Hegel:

> So that in the nature of man we find three principal causes of quarrel: first, competition; secondly, diffidence; thirdly, *glory* . . . the third [makes men invade] for trifles, as a word, a smile, a different opinion, and any other sign of undervalue, either direct in their persons or by reflection in their kindred, their friends, their nation, their profession, or their name.[3]

According to Hobbes, men may fight over necessities, but more
often than not, they fight over "trifles"—in other words, over
recognition. Hobbes the great materialist ends up describing the
nature of the "first man" in terms that are not much different
from those of the idealist Hegel. That is, the passion that first and
foremost drives men into the war of all against all is not covet-
ousness for material possessions, but the satisfaction of the pride
and vanity of a few ambitious men.[4] For Hegel's "desire for a
desire," or the quest for "recognition," can be understood as none
other than the human passion that we generally call "pride" or
"self-respect" (when we approve of it), and "vanity," "vainglory,"
or *"amour-propre"* (when we don't).[5]

In addition, both philosophers understand that the instinct
for self-preservation is in some sense the strongest and most
widely shared of the natural passions. For Hobbes, this instinct,
along with "such things as are necessary to commodious living,"
was the passion that most strongly inclined man toward peace.
Both Hegel and Hobbes see in the primordial battle a fundamental tension between, on the one hand, man's pride or desire for
recognition, which induces him to risk his life in a prestige battle,
and his fear of violent death, which inclines him to back down and
accept a life of slavery in return for peace and security. And
finally, Hobbes would accept Hegel's contention that the bloody
battle led, historically, to the relationship of lordship and bondage
as one combatant, fearful of his life, submitted to the other. The
domination of slaves by masters for Hobbes is despotism, a condition which does not remove man from the state of nature because slaves serve masters only under the implicit threat of force.[6]

Where Hobbes and Hegel differ fundamentally, however, and
where the Anglo-Saxon tradition of liberalism takes its decisive
turn, is in the relative moral weight assigned to the passions of
pride or vanity (i.e., "recognition") on the one hand, and the fear
of violent death, on the other. Hegel, as we have seen, believes
that the willingness to risk one's life in a battle for pure prestige is
in some sense what makes human beings human, the foundation
of human freedom. Hegel does not "approve," in the end, the
highly unequal relationship of master and slave, and knows full
well it is both primitive and oppressive. He understands, however,
that it is a necessary stage of human history in which both terms
of the class equation, masters and slaves, preserve something importantly human. The consciousness of the master is for him in a

certain sense higher and more human than that of the slave, for by submitting to the fear of death the slave does not succeed in rising above his animal nature, and therefore is less free than the master. Hegel, in other words, finds something morally praiseworthy in the pride of the aristocrat-warrior who is willing to risk his life, and something ignoble in the slavish consciousness that seeks self-preservation above all else.

Hobbes, on the other hand, finds nothing whatsoever morally redeeming in the pride (or more properly, vanity) of the aristocratic master: indeed, it is precisely this desire for recognition, this willingness to fight over a "trifle" like a medal or a flag, that is the source of all violence and human misery in the state of nature.[7] For him, the strongest human passion is the fear of violent death, and the strongest moral imperative—the "law of nature"—is the preservation of one's own physical existence. Self-preservation is the fundamental moral fact: all concepts of justice and right for Hobbes are founded in the rational pursuit of self-preservation, while injustice and wrong are those things that lead to violence, war, and death.[8]

The centrality of the fear of death is what leads Hobbes to the modern liberal state. For in the state of nature, prior to the establishment of positive law and government, the "right of nature" for every man to preserve his own existence, gives him the right to whatever means he judges necessary to accomplish that end, including violent ones. Where men have no common master, the inevitable result is the anarchic war of all against all. The cure for this anarchy is government, established on the basis of a social contract, under which all men agree to "lay down this right to all things, and be contented with so much liberty against other men as he would allow other men against himself." The only source of a state's legitimacy is its ability to protect and preserve those *rights* that individuals possess as human beings. For Hobbes, the fundamental human right was the right to life, that is, to the preservation of every human being's physical existence, and the only legitimate government was one that could adequately preserve life and prevent a return to the war of all against all.[9]

Peace and preservation of the right to life does not come cost-free, however. Fundamental to Hobbes's social contract is an agreement that in return for the preservation of their physical existences, men will give up their unjust pride and vanity. Hobbes demands, in other words, that men give up their struggle to be recognized, in particular, their struggle to be recognized as superior on the basis of their willingness to risk their lives in a prestige battle. The side of man that seeks to show himself superior to other men, to dominate them on the basis of superior virtue, the noble character who struggles against his "human all too human" limitations, is to be persuaded of the folly of his pride. The liberal tradition that springs from Hobbes therefore explicitly takes aim at those few who would seek to transcend their "animal" natures, and constrains them in the name of a passion that constitutes man's lowest common denominator—self-preservation. Indeed, it is a denominator common not only to human beings, but to the "lower" animals as well. Contrary to Hegel, Hobbes believes that the desire for recognition and the noble contempt for "mere" life is not the beginning of man's freedom but the source of his misery.[10] Hence the title of Hobbes's most famous book: explaining that "God having set forth the great power of Leviathan, called him King of the *Proud*," Hobbes compares his state to the Leviathan because it is "King of all the children of pride."[11] The Leviathan does not satisfy that pride, but subdues it.

The distance from Hobbes to the "spirit of 1776" and to modern liberal democracy is a very short one. Hobbes believed in absolute monarchical sovereignty, not because of any inherent right of kings to rule, but because he believed that a monarch could be invested with something approaching popular consent. Consent of the governed, he believed, could not only be obtained, as we would have it today, through free, secret-ballot, multi-party elections on the basis of universal suffrage, but through a kind of tacit consent expressed in a citizen's willingness to live under a particular government and abide by its laws.[12] For Hobbes there was a very clear difference between despotism and legitimate government, even though the two might look similar on the outside (i.e., both taking the form of absolute monarchy): a legitimate ruler had popular consent, while the despot did not. Hobbes's preference for one-man rule over parliamentary or democratic rule reflected his belief in the necessity of strong government to suppress the proud, and not because he contested the principle of popular sovereignty as such.

The weakness in Hobbes's argument was the tendency of legitimate monarchs to quietly slide over into being despots; without an institutional mechanism like elections for registering popular consent, it would frequently be difficult to know whether

a particular monarch had such consent or not. Thus it was relatively easy for John Locke to modify Hobbes's doctrine of monarchical sovereignty into one of parliamentary or legislative
sovereignty based on majority rule. Locke agreed with Hobbes
that self-preservation was the most fundamental passion, and that
the right to life was the fundamental right from which all others
were derived. While his vision of the state of nature is softer than
that of Hobbes, he agreed that it tended to degenerate into a state
of war or anarchy, and that legitimate government grew out of
the need to protect man from his own violence. But Locke pointed
out that absolute monarchs could violate man's right to self-
preservation, as when a king arbitrarily stripped a subject of his
possessions and life. The cure for this was not absolute monarchy
but limited government, a constitutional regime providing safeguards for the citizen's fundamental human rights and whose
authority derived from the consent of the governed. According to
Locke, Hobbes's natural right to self-preservation implied a right
of revolution against a tyrant who used his power unjustly against
the interests of his people. It is this right that is referred to in the
first paragraph of the Declaration of Independence, which speaks
of the necessity for "one people to dissolve the political bonds
which have connected them with another."[13]

Locke would not quarrel with Hobbes's relative evaluation of
the moral merits of recognition versus self-preservation: the
former had to be sacrificed to the latter, which was the fundamental right of nature from which all other rights are derived.
Locke, in contrast to Hobbes, would argue that man had a right
not simply to a bare physical existence, but to a comfortable and
potentially wealthy one as well; civil society existed not just to
preserve social peace, but to protect the right of the "industrious
and rational" to create abundance for all men through the institution of private property. Natural poverty is replaced by social
plenty, such that "a king of a large and fruitful territory [in Amer-
ica] feeds, lodges, and is clad worse than a day laborer in England."

The first man of Locke is similar to that of Hobbes and differs
radically from that of Hegel, however: while he struggles for recognition in the state of nature, he must be educated to subordinate his desire for recognition to the desire to preserve his own
life, and to the desire to endow that life with material comfort.

Hegel's first man desires not material possessions but another desire, the recognition by others of his freedom and humanity, and in pursuit of recognition shows himself to be indifferent to the "things of this world," beginning with private property and ending with his own life. The first man of Locke, by contrast, enters into civil society not simply to protect those material possessions he has in the state of nature, but to open up the possibility of obtaining more without limit.

Despite the efforts of some recent scholars to see the roots of the American regime in classical republicanism, the American founding was thoroughly if not wholly imbued with the ideas of John Locke.[14] Thomas Jefferson's "self-evident" truths about the right of men to life, liberty, and the pursuit of happiness were not essentially different from Locke's natural rights to life and property. The American founders believed that Americans possessed these rights as human beings, prior to the establishment of any political authority over them, and that the primary purpose of government was to protect those rights. The list of rights with which Americans believe themselves imbued by nature has expanded beyond life, liberty, and the pursuit of happiness to include not only those enumerated in the Bill of Rights, but others like the "right to privacy" of more recent invention. Whatever the specific set of rights enumerated, however, American liberalism and that of other constitutional republics similar to it share a common self-understanding that these rights stake out a sphere of individual choice where the power of the state is strictly limited.

To an American schooled in the thought of Hobbes, Locke, Jefferson, and the other American Founding Fathers, Hegel's honoring of the aristocratic master who risks his life in a prestige battle must sound very Teutonic and perverse. It is not that any of these Anglo-Saxon thinkers failed to recognize Hegel's first man as an authentic human type. It is rather that they saw the problem of politics as being in some sense the effort to persuade the would-be master to accept the life of the slave in a kind of classless society of slaves. This is because they rated the satisfaction derived from recognition much lower than Hegel, particularly when weighed against the pain of "man's lord and master," death. Indeed, they believed the fear of violent death and the desire for comfortable self-preservation to be so strong that these passions would override man's desire for recognition in the mind of any

rational man schooled in his own self-interest. This is the origin of
our almost instinctive reaction that Hegel's prestige battle is irrational.

In fact, opting for the life of a slave over that of a master is not
obviously more rational, unless one accepts the higher relative
moral weight given to self-preservation over recognition in the
Anglo-Saxon tradition. It is precisely the moral primacy accorded
self-preservation or comfortable self-preservation in the thought
of Hobbes and Locke that leaves us unsatisfied. Beyond establishing rules for mutual self-preservation, liberal societies do not attempt to define any positive goals for their citizens or promote a
particular way of life as superior or desirable to another. Whatever positive content life may have has to be filled by the individual himself. That positive content can be a high one of public
service and private generosity, or it can be a low one of selfish
pleasure and personal meanness. The state as such is indifferent.
Indeed, government is committed to the tolerance of different
"lifestyles," except when the exercise of one right impinges on
another. In the absence of positive, "higher" goals, what usually
fills the vacuum at the heart of Lockean liberalism is the open-
ended pursuit of wealth, now liberated from the traditional constraints of need and scarcity.[15]

The limitations of the liberal view of man become more obvious if we consider liberal society's most typical product, a new type
of individual who has subsequently come to be termed pejora-
tively as the *bourgeois*: the human being narrowly consumed with
his own immediate self-preservation and material well-being, interested in the community around him only to the extent that it
fosters or is a means of achieving his private good. Lockean man
did not need to be public-spirited, patriotic, or concerned for the
welfare of those around him; rather, as Kant suggested, a liberal
society could be made up of devils, provided they were rational. It
was not clear why the citizen of a liberal state, particularly in its
Hobbesian variant, would ever serve in the army and risk his life
for his country in war. For if the fundamental natural right was
self-preservation of the individual, on what grounds could it ever
be rational for an individual to die for his country rather than
trying to run away with his money and his family? Even in times
of peace, Hobbesian or Lockean liberalism provided no reason
why society's best men should choose public service and states-
manship over a private life of money-making. Indeed, it was not

clear why Lockean man should become active in the life of his community, be privately generous to the poor, or even make the sacrifices necessary to raise a family.[16]

Beyond the practical question of whether one can create a viable society in which all public-spiritedness is missing, there is an even more important issue as to whether there was not something deeply contemptible about a man who cannot raise his sights higher than his own narrow self-interests and physical needs. Hegel's aristocratic master risking his life in a prestige battle is only the most extreme example of the human impulse to transcend merely natural or physical need. Is it not possible that the struggle for recognition reflects a longing for self-transcendence that lies at the root not only of the violence of the state of nature and of slavery, but also of the noble passions of patriotism, courage, generosity, and public-spiritedness? Is recognition not somehow related to the entire moral side of man's nature, the part of man that finds satisfaction in the sacrifice of the narrow concerns of the body for an objective or a principle that lies beyond the body? By not rejecting the perspective of the master in favor of that of the slave, by identifying the master's struggle for recognition as somehow at the core of what is human, Hegel seeks to honor and preserve a certain moral dimension to human life that is entirely missing in the society conceived of by Hobbes and Locke. Hegel, in other words, understands man as a moral agent whose specific dignity is related to his inner freedom from physical or natural determination. It is this moral dimension, and the struggle to have it recognized, that is the motor driving the dialectical process of history.

But how are the struggle for recognition and the risk of death in the primordial bloody battle related to moral phenomena that are more familiar to us? To answer this question, we need to look more deeply at recognition and try to understand the side of the human personality out of which it arises.

15

A Vacation in Bulgaria

"Then we'll expunge all such things [from the just city]," I said, "beginning with the verse:

> *I would rather be on the soil, a slave to another*
> *To a man without lot whose means of life are not great*
> *Than rule over all the dead who have perished . . ."*

—Socrates, in Plato's Republic, Book III[1]

The "desire for recognition" sounds like a strange and somewhat artificial concept, the more so when it is said to be the primary motor driving human history. "Recognition" enters our vocabulary from time to time, for example when one of our colleagues retires and is given a watch "in recognition for years of service." But we do not normally think about political life as a "struggle for recognition." To the extent we generalize about politics, we are much more likely to view it as a competition for power between economic interests, a struggle to divide up wealth and the other good things in life.

The concept underlying "recognition" was not invented by Hegel. It is as old as Western political philosophy itself, and refers to a thoroughly familiar part of the human personality. Over the millennia, there has been no consistent word used to refer to the psychological phenomenon of the "desire for recognition": Plato spoke of *thymos*, or "spiritedness," Machiavelli of man's desire for glory, Hobbes of his pride or vainglory, Rousseau of his *amour-propre*, Alexander Hamilton of the love of fame and James Madison of ambition, Hegel of recognition, and Nietzsche of man as the "beast with red cheeks." All of these terms refer to that part of man which feels the need to place *value* on things—himself in the first instance, but on the people, actions, or things around him as well. It is the part of the personality which is the fundamental source of the emotions of pride, anger, and shame, and is not reducible to desire, on the one hand, or reason on the other. The desire for recognition is the most specifically political part of the human personality because it is what drives men to want to assert themselves over other men, and thereby into Kant's condition of "asocial sociability." It is not surprising that so many political philosophers have seen the central problem of politics as one of taming or harnessing the desire for recognition in a way that would serve the political community as a whole. Indeed, the project of taming the desire for recognition has been so successful in the hands of modern political philosophy that we citizens of modern egalitarian democracies often fail to see the desire for recognition in ourselves for what it is.[2]

The first extended analysis of the phenomenon of the desire for recognition in the Western philosophical tradition appears, quite appropriately, in the book that stands at the very head of that tradition, Plato's *Republic*. The *Republic* records a conversation between the philosopher Socrates and two young aristocratic Athenians, Glaucon and Adeimantus, who seek to describe the nature of a just city "in speech." Such a city, like cities "in reality," needs a class of guardians or warriors to defend it from external enemies. According to Socrates, the chief characteristic of these guardians is *thymos,* a Greek word that may somewhat awkwardly be translated as "spiritedness."[3] He compares a man with *thymos* to a noble dog who is capable of great courage and anger fighting strangers in defense of his own city. In his first approach to the problem, Socrates describes *thymos* from the outside: we only know that it is associated with courage—that is, the willingness to risk one's life—and with the emotion of anger or indignation on behalf of one's own.[4]

Socrates then returns to a more detailed analysis of *thymos* in Book IV, which contains his famous tripartite division of the soul.[5] Socrates notes that the human soul has a desiring part which is made up of many different desires, the most vivid of which are hunger and thirst. These desires all take a similar form of impelling man *toward* something—food or drink—outside of himself. But, Socrates notes, there are times when a man refrains from drinking even when he is thirsty. He and Adeimantus readily agree that there is a separate part of the soul, the reasoning or calculating part, that may induce a human being to act contrary to desire—for example, when the thirsty man fails to drink because he knows the water is contaminated. Are desire and reason then the only two parts of the soul, sufficient to explain human behavior? Can one, for example, explain all cases of self-restraint as reason's pitting one desire against another desire, for example greed against lust or long-term security against short-term pleasure?

Adeimantus is ready to agree that *thymos* is really just another kind of desire, when Socrates tells the story of a certain Leontius who wants to look at a pile of corpses lying by the public executioner:

> He desired to look, but at the same time he was disgusted and made himself turn away; and for a while he struggled and covered his face. But finally, overpowered by the desire, he opened his eyes wide, ran toward the corpses and said: "Look, you damned wretches, take your fill of the fair sight."[6]

One could interpret the internal struggle going on within Leontius as nothing more than the struggle between two desires: the desire to look at the corpses, competing with a natural disgust at viewing a dead human body. This would be in keeping with Hobbes's somewhat mechanistic psychology: he interprets the will as simply "the *last appetite in deliberating*," and therefore as the victory of the most powerful or tenacious desire. But to interpret Leontius's behavior as nothing more than a clash of desires does not explain his *anger* with himself.[7] For he presumably would not have been angry had he succeeded in restraining himself: on the contrary, he would have felt a different but related emotion, pride.[8] A moment's reflection will indicate that Leontius's anger could come from neither the desiring part nor from the calculating part of the soul, because Leontius was not indifferent to the outcome of his inner struggle. It therefore had to come from a third and altogether different part, which Socrates calls *thymos*. This anger arising from *thymos* is, as Socrates points out, potentially an ally of reason in helping to suppress wrong or foolish desires, but nonetheless is distinct from reason.

Thymos emerges in the *Republic* as being somehow related to the value one sets on oneself, what we today might call "self-esteem." Leontius believed himself to be the type of individual who could comport himself with a certain dignity and self-restraint, and when he failed to live up to his own sense of self-esteem, he grew angry with himself. Socrates suggests a relationship between anger and "self-esteem" by explaining that the nobler a man is—that is, the more highly he evaluates his own worth—the more angry he will become when he has been dealt with unjustly: his spirit "boil[s] and become[s] harsh," forming an "alliance for battle with what seems just" even if he "suffers in hunger, cold, and everything of the sort . . ."[9] *Thymos* is something like an innate human sense of justice: people believe that they have a certain worth, and when other people act as though they are worth less—when they do not *recognize* their worth at its correct value—then they become angry. The intimate relationship between self-evaluation and anger can be seen in the English word synonymous with anger, "indignation." "Dignity" refers to a person's sense of self-worth; "in-dignation" arises when something happens to offend that sense of worth. Conversely, when other people see that we are not living up to our own sense of self-esteem, we feel *shame;* and when we are evaluated justly (i.e., in proportion to our true worth), we feel *pride.*

Anger is a potentially all-powerful emotion, capable of overwhelming, as Socrates points out, natural instincts like hunger, thirst, and self-preservation. But it is not a desire for any material object outside the self; if we can speak of it at all as a desire, it is a *desire for a desire,* that is, a desire that that person who evaluated us too low should change his opinion and recognize us according to our own estimate of our worth. Plato's *thymos* is therefore nothing other than the psychological seat of Hegel's desire for recognition: for the aristocratic master in the bloody battle is driven by the desire that other people evaluate him at his own sense of self-worth. Indeed, he is driven into a bloody rage when that sense of self-worth is denigrated. *Thymos* and the "desire for recognition" differ somewhat insofar as the former refers to a part of the soul that invests objects with value, whereas the latter is an activity of *thymos* that demands that another consciousness share the same valuation. It is possible for one to feel thymotic pride in oneself without demanding recognition. But esteem is not a "thing" like an apple or a Porsche: it is a state of consciousness, and to have subjective certainty about one's own sense of worth, it must be recognized by another consciousness. Thus *thymos* typically, but not inevitably, drives men to seek recognition.

Let us consider, for a moment, a small but revealing example of *thymos* in the contemporary world. Václav Havel, before he became president of Czechoslovakia in the fall of 1989, spent a great deal of time in and out of jails for his activities as a dissident and founding member of the human rights organization Charter '77. His sojourns in prison evidently gave him considerable time to think about the system that had jailed him, and about the real nature of the evil that it represented. In his essay "The Power of the Powerless," published in the early 1980s before the democratic revolutions in Eastern Europe were a twinkle in Gorbachev's eye, Havel tells the following story of a greengrocer:

> The manager of a fruit and vegetable shop places in his window, among the onions and carrots, the slogan: "Workers of the World, Unite!" Why does he do it? What is he trying to communicate to the world? Is he genuinely enthusiastic about the idea of unity among the workers of the world? Is his enthusiasm so great that he feels an irrepressible impulse to acquaint the public with his ideals? Has he really given more than a moment's thought to how such a unification might occur and what it would mean? . . .
>
> Obviously, the greengrocer is indifferent to the semantic content of the slogan on exhibit; he does not put the slogan in this window from any personal desire to acquaint the public with the ideal it expresses. This, of course, does not mean that his action has no motive or significance at all, or that the slogan communicates nothing to anyone. The slogan is really a *sign,* and as such it contains a subliminal but very definite message. Verbally, it might be expressed this way: "I, the greengrocer XY, live here and I know what I must do. I behave in the manner expected of me. I can be depended upon and am beyond reproach. I am obedient and therefore I have the right to be left in peace." This message, of course, has an addressee: it is directed above, to the greengrocer's superior, and at the same time it is a shield that protects the greengrocer from potential informers. The slogan's real meaning, therefore, is rooted firmly in the greengrocer's existence. It reflects his vital interests. But what are those vital interests?
>
> Let us take note: if the greengrocer had been instructed

to display the slogan, "I am afraid and therefore unquestion-
ingly obedient," he would not be nearly as indifferent to its
semantics, even though the statement would reflect the truth.
*The greengrocer would be embarrassed and ashamed to put such an
unequivocal statement of his own degradation in the shop window,
and quite naturally so, for he is a human being and thus has a sense
of his own dignity.* To overcome this complication, his expression of loyalty must take the form of a sign which, at least on
its textual surface, indicates a level of disinterested conviction.
It must allow the greengrocer to say, "What's wrong with the
workers of the world uniting?" Thus the sign helps the greengrocer to conceal from himself the low foundations of his
obedience, at the same time concealing the low foundations of
power. It hides them behind the facade of something high.
And that something is *ideology.*[10]

In reading this passage one is struck immediately by Havel's
use of the word "dignity." Havel depicts the greengrocer as an
ordinary man of no particular education or stature, who nonetheless would feel ashamed to display a sign saying "I am afraid."
What is the nature of this dignity that is the source of the man's
inhibition? Havel notes that such a sign would be a more honest
statement than displaying the communist slogan. Moreover, in
communist Czechoslovakia everyone understood that one was
forced to do things one didn't want to do out of fear. Fear itself,
the instinct for self-preservation, is a natural instinct universally
shared by all men: Why, then, not admit that one is a human
being and therefore afraid?

   The reason, ultimately, has to do with the fact that the greengrocer believes he has a certain *worth*. That worth is related to his
belief that he is something more than a fearful and needy animal
who can be manipulated by his fears and needs. He believes, even
if he cannot articulate this belief, that he is a moral agent who is
capable of choice, who can resist his natural needs for the sake of
principle.

   Of course, as Havel points out, the greengrocer is able to
sidestep this internal debate because he can simply display a high-
minded communist slogan and fool himself that he is principled
rather than fearful and abject. In a way, his situation is like that of
Socrates' character Leontius who gave in to his desire to view the
corpses. Both the greengrocer and Leontius believed they had a
certain worth related to their capacity for choice, that they were

"better than" their natural fears and desires. Both, in the end, were vanquished by their natural fear or desire. The only difference was that Leontius was honest about his own weakness and condemned himself for it, while the greengrocer failed to confront his own degradation because ideology provided him a convenient excuse. Havel's story teaches us two things: first, that the feeling of dignity or self-worth that is at the root of *thymos* is related to man's view that he is in some way a moral agent capable of real choice, and second, that this self-perception is innate to or characteristic of all human beings, whether they are great and proud conquerors or humble greengrocers. As Havel puts it,

> The essential aims of life are present naturally in every person. In everyone there is some longing for humanity's rightful dignity, for moral integrity, for free expression of being and a sense of transcendence over the world of existences.[11]

On the other hand, Havel notes that "each person is capable, to a greater or lesser degree, of coming to terms with living within the lie." His condemnation of the post-totalitarian communist state revolves around the damage that communism has done to people's moral character, to their belief in their capacity to act as moral agents—the greengrocer's absent sense of dignity when he agrees to put up the sign "Workers of the World, Unite!" Dignity and its opposite, humiliation, are the two most common words used by Havel in describing life in communist Czechoslovakia.[12] Communism *humiliated* ordinary people by forcing them to make a myriad of petty, and sometimes not so petty, moral compromises with their better natures. These took the form of putting up a sign in one's store window, or signing a petition denouncing a colleague for doing something the state did not like, or simply remaining silent when that colleague was unjustly persecuted. The seedy post-totalitarian states of the Brezhnev era tried to make everybody morally complicit not through terror but, ironically enough, by dangling before them the fruits of modern consumer culture. These were not the spectacular baubles that fueled the greed of the American investment banker of the 1980s, but small things like a refrigerator, a bigger apartment, or a vacation in Bulgaria, which loomed large to people with few material possessions. Communism, in a much more thoroughgoing way than "bourgeois" liberalism, fortified the desiring part of the soul against the thymotic part. Havel's charge against communism is not at all that it failed in its promise to deliver the material plenty of industrial efficiency, or that it disappointed the hopes of the working class or the poor for a better life. On the contrary, it did offer them these things in a Faustian bargain, requiring them to compromise their moral worth in return. And in making this bargain, the victims of the system became its perpetuators, while the system itself took on a life of its own independently of anyone's desire to participate in it.

Of course, what Havel identifies as "the general unwillingness of consumption-oriented people to sacrifice some material certainties for the sake of their own spiritual and moral integrity" is a phenomenon that is hardly unique to communist societies. In the West, consumerism induces people to make moral compromises with themselves daily, and they lie to themselves not in the name of socialism but of ideas like "self-realization" or "personal growth." And yet, there is an important difference: in communist societies, it was difficult to have a normal life, and next to impossible to have a "successful" one, without suppressing one's *thymos* to a greater or lesser degree. One could not be a simple carpenter or electrician or doctor without "going along" in some fashion, just as the greengrocer did, and one certainly could not be a successful writer or professor or television journalist without implicating oneself rather fully in the system's deceit.[13] If one were thoroughly honest and wanted to retain one's sense of inner self-worth, there was only one alternative (assuming one was not among the increasingly small circle of people who still believed sincerely in Marxist-Leninist ideology). That was to drop out of the system altogether and become, like Vladimir Bukovsky, Andrey Sakharov, Aleksandr Solzhenitsyn, or Havel himself, professional dissidents. But this meant breaking with the desiring side of life altogether, and exchanging such simple material gratifications as a regular job and apartment for an ascetic life of jail, mental institution, or exile. For the great mass of people whose thymotic sides were not nearly so well developed, normal life meant acceptance of a petty, day-to-day moral degradation.

In Plato's story of Leontius and Havel's fable of the greengrocer—at the beginning and the end of the Western tradition of political philosophy, so to speak—we see a humble form of *thymos* emerge as a central factor in political life. *Thymos* appears to be related to a good political order in some way, because it is the source of courage, public-spiritedness, and a certain unwilling-ness to make moral compromises. The good political order needs to be something more than a mutual non-aggression pact, accord-ing to these writers; it must also satisfy man's just desire for rec-ognition of his dignity and worth.

But *thymos* and the desire for recognition are much broader phenomena than these two examples would suggest. The process of valuation and self-valuation pervades many aspects of day-to-day life that we commonly think of as economic: man is truly "the beast with red cheeks."

16

The Beast with Red Cheeks

Yet, if God wills that [this war] continue until the wealth piled up by the bondsman's two hundred and fifty years of unrequited toil shall be sunk, and until every drop of blood drawn by the lash shall be paid by another drawn by the sword, still it must be said, as was said three thousand years ago, "The judgments of the Lord are true and righteous altogether."

—Abraham Lincoln, Second Inaugural Address, March 1865[1]

Thymos as it emerges in the *Republic* or in Havel's account of the greengrocer constitutes something like an innate human sense of justice, and as such is the psychological seat of all the noble virtues like selflessness, idealism, morality, self-sacrifice, courage, and honorability. *Thymos* provides an all-powerful emotional support to the process of valuing and evaluating, and allows human beings to overcome their most powerful natural instincts for the sake of what they believe is right or just. People evaluate and assign worth to *themselves* in the first instance, and feel indignation on *their own* behalf. But they are also capable of assigning worth to *other* people, and feeling anger on behalf of *others*. This occurs most often when an individual is a member of a class of people that perceives itself as being treated unjustly, for example, a feminist on behalf of all women, or a nationalist on behalf of his ethnic group. Indignation on one's own behalf then extends to the class as a whole and engenders feelings of solidarity. There are also instances of anger on behalf of classes of people to which one does not belong. The just rage of radical white abolitionists against slavery before the American Civil War, or the indignation that people around the world have felt against the apartheid system in South

171

Africa, are both manifestations of *thymos*. Indignation in these cases arises because the victim of racism is not being treated with the worth that the person feeling indignation believes they are due as human beings, that is, because the victim of racism is not *recognized*.

The desire for recognition arising out of *thymos* is a deeply paradoxical phenomenon because the latter is the psychological seat of justice and selflessness while at the same time being closely related to selfishness. The thymotic self demands recognition for its *own* sense of the worthiness of things, both itself and of other people. The desire for recognition remains a form of self-assertion, a projection of one's own values on the outside world, and gives rise to feelings of anger when those values are not recognized by other people. There is no guarantee that the thymotic self's sense of justice will correspond to that of other selves: What is just for the anti-apartheid activist, for example, is completely different for the pro-apartheid Afrikaner, based on differing evaluations of black dignity. In fact, since the thymotic self usually begins by evaluating itself, the likelihood is that it will *overvalue* itself: as Locke says, no man is a good judge in his own case.

The self-assertive nature of *thymos* leads to the common confusion of *thymos* and desire. In fact, the self-assertion arising from *thymos* and the selfishness of desire are very distinct phenomena.[2] Take the example of a wage dispute between management and organized labor in an automobile factory. Most contemporary political scientists, following a Hobbesian psychology that reduces the will to desire and reason alone, would interpret such disputes as conflicts between "interest groups," that is, between the desire of the managers and the desire of the workers to have a greater part of the economic pie. Reason, such a political scientist would assert, induces each side to follow a bargaining strategy that maximizes the economic benefits to itself or, in the case of a strike, minimizes the costs, until the relative strength of each produces a compromise outcome.

But in fact, this is a considerable simplification of the psychological process that goes on internally on both sides. The striking worker does not carry a sign saying "I am a greedy person and want all the money I can extract from management," any more than Havel's greengrocer was willing to put out the sign saying "I am afraid." Rather, the striker says (and thinks to himself): "I am a good worker; I am worth much more to my employer than I am currently being paid. Indeed, given the profits that I have allowed the company to earn, and given the kinds of wages that are paid for comparable work in other industries, I am being unfairly underpaid; indeed, I am being . . ." at which point the worker would resort to a biological metaphor whose meaning is that his human dignity is being violated. The worker, just like the greengrocer, believes that he has a certain worth. The worker demands higher pay, of course, because it pays his mortgage and buys food for his children, but he wants it also as a sign of his worth. The anger that arises in job disputes seldom has to do with the absolute level of wages, but rather arises because management's wage offer does not adequately "recognize" the dignity of the worker. And this explains why strikers feel much more intense anger at a strikebreaker than at the management itself. Even though the strikebreaker is nothing more than a tool of management, he is despised as an abject person whose own sense of dignity was overwhelmed by his desire for immediate economic gain. Unlike the other strikers, the strikebreaker's desire won out over his *thymos*.

We readily understand economic self-interest, but frequently ignore the way it is intimately bound up with thymotic self-assertion. Higher wages satisfy both the desire for material things of the desiring part of the soul, *and* the desire for recognition of the thymotic part. In political life, economic claims are seldom presented as simple demands for more; they are usually couched in terms of "economic justice." To dress up an economic demand as a claim on behalf of justice toward oneself can be done as an act of pure cynicism, but more often than not it reflects the real power of thymotic anger on the part of people who believe, consciously or not, that their dignity is ultimately at stake in disputes over money. Indeed, much of what is commonly interpreted as economic motivation dissolves into a kind of thymotic desire for recognition. This was understood perfectly well by the father of political economy, Adam Smith. In *The Theory of Moral Sentiments*, Smith argues that the reason men seek riches and shun poverty has very little to do with physical necessity. This is because "the wages of the meanest labourer" can supply the necessities of nature, such as "food and clothing, the comfort of a house, and of a family," and that much of the income even of poor people is spent on things that are, strictly speaking, "conveniences, which may be regarded as superfluities." Why, then, do men seek to "better their condition" by seeking the toil and bustle of economic life? The answer is:

> To be observed, to be attended to, to be taken notice of with sympathy, complacency, and approbation, are all the advantages which we can propose to derive from it. It is the *vanity, not the ease or the pleasure*, which interests us. But vanity is always founded upon the belief of our being the object of attention and approbation. The rich man *glories* in his riches, because he feels that they naturally draw upon him the attention of the world, and that mankind are disposed to go along with him in all the agreeable emotions with which the advantages of his situation so readily inspire him. . . . The poor man, on the contrary, is *ashamed* of his poverty. He feels that it either places him out of sight of mankind, or, that if they take any notice of him, they have, however, scarce any fellow-feeling with the misery and distress which he suffers . . .[3]

There is a level of poverty where economic activity is undertaken for the fulfillment of natural needs, such as in the drought-stricken African Sahel during the 1980s. But for most other regions in the world, poverty and deprivation are relative rather than absolute concepts arising from money's role as a symbol for worth.[4] The official "poverty line" in the United States represents a standard of living much higher than that of well-off people in certain Third World countries. This does not mean that poor people in the United States are more satisfied than well-to-do people in Africa or South Asia, however, for their sense of self-worth receives many more daily affronts. Locke's observation that a king in America "feeds, lodges, and is clad worse than a day-laborer in England" neglects *thymos* and thus misses the point entirely. The king in America has a sense of dignity missing entirely from the English day-laborer, a dignity that is born of his freedom, self-sufficiency, and the respect and recognition he receives from the community around him. The day-laborer may eat better, but he is totally dependent on an employer to whom he is virtually invisible as a human being.

The failure to understand the thymotic component of what is normally thought of as economic motivation leads to vast misinterpretations of politics and historical change. For example, it is very common to assert that revolutions are caused by poverty and deprivation, or to believe that the greater the poverty and depri-

vation, the greater the revolutionary potential. Tocqueville's famous study of the French Revolution, however, shows that just
the reverse happened: in the thirty or forty years preceding the
revolution, France experienced an unprecedented period of economic growth, coupled with a series of well-intentioned but poorly
thought-through liberalizing reforms on the part of the French
monarchy. The French peasantry was far more prosperous and
independent on the eve of the revolution than their counterparts
in Silesia or East Prussia, as was the middle class. They became
combustible material for the revolution, however, because the liberalization of political life that took place toward the end of the
eighteenth century allowed them to feel their *relative* deprivation
much more acutely than anyone in Prussia, and to express their
anger over it.[5] In the contemporary world, only the poorest and
richest countries tend to be stable. Those countries that are modernizing economically tend to be the least stable politically because
growth itself promotes new expectations and demands. People
compare their situation not with that of traditional societies, but
with that of wealthy countries, and grow angry as a result. The
commonly perceived "revolution of rising expectations" is as
much a thymotic phenomenon as one arising out of desire.[6]

There are other cases where *thymos* has been confused with
desire. Historians attempting to explain the American Civil War
must give an account of why Americans were willing to endure
the appalling suffering brought on by a war that killed six hundred thousand men out of a population of thirty-one million, or
almost 2 percent of the total. A number of twentieth-century historians, emphasizing economic factors, have tried to interpret the
war as a struggle between an industrializing, capitalist North and
a traditional, planter South. But these sorts of explanations are
somehow unsatisfactory. The war was initially fought under the
banner of largely non-economic goals—for the North, preservation of the Union, and, in the South, maintenance of their "pe-
culiar institution" and the way of life it represented. But there was
a further issue as well, which Abraham Lincoln, wiser than many
of his later interpreters, pointed to when he said that "everyone
knew" that slavery was "somehow the cause" of the conflict. Many
Northerners were, of course, opposed to emancipation and hoped
to settle the war early through compromise. But Lincoln's determination to see the war through to the end, evident in his own
stern admonition that he would be willing to see the war go on

even if it consumed the fruits of "the bondsman's two hundred and fifty years of unrequited toil," was, economically speaking, incomprehensible. Such exchanges make sense only to the thymotic part of the soul.[7]

There are any number of examples of the desire for recognition operating in contemporary American politics. Abortion, for example, has been one of the most neuralgic issues on the American social agenda for the past generation, and yet it is an issue with almost no economic content.[8] The debate over abortion centers over a conflict in rights between the unborn and women, but in fact reflects a deeper disagreement over the relative dignity of the traditional family and the woman's role in it, on the one hand, and that of the self-sufficient, working woman on the other. The sides in this debate feel indignation on behalf of either aborted fetuses or women dying at the hands of incompetent abortionists, but they feel indignation on their own behalf as well: the traditional mother because she feels abortion somehow degrades the respect due motherhood, and the working woman because the absence of abortion rights diminishes her dignity as the equal of men. The indignity of racism in modern America lies only partly in the physical deprivation brought on by poverty among blacks: much of its pain lies in the fact that in the eyes of many whites, a black is (in Ralph Ellison's phrase) an "invisible man," not actively hated but unseen as a fellow human being. Poverty merely adds to that invisibility. Virtually the entire civil liberties and civil rights agendas, while having certain economic components, are essentially thymotic contests over recognition of competing understandings of justice and human dignity.

There is a thymotic aspect to many other activities that are normally seen as instances of natural desire. For example, sexual conquest is usually not just a matter of physical gratification—one does not always need a partner for that—but reflects in addition the need to have one's desirability "recognized" by the other. The self that is being recognized is not necessarily the same as the self of Hegel's aristocratic master, or the moral self of Havel's greengrocer. But the deepest forms of erotic love involve a longing for the lover's recognition of something more than one's physical characteristics, a longing for what amounts to a recognition of one's worth.

These examples of *thymos* are not meant to prove that all economic activity, all erotic love, and all politics can be reduced to the desire for recognition. Reason and desire remain parts of the soul distinct from *thymos*. Indeed, in many ways they constitute the *dominant* parts of the soul for modern, liberal man. Human beings covet money because they want *things*, not just recognition, and with the liberation of human acquisitiveness that took place in early modern times, the growth in the number and variety of material desires has been explosive. And they crave sex because it—well, feels good. I have taken note of the thymotic dimensions of greed and lust precisely because the primacy of desire and reason in the modern world tends to obscure the role that *thymos* or recognition plays in day-to-day life. *Thymos* frequently manifests itself as an ally of desire—as in the case of the worker's demand for "economic justice"—and is thus easily confused with desire.

The desire for recognition has also played a critical role in bringing about the anti-communist earthquake in the Soviet Union, Eastern Europe, and China. Certainly, many Eastern Europeans wanted an end to communism for less than elevated economic reasons, that is, because they thought that this would pave the way toward West German living standards. The fundamental impulse for the reforms undertaken in the Soviet Union and China was in a certain sense economic, what we have identified as the inability of centralized command economies to meet the requirements of "post-industrial" society. But the desire for prosperity was accompanied by a demand for democratic rights and political participation as ends in themselves, in other words, for a system that implemented recognition on a routine and universal basis. The would-be coup makers of August 1991 deceived themselves that the Russian people would trade "their freedom for a piece of sausage," in the words of one of the defenders of the Russian parliament.

We cannot understand the totality of the revolutionary phenomenon unless we appreciate the working of thymotic anger and the demand for recognition that accompanied communism's economic crisis. It is a curious characteristic of revolutionary situations that the events which provoke people to take the greatest risks and set in motion the crumbling of governments are seldom the large ones that historians later describe as fundamental causes, but rather small and seemingly incidental ones. For example, in Czechoslovakia, the Civic Forum opposition group was formed out of popular indignation at the jailing of Havel himself, which occurred despite the communist Jakes regime's earlier promise of liberalization. Large crowds began to gather in the streets of Prague in November 1989 initially after rumors—subsequently discovered to be false—that a student had been killed by the security police. In Romania, the chain of events that brought down the Ceaucescu regime in December 1989 began with protests in the town of Timisoara over the jailing of an ethnic Hungarian cleric, Father Tokes, who had been an active campaigner for the rights of the Hungarian community there.[9] In Poland, hostility toward the Soviets and their Polish communist allies was fed for decades by Moscow's unwillingness to admit responsibility for the Soviet NKVD 's murder of Polish officers in the Katyn forest in 1940. One of the first acts undertaken by Solidarity when it entered the government after the round table agreement in the spring of 1989 was to demand from the Soviets a full accounting of the Katyn murders. A similar process was going on in the Soviet Union itself, where many of the survivors of the Stalin years were demanding an accounting from those who had committed the crimes, and rehabilitation for those who were the victims. *Perestroika* and political reform cannot be understood separately from the desire to simply tell the truth about the past, and to restore dignity to those who had disappeared voicelessly into the Gulag. The anger that swept aside countless local party officials in 1990 and 1991 arose not only over systemic economic grievances, but over issues of personal corruption and arrogance, like the party first secretary in Volgograd who was drummed out of office for using party funds to buy himself a Volvo.

The Honecker regime in East Germany was critically weakened by a series of events in 1989: a refugee crisis, in which hundreds of thousands fled to West Germany, its loss of Soviet support, and finally by the opening of the Berlin Wall. Even at that point, however, it was not clear that socialism was dead in East Germany; what swept the Socialist Unity party out of power completely and discredited its new leaders Krenz and Modrow were revelations about the opulence of Honecker's personal residence in the suburb of Wandlitz.[10] Now, strictly speaking, the enormous anger that these revelations provoked was somewhat irrational. There were many causes for complaint against communist East Germany, above all relating to the country's lack of political freedom and its low standard of living when compared to West Germany. Honecker for his part did not live in a modern version of the Palace of Versailles; his home was that of a well-to-do burgher in Hamburg or Bremen. But the well-known and long-standing charges against communism in East Germany did not raise nearly the degree of thymotic anger on the part of average East Germans as viewing the Honecker residence on their television screens. For the tremendous hypocrisy those images revealed, on the part of a regime that was explicitly devoted to equality, deeply offended people's sense of justice and was sufficient to get them into the streets to demand a total end to the Communist party's power.

Finally, there was the case of China. Deng Xiaoping's economic reform created a whole new horizon of economic opportunities for a generation of young Chinese coming of age in the 1980s, who could now start businesses, read foreign newspapers, and study in the United States and other Western countries for the first time since the revolution. The students reared in this climate of economic freedom had economic complaints, of course, particularly concerning the mounting inflation in the late 1980s that was steadily eroding the purchasing power of most city dwellers. But reformed China was a place of vastly greater dynamism and opportunity than under Mao, particularly for those privileged children of the elite attending universities in Beijing, Xian, Canton, and Shanghai. And yet, these students were precisely the ones who demonstrated for greater democracy, first in 1986, and then again in the spring of 1989 on the anniversary of Hu Yaobang's death. As the protest went on, however, they became angry with their lack of a voice, and with the party and government for failing to *recognize* them and the justice of their complaints. They wanted Deng Xiaoping, Zhao Ziyang, or other top Chinese leaders to meet with them personally, and began to demand that in the longer run their participation be institutionalized. Whether all of them wanted institutionalization to ultimately take the form of representative democracy was unclear, but the underlying demand was that they be taken seriously as adults whose opinions were due a degree of respect and deference.

All of these cases from the communist world illustrate in one way or another the workings of the desire for recognition. Both reform and revolution were undertaken for the sake of a political system that would institutionalize universal recognition. More than that, however, thymotic anger played a critical role in catalyzing revolutionary events. People did not go into the streets of

Leipzig, Prague, Timisoara, Beijing, or Moscow demanding that
the government give them a "post-industrial economy," or that
the supermarkets be full of food. Their passionate anger was
aroused over their perceptions of relatively small acts of injustice
like the jailing of a priest or the refusal of powerful officials to
accept a list of demands.

Historians later interpret these as secondary or triggering
causes, which they are; but that does not make them less necessary
in bringing about the final revolutionary chain of events. Revolutionary situations cannot occur unless at least some people are
willing to risk their lives and their comfort for a cause. The courage to do so cannot arise out of the desiring part of the soul, but
must come from the thymotic part. The man of desire, Economic
Man, the true *bourgeois*, will perform an internal "cost-benefit analysis" which will always give him a reason for working "within the
system." It is only thymotic man, the man of anger who is jealous
of his own dignity and the dignity of his fellow citizens, the man
who feels that his worth is constituted by something more than the
complex set of desires that make up his physical existence—it is
this man alone who is willing to walk in front of a tank or confront
a line of soldiers. And it is frequently the case that without such
small acts of bravery in response to small acts of injustice, the
larger train of events leading to fundamental changes in political
and economic structures would never occur.

17

The Rise and Fall of *Thymos*

Man does not *strive after happiness; only the Englishman does that.*

—*Nietzsche,* Twilight of the Idols[1]

Man's sense of self-worth and the demand that it be recognized has, up till now, been presented as the source of the noble virtues like courage, generosity, and public-spiritedness, as the seat of resistance to tyranny, and as a reason for the choice of liberal democracy. But there is a dark side to the desire for recognition as well, a dark side that has led many philosophers to believe that *thymos* is the fundamental source of human evil.

Thymos initially came into being for us as an evaluation of one's own worth. Havel's example of the greengrocer indicates that this sense of worth is frequently related to the feeling that one is "more than" one's natural desires, that one is a moral agent capable of free choice. This rather humble form of *thymos* can be thought of as a feeling of self-respect, or, in currently fashionable language, "self-esteem." It is possessed to a greater or lesser degree by virtually all human beings. Having a modest sense of self-respect seems to be important to everybody, important to their ability to function in the world and the satisfaction they feel with their lives. It is, according to Joan Didion, what enables us to say "no" to other people without self-reproach.[2]

The existence of a moral dimension in the human personality that constantly evaluates both the self and others does not, however, mean that there will be any agreement on the substantive content of morality. In a world of thymotic moral selves, they will be constantly disagreeing and arguing and growing angry with

181

one another over a host of questions, large and small. Hence *thymos* is, even in its most humble manifestations, the starting point for human conflict.

Moreover, there is no guarantee that a human being's evaluation of his own worth will remain within the bounds of this "moral" self. Havel believes that there is a germ of moral judgment and sense of "rightness" in all men; but even if we accept this generalization, we would have to admit that it is much less developed in some people than in others. One can demand recognition not only for one's moral worth, but also for one's wealth, or power, or physical beauty as well.

More importantly, there is no reason to think that all people will evaluate themselves as the *equals* of other people. Rather, they may seek to be recognized as *superior* to other people, possibly on the basis of true inner worth, but more likely out of an inflated and vain estimate of themselves. The desire to be recognized as superior to other people we will henceforth label with a new word with ancient Greek roots, *megalothymia*. *Megalothymia* can be manifest both in the tyrant who invades and enslaves a neighboring people so that they will recognize his authority, as well as in the concert pianist who wants to be recognized as the foremost interpreter of Beethoven. Its opposite is *isothymia*, the desire to be recognized as the equal of other people. *Megalothymia* and *isothymia* together constitute the two manifestations of the desire for recognition around which the historical transition to modernity can be understood.

It is clear that *megalothymia* is a highly problematic passion for political life, for if recognition of one's superiority by another person is satisfying, it stands to reason that recognition by *all* people will be more satisfying still. *Thymos*, which first came to light as a humble kind of self-respect, can thus also manifest itself as the desire to dominate. This latter, dark side of *thymos* was of course present right from the outset in Hegel's description of the bloody battle, since the desire for recognition provoked the primordial battle and ultimately led to the domination by the master of the slave. The logic of recognition ultimately led to the desire to be *universally* recognized, that is, to imperialism.

Thymos, either in the humble form of the greengrocer's sense of dignity, or in the form of *megalothymia*—the tyrannical ambition of a Caesar or a Stalin—has been a central subject of Western political philosophy, even if the phenomenon has been given a different name by each thinker. Virtually everyone who has thought seriously about politics and the problems of a just political order has had to contend with the moral ambiguities of *thymos*, trying to make use of its positive aspects and seeking a way to neutralize its dark side.

Socrates enters into an extended discussion of *thymos* in the *Republic* because the thymotic part of the soul turns out to be crucial for the construction of his just city "in speech."[3] This city, like any city, has foreign enemies and needs to be defended from outside attack. It therefore needs a class of guardians who are courageous and public-spirited, who are willing to sacrifice their material desires and wants for the sake of the common good. Socrates does not believe that courage and public-spiritedness can arise out of a calculation of enlightened self-interest. Rather, they must be rooted in *thymos*, in the just pride of the guardian class in themselves and in their own city, and their potentially irrational anger against those who threaten it.[4] Thus for Socrates, *thymos* is an innately political virtue necessary for the survival of any political community, because it is the basis on which private man is drawn out from the selfish life of desire and made to look toward the common good. But Socrates also believes that *thymos* has the capability to destroy political communities as well as to cement them together. He hints at the various points in the *Republic*, for instance when he compares the thymotic guardian to a ferocious watchdog who can bite his master as well as a stranger if not properly trained.[5] Construction of a just political order therefore requires both the cultivation and the taming of a *thymos*, and the greater part of the first six books of the *Republic* is devoted to the proper thymotic education of the guardian class.

The *megalothymia* of would-be masters to dominate other people through imperialism was an important theme in a good deal of medieval and early modern political thought, which referred to the phenomenon as the quest for *glory*. The struggle of ambitious princes for recognition was broadly assumed to be a general characteristic both of human nature and of politics. It did not necessarily connote tyranny or injustice in an era when the legitimacy of imperialism was frequently taken for granted.[6] St. Augustine, for example, lists the desire for glory among the vices, but one of the least pernicious and potentially a source of human greatness.[7]

Megalothymia understood as the desire for glory was central to the thought of the first early modern thinker to break decisively

with the Aristotelian tradition of medieval Christian political philosophy, Niccoló Machiavelli. Machiavelli is known at present primarily as the author of a number of shockingly frank maxims
about the ruthless nature of politics, for example that it is better
to be feared than loved, or that one should keep one's word only
when it is in one's interest to do so. Machiavelli was the founder of
modern political philosophy, who believed that man could become master of his own earthly house if he took his cues not from
the way men ought to live, but the way they actually live. Rather
than trying to make human beings good through education, as
Plato taught, Machiavelli sought to create a good political order
out of man's badness: badness could be made to serve good ends
if it were channeled through the appropriate institutions.[8]

Machiavelli understood that *megalothymia* in the form of the
desire for glory was the basic psychological drive behind the ambition of princes. Nations may on occasion conquer their neighbors as a matter of necessity, in self-defense, or to build up
population and resources for the future. But above and beyond
such considerations was the desire of man to be recognized—the
pleasure that a Roman general felt during his triumph when his
opponent was paraded through the streets in chains to the cheers
of the multitude. For Machiavelli, the desire for glory was not an
exclusive characteristic of princes or aristocratic governments. It
infected republics as well, as in the case of the rapacious Athenian
and Roman empires, where democratic participation had the effect of increasing the state's ambition and providing a more effective military instrument for expansion.[9]

While the desire for glory is a universal characteristic of
man,[10] Machiavelli saw that it created special problems by leading
ambitious men to tyranny, and the rest to slavery. His solution to
this problem was different from Plato's, and became characteristic
of subsequent republican constitutionalism. Rather than try to
educate the thymotic princes or guardians, as Plato had suggested,
thymos would be counterpoised to *thymos*. Mixed republics, in which
the thymotic ambitions of princes and the aristocratic few could
be balanced against the thymotic desire for independence on the
part of the people, could ensure a degree of liberty.[11] Machiavelli's mixed republic was, therefore, an early version of the separation of powers familiar in the American Constitution.

After Machiavelli there began another, perhaps more ambitious project with which we are already familiar. Hobbes and

Locke, the founders of modern liberalism, sought to eradicate *thymos* from political life altogether, and to replace it with a combination of desire and reason. These early modern English liberals saw *megalothymia* in the form of passionate and stubborn pride of princes, or the otherworldly fanaticism of militant priests, as the chief cause of war, and in the process took aim at all forms of pride. Their denigration of aristocratic pride was continued by any number of Enlightenment writers, including Adam Ferguson, James Steuart, David Hume, and Montesquieu. In the civil society envisioned by Hobbes, Locke, and other early modern liberal thinkers, man needs only desire and reason. The *bourgeois* was an entirely deliberate creation of early modern thought, an effort at social engineering that sought to create social peace by changing human nature itself. Instead of pitting the *megalothymia* of the few against that of the many, as Machiavelli had suggested, the founders of modern liberalism hoped to overcome *megalothymia* altogether by pitting, in effect, the interests of the desiring part of human nature against the passions of its thymotic part.[12]

The social embodiment of *megalothymia*, and the social class against which modern liberalism declared war, was the traditional aristocracy. The aristocratic warrior did not create wealth, he stole it from other warriors, or more precisely from the peasantry whose surplus he appropriated. He did not act on the basis of economic rationality, selling his labor to the highest bidder: indeed, he did not work at all but fulfilled himself in his leisure. His behavior was fenced in by dictates of pride and codes of honor, which did not permit him to do things beneath his dignity like engage in commerce. And for all the decadence of many aristocratic societies, the core of the aristocrat's being was related, as for Hegel's primordial master, to his willingness to risk his life in a bloody battle. War therefore remained central to the aristocratic way of life, and war, as we well know, is "economically suboptimal." Much better, then, to convince the aristocratic warrior of the vanity of his ambitions, and to transform him into a peaceful businessman, whose self-enriching activities would serve to enrich those around him as well.[13]

The "modernization" process described by contemporary social science can be understood as the gradual victory of the desiring part of the soul, guided by reason, over the soul's thymotic part, played out in countless countries around the world. Aristocratic societies were virtually universal across different human cultures, from Europe to the Middle East to Africa to South and East Asia. Economic modernization required not just the creation of modern social structures like cities and rational bureaucracies, but the ethical victory of the bourgeois way of life over the thymotic life of the aristocrat. In one society after another, Hobbes's deal has been offered to the old class of aristocrats: namely, that they trade in their thymotic pride for the prospect of a peaceful life of unlimited material acquisition. In some countries like Japan, this trade was made overtly: the modernizing state set up members of the former *samurai* or warrior class as businessmen, whose enterprises grew into the twentieth-century *zaibatsus*.[14] In countries like France, the trade was declined by many parts of the aristocracy, which fought a series of hopeless rearguard actions to preserve their thymotic ethical order. That struggle continues today in many Third World countries, where the descendants of warriors face the same decision as to whether they should hang up their swords as family heirlooms and take up instead the computer terminal and office.

By the time we arrive at the American founding, the victory of Lockean principles in North America—and thereby the victory of the desiring part of the soul over the thymotic part—was almost complete. The right to "the pursuit of happiness" proclaimed in the American Declaration of Independence was conceived largely in terms of the acquisition of property. Lockeanism is the broad framework for the *Federalist* papers, that great defense of the American Constitution written by Alexander Hamilton, James Madison, and John Jay. For example, in the famous *Federalist* 10, which defends representative government as the cure for popular government's disease of faction, James Madison asserts that protection of man's diverse faculties, and particularly the "different and unequal faculties of acquiring property," was the "first object of government."[15]

While the American Constitution's Lockean heritage is undeniable, the authors of the *Federalist* nonetheless demonstrated an awareness that the desire for recognition could not simply be banished from political life. Indeed, prideful self-assertion was understood to be one end of or motive for political life, and good government required that it have adequate scope. They sought to channel the desire for recognition into positive or at least harmless directions, much as Machiavelli had sought to do. While Madison referred to factions based on economic "interests" in *Federalist* 10, he distinguished them from other factions based on "passions," or more precisely, people's passionate opinions about right and wrong: "A zeal for different opinions concerning religion, concerning government, and many other points" or "an attachment to different leaders." Political opinions were an expression of self-love, and became inextricably bound up with a person's evaluation of himself and his own worth: "As long as the connection subsists between his reason and his self-love, [man's] opinions and his passions will have a reciprocal influence on each other; and the former will be objects to which the latter will attach themselves."[16] Thus factions result not just from the clash between the desiring parts of different men's souls (i.e., economic interests), but between their thymotic parts as well.[17] And so in Madison's day, American politics was dominated by differences over issues like temperance, religion, slavery, and the like, just as ours is dominated by abortion rights, school prayer, and freedom of speech.

In addition to the myriad of passionate opinions that will be asserted by a large number of relatively weak individuals, the authors of the *Federalist* believed that political life had to contend with the "love of fame" which was, according to Hamilton, "the ruling passion of the noblest minds"[18]—that is, the desire for glory on the part of strong and ambitious men. *Megalothymia* as well as *isothymia* remained a problem for the founders. The American Constitution was seen by Madison and Hamilton as an institutional means not of repressing these different expressions of *thymos*, but rather of channeling them into safe, indeed productive, outlets. Thus Madison saw popular government—the process of running for office, making political speeches, debating, writing editorials, voting in elections, and the like—as a benign way to indulge man's natural pride and inclination toward thymotic self-assertion, provided it could be spread out over a relatively large republic. The democratic political process was important not just as a means of making decisions or "aggregating interests," but *as a process*, that is, as a stage for the expression of *thymos*, where men could seek recognition for their own views. On the higher and potentially more dangerous level of the *megalothymia* of great and ambitious men, constitutional government was explicitly established as a way of using ambition "to counteract ambition." The different branches of government were seen as avenues for the advancement of powerful ambitions, but the system of checks and balances would ensure that these ambitions canceled each other out and prevented the emergence of tyranny. An American politician could harbor ambitions to be a Caesar or a Napoleon, but the system would allow him or her to be no more than a Jimmy Carter or Ronald Reagan—hemmed in by powerful institutional constraints and political forces on all sides, and forced to realize their ambition by being the people's "servant" rather than their master.

The attempt of liberal politics in the Hobbes-Locke tradition to banish the desire for recognition from politics or to leave it constrained and impotent left many thinkers feeling quite uneasy. Modern society would henceforth be composed of what C. S. Lewis called "men without chests": that is, people who were composed entirely of desire and reason, but lacking that proud self-assertiveness that was somehow at the core of man's humanity in earlier ages. For the chest was what made man man: "by his intellect he is mere spirit and by his appetite mere animal."[19] The greatest and most articulate champion of *thymos* in modern times, and the prophet of its revival, was Friedrich Nietzsche, the godfather of present-day relativism and nihilism. Nietzsche was once described by a contemporary as an "aristocratic radical," a characterization he did not dispute. Much of his work can be seen, in a certain sense, as a reaction to what he saw as the rise of an entire civilization of "men without chests," a society of *bourgeois* who aspired to nothing more than their own comfortable self-preservation. For Nietzsche, the very essence of man was neither his desire nor his reason, but his *thymos*: man was above all a *valuing* creature, the "beast with red cheeks" who found life in his ability to pronounce the words "good" and "evil." As his character Zarathustra says,

> Verily, men gave themselves their good and evil. Verily, they did not take it, they did not find it, nor did it come to them as a voice from heaven. Only man placed values in things to preserve himself—he alone created a meaning for things, a human meaning. Therefore he calls himself "man," which means: the esteemer.
>
> To esteem is to create: hear this, you creators! Esteeming itself is of all esteemed things the most estimable treasure.

> Through esteeming alone is there value: and without esteem-
> ing, the nut of existence would be hollow. Hear this, you
> creators![20]

Which values men created was not, for Nietzsche, the central
issue, for there were a "thousand and one goals" which men followed. Each of the peoples of the earth had its own "language of
good and evil," which their neighbors could not understand. What
constituted the essence of man was the act of valuing itself, of
giving oneself worth and demanding recognition for it.[21] The act
of evaluating was inherently inegalitarian, for it required distin-
guishing between better and worse. And therefore Nietzsche was
interested only in the manifestation of *thymos* that led men to say
that they were better than others, *megalothymia*. The terrible consequence of modernity was the effort of its creators Hobbes and
Locke to strip man of his evaluative powers in the name of physical security and material accumulation. Nietzsche's well-known
doctrine of the "will to power" can be understood as the effort to
reassert the primacy of *thymos* as against desire and reason, and to
undo the damage that modern liberalism had done to man's pride
and self-assertiveness. His work is a celebration of Hegel's aristocratic master and his struggle to the death for pure prestige, and
a thunderous condemnation of a modernity that had so fully accepted the morality of the slave that it was not even aware such a
choice had been made.

Despite the changing vocabulary that has been used to describe the phenomenon of *thymos* or the desire for recognition, it
should be very clear that this "third part" of the soul has been a
central concern of the philosophical tradition that stretches from
Plato to Nietzsche. It suggests a very different way of reading the
historical process, not as the story of the unfolding of modern
natural science or of the logic of economic development, but
rather as the emergence, growth, and eventual decline of *megalothymia*. Indeed, the modern economic world could only emerge
after desire had been liberated, so to speak, at the expense of
thymos. The historical process that begins with the master's bloody
battle ends in some sense with the modern *bourgeois* inhabitant of
contemporary liberal democracies, who pursues material gain
rather than glory.

Today nobody studies the *thymos* systematically as part of their
education, and the "struggle for recognition" is not part of our

contemporary political vocabulary. The desire for glory that for Machiavelli was so normal a part of the human makeup—that inordinate striving to be better than others, to make as many people as possible recognize one's superiority—is no longer an acceptable way to describe one's personal goals. It is in fact a characteristic we attribute to people that we don't like, those tyrants who have arisen among us like Hitler, Stalin, or Saddam Hussein. *Megalothymia*—the desire to be recognized as superior—lives on under a variety of guises in day-to-day life, and, as we shall see in Part Five, much of what we find satisfying in our lives would not be possible without it. But in terms of what we say about ourselves, it has been ethically vanquished in the modern world.

The attack on *megalothymia* and its lack of respectability in our present-day world therefore should incline us to agree with Nietzsche that those early modern philosophers who wanted to banish the more visible forms of *thymos* from civil society have been quite successful. What has taken the place of *megalothymia* is a combination of two things. The first is a blossoming of the desiring part of the soul, which manifests itself as a thorough-going *economization* of life. This economization extends from the highest things to the lowest, from the states of Europe who seek not greatness and empire, but a more integrated European Community in 1992, to the college graduate who performs an internal cost-benefit analysis of the career options open to him or her.

The second thing that remains in place of *megalothymia* is an all-pervasive *isothymia*, that is, the desire to be recognized as the equal of other people. This in its various manifestations includes the *thymos* of Havel's greengrocer, the anti-abortion protester, or the animal rights advocate. While we do not use the words "recognition" and "*thymos*" to describe our personal goals, we do use words like "dignity," "respect," "self-respect," and "self-esteem" all too frequently, and these non-material factors even enter into the career calculations of the typical college graduate. Such concepts permeate our political life and are indispensable to an understanding of the democratic transformation that has occurred around the world in the late twentieth century.

We are thus left with an apparent contradiction. The founders of the Anglo-Saxon tradition of modern liberalism sought to banish *thymos* from political life, and yet the desire for recognition remains all around us in the form of *isothymia*. Was this an unexpected outcome, the result of failure to suppress what ultimately could not be suppressed in human nature? Or is there a higher understanding of modern liberalism that tries to preserve the thymotic side of the human personality rather than exiling it from the realm of politics?

There is in fact such a higher understanding, and to see it, we must return to Hegel and to the unfinished account of his historical dialectic in which the struggle for recognition plays a key role.

18

Lordship and Bondage

The complete, absolutely free man, definitively and completely satisfied by what he is, the man who is perfected and completed in and by this satisfaction, will be the Slave who has "overcome" his Slavery. If idle Mastery is an impasse, laborious Slavery, in contrast, is the source of all human, social, historical progress. History is the history of the working Slave.

—*Alexandre Kojève,* Introduction to the Reading of Hegel[1]

We left off our account of the Hegelian dialectic several chapters ago at a very early point in the historical process—in fact, at the conclusion of the beginning period of human history, when man first risked his life in a battle for pure prestige. The state of war that prevailed in Hegel's "state of nature" (remembering that Hegel himself never used such a term) did not lead directly to the establishment of civil society based on a social contract, as it did for Locke. Rather, it led to the relationship of lordship and bondage, when one of the primordial combatants, fearing for his life, "recognized" the other and agreed to be his slave. The social relationship of lordship and bondage was not a stable one in the long term, however, because neither the master nor the slave was ultimately satisfied in his desire for recognition.[2] This absence of satisfaction constituted a "contradiction" in slave-owning societies, and generated the impulse toward further historical progress. Man's first human act may have been his willingness to risk his life in the bloody battle, but he did not thereby become a fully free and therefore satisfied man. This could come about only in the course of subsequent historical evolution.[3]

The master and the slave are left unsatisfied for different

192

reasons. The master is in some sense more human than the slave because he is willing to overcome his biological nature for the sake of a non-biological end, recognition. By risking his life, he demonstrates that he is free. The slave, by contrast, follows Hobbes's advice and gives in to his fear of violent death. In so doing he remains a needy and fearful animal, incapable of overcoming his biological or natural determination. But the slave's lack of freedom, his incomplete humanity, is the source of the master's dilemma. For the master desires recognition by another human being, that is, recognition of his worth and human dignity by another human being possessing worth and dignity. But by winning the prestige battle, he is recognized by one who has become a slave, whose humanity was unachieved due to his having given in to his natural fear of death. The master's worth is therefore recognized by someone not quite human.[4]

This corresponds to our own commonsense experience of recognition: we value praise or recognition of our worth much more highly if it comes from somebody we respect, or whose judgment we trust, and most of all if it is freely given rather than coerced. Our pet dog "recognizes" us in some sense when he wags his tail in greeting when we come home; but he recognizes everybody as well in a similar fashion—the postman, or a burglar—because the dog is instinctually conditioned to do so. Or, to take a more political example, the satisfaction of a Stalin or a Saddam Hussein on hearing the adulation of a crowd that has been bused into a stadium and forced to cheer on pain of death is presumably less than that experienced by a democratic leader like a Washington or a Lincoln when accorded genuine respect by a free people.

This then constitutes the tragedy of the master: he risks his life for the sake of recognition on the part of a slave who is not worthy of recognizing him. The master remains less than satisfied. Moreover, the master remains fundamentally unchanging over time. He does not need to work, because he has a slave to work for him, and he has easy access to all of the things that are necessary to maintain his life. His life therefore becomes a static and unchanging one of leisure and consumption; he can be killed, as Kojève points out, but he cannot be educated. The master can of course risk his life again and again in mortal combats with other masters, for control of a province or for the succession to someone's throne. But the act of risking one's life, while deeply human, is also perpetually identical to itself. The ceaseless conquest and re-conquest of provinces does not change man's qualitative relationship to other men or to his natural environment, and therefore does not provide a motor for historical progress.

The slave is also unsatisfied. His lack of satisfaction, however, leads not to deadening stasis, as in the case of the master, but to creative and enriching change. By submitting to the master, the slave of course is not recognized as a human being: on the contrary, he is treated as a *thing*, a tool for the satisfaction of the master's wants. Recognition is entirely one-way. But this total absence of recognition is what leads the slave to desire change.

The slave recovers his humanity, the humanity he lost on account of the fear of violent death, through *work*.[5] Initially, the slave is forced to work for the master's satisfaction on account of the former's fear of death. But the motive for his labor eventually changes. Instead of working for fear of immediate punishment, he begins to do it out of a sense of duty and self-discipline, in the course of which he learns to suppress his animal desires for the sake of work.[6] In other words, he develops something like a work ethic. More importantly, through work the slave begins to realize that as a human being, he is capable of transforming nature, that is, of taking the materials of nature and freely changing them into something else based on a pre-existing idea or concept. The slave uses tools; he can use tools to make tools, and thereby invents technology. Modern natural science is not the invention of idle masters, who have everything they want, but of slaves who are forced to work and who do not like their present condition. Through science and technology, the slave discovers that he can change nature, not only the physical environment into which he is born, but his own nature as well.[7]

For Hegel, in contrast to Locke, work became totally liberated from nature. The point of work was not simply to satisfy natural needs, or even newly minted desires. Work itself represented freedom because it demonstrated man's ability to overcome natural determination, to create through his labor. There was no such thing as work "in accordance with nature"; truly human work began only when man demonstrated his mastery over nature. Hegel also had a very different understanding of the meaning of private property than did Locke. Lockean man acquired property in order to satisfy his desires; Hegelian man sees property as a kind of "objectification" of himself in a thing—for example, a house, a car, a piece of land. Property is not an intrinsic characteristic of things; it exists only as a matter of social convention when men agree to respect each other's property rights. Man derives satisfaction owning property not only for the needs that it satisfies, but because other men recognize it. The protection of private property is a legitimate end of civil society for Hegel, as it is for Locke and for Madison. But Hegel sees property as a stage or aspect of the historical struggle for recognition, as something that satisfies *thymos* as well as desire.[8]

The master demonstrates his freedom by risking his life in a bloody battle, thereby indicating his superiority to natural determination. The slave, by contrast, conceives of the *idea* of freedom by working for the master, and in the process realizes that as a human being he is capable of free and creative labor. The slave's mastery of nature is the key to his understanding of mastery *tout court*. The potential freedom of the slave is historically much more significant than the actual freedom of the master. The master *is* free; he enjoys his freedom in an immediate, unreflective sense by doing what he pleases and consuming what he wants. On the other hand, the slave only conceives of the *idea* of freedom, an idea that occurs to him as a result of his work. The slave, however, is not free in his own life; there is a discrepancy between his idea of freedom and his actual condition. The slave is therefore more philosophic: he must consider freedom in the abstract before he is able to enjoy it in reality, and must invent for himself the principles of a free society before living in one. The slave's consciousness is therefore higher than the consciousness of the master, because it is more self-conscious, that is, reflective of itself and its own condition.

The principles of 1776 or 1789, of liberty and equality, did not spring into the heads of slaves spontaneously. The slave does not begin by challenging the master, but rather goes through a long and painful process of self-education as he teaches himself to overcome his fear of death and claim his rightful freedom. The slave, reflecting on his condition and the abstract *idea* of freedom, throws up several preliminary versions of freedom before he hits on the right one. The preliminary versions are for Hegel as for Marx *ideologies*, that is, intellectual constructs not true in themselves but reflective of the underlying substructure of reality, the reality of lordship and bondage. While containing the germ of the idea of freedom, they serve to reconcile the slave to the reality of his lack of freedom. Hegel in the *Phenomenology* identifies several of these slave ideologies, including philosophies like Stoicism and skepticism. But the most important slave ideology, and the one that leads most directly to the realization of societies based on liberty and equality here on earth, is Christianity, the "absolute religion."

Hegel speaks of Christianity as the "absolute religion" not out of any kind of narrow-minded ethnocentrism, but because of the objective historical relationship that existed between Christian doctrine and the emergence of liberal democratic societies in Western Europe—a relationship that was accepted by any number of later subsequent thinkers such as Weber and Nietzsche. The idea of freedom received its penultimate form in Christianity, according to Hegel, because this religion was the first to establish the principle of the universal equality of all men in the sight of God, on the basis of their faculty for moral choice or belief. That is, Christianity maintained that man was free: free not in the formal Hobbesian sense of freedom from physical constraint, but morally free to choose between right or wrong. Man was fallen, a naked and needy animal, but he was also capable of spiritual regeneration through his capacity for choice and belief. Christian freedom was an inner condition of the spirit, and not an external condition of the body. The thymotic sense of self-worth felt by both Socrates' Leontius and Havel's greengrocer has something in common with the inner dignity and freedom of the Christian believer.

The Christian understanding of freedom implies universal human equality, but for different reasons than for Hobbesian-Lockean liberals. The American Declaration of Independence asserts that "all men are created equal," presumably because they are endowed by their creator with certain inalienable rights. Hobbes and Locke based their belief in human equality on the equality of natural endowments: the former said men were equal because they were equally capable of killing one another, while the latter pointed to their equality of faculties. Locke noted, however, that children are not the equals of their parents, and he like Madison believed that men had unequal faculties for acquiring property. Equality in a Lockean state therefore means something like equality of opportunity.

Christian equality, by contrast, is based on the fact that all men are equally endowed with one specific faculty, the faculty for moral choice.[9] All men can accept or reject God, do good or evil. The Christian perspective on equality is illustrated by Dr. Martin

Luther King's "I have a dream" speech on the steps of the Lincoln Memorial in 1964. In one memorable phrase, he said he had a dream that his four little children "will one day live in a nation where they will not be judged by the color of their skin but by the content of their character." Note that King did not say that they should be judged according to their talent or merit, or that he wanted them to rise as far as their ability would permit. For King, a Christian minister, human dignity did not reside in man's reason or cleverness, but in his character, that is, his moral character, his ability to distinguish right from wrong. People who are manifestly unequal in terms of beauty, talent, intelligence, or skill, are nonetheless equal insofar as they are moral agents. The homeliest and most awkward orphan can have a more beautiful soul in the eyes of God than the most talented pianist or the most brilliant physicist.

Christianity's contribution, then, to the historical process was to make clear to the slave this vision of human freedom, and to define for him in what sense all men could be understood to have dignity. The Christian God *recognizes* all human beings universally, recognizes their individual human worth and dignity. The Kingdom of Heaven, in other words, presents the prospect of a world in which the *isothymia* of every man—though not the *megalothymia* of the vainglorious—will be satisfied.

The problem with Christianity, however, is that it remains just another slave ideology, that is, it is untrue in certain crucial respects. Christianity posits the realization of human freedom not here on earth but only in the Kingdom of Heaven. Christianity, in other words, had the right *concept* of freedom, but ended up reconciling real-world slaves to their lack of freedom by telling them not to expect liberation in this life. According to Hegel, the Christian did not realize that God did not create man, but rather that man had created God. He created God as a kind of projection of the idea of freedom, for in the Christian God we see a being who is the perfect master of himself and of nature. But the Christian then proceeded to enslave himself to this God that he himself created. He reconciled himself to a life of slavery on earth in the belief that he would be redeemed later by God, when in fact he could be his own redeemer. Christianity was thus a form of *alienation*, that is, a new form of slavery where man enslaved himself to something that he himself created, thereby becoming divided against himself.

The last great slave ideology, Christianity, articulated for the slave a vision of what human freedom should be. Even though it did not provide him with a practical way out of his slavery, it permitted him to see more clearly his objective: the free and autonomous individual who is recognized for his freedom and autonomy, recognized universally and reciprocally by all men. The slave, through his work, did much of the job of liberating himself: he mastered nature and transformed it according to his own ideas, and he came to a self-awareness of the possibility of his own freedom. For Hegel, then, completion of the historical process required only a secularization of Christianity, that is, a translation of the Christian idea of freedom into the here-and-now. It also required one more bloody battle, the battle in which the slave liberates himself from the master. And Hegel regarded his own philosophy as a transformation of Christian doctrine, one that was no longer based on myth and scriptural authority, but on the slave's achievement of absolute knowledge and self-consciousness.

The human historical process started with the battle for pure prestige, in which the aristocratic master sought recognition for his willingness to risk his life. By overcoming his nature, the master showed he was the freer and more authentic human being. But it was the slave and his work, not the master and his fighting, that propelled the historical process forward. The slave initially accepted his slavery out of fear of death, but unlike Hobbes's rational man seeking self-preservation, Hegel's slave was never content with himself. That is, the slave still possessed *thymos*, a sense of his own worth and dignity, and a desire to live something other than a merely slavish life. His *thymos* was expressed in the pride he took in his own work, in his ability to manipulate the "almost worthless materials" of nature and transform them into something bearing his imprint. It was also revealed in the idea he had of freedom: his *thymos* led him to imagine the abstract possibility of a free being with worth and dignity, long before his own worth and dignity were recognized by anyone else. Unlike Hobbes's rational man, he did not try to repress his own pride. On the contrary, he did not feel himself a full human being until he had achieved recognition. It was the slave's continuing desire for recognition that was the motor which propelled history forward, not the idle complacency and unchanging self-identity of the master.

19

The Universal and Homogeneous State

Es ist der Gang Gottes in der Welt, daß der Staat ist.

—G. W. F. Hegel, The Philosophy of Right[1]

For Hegel, the French Revolution was the event that took the Christian vision of a free and equal society, and implemented it here on earth. In making this revolution, the former slaves risked their lives, and in so doing proved that they had overcome the very fear of death that had served originally to define them as slaves. The principles of liberty and equality were then carried to the rest of Europe by Napoleon's victorious armies. The modern liberal democratic state that came into being in the aftermath of the French Revolution was, simply, the realization of the Christian ideal of freedom and universal human equality in the here-and-now. This was not an attempt to deify the state or give it a "metaphysical" significance absent in Anglo-Saxon liberalism. Rather, it constituted a recognition that it was man who had created the Christian God in the first place, and therefore man who could make God come down to earth and live in the parliament buildings, presidential palaces, and bureaucracies of the modern state.

Hegel gives us the opportunity to reinterpret modern liberal democracy in terms that are rather different from the Anglo-Saxon tradition of liberalism emanating from Hobbes and Locke. This Hegelian understanding of liberalism is at the same time a more noble vision of what liberalism represents, and a more accurate account of what people around the world mean when they

199

say they want to live in a democracy. For Hobbes and Locke, and for their followers who wrote the American Constitution and Declaration of Independence, liberal society was a social contract between individuals who possessed certain natural rights, chief among which were the right to life—that is, self-preservation—and to the pursuit of happiness, which was generally understood as the right to private property. Liberal society is thus a reciprocal and equal agreement among citizens not to interfere with each other's lives and property.

For Hegel, by contrast, liberal society is a reciprocal and equal agreement among citizens to mutually recognize each other. If Hobbesian or Lockean liberalism can be interpreted as the pursuit of rational self-interest, Hegelian "liberalism" can be seen as the pursuit of *rational recognition*, that is, recognition on a universal basis in which the dignity of each person as a free and autonomous human being is recognized by all. What is at stake for us when we choose to live in a liberal democracy is not merely the fact that it allows us the freedom to make money and satisfy the desiring parts of our souls. The more important and ultimately more satisfying thing it provides us is recognition of our dignity. Life in a liberal democracy is potentially the road to great material abundance, but it also shows us the way to the completely non-material end of recognition of our freedom. The liberal democratic state values us at our own sense of self-worth. Thus both the desiring and thymotic parts of our souls find satisfaction.

Universal recognition solves the severe defect in recognition that existed in slave-holding societies and its many variants. Virtually every society prior to the French Revolution was either a monarchy or aristocracy, in which either one person (the king), or a few persons (the "ruling class" or the elite), were recognized. Their satisfaction at being recognized came at the expense of the great mass of people whose humanity was not acknowledged in return. Recognition could be rationalized only if it were put on a universal and equal basis. The internal "contradiction" of the master-slave relationship was solved in a state which successfully synthesized the morality of the master and the morality of the slave. The very distinction between masters and slaves was abolished, and the former slaves became the new masters—not of other slaves, but of themselves. This was the meaning of the "Spirit of 1776"—not the victory of yet another group of masters, not the rise of a new slavish consciousness, but the achievement of self-mastery in the form of democratic government. Something of both lordship and bondage was preserved in this new synthesis—the satisfaction of recognition on the part of the master, and the work of the slave.

We can better understand the rationality of the universal recognition by contrasting it with other forms of recognition that are not rational. For example, a nationalist state, that is, a state in which citizenship is restricted to members of a particular national, ethnic, or racial group, constitutes a form of *irrational* recognition. Nationalism is very much a manifestation of the desire for recognition, arising out of *thymos*. The nationalist is primarily preoccupied not with economic gain, but with recognition and dignity.[2] Nationality is not a natural trait; one has nationality only if one is recognized by other people as having it.[3] The recognition one seeks, however, is not for oneself as an individual, but for the group of which one is a member. In a sense, nationalism represents a transmutation of the *megalothymia* of earlier ages into a more modern and democratic form. Instead of individual princes struggling for personal glory, we now have entire nations demanding recognition of their nationhood. Like the aristocratic master, these nations have shown themselves willing to accept the risk of violent death for the sake of recognition, for their "place in the sun."

The desire for recognition based on nationality or race, however, is not a rational one. The distinction between human and non-human is fully rational: only human beings are free, that is, able to struggle for recognition in a battle for pure prestige. This distinction is based on nature, or rather, on the radical disjunction between the realm of nature and the realm of freedom. The distinction between one human group and another, on the other hand, is an accidental and arbitrary by-product of human history. And the struggle between national groups for recognition of their national dignity leads, on an international scale, to the same impasse as the prestige battle between aristocratic masters: one or another nation becomes a master, so to speak, and the other becomes a slave. The recognition available to either is defective for the same reasons that the original, individual relationship of lordship and bondage was unsatisfactory.

The liberal state, on the other hand, is rational because it reconciles these competing demands for recognition on the only mutually acceptable basis possible, that is, on the basis of the individual's identity as a human being. The liberal state must be *universal*, that is, grant recognition to all citizens because they are human beings, and not because they are members of some particular national, ethnic, or racial group. And it must be *homogeneous* insofar as it creates a classless society based on the abolition of the distinction between masters and slaves. The rationality of this universal and homogeneous state is further evident in the fact that it is consciously founded on the basis of open and publicized principles, such as occurred in the course of the constitutional convention that led to the birth of the American republic. That is, the authority of the state does not arise out of age-old tradition or from the murky depths of religious faith, but as the result of a public debate in which the citizens of the state agree amongst one another on the explicit terms under which they will live together. It represents a form of rational self-consciousness because for the first time human beings as a society are aware of their own true natures, and are able to fashion a political community that exists in conformity with those natures.

In what way can we say that modern liberal democracy "recognizes" all human beings universally?

It does this by granting and protecting their *rights*. That is, any human child born on the territory of the United States or France or any of a number of other liberal states is by that very act endowed with certain rights of citizenship. No one may harm the life of that child, whether he or she is poor or rich, black or white, without being prosecuted by the criminal justice system. In time, that child will have the right to own property, which must be respected both by the state and by fellow citizens. This child will have the right to have thymotic options (i.e., opinions concerning value and worth) about any topic he or she conceives, and will have the right to publish and disseminate those opinions as broadly as possible. These thymotic opinions can take the form of religious belief, which may be exercised with complete freedom. And finally, when this child reaches adulthood, he or she will have the right to participate in the very government that establishes these rights in the first place, and to contribute to deliberations on the highest and most important questions of public policy. This participation can take the form of either voting in periodic elections, or the more active form of entering into the political process directly, for instance by running for office, or writing editorials in support of a person or position, or by serving in a public-sector bureaucracy. Popular self-government abolishes the distinction between masters and slaves; everyone is entitled to at least some share in the role of master. Mastery now takes the form of the promulgation of democratically determined laws, that is, sets of universal rules by which man self-consciously masters himself. Recognition becomes *reciprocal* when the state and the people recognize each other, that is, when the state grants its citizens rights and when citizens agree to abide by the state's laws. The only limitations on these rights occur when they become self-contradictory, in other words, when the exercise of one right interferes with the exercise of another.

This description of the Hegelian state sounds virtually identical to the Lockean liberal state, which is similarly defined as a system for protecting a set of individual rights. The Hegel specialist will immediately object that Hegel was critical of Lockean or Anglo-Saxon liberalism, and would have rejected the notion that a Lockean United States of America or England constituted the final stage of history. He would of course be right in a certain sense. Hegel would never have endorsed the view of certain liberals in the Anglo-Saxon tradition, now primarily represented on the libertarian Right, who believe that government's only purpose is to get out of the way of individuals, and that the latter's freedom to pursue their selfish private interests is absolute. He would have rejected the version of liberalism that viewed political rights simply as a means by which men could protect their lives and their money or, in more contemporary language, their personal "lifestyles."

On the other hand, Kojève identified an important truth when he asserted that postwar America or the members of the European Community constituted the embodiment of Hegel's state of universal recognition. For while the Anglo-Saxon democracies may have been founded on explicitly Lockean grounds, their self-understanding has never been purely Lockean. We have seen, for example, how both Madison and Hamilton in the *Federalist* took account of the thymotic side of human nature, and how the former believed that one of the purposes of representative government was to give an outlet to men's thymotic and passionate opinions. When people in contemporary America talk about their society and form of government, they frequently use language that is more Hegelian than Lockean. For example, during the civil

rights era, it was perfectly normal for people to say that the purpose of a particular piece of civil rights legislation was to recognize
the dignity of black people, or to fulfill the promise of the Declaration of Independence and the Constitution to allow all Americans to live in dignity and freedom. One did not need to be a
Hegel scholar to understand the force of this argument; it was
part of the vocabulary of the least educated and most humble
citizen. (The constitution of the Federal Republic of Germany
makes explicit reference to human dignity.) The right to vote, in
the United States and in other democratic countries, first for
people who did not meet property qualifications, then for blacks
and other ethnic or racial minorities, and for women, was never
seen as an exclusively economic matter (i.e., that the right to
vote allowed these groups to protect their economic interests),
but was generally perceived as a symbol of their worth and
equality, and was valued as an end in itself. The fact that the
American Founding Fathers did not use the terms "recognition"
and "dignity" did not prevent the Lockean language of rights
from sliding effortlessly and invisibly into the Hegelian language
of recognition.

The universal and homogeneous state that appears at the end
of history can thus be seen as resting on the twin pillars of economics and recognition. The human historical process that leads
up to it has been driven forward equally by the progressive unfolding of modern natural science, and by the struggle for recognition. The former emanates from the desiring part of the soul,
which was liberated in early modern times and turned to the
unlimited accumulation of wealth. This unlimited accumulation
was made possible because of an alliance that was formed between
desire and reason: capitalism is inextricably bound to modern
natural science. The struggle for recognition, on the other hand,
originated in the thymotic part of the soul. It was driven forward
by the reality of slavery, which contrasted with the slave's vision of
mastery in a world where all men were free and equal in the sight
of God. A full description of the historical process—a true Universal History—cannot really be complete without giving an account of both of these pillars, just as a description of the human
personality is not complete that does not take account of desire,
reason, and *thymos*. Marxism, "modernization theory," or any
other theory of history based primarily on economics will be radically incomplete unless it takes account of the thymotic part of

the soul, and of the struggle for recognition as a major driver of history.

We are now in a position to explicate more fully the interrelationship between liberal economics and liberal politics, and to give an account of the high degree of correlation between advanced industrialization and liberal democracy. There is, as stated earlier, no *economic* rationale for democracy; if anything, democratic politics is a drag on economic efficiency. The choice of democracy is an autonomous one, undertaken for the sake of recognition and not for the sake of desire.

But economic development creates certain conditions that make that autonomous choice more likely. This happens for two reasons. In the first place, economic development demonstrates to the slave the concept of mastery, as he discovers he can master nature through technology, and master himself as well through the discipline of work and education. As societies become better educated, slaves have the opportunity to become more conscious of the fact that they are slaves and would like to be masters, and to absorb the ideas of other slaves who have reflected on their condition of servitude. Education teaches them that they are human beings with dignity, and that they ought to struggle to have that dignity recognized. The fact that modern education teaches the ideas of liberty and equality is not accidental; these are slave ideologies that have been thrown up in reaction to the real situation in which slaves found themselves. Christianity and communism were both slave ideologies (the latter unanticipated by Hegel) that captured part of the truth. But in the course of time the irrationalities and self-contradictions of both were revealed: Communist societies, in particular, despite their commitment to principles of freedom and equality, were exposed as modern variants of slave-holding ones, in which the dignity of the great mass of people went unrecognized. The collapse of Marxist ideology in the late 1980s reflected, in a sense, the achievement of a higher level of rationality on the part of those who lived in such societies, and their realization that rational universal recognition could be had only in a liberal social order.

The second way in which economic development encourages liberal democracy is because it has a tremendous leveling effect through its need for universal education. Old class barriers are broken down in favor of a general condition of equality of opportunity. While new classes arise based on economic status or education, there is an inherently greater mobility in society that promotes the spread of egalitarian ideas. The economy thus creates a kind of *de facto* equality before such equality arises *de jure*.

If human beings were nothing but reason and desire, they would be perfectly content to live in a South Korea under military dictatorship, or under the enlightened technocratic administration of Francoist Spain, or in a Guomindang-led Taiwan, hellbent on rapid economic growth. And yet, citizens of these countries are something more than desire and reason: they have a thymotic pride and belief in their own dignity, and want that dignity to be recognized, above all by the government of the country they live in.

The desire for recognition, then, is the missing link between liberal economics and liberal politics. We have seen how advanced industrialization produces societies that are urban, mobile, increasingly well-educated, and free from traditional forms of authority like that of tribe, priest, or guild. We saw that there was a high degree of empirical correlation between such societies and liberal democracy, without being able to fully explain the reason for that correlation. The weakness in our interpretive framework lay in the fact that we were seeking an economic explanation for the choice of liberal democracy, that is, an explanation that in one way or another arose out of the desiring part of the soul. But we should instead have looked at the thymotic part, at the soul's desire for recognition. For the social changes that accompany advanced industrialization, in particular education, appear to liberate a certain demand for recognition that did not exist among poorer and less educated people. As people become wealthier, more cosmopolitan, and better educated, they demand not simply more wealth but recognition of their status. It is this completely non-economic, non-material drive that can explain why people in Spain, Portugal, South Korea, Taiwan, and the People's Republic of China have all expressed a demand not just for market economics but for free governments by and for the people as well.

Alexandre Kojève, interpreting Hegel, maintained that the universal and homogeneous state would be the last stage in human history because it was *completely satisfying* to man. This was based, in the end, on his belief in the primacy of *thymos*, or the desire for recognition, as the most deep-seated and fundamental human longing. In pointing to the metaphysical, as well as psychological, importance of recognition, Hegel and Kojève perhaps saw more profoundly into the human personality than other philosophers like Locke or Marx, for whom desire and reason were paramount. While Kojève claimed that he had no trans-historical standard by which to measure the adequacy of human institutions, the desire for recognition in fact constituted such a standard. *Thymos* was in the end for Kojève a permanent part of human nature. The struggle for recognition arising out of *thymos* may have required an historical march of ten thousand years or more, but it was no less a constitutive part of the soul for Kojève than for Plato.

Kojève's claim that we are at the end of history therefore stands or falls on the strength of the assertion that the recognition provided by the contemporary liberal democratic state adequately satisfies the human desire for recognition. Kojève believed that modern liberal democracy successfully synthesized the morality of the master and the morality of the slave, overcoming the distinction between them even as it preserves something of both forms of existence. Is this really true? In particular, has the *megalothymia* of the master been successfully sublimated and channeled by modern political institutions so that it no longer presents a problem for contemporary politics? Will man be forever content to be recognized simply as the equal of all other men, or will he not demand more in time? And if *megalothymia* has been so totally sublimated or channeled by modern politics, should we agree with Nietzsche that his is not a cause for celebration, but an unparalleled disaster?

These are very long-term considerations, to which we will return in Part Five of this book.

In the meantime, we will look more closely at the actual transition in consciousness as it moves toward liberal democracy. The desire for recognition can take a variety of irrational forms before it is transformed into universal and equal recognition, such as those represented under the broad rubrics of religion and nationalism. That transition is never a smooth one, and it turns out that rational recognition co-exists with irrational forms in most real-word societies. More than that: the emergence and durability of a society embodying rational recognition appears to *require* the survival of certain forms of irrational recognition, a paradox that Kojève does not fully address.

In the preface to the *Philosophy of Right*, Hegel explains that philosophy "is its own time apprehended in thought," and that as a philosopher one can no more go beyond one's time and predict the future than a man could leap over the giant statue that once stood on the island of Rhodes. Despite this warning we will look ahead to try to understand both the prospects and limitations of the current worldwide liberal revolution, and what effect it will have on international relations.

Part IV
LEAPING OVER RHODES

Hic Rhodus, hic saltus

20

The Coldest of
All Cold Monsters

Somewhere there are still peoples and herds, but not where we live, my brothers: here there are states. State? What is that? Well then, open your ears to me, for now I shall speak to you about the death of peoples.

State is the name of the coldest of all cold monsters. Coldly it tells lies too; and this lie crawls out of its mouth: "I, the state, am the people." This is a lie! It was creators who created peoples and hung a faith and a love over them: thus they served life.

It is annihilators who set traps for the many and call them "state": they hang a sword and a hundred appetites over them . . .

This sign I give you: every people speaks its language of good and evil, which the neighbor does not understand. It has invented its own language of customs and rights. But the state tells lies in all the languages of good and evil; and whatever it says it lies—and whatever it has it has stolen.

—Nietzsche, Thus Spoke Zarathustra[1]

At the end of history, there are no serious ideological competitors left to liberal democracy. In the past, people rejected liberal democracy because they believed that it was inferior to monarchy, aristocracy, theocracy, fascism, communist totalitarianism, or whatever ideology they happened to believe in. But now, outside the Islamic world, there appears to be a general consensus that accepts liberal democracy's claims to be the most rational form of government, that is, the state that realizes most fully either ratio-

211

nal desire or rational recognition. If this is so, why then are all
countries outside the Islamic world not democratic? Why does the
transition to democracy remain so difficult for many nations
whose people and leaderships have accepted democratic principles in the abstract? Why do we have the suspicion that certain
regimes around the world currently proclaiming themselves democratic are unlikely to remain that way, while others are scarcely
conceivable as anything other than stable democracies? And why
is the current trend toward liberalism eventually likely to recede,
even if it promises to be victorious in the long run?

The founding of a liberal democracy is meant to be a su-
premely rational political act, in which the community as a whole
deliberates on the nature of the constitution and set of basic laws
that will govern its public life. But one is frequently struck by the
weakness of both reason and politics to achieve their ends, and for
human beings to "lose control" of their lives, not just on a personal but on a political level. For example, many countries in
Latin America were established as liberal democracies shortly after winning independence from Spain or Portugal in the nineteenth century, with constitutions modeled on those of the United
States or Republican France. And yet, not one of them has succeeded in maintaining an unbroken democratic tradition up to
the present. Opposition to liberal democracy in Latin America on
a theoretical level has never been strong, except for brief challenges from fascism and communism, and yet liberal democrats
have faced an uphill battle winning and keeping power. There are
a number of nations like Russia which have known a variety of
authoritarian forms of government, but until recently never true
democracy. Other nations like Germany have had terrible difficulties achieving stable democracy, despite their firm rooting in
the Western European tradition, while France, the birthplace of
liberty and equality, has seen five different democratic republics
come and go since 1789. These cases stand in sharp contrast to the
experience of most democracies of Anglo-Saxon origin, which
have had a relatively easy time maintaining the stability of their
institutions.

The reason why liberal democracy has not become universal,
or remained stable once it has achieved power, lies ultimately in
the incomplete correspondence between peoples and states. States
are purposeful political creations, while peoples are pre-existing
moral communities. That is, peoples are communities with com-

mon beliefs about good and evil, about the nature of the sacred
and the profane, which may have arisen from a deliberate founding in the distant past but which now exist largely as a matter of
tradition. As Nietzsche says, "every people speaks its language of
good and evil," and has "invented its own language of customs
and rights" that are reflected not just in the constitution and laws,
but in the family, in religion, in class structure, in the daily habits
and the ways of life that are honored. The realm of states is the
realm of the political, the sphere of self-conscious choice about
the proper mode of governance. The realm of peoples is sub-
political: it is the domain of culture and of society, whose rules are
seldom explicit or self-consciously recognized even by those who
participate in them. When Tocqueville talks about America's constitutional system of checks and balances, or the division of re-
sponsibilities between federal and state government, he is talking
about states; but when he describes the sometimes fanatical spir-
itualism of Americans, their passion for equality, or the fact that
they are addicted to practical rather than theoretical science, he is
describing them as a people.

States impose themselves on top of peoples. In some cases, the
state forms the people, as the laws of Lycurgus and Romulus were
held to have formed the *ethos* of the people of Sparta and Rome,
respectively, or as the rule of liberty and equality has shaped a
democratic consciousness among the various immigrant peoples
making up the United States of America. But states in many cases
sit in uneasy tension with peoples, and in some instances might be
said to be at war with their peoples—as when the Russian and
Chinese communists sought forcibly to convert their populations
to Marxist ideals. The success and the stability of liberal democracy therefore never depends simply on the mechanical application of a certain set of universal principles and laws, but requires
a degree of conformity between peoples and states.

If we, following Nietzsche, define a people as a moral community sharing ideas of good and evil, then it becomes clear that
peoples, and the cultures they create, originate in the thymotic
part of the soul. That is to say, *culture* arises out of the capacity to
evaluate, to say for instance that the person who defers to his
elders is worthy, or that the human being who eats unclean animals like pigs is not. *Thymos* or the desire for recognition is thus
the seat of what social scientists call "values." It was the struggle
for recognition, as we have seen, that produced the relationship

of lordship and bondage in all of its various manifestations, and
the moral codes that arose out of it—the deference of a subject to
his monarch, the peasant to his landlord, the haughty superiority
of the aristocrat, and so forth.

The desire for recognition is also the psychological seat of two
extremely powerful passions—religion and nationalism. By this I
do not mean that religion and nationalism can be reduced to the
desire for recognition; but the rootedness of these passions in
thymos is what gives them their great power. The religious believer
assigns dignity to whatever his religion holds sacred—a set of
moral laws, a way of life, or particular objects of worship. He
grows angry when the dignity of what he holds sacred is violated.[2]
The nationalist believes in the dignity of his national or ethnic
group, and therefore in his own dignity *qua* member of that
group. He seeks to have this particular dignity recognized by
others, and, like the religious believer, grows angry if that dignity
is slighted. It was a thymotic passion, the desire for recognition on
the part of the aristocratic master, that started the historical process, and it was the thymotic passions of religious fanaticism and
nationalism that have propelled it along through war and conflict
over the centuries. The thymotic origins of religion and nationalism explain why conflicts over "values" are potentially much
more deadly than conflicts over material possessions or wealth.[3]
Unlike money, which can simply be divided, dignity is something
inherently uncompromisable: either you recognize my dignity, or
the dignity of that which I hold sacred, or you do not. Only *thymos*,
searching for "justice," is capable of true fanaticism, obsession,
and hatred.

Liberal democracy in its Anglo-Saxon variant represents the
emergence of a kind of cold calculation at the expense of earlier
moral and cultural horizons. Rational desire must win out over
the irrational desire for recognition, particularly the *megalothymia*
of prideful masters seeking recognition of their superiority. The
liberal state growing out of the tradition of Hobbes and Locke
engages in a protracted struggle with its own people. It seeks to
homogenize their variegated traditional cultures and to teach
them to calculate instead their own long-term self-interest. In
place of an organic moral community with its own language of
"good and evil," one had to learn a new set of democratic values:
to be "participant," "rational," "secular," "mobile," "empathetic,"
and "tolerant."[4] These new democratic values were initially not

values at all in the sense of defining the final human virtue or
good. They were conceived as having a purely instrumental function, habits that one had to acquire if one was to live successfully
in a peaceful and prosperous liberal society. It was for this reason
that Nietzsche called the state the "coldest of all cold monsters"
that destroyed peoples and their cultures by hanging "a thousand
appetites" in front of them.

For democracy to work, however, citizens of democratic states
must forget the instrumental roots of their values, and develop a
certain irrational thymotic pride in their political system and a
way of life. That is, they must come to love democracy not because
it is necessarily better than the alternatives, but because it is
theirs. Moreover, they must cease to see values like "tolerance" as
merely a means to an end; tolerance in democratic societies becomes the defining virtue.[5] Development of this kind of pride in
democracy, or the assimilation of democratic values into the citizen's sense of his own self, is what is meant by the creation of a
"democratic" or "civic culture." Such a culture is critical to the
long-term health and stability of democracies, since no real-world
society can long survive based on rational calculation and desire
alone.

Culture—in the form of resistance to the transformation of
certain traditional values to those of democracy—thus can constitute an obstacle to democratization. What, then, are some of the
cultural factors that inhibit the establishment of stable liberal democracies?[6] These fall into several categories.

The first has to do with the degree and character of a country's national, ethnic, and racial consciousness. There is nothing
inherently incompatible between nationalism and liberalism; nationalism and liberalism were in fact closely allied in the national
unity struggles of Germany and Italy in the nineteenth century.
Nationalism and liberalism were also associated in Poland's drive
for national rebirth in the 1980s, and are today closely connected
in the independence struggles of the Baltic states from the USSR.
The desire for national independence and sovereignty can be
seen as one possible manifestation of the desire for self-
determination and freedom, provided that nationality, race, or
ethnicity do not become the exclusive basis for citizenship and
legal rights. An independent Lithuania can be a fully liberal state
provided it guarantees the rights of all its citizens, including any
Russian minority that chooses to remain.

On the other hand, democracy is not likely to emerge in a country where the nationalism or ethnicity of its constituent groups is so highly developed that they do not share a sense of nation or accept one another's rights. A strong sense of national unity is therefore necessary prior to the emergence of stable democracy, just as it preceded the emergence of democracy in countries such as Britain, the United States, France, Italy, and Germany. The absence of such a sense of unity in the Soviet Union was one of the reasons why stable democracy could not emerge prior to that country's breakup into smaller national units.[7] Only 11 percent of Peru's population are whites, descended from the Spanish conquerors; the remainder of the population is Indian, separated geographically, economically, and spiritually from the rest of the country. This separation will be a serious long-term obstacle to stable democracy in Peru. The same can be said about South Africa: not only is there a fundamental cleavage between blacks and whites, but the blacks themselves are divided into ethnic groups that have a long history of mutual antagonism.

The second cultural obstacle to democracy has to do with religion. Like nationalism, there is no inherent conflict between religion and liberal democracy, except at the point where religion ceases to be tolerant or egalitarian. We have already noted how Hegel believed that Christianity paved the way for the French Revolution by establishing the principle of the equality of all men on the basis of their capacity for moral choice. A great majority of today's democracies have Christian religious heritages, and Samuel Huntington has pointed out that most of the new democracies since 1970 have been Catholic countries.[8] In some ways, then, religion would appear to be not an obstacle but a spur to democratization.

But religion *per se* did not create free societies; Christianity in a certain sense had to abolish itself through a secularization of its goals before liberalism could emerge. The generally accepted agent for this secularization in the West was Protestantism. By making religion a private matter between the Christian and his God, Protestantism eliminated the need for a separate class of priests, and religious intervention into politics more generally. Other religions around the world have lent themselves to a similar process of secularization: Buddhism and Shinto, for example,

have confined themselves to a domain of private worship centering around the family. The legacy of Hinduism and Confucianism is mixed: while they are both relatively permissive doctrines
that have proven to be compatible with a wide range of secular
activities, the substance of their teachings is hierarchical and inegalitarian. Orthodox Judaism and fundamentalist Islam, by contrast, are totalistic religions which seek to regulate every aspect of
human life, both public and private, including the realm of politics. These religions may be compatible with democracy—Islam,
in particular, establishes no less than Christianity the principle of
universal human equality—but they are very hard to reconcile
with liberalism and the recognition of universal rights, particularly freedom of conscience or religion. It is perhaps not surprising that the only liberal democracy in the contemporary Muslim
world is Turkey, which was the only country to have stuck with an
explicit rejection of its Islamic heritage in favor of a secular society
early in the twentieth century.[9]

The third constraint on the emergence of stable democracy
has to do with the existence of a highly unequal social structure,
and all of the habits of mind that arise from it. According to
Tocqueville, the strength and stability of American democracy
was due to the fact that American society was thoroughly egalitarian and democratic long before the Declaration of Independence and Constitution were written: Americans were "born
equal." That is, the dominant cultural traditions brought to North
America were those of liberal England and Holland, rather than,
say, those of absolutist seventeenth-century Portugal and Spain.
Brazil and Peru, by contrast, inherited highly stratified class structures in which the different classes were mutually hostile and
self-regarding.

Masters and slaves persisted, in other words, in more naked
and deeply rooted forms in some countries than in others. In
many parts of Latin America, as in the American South prior to
the Civil War, overt slavery existed, or else some form of large-
scale hacienda agriculture which tied peasants to a class of landowners in virtual serfdom. This led to the situation described by
Hegel as characteristic of the early periods of lordship and bondage: violent and idle masters, and a class of fearful and dependent
slaves with little concept of their own freedom. By contrast, the
absence of hacienda agriculture in Costa Rica, an isolated and

neglected part of the Spanish Empire, and the equality of poverty that resulted, is one explanation for the relative success of democracy in that country.[10]

A final cultural factor affecting the prospects for stable democracy has to do with a society's ability to autonomously create a healthy civil society—a sphere in which a people are able to exercise Tocqueville's "art of associating," free from reliance on the state. Tocqueville argued that democracy works best when it proceeds not from the top down, but from the bottom up, with the central state arising naturally out of a myriad of local governmental bodies and private associations that serve as schools for freedom and self-mastery. Democracy is, after all, a matter of self-government, and if people are capable of governing themselves in their towns, corporations, professional associations, or universities, they are more likely to succeed in doing so at a national level.

This ability, in turn, has frequently been related to the character of the pre-modern society out of which democracy arose. The argument has been made that those pre-modern societies that were governed by strong, centralized states which systematically destroyed all intermediate sources of power, such as the feudal aristocracy or regional warlords, were more likely to produce authoritarian rule once they modernized than were feudal societies, in which power was divided between the king and a number of powerful feudal chiefs.[11] Thus Russia and China, which were vast, centralized bureaucratic empires in pre-revolutionary times, developed into communist totalitarian states, while England and Japan, which were predominantly feudal, sustained stable democracies.[12] This explanation accounts for the difficulties that West European countries like France and Spain have had establishing stable democracy. In both cases, feudalism was destroyed by a centralizing, modernizing monarchy in the sixteenth and seventeenth centuries, which left these countries with a legacy of strong state power, and a weak and dispirited civil society made dependent on state authority. These centralizing monarchies induced a certain habit of mind where people lost the ability to organize themselves privately and spontaneously, to work together at local levels, and to take responsibility for their own lives. The centralizing tradition in France, where traditionally no road or bridge in any provincial backwater could be built without permission from Paris, continued in an unbroken line from Louis XIII to Napoleon to the current Fifth Republic, where it remains embodied in the *Conseil d'Etat*.[13] Spain bequeathed a similar legacy to many states in Latin America.

The strength of a "democratic" culture often depends heavily on the sequence in which the various elements of liberal democracy came to be. The strongest contemporary liberal democracies—for example, those of Britain or the United States—were ones in which liberalism preceded democracy, or in which freedom preceded equality. That is, liberal rights of free speech, free association, and political participation in government were practiced among a small elite—largely male, white, and landed—before they spread to other parts of the population.[14] The habits of democratic contestation and compromise, where the rights of losers are carefully protected, were more readily learned first by a small, elite group with similar social backgrounds and inclinations, than by a large and heterogeneous society full of, say, long-standing tribal or ethnic hatreds. This kind of sequencing allowed liberal democratic practice to become ingrained and associated with the oldest national traditions. The identification of liberal democracy with patriotism strengthens its thymotic appeal for newly enfranchised groups, and binds them to democratic institutions more firmly than had they participated from the start.

All of these factors—sense of national identity, religion, social equality, the propensity for civil society, and the historical experience of liberal institutions—collectively constitute the culture of a people. The fact that peoples can be so different in these respects accounts for why identical liberal democratic constitutions will work smoothly for some peoples but not for others, or why the same people reject democracy in one age and adopt it without hesitation in another. Any statesman seeking to expand the sphere of liberty and to consolidate its advances must be sensitive to these kinds of subpolitical constraints on the ability of states to arrive at the end of history successfully.

There are, nonetheless, several fallacies about culture and democracy that should be avoided. The first is the notion that cultural factors constitute *sufficient* conditions for the establishment of democracy. Thus one well-known Sovietologist persuaded himself that an effective form of pluralism existed in the Soviet Union during the Brezhnev years simply because the Soviet Union had reached a certain level of urbanization, education, per capita income, secularization, and so forth. But we should remember that

Nazi Germany met virtually all of the cultural preconditions usually put forward as necessary for stable democracy: it was nationally integrated, economically developed, largely Protestant, had a
healthy civil society, and was no more socially inegalitarian than
other countries in Western Europe. And yet the enormous outpouring of thymotic self-assertion and anger that constituted German National Socialism was able to overwhelm completely the
desire for rational and reciprocal recognition.

Democracy can never enter through the back door; at a certain point, it must arise out of a deliberate political decision to
establish democracy. The realm of politics remains autonomous
from that of culture, and has its own special dignity as the point
of intersection between desire, *thymos*, and reason. Stable liberal
democracy cannot come into being without the existence of wise
and effective statesmen who understand the art of politics and are
able to convert the underlying inclinations of peoples into durable
political institutions. Studies of successful transitions to democracy underline the importance of such thoroughly political factors
as the new democratic leadership's ability to neutralize the armed
forces while seeking an accounting for past abuses, its ability to
maintain symbolic continuity (flags, anthems, and the like) with
the past, the nature of the party system that was established, or
whether the democracy is presidential or parliamentary.[15] Conversely, studies of the breakdown of democracies have constantly
shown that such events were in no way inevitable as a result of the
cultural or economic environment, but frequently stemmed from
specific bad decisions on the part of individual politicians.[16] The
states of Latin America were never forced to adopt policies of
protectionism and import substitution when faced with the world
depression of the 1930s, yet such policies undermined their prospects for stable democracy for years to come.[17]

The second, and probably more common mistake, is to view
cultural factors as *necessary* conditions for the establishment of
democracy. Max Weber gives a long account of the historical origins of modern democracy, which he sees as having arisen out of
certain very specific social conditions that existed in the Occiden-
tal city.[18] Weber's account of democracy is, as usual, historically
rich and insightful. But he portrays democracy as something that
could only have arisen in the specific cultural and social milieu of
a small corner of Western civilization. The fact that democracy
took off because it was the most rational possible political system

and "fit" a broader human personality shared across cultures is not seriously considered.

There are numerous examples of countries which do not meet a number of so-called cultural "preconditions" for democracy, and which nonetheless have managed to achieve a surprisingly high level of democratic stability. The chief example of this is India, which is neither rich and highly industrialized (although certain sectors of its economy are technologically very advanced), nor nationally integrated, nor Protestant, and which nonetheless has been able to sustain an effective working democracy since independence in 1947. At other times in the past, entire peoples have been written off as culturally unqualified for stable democracy: the Germans and Japanese were said to be hobbled by their authoritarian traditions; Catholicism was held to be an insuperable obstacle to democracy in Spain, Portugal, and any number of Latin American countries, as was Orthodoxy in Greece and Russia. Many of the peoples of Eastern Europe were held to be either incapable of or uninterested in the liberal democratic traditions of Western Europe. As Gorbachev's *perestroika* continued without producing any clear-cut reform, many people both inside and outside the Soviet Union said that the Russian people were culturally incapable of sustaining democracy: They had no democratic tradition and no civil society, having been broken to tyranny over the centuries. And yet, democratic institutions emerged in all of these places. In the Soviet Union, the Russian Parliament under Boris Yeltsin functioned as if it were a legislative body of long standing, while an increasingly broad and vigorous civil society began to spring up spontaneously in 1990–1991. The degree to which democratic ideas had taken root among the broader population was made evident in the widespread resistance to the hardline coup that was attempted in August 1991.[19]

An argument that is heard all too frequently is that a given country cannot democratize because it has no preexisting democratic tradition. Were the latter necessary, then *no* country could become a democracy since there is no people or culture (including those of Western Europe) that did not start out with or come to adopt strongly authoritarian traditions.

Further consideration suggests that the dividing line between culture and politics, between peoples and states, is not all that clear. States can play a very important role in *forming* peoples, that is, in establishing their "language of good and evil" and creating new habits, customs, and cultures *de novo*. Americans were not simply "born equal," they were also "made equal" prior to the establishment of the United States by the practice of self-government on a state and local level in the years before the colonies got their independence from Britain. And the overtly democratic nature of the American founding was responsible for the formation of the democratic American of later generations, a human type (so brilliantly described by Tocqueville) which had not existed before in the course of history. Cultures are not static phenomena like the laws of nature; they are human creations that undergo a continuous process of evolution. They can be modified by economic development, wars and other national traumas, immigration or by conscious choice. Hence cultural "prerequisites" for democracy, while definitely important, need to be treated with some skepticism.

On the other hand, the importance of peoples and their cultures underscores the limits of liberal rationalism, or to put it differently, the dependence of rational liberal institutions on irrational *thymos*. The rational liberal state cannot be brought about by a single election. Nor can it survive without some degree of irrational love of country, or without an instinctive attachment to values like tolerance. If the health of contemporary liberal democracy rests on the health of civil society, and the latter depends on people's spontaneous ability to associate, then it is clear that liberalism must reach beyond its own principles to succeed. The civil associations or communities noted by Tocqueville were often not founded on liberal principles, but were based on religion, ethnicity, or some other irrational basis. Successful political modernization thus requires the preservation of something premodern within its framework of rights and constitutional arrangements, the survival of peoples and the incomplete victory of states.

21

The Thymotic Origins of Work

Hegel . . . believed that Work was the essence, *the true essence of Man.*

—Karl Marx[1]

Given the strong correlation between advanced industrialization and democracy, the ability of countries to grow economically over prolonged periods of time would seem to be very important to their ability to create and sustain free societies. And yet, while the most successful modern economies may be capitalist, not all capitalist economies are successful—or, at any rate, as successful as others. Just as there are sharp distinctions between the ability of formally democratic countries to sustain democracy, so there are equally sharp differences between the ability of formally capitalist economies to grow.

It was the view of Adam Smith that the chief source of the differences in the wealth of nations was the wisdom or foolishness of government policies, and that human economic behavior, once free from the constraints of bad policy, was more or less universal. Many of the differences in performance between capitalist economies can in fact be traced to differences in government policy. As noted earlier,[2] many ostensibly capitalist economies in Latin America are actually mercantilist monstrosities in which years of state intervention have reduced efficiency and deadened entrepreneurship. Conversely, a good deal of postwar East Asian economic success can be traced to that region's adoption of sensible economic policies, such as the maintenance of competitive internal markets. The importance of government policy is most evident when a Spain, South Korea, or Mexico opens up its economy and booms, or when an Argentina nationalizes industries and crashes.

And yet, one gets the sense that policy differences are only part of the story, and that culture affects economic behavior in certain critical ways just as it affects the ability of a people to sustain stable democracy. This is nowhere more evident than in attitudes toward work. Work, according to Hegel, is the *essence* of man: it is the working slave who creates human history by transforming the natural world into a world habitable by man. Apart from a few idle masters, all human beings work: and yet, there are tremendous differences in the manner and degree to which they work. These differences have traditionally been discussed under the rubric of the "work ethic."

In the contemporary world, it is not considered acceptable to talk about "national character": such generalizations about a people's ethical habits are said not to be measurable "scientifically," and are therefore prone to crude stereotyping and abuse when based, as they usually are, on anecdotal evidence. Generalizations about national character also run counter to the relativistic and egalitarian temper of our times, because they almost always contain implicit value judgments concerning the relative worth of the cultures in question. No one likes to be told that his culture promotes laziness and dishonesty; and indeed, such judgments are liable to considerable abuse.

Nonetheless, anyone who has spent time traveling or living abroad cannot help but notice that attitudes toward work are decisively influenced by national cultures. To some extent, these differences are measurable empirically, for example in the relative economic performance of different groups in multi-ethnic societies like Malaysia, India, or the United States. The superior economic performance of certain ethnic groups like the Jews in Europe, or the Greeks and Armenians in the Middle East, or the Chinese in Southeast Asia, is familiar enough not to need elaborate documentation. In the United States, Thomas Sowell has pointed to the sharp differences in income and education between the descendants of blacks who voluntarily immigrated from the West Indies, and those who were brought directly to the country from Africa as slaves.[3] Such differences suggest that economic performance is related not exclusively to environmental conditions, like the presence or absence of economic opportunity, but to differences in culture of the ethnic groups themselves as well.

Beyond gross measures of economic performance like per capita income, there is a host of subtle contrasts in the approaches taken toward work in different cultures. To give one small example, R. V. Jones, one of the founders of British scientific intelligence in World War II, recounted a story of how the British were able to capture an entire German radar set intact and bring it back to England in the early years of the war. The British had invented radar and were well ahead of the Germans in technology, yet the German machine was surprisingly good because the antenna was machined to tolerances superior to anything that could be produced in England.[4] Germany's long-standing superiority over its European neighbors in maintaining a tradition of highly skilled industrial craftsmanship, still evident in its automobile and machine tool industries, is one of those phenomena that defy explanation in terms of "macro" economic policies. Its ultimate cause would have to be found in the realm of culture.

Traditional liberal economic theory, beginning with Adam Smith, maintains that work is an essentially unpleasant activity,[5] undertaken for the sake of the utility of the things created by work.[6] That utility can primarily be enjoyed in leisure; the aim of human labor, in a certain sense, is not to work but to enjoy leisure. A man will work up to the point where the marginal disutility of labor—that is, the unpleasantness of having to stay late at the office, or working on a Saturday—exceeds the utility of the material benefit arising out of work. Men differ in the productivity of their labor, and in their subjective evaluation of the disutility of labor, but the degree to which they will work is essentially the result of a rational calculation in which they weigh the unpleasantness of work against the pleasurability of its results. Harder work is stimulated by higher material benefits to the individual worker: a person is more likely to stay late in the office if his or her employer offers to pay double for overtime. Desire and reason, by traditional liberal economic theory, are therefore adequate to give an account of differing propensities to work.

The very term "work ethic," by contrast, implies that differences in the manner and degree to which people work are determined by culture and custom, and are therefore related in some way to *thymos*. And in fact, it is very difficult to give an adequate account of an individual or a people with a strong work ethic in the strictly utilitarian terms of traditional liberal economics. Take the contemporary "type-A" personality—the hard-charging law-

yer or corporate executive, or the Japanese "salaryman" employed
by a competitive Japanese multinational corporation. Such individuals can easily work seventy- or eighty-hour weeks, with few or
short vacations, as they move up the career ladder. They may be
paid high salaries relative to others who work less hard, but the
degree to which they work is not strictly related to their compensation. In fact, their behavior is irrational in strictly utilitarian
terms:[7] they work so hard that they are never able to make use of
their money; they can't enjoy their leisure because they have none;
and in the process they ruin their health and their prospects for
a comfortable retirement, because they are likely to die sooner.
One could argue that they are working on behalf of their families,
or of future generations, and this undoubtedly does constitute
something of a motive, but most "workaholics" almost never see
their children and are so driven by their careers that their family
lives all too often suffer. The reason such people work as hard as
they do is only partially related to their monetary compensation:
they clearly derive satisfaction from the work itself, or from the
status and recognition that it provides. Their sense of self-worth
is tied up in how hard and how skillfully they work, how quickly
they are moving up the corporate ladder, and the respect with
which they are held by other people. Even their material possessions are enjoyed more for the reputation they confer than for
any actual use made of them, since their time to enjoy them is so
short. Work, in other words, is undertaken to satisfy their *thymos*
rather than desire.

In fact, many empirical studies of work ethics have seen them
as non-utilitarian in origin. The most famous of these is undoubtedly Max Weber's *The Protestant Ethic and the Spirit of Capitalism*
(1904–05). Weber was by no means the first to observe a relationship between Protestantism, particularly in its Calvinist or Puritan
variety, and capitalist economic development. Indeed, the observation was so commonplace at the time Weber wrote his book that
he felt the burden was on others to disprove it.[8] Since its publi-
cation, his thesis has been endlessly debated. While many have
challenged the specific causal relationship Weber posited as linking religion and economic behavior, few would deny altogether
the existence of a strong relationship between the two.[9] The relationship between Protestantism and economic growth continues
to be evident today in Latin America, where large-scale conver-
sions to Protestantism (usually by evangelical North American

sects) have been followed by occasionally dramatic increases in personal income, and decreases in criminal behavior, drug use, and so forth.[10]

What Weber sought to explain was why many early capitalist entrepreneurs who devoted their lives to the endless accumulation of wealth appeared to have little interest in consuming that wealth. Their frugality, self-discipline, honesty, cleanliness, and aversion to simple pleasures constituted a "this-worldly asceticism" which he understood as a transmutation of the Calvinist doctrine of predestination. Work was not an unpleasant activity undertaken for the sake of utility or consumption; rather, it was a "calling" which the believer hoped would reflect his status as either saved or damned. Work was undertaken for a totally non-material and "irrational" goal, that is, to demonstrate that one had been "elected." The dedication and discipline with which the believer worked could not be explained by any mundane rational calculation of pleasures and pains. Weber believed that the original spiritual impulse that underlay capitalism had atrophied in subsequent years, and that work for the sake of material wealth had reinserted itself into capitalism. Nonetheless, "the idea of duty in one's calling" lived on "like the ghost of dead religious beliefs" in the contemporary world, and the work ethic of modern Europe could not be fully explained without reference to its spiritual origins.

Analogies to the "Protestant ethic" have been identified in other cultures to explain their economic success.[11] Robert Bellah, for example, has shown how the contemporary Japanese work ethic can be traced back to certain Japanese religious sources that were the functional equivalent of Calvinism. The *Jodo Shinshu* or "Pure Land" sect of Buddhism, for example, stressed economy, frugality, honesty, hard work, and an ascetic attitude toward consumption, while legitimating profit-making in a way that Japan's earlier Confucian traditions did not.[12] The *Shingaku* movement of Ishida Baigan, while less influential than *Jodo Shinshu*, also preached a form of "this-worldly mysticism," emphasizing economy and diligence, while downplaying consumption.[13] These religious movements dovetailed with the *Bushido* ethic of the *samurai* class. The latter was an aristocratic warrior ideology stressing the risk of death, which nonetheless encouraged not idle mastery but asceticism, economy, and above all, learning. The "spirit of capitalism," then, with its ascetic work ethic and rationality, did not have to be imported into Japan along with naval technology and the Prussian constitution; it was there from the beginning in Japanese religious and cultural traditions.

In contrast to these instances where religious belief encouraged or made possible economic development, there are a legion of cases where religion and culture have acted as obstacles. Hinduism, for example, is one of the few great world religions that is not based on a doctrine of the universal equality of man. To the contrary, Hindu doctrine divides human beings into a complex series of castes that define their rights, privileges, and ways of life. In a curious paradox, Hinduism has not posed much of an obstacle to the practice of liberal politics in India—though a growing degree of religious intolerance suggests this may be breaking down—but it has seemingly constituted a barrier to economic growth. This is usually attributed to the fact that Hinduism sanctifies the poverty and social immobility of the lower castes: while promising them the possibility of higher rebirth in later lives, it reconciles them to whatever station they are born to in this life. This traditional Hindu sanctification of poverty was encouraged and given a somewhat more modern form by the father of modern India, Gandhi, who preached the virtues of the simple peasant life as spiritually fulfilling. Hinduism may have eased the daily burden of life for those Indians living under crushing poverty, and the religion's "spirituality" is tremendously appealing to middle-class young people in the West. But it induces in its believers a certain kind of "this-worldly" torpor and inertia which is in many respects the opposite of the spirit of capitalism. There are many highly successful Indian entrepreneurs, but they (like the overseas Chinese) seem to be more enterprising outside of the confines of Indian culture. Noting that many of India's great scientists did their work abroad, the novelist V. S. Naipaul was led to remark:

> Indian poverty is more dehumanizing than any machine; and, more than in any machine civilization, men in India are units, locked up in the straitest obedience by their idea of the *dharma*. The scientist returning to India sheds the individuality he acquired during his time abroad; he regains the security of his caste identity, and the world is once more simplified. There are minute rules, as comforting as bandages; individual perception and judgment, which once called forth his creativity, are relinquished as burdens. . . . The

blight of caste is not only untouchability and the consequent deification in India of filth; the blight, in an India that tries to grow, is also the over-all obedience it imposes, its ready-made satisfactions, the diminishing of adventuresomeness, the pushing away from men of individuality and the possibility of excellence.[14]

Gunnar Myrdal, in his great study of South Asian poverty, was left to conclude that overall, Indian religion constituted "a tremendous force for social inertia," and nowhere acted as a positive agent for change in the way that Calvinism or *Jodo Shinshu* did.[15]

   With examples like the Hindu sanctification of poverty in mind, most social scientists have assumed that religion was one of those aspects of "traditional culture" that would decline under the impact of industrialization. Religious belief was fundamentally irrational, and would therefore eventually have to give way before the rational acquisitiveness that constituted modern capitalism. But if Weber and Bellah are right, there was no fundamental tension between *certain* forms of religious belief and capitalism: indeed, capitalism in both its European and Japanese varieties were greatly facilitated by religious doctrines that encouraged labor "in a calling," that is, for its own sake and not for the sake of consumption. Bare economic liberalism—the doctrine that calls on human beings to enrich themselves *ad infinitum* through the application of reason to the problem of satisfying their private desire for property—may be enough to explain the functioning of most capitalist societies, but it does not give a complete account of the most competitive and dynamic ones. The most successful capitalist societies have risen to the top because they happen to have a fundamentally *irrational* and "pre-modern" work ethic, which induces people to live ascetically and drive themselves to an early death because work itself is held to be redeeming. This suggests that even at the end of history, some form of irrational *thymos* is still necessary in order to keep our rational, liberal economic world going, or at least if we are to be in the front ranks of world economic powers.

   One can object that whatever the religious origins of the work ethic in Europe and Japan, they are now totally divorced from their spiritual sources due to the overall secularization of modern societies. People no longer believe they are working "in a calling," but are laboring, just as the laws of capitalism dictate, in the rational pursuit of their own self-interest.

The divorce of the capitalist work ethic from its spiritual roots, and the growth of a culture stressing the legitimacy and desirability of immediate consumption, have led any number of observers to predict a sharp decline in the work ethic and thereby an undermining of capitalism itself.[16] Achievement of an "affluent society" would remove any remaining sting of natural necessity, and lead people to pursue the gratifications of leisure rather than work. Predictions about a decline in the work ethic seemed to receive support from a number of studies in the 1970s which indicated a general perception on the part of American managers that standards of professionalism, self-discipline, and drive were deteriorating among their workers.[17] Few of today's corporate managers would appear to be the paragons of ascetic thrift described by Weber. The work ethic, it was believed, would be eroded not through frontal attack, but through the promotion of other values inconsistent with this-worldly asceticism, such as "self-realization," or the desire not just to have work but "meaningful work." Though the work ethic remains very strong in Japan, the same process of gradual degeneration of work values would presumably be a problem in the future there as well, where present-day executives and managers are every bit as secular and divorced from their culture's spiritual roots as their American or European counterparts.

Whether these predictions about the decline of the work ethic will prove to be true in the United States remains to be seen. For the time being, the trend toward a weaker work ethic noted in the 1970s appears to have been reversed, at least among the professional and managerial classes in the United States.[18] The reasons for this appear to be primarily economic rather than cultural. For many sectors of the population, real living standards and job security declined during the 1980s, and people found themselves having to work harder just to stay where they were. Even for those enjoying ever-higher levels of material prosperity in this period, the pull of rational self-interest continued to stimulate people to work diligently and long. Those who feared the consequences of consumerism for the work ethic tended, like Marx, to forget the infinitely elastic nature of human desire and insecurity, which continues to push people to work up to their physical limits. The importance of rational self-interest in stimulating a work ethic is evident if one contrasts the productivity of East and West German workers, who shared a common culture but differed in the material incentives they faced. The persistence of a strong work ethic in the capitalist West may be less a testament to the durability of the "ghosts of dead religious beliefs" referred to by Weber, than to the power of desire linked to reason.

Nonetheless, there remain important differences in the propensity to work *between* countries that share a common commitment to economic liberalism, and where rational self-interest can be taken for granted. This appears to reflect the fact that in some countries, *thymos* has found new objects beyond religion to which it can attach itself in the modern world.

For example, Japanese culture (like many others in East Asia) is much more oriented toward groups rather than individuals. These groups begin with the smallest and most immediate, the family, and extend through the various patron-client relationships established during one's upbringing and education, include the corporation one works for, and the largest group with any meaning to Japanese culture, the nation. An individual's identity is to a very high degree smothered in that of the group: he does not work so much for his own short-term benefit, but for the well-being of the larger group or groups of which he is a member. His status is determined less by his performance as an individual, than by the performance of his group. His attachment to the group therefore has a highly thymotic character: he works for the recognition that the group accords him, and for the recognition of the group by other groups, and not simply for the short-run material benefit constituted by his salary. When the group for which he seeks recognition is the nation, the result is economic nationalism. And indeed, Japan tends to be more economically nationalistic than the United States. This nationalism is expressed not in overt protectionism but in less visible forms, like the networks of traditional domestic suppliers retained by Japanese manufacturers, and their greater willingness to pay higher prices to buy Japanese products.

It is this group identity that makes practices like permanent lifetime employment, used by certain large Japanese corporations, effective. According to the precepts of Western economic liberalism, lifetime employment should damage economic efficiency by making employees too secure, like professors at universities who stop writing the moment they receive tenure. The experience of the communist world, where everyone was in effect granted permanent lifetime employment, also confirms this view. The best talent ought to be attracted to the most challenging jobs and rewarded with the highest salaries; conversely, companies need to be able to cut out dead wood. Patron-client loyalties, in terms of classical liberal economics, constitute market rigidities constraining economic efficiency. And yet, in the context of the group consciousness fostered by Japanese culture, the paternalistic loyalty shown by a company to its worker is repaid by a higher level of effort on the part of the worker, who is working not only for himself but for the glory and reputation of the larger organization. This larger organization does not simply represent a biweekly paycheck, but is a source of recognition and a protective umbrella for family and friends. And the highly developed national self-consciousness of the Japanese provides a further source of identity and motivation, beyond family or company. Thus, even in an age when religious spirituality has all but disappeared, the work ethic has been sustained by creating a pride in labor based on recognition by an overlapping set of larger communities.

This highly developed group consciousness is typical in other parts of Asia, but considerably less so in Europe, and is almost totally absent in the United States, where the idea of lifetime loyalty to a single corporation would often be regarded with incomprehension. Outside of Asia, however, there are certain forms of group consciousness that have served to sustain the work ethic. Economic nationalism, taking the form of a common desire on the part of management and labor to work together to expand export markets, is fairly well developed in certain European countries like Sweden and Germany. Craft guilds have traditionally been another source of group identity: a highly skilled machinist works not simply to punch the clock, but because he takes pride in the results of his labor. The same could be said for the liberal professions, whose relatively high standards for qualification support the gratification of *thymos*.

The economic collapse of communism teaches us that certain forms of group consciousness are far inferior to the individual self-interest in stimulating a strong work ethic. The East German or Soviet worker, hectored by his local party official to work for the sake of building socialism, or asked to give up his Saturdays to demonstrate solidarity with the Vietnamese or Cubans, regarded work only as a burden to be avoided in whatever way possible.

The democratizing countries of Eastern Europe all face the problem of reconstructing a work ethic on the basis of individual self-interest, after decades of habituation to state welfare.

But the experience of certain successful Asian and European economies suggests that among countries that share a capitalist economic system with its network of personal incentives, the individual self-interest at the heart of Western liberal economic theory may be an inferior source of motivation to certain forms of group interest. It has long been recognized in the West that people will work harder for their families than for themselves alone, and that in times of war or crisis they can be called upon to work on behalf of the nation. On the other hand, the highly atomistic economic liberalism of the United States or Britain, based exclusively on rational desire, becomes economically counterproductive at a certain point. This can happen when workers don't take pride in the labor for its own sake, but come to regard it as nothing more than a commodity to be sold, or when workers and managers see each other as antagonists in a zero-sum game, rather than as potential collaborators in competition with workers and managers in another country.[19]

Just as culture affects the ability of countries to establish and sustain political liberalism, culture affects their ability to make economic liberalism work. Just as in the case of political democracy, the success of capitalism depends in some measure on the survival of pre-modern cultural traditions into the modern age. Like political liberalism, economic liberalism is not totally self-sustaining, but depends on a degree of irrational *thymos*.

The broad acceptance of liberalism, political or economic, by a large number of nations will not eliminate differences between them based on culture, differences which will undoubtedly become more pronounced as ideological cleavages are muted. Already, trade disputes with Japan loom larger in the minds of many Americans than the question of freedom around the world, despite the fact that Japan and the United States share, in formal terms, a common political and economic system. Japan's persistent and apparently unremovable trade surplus with the United States is, at this point, more the product of cultural factors such as the high savings rate, or the closed nature of Japanese supplier relationships, than of any legal protectionism. The ideological conflicts of the Cold War could be settled altogether when one side or the other compromised on a specific political issue like the

Berlin Wall, or else abandoned its ideology wholesale. But persistent cultural differences between ostensibly liberal democratic capitalist states will prove much harder to eradicate.

These cultural differences in attitudes toward work between Japan and the United States look positively minuscule when compared with the cultural differences separating Japan and the United States, on the one hand, from any number of Third World countries that have been much less successful at making capitalism work, on the other. Economic liberalism provides the optimal route to prosperity to any people willing to take advantage of it. For many countries, the problem is simply one of adopting the right market-oriented policy. But policy is only the necessary precondition for high rates of growth. "Irrational" forms of *thymos*—religion, nationalism, the ability of craft occupations and the professions to maintain standards and pride in work—continue to influence economic behavior in countless ways that contribute to the wealth or poverty of nations. And the persistence of these differences may mean that international life will be seen increasingly as a competition not between rival ideologies—since most economically successful states will be organized along similar lines—but between different cultures.

22

Empires of Resentment, Empires of Deference

The impact of culture on economic development, either as a stimulus or a constraint, points to potential obstacles in the march of the Universal History described in Part Two. Modern economics—the process of industrialization determined by modern natural science—is forcing the homogenization of mankind, and is destroying a wide variety of traditional cultures in the process. But it may not win every battle, finding instead that certain cultures and certain manifestations of *thymos* are difficult to digest. And if the process of economic homogenization stops, the process of democratization will face an uncertain future as well. Many as are the peoples in the world who believe they want capitalist prosperity and liberal democracy on an intellectual level, not everyone will be able to obtain it.

Thus, despite the apparent absence of systematic alternatives to liberal democracy at present, some new authoritarian alternatives, perhaps never before seen in history, may assert themselves in the future. These alternatives, if they come about, will be created by two distinct groups of people: those who for cultural reasons experience persistent economic failure, despite an effort to make economic liberalism work, and those who are inordinately successful at the capitalist game.

The first phenomenon, the emergence of illiberal doctrines out of economic failure, has occurred in the past. The current revival of Islamic fundamentalism, touching virtually every coun-

235

try in the world with a substantial Muslim population, can be seen as a response to the failure of Muslim societies generally to maintain their dignity vis-à-vis the non-Muslim West. Under the pressure of competition from a militarily dominant Europe, a number of Islamic countries in the nineteenth and early twentieth centuries undertook crash modernization efforts to assimilate the Western practices seen as necessary to remain competitive. Like the reforms of Meiji Japan, these modernization programs involved thoroughgoing attempts to introduce principles of Western rationalism into all walks of life, from the economy, bureaucracy, and military, to education and social policy. The most systematic endeavor in this direction was undertaken by Turkey: the Ottoman reforms of the nineteenth century were followed in the twentieth by those of the founder of the present-day Turkish state, Kemal Ataturk, who sought to create a secular society based on Turkish nationalism. The last major intellectual import accepted from the West by the Islamic world was secular nationalism, represented by the great pan-Arab nationalist movements of Egypt's Nasser, and the Baʿath parties of Syria, Lebanon, and Iraq.

Unlike Meiji Japan, however, which used Western technology to defeat Russia in 1905 and to challenge the United States in 1941, most of the Islamic world never assimilated these Western imports in a convincing way, or produced the kind of political or economic success for which the modernizers of the nineteenth and early twentieth centuries had hoped. Until the advent of oil wealth in the 1960s and 70s, no Islamic society was able to challenge the West militarily or economically. Many indeed remained colonial dependencies through World War II, and the project of secular pan-Arab unity foundered after Egypt's humiliating defeat by Israel in 1967. The Islamic fundamentalist revival, that came into view with the Iranian Revolution of 1978–79, was not a case of "traditional values" surviving into the modern age. Those values, corrupt and latitudinarian, had been soundly defeated in the course of the previous hundred years. The Islamic revival was rather the nostalgic re-assertion of an older, purer set of values, said to have existed in the distant past, that were neither the discredited "traditional values" of the recent past, nor the Western values that had been so poorly transplanted to the Middle East. In this respect, Islamic fundamentalism bears a more than superficial resemblance to European fascism. As in the case of European fascism, it is no surprise that the fundamentalist revival hit the most apparently modern countries the hardest, for it was they whose traditional cultures had been most thoroughly threatened by the import of Western values. The strength of the Islamic revival can only be understood if one understands how deeply the dignity of Islamic society had been wounded in its double failure to maintain the coherence of its traditional society and to successfully assimilate the techniques and values of the West.

Even in the United States, it is possible to see the beginnings of new illiberal ideologies emerging as the distant result of different cultural attitudes toward economic activity. In the heyday of the civil rights movement, most American blacks aspired to complete integration into white society, implying a full acceptance of the dominant cultural values of American society. The problem for black Americans was understood not as one concerning the values themselves, but the willingness of white society to recognize the dignity of blacks who accepted those values. Despite the abolition of legally sanctioned barriers to equality in the 1960s, however, and the rise of a variety of affirmative action programs giving preference to blacks, a certain sector of the American black population not only failed to advance economically, but actually lost ground.

One political result of persistent economic failure, however, is the now more frequently heard assertion that the traditional measures of economic success, such as work, education, and employment, represent not universal but "white" values. Rather than seeking integration in a color-blind society, some black leaders stress instead the need to take pride in a distinct Afro-American culture with its own history, traditions, heroes, and values, equal to but separate from the culture of white society. In some cases this shades over into an "Afro-centrism" which asserts the superiority of indigenous African culture over "European" ideas like socialism and capitalism. Desire for recognition of the dignity of this separate culture by the educational system, by employers, and by the state itself has for many blacks replaced the desire for recognition of their undifferentiated *human* dignity, for example the Christian dignity of man as a moral agent referred to by Martin Luther King. The result of this kind of thinking has been an increasing self-segregation by blacks—evident on most American college campuses today—and an emphasis on the politics of group dignity rather than on individual achievement or economic activity as the main route to social advancement.

But if new, illiberal ideologies may be spun out by those who find themselves culturally hobbled in the economic competition, the other potential source of authoritarian ideas may be those who have been more than ordinarily successful economically. The most significant challenge being posed to the liberal universalism of the American and French revolutions today is not coming from the communist world, whose economic failures are evident for everyone to see, but from those societies in Asia which combine liberal economies with a kind of paternalistic authoritarianism. It was the case for many years after World War II that Japan and other Asian societies looked to the United States and Europe as models for fully modernized societies, and believed that they had to borrow everything, from technology to Western management techniques and, ultimately, Western political systems, in order to stay competitive. But Asia's tremendous economic success has led to a growing recognition that that success was due not simply to the successful borrowing of Western practices, but to the fact that Asian societies *retained* certain traditional features of their own cultures—like a strong work ethic—and integrated them into a modern business environment.

Political authority has special origins in much of Asia when compared to Europe or North America, and liberal democracy is interpreted rather differently there than in the countries of its historical birth.[1] Those groups that in in Confucian societies are so important in sustaining the work ethic are also critical as the bases for political authority as well. An individual derives his status primarily not on the basis of his individual ability or worth, but insofar as he is a member of one of a series of interlocking groups. For example, while the Japanese constitution and legal system may recognize individual rights just like the United States, Japanese society tends to grant recognition primarily to groups. An individual in such a society has dignity insofar as he is a member of an established group and conforms to its rules. But the moment he seeks to assert his personal dignity and rights against the group, he is subject to a social ostracism and loss of status that can be as devastating as the overt tyranny of traditional despotisms. This produces tremendous pressures for conformity that children in such cultures internalize at a very young age. Individuals in Asian societies are, in other words, subject to what Tocqueville called the "tyranny of the majority"—or rather, majorities in all the social groups, large and small, with which an individual has dealings in the course of his or her life.

This tyranny may be illustrated by a couple of examples from Japanese society, which has parallels in every other culture in East Asia. The primary social group to which individuals in Japan owe deference is the family, and the benevolent authority of a father over his children was the original model for authority relations throughout society, including those between ruler and ruled.[2] (Paternal authority was a model for political authority in Europe as well, but modern liberalism represented an overt break with that tradition.)[3] In the United States, young children are expected to defer to the authority of their parents, but as they start growing older, they begin to assert their own identity *against* their parents. An act of teenage rebellion, in which the child openly rejects the parents' values and wishes, is an almost necessary part of the process of forming the personality of an adult human being.[4] For it is only in that act of rebellion that the child develops the psychological resources of self-sufficiency and independence, a thymotic sense of individual self-worth based on the child's ability to leave the protective umbrella of the home, that will sustain the individual later on as an adult. Only after that rebellion has played itself out can the child return to a relationship of mutual respect with his or her parents, this time, however, not as a dependent but as an equal. In Japan, by contrast, the incidence of teenage rebellion is much lower: the early deference to elders is expected to continue throughout one's adult life. One's *thymos* is attached not so much to an individual self in whose personal qualities one takes pride, but to the family and other groups whose reputation takes precedence over that of any of its members.[5] Anger arises not when other people fail to recognize one's own worth, but when these groups are slighted; conversely, the greatest sense of shame arises not as a matter of personal failure, but because of the disgrace brought upon one's group.[6] Thus parents in Japan continue to influence important decisions for their children, like the choice of a marriage partner, which no self-respecting young American would permit.

The second manifestation of group consciousness in Japan is the muting of democratic "politics" in the conventional Western understanding of the word. That is, Western democracy is built upon the contestation of different thymotic opinions about right and wrong, carried out on editorial pages and ultimately in elections at various levels, where political parties representing different interests or thymotic points of view alternate with one another in office. This contestation is held to be a natural, indeed, a necessary adjunct to the normal functioning of democracy. In Japan, by contrast, society as a whole tends to regard itself as a single, large group with a single, stable source of authority. The emphasis on group harmony tends to push open confrontation to the fringes of politics; there is no alternation of political parties in power based on clashes over "issues," but rather the decades-long dominance of the Liberal Democratic party (LDP). There is of course open contestation between the LDP and the socialist and communist opposition parties, but the latter have marginalized themselves by their extremism. Serious politics, generally speaking, takes place out of public view, in the central bureaucracies or in the back rooms of the LDP.[7] Within the LDP, politics revolves around the constant maneuvering of factions that are based on personalistic patron-client relationships, that are largely devoid of what anyone in the West would understand as political content.

In Japan, emphasis on group consensus is partially balanced by respect for individuals who go against the grain, like the late novelist Yukio Mishima. But in many other Asian societies, there would be little respect for the principled individualism of a Solzhenitsyn or Sakharov who stands alone against the injustice of the society around him. In Frank Capra's movie *Mr. Smith Goes to Washington,* Jimmy Stewart plays a small-town innocent who is appointed to represent his state by the political bosses when the elected senator dies. Arriving in Washington, Stewart rebels at the corruption he sees and, to the dismay of his would-be manipulators, single-handedly filibusters the Senate in order to block a piece of unprincipled legislation. The Stewart character is in some sense an archetypical American hero. In many Asian societies, by contrast, such wholesale rejection of the prevailing consensus by a lone individual would be regarded as lunacy.

Japanese democracy looks somewhat authoritarian by American or European standards. The most powerful men in the country are either senior bureaucrats or faction leaders within the LDP, who arrived at their positions not through popular choice, but either as a result of their educational backgrounds or through personal patronage. These men make major decisions affecting the welfare of the community with relatively little feedback from voters or other forms of popular pressure. The system remains fundamentally democratic because it is *formally* democratic, that is, it meets the criteria for liberal democracy of periodic multi-party elections and guarantees of basic rights. Western concepts of universal individual rights have been accepted and internalized throughout large parts of Japanese society. On the other hand, there are respects in which one could say Japan is governed by a benevolent one-party dictatorship, not because that party has imposed itself upon society in the manner of the Soviet Communist party, but because the people of Japan *choose* to be ruled in that fashion. The current Japanese system of government reflects a broad social consensus rooted in Japan's group-oriented culture, a culture that would feel profoundly uncomfortable with more "open" contestation or the alternation of parties in power.

Given the widespread consensus that exists in most Asian societies concerning the desirability of group harmony, however, it is not surprising that authoritarianism of a more overt variety is widespread in the region. The argument can and has been made—most notably by former Prime Minister Lee Kuan Yew of Singapore—that a form of paternalistic authoritarianism is more in keeping with Asia's Confucian traditions, and, most importantly, that it is more compatible with consistently high rates of economic growth than liberal democracy. Democracy is a drag on growth, Lee has argued, because it interferes with rational economic planning and promotes a kind of egalitarian self-indulgence in which a myriad of private interests assert themselves at the expense of the community as a whole. Singapore itself has become notorious in recent years for its efforts to stifle press criticism, and for violations of the human rights of the regime's political opponents. In addition, the Singaporean government interferes in the private lives of its citizens to a degree that would be completely unacceptable in the West, for example, by mandating how long boys can grow their hair, outlawing video parlors, and imposing stiff fines for petty crimes like littering or failing to flush a public toilet. Singapore's authoritarianism is mild by the standards of the twentieth century, but is distinctive in two ways. First, it has been accompanied by extraordinary economic success, and second, it has been justified unapologetically, not just as a transitional arrangement, but as a system superior to liberal democracy.

Asian societies lose a great deal by their group orientation. They impose a high degree of conformity on their members and beat back the mildest forms of individual expression. The constraints of such a society are most evident in the situation of women, where emphasis on the traditional patriarchal family has limited their opportunities for a life outside the home. Consumers have few rights and must accept economic policies over which they have little say. Recognition based on groups is ultimately irrational: at one extreme, it can become the source of chauvinism and war, as it was in the 1930s. Short of war, group-oriented recognition can be highly dysfunctional. For example, all developed countries are now experiencing an influx of large numbers of people from poorer and less stable countries, attracted by jobs and security. Japan no less than the United States needs low-wage workers for certain occupations, but is perhaps the least able to accommodate immigrants because of the fundamentally intolerant nature of its constituent groups. The atomistic liberalism of the United States, by contrast, is the only conceivable basis on which large immigrant populations can be successfully assimilated.

But the long-predicted breakdown of traditional Asian values in the face of modern consumerism has been very slow in materializing. This is perhaps because Asian societies have certain strengths which their members will not easily dismiss, especially when they observe the non-Asian alternatives. While American workers do not have to sing their company's song while doing group exercises, one of the most common complaints about the character of contemporary American life is precisely its lack of *community*. The breakdown of community life in the United States begins with the family, which has been steadily fractured and atomized over the past couple of generations in ways that are thoroughly familiar to all Americans. But it is evident as well in the absence of any meaningful sense of local attachment for many Americans, and the disappearance of outlets for sociability beyond the immediate family. Yet it is precisely a sense of community that is offered by Asian societies, and for many of those growing up in that culture, social conformity and constraints on individualism seem to be a small price to pay

In light of such considerations, it would appear that Asia, and Japan in particular, are at a particularly critical turning point with respect to world history. It is possible to imagine Asia moving in two rather different directions as it continues to grow economically in the next couple of generations. On the one hand, Asia's increasingly cosmopolitan and educated populations can continue to absorb Western ideas of universal and reciprocal recognition, leading to the further spread of formal liberal democracy. Groups will decline in importance as sources of thymotic identification; Asians will become more concerned with personal dignity, women's rights, and private consumption, internalizing the principles of the universal rights of man. This is the process that has been pushing South Korea and Taiwan toward formal democracy over the past generation. Japan has already moved very far down that road in the postwar period, and the decay of patriarchal institutions makes it a far more "modern" country than, say, Singapore.

On the other hand, if Asians become convinced that their success was due more to their own than to borrowed cultures, if economic growth in America and Europe falters relative to that in the Far East, if Western societies continue to experience the progressive breakdown of basic social institutions like the family, and if they themselves treat Asia with distrust or hostility, then a systematic illiberal and non-democratic alternative combining technocratic economic rationalism with paternalistic authoritarianism may gain ground in the Far East. Up until now, many Asian societies have at least paid lip service to Western principles of liberal democracy, accepting the form while modifying the content to accommodate Asian cultural traditions. But an overt rupture with democracy could occur in which the form itself would be rejected as a Western imposition, as irrelevant to the successful functioning of Asian societies as Western business management techniques are to their economies. The beginnings of a systematic Asian rejection of liberal democracy can be heard in Lee Kuan Yew's theoretical pronouncements, and in the writings of certain Japanese like Shintaro Ishihara. Japan will play a crucial role if such an alternative emerges in the future, since that country has already replaced the United States as the model for modernization in much of Asia.[8]

A new Asian authoritarianism would most likely not be the harsh totalitarian police state with which we have become familiar. The tyranny would be one of deference, the willing obedience of people to higher authority and their conformity to a rigid set of social norms. It is doubtful whether such a political system would be exportable to other cultures that did not share Asia's Confucian heritage, any more than Islamic fundamentalism has been exportable to the non-Islamic parts of the world.[9] The empire of deference that it represents may produce unprecedented prosperity, but it also means a prolonged childhood for most citizens, and therefore an incompletely satisfied *thymos*.

In the contemporary world, we see a curious double phenomenon: both the victory of the universal and homogeneous state, and the persistence of peoples. On the one hand, there is the ever-increasing homogenization of mankind being brought about by modern economics and technology, and by the spread of the idea of rational recognition as the only legitimate basis of government around the world. On the other hand, there is everywhere a resistance to that homogenization, and a reassertion, largely on a sub-political level, of cultural identities that ultimately reinforce existing barriers between people and nations. The triumph of the coldest of all cold monsters has been incomplete. While the forms of acceptable economic and political organization have been growing steadily fewer in number over the past hundred years, the possible interpretations of the surviving forms, capitalism and liberal democracy, continue to be varied. This suggests that even as ideological differences between states fade into the background, important differences between states will remain, shifted however to the plane of culture and economics. These differences further suggest that the existing state system will not collapse anytime soon into a *literally* universal and homogenous state.[10] The nation will continue to be a central pole of identification, even if more and more nations come to share common economic and political forms of organization.

We need, then, to consider what relations between such states will look like, and how they will differ from the international order with which we are familiar.

23

The Unreality of "Realism"

For of the gods we believe, and of men we know, that by a necessity of their nature wherever they have power they always rule. And so in our case since we neither enacted this law nor when it was enacted were the first to use it, but found it in existence and expect to leave it in existence for all time, so we make use of it, well aware that both you and others, if clothed with the same power as we are, would do the same thing.

—*Speech of the Athenians to the Melians,* Thucydides' History of the Peloponnesian War[1]

The existence of a directional history should have important consequences for international relations. If the advent of the universal and homogeneous state means the establishment of rational recognition on the level of individuals living within one society, and the abolition of the relationship of lordship and bondage between them, then the spread of that type of state throughout the international system of states should imply the end of relationships of lordship and bondage *between* nations as well—that is, the end of imperialism, and with it, a decrease in the likelihood of war based on imperialism.

But just as the events of the twentieth century have engendered a deep pessimism regarding the possibility of a Universal History and progressive change within countries, so too has it fostered a pessimism concerning relations between countries. The latter type of pessimism is, in a way, much more thoroughgoing than the pessimism concerning domestic politics. For while the main currents of theory in economics and sociology have, over the past century, been struggling with the problem of history and historical change, theorists of international relations talk as if history did not exist—for example, as if war and imperialism were permanent aspects of the human horizon, whose fundamental causes were no different today than in the time of Thucydides. While all other aspects of the human social environment—religion, the family, economic organization, concepts of political legitimacy—are subject to historical evolution, international relations is regarded as forever identical to itself: "war is eternal."[2]

This pessimistic view of international relations has been given a systematic formulation that goes variously under the titles of "realism," *realpolitik*, or "power politics." Realism, whether consciously called by that name, is the dominant framework for understanding international relations, and shapes the thinking of virtually every foreign policy professional today in the United States and much of the rest of the world. In order to understand the impact of spreading democracy on international politics, we need to analyze the weaknesses of this dominant realist school of interpretation.

The true progenitor of realism was Machiavelli, who believed that men should take their bearings not by how philosophers have imagined they ought to live, but by how they actually live, and who taught that the best states would have to emulate the policies of the worst states if they were to survive. As a doctrine meant to apply to problems of contemporary politics, however, realism did not arrive on the scene until after World War II. Since then, it has taken several forms. The original formulation was that of pre- and early postwar writers like the theologian Reinhold Niebuhr, the diplomat George Kennan, and Professor Hans Morgenthau, whose textbook on international relations was perhaps the single greatest influence on the way Americans thought about foreign policy during the Cold War.[3] Since then, there have been a variety of academic versions of this theory, such as "neo-" or "structural" realism, but the single most articulate advocate of realism in the past generation has been Henry Kissinger. As secretary of state, Kissinger saw his long-term task as one of educating the American public away from its traditional Wilsonian liberalism and toward a more "realistic" understanding of foreign policy. Realism characterize the thinking of Kissinger's many students and protégés, who continued to shape American foreign policy long after Kissinger's departure from office.

All realist theories start from the assumption that insecurity is a universal and permanent feature of the international order, due to the latter's abidingly anarchic character.[4] In the absence of an international sovereign, each state will be potentially threatened by every other state, and will have no other remedy for its insecurity other than taking up arms in its own defense.[5] This sense of threat is in some way inevitable, because every state will misinterpret the "defensive" actions of other states as threatening to itself, and undertake defensive measures which will in turn be misinterpreted as offensive. Threat thus becomes a self-fulfilling prophecy. The consequence of this situation is that all states will seek to maximize their power relative to other states. Competition and war are inevitable by-products of the international system, not on account of the nature of the states themselves, but due to the anarchic character of the state system as a whole.

This striving for power is not affected by the internal characteristics of states—whether countries arc theocracies, slave-holding aristocracies, fascist police states, communist dictatorships or liberal democracies. Morgenthau explained that "it is the very nature of politics to compel the actor on the political scene to use ideologies in order to disguise the immediate goal of his action," which was always power.[6] For example, Russia expanded under Tsarist rule, much as it expanded under the Bolsheviks; what was constant was the expansion and not the particular form of government.[7] The expectation is that a future government of Russia, shorn completely of Marxism-Leninism, will remain equally expansionist because that expansionism represents an expression of the Russian people's will to power.[8] Japan may be a liberal democracy now rather than a military dictatorship as it was in the 1930s, but it remains Japan first and foremost, dominating Asia now not with bullets but with yen.[9]

If the drive for power is essentially the same for all states, the real factor determining the likelihood of war is not the aggressive behavior of certain states, but rather whether power is balanced or not within the system of states. If it is, then aggression is not likely to pay; if it is not, then states will be tempted to take advantage of their neighbors. In its purest form, realists maintain that the *distribution* of power is the single most important determinant of war and peace. Power can be distributed in a "bipolar" fashion, when two states in the system predominate over all the rest. This was true of Athens and Sparta at the time of the Peloponnesian War, Rome and Carthage a couple of centuries later, or the Soviet Union and the United States in the Cold War. The alternative is a "multipolar" system in which power is distributed among a larger number of nations, such as was the case in Europe during the eighteenth and nineteenth centuries. There have been extended arguments among realists as to whether bipolarity or multipolarity is more productive of long-term international stability. Most have concluded that bipolar systems are more likely to be stable, though the reasons for this probably have to do with historically contingent factors like the inability of modern nation states to be perfectly flexible in their system of alliances.[10] The bipolar distribution of power after World War II is therefore held to be one of the reasons why Europe remained peaceful for an unprecedented half century after 1945.

In its most extreme form, realism treats nation-states like billiard balls, whose internal contents, hidden by opaque shells, are irrelevant in predicting their behavior. The science of international politics does not require knowledge of those insides. One needs only to understand the mechanical laws of physics governing their interaction: how bouncing a ball off one cushion will leave it ricocheting at a complementary angle, or how the energy of one ball becomes differentially imparted to the two balls it strikes simultaneously. International politics, then, is not about the interaction of complex and historically developing human societies, nor are wars about clashes of values. Under the "billiard ball" approach, the slender knowledge of whether an international system is bipolar or multipolar is sufficient to determine the likelihood of peace or war.

Realism takes the form both of a *de*scription of international politics, and as a *pre*scription for how states ought to run their foreign policies. The prescriptive value of realism obviously proceeds from its descriptive accuracy. No good person, presumably, would want to operate by the cynical tenets of realism unless they were forced to do so, as Machiavelli says, by the behavior of "the many who are not good." Prescriptive realism results in several familiar rules of the road to guide policy.

The first rule is that the ultimate solution to the problem of international insecurity is to be found through maintenance of a balance of power against one's potential enemies. Since war is the final arbiter in disputes between states, states must have sufficient power to defend themselves. They cannot rely on international agreements alone, or on international organizations like the United Nations which have no power to enforce or to sanction. Reinhold Niebuhr, citing the failure of the League of Nations to punish the Japanese invasion of Manchuria, argued that "the prestige of the international community is not great enough . . . to achieve a communal spirit sufficiently unified, to discipline recalcitrant nations."[11] The true coin of the realm in international politics is military power. Other forms of power such as natural resources or industrial capacity are important, but primarily as a means of creating the military capabilities for self-defense.

The second precept of realism is that friends and enemies ought to be chosen primarily on the basis of their power, rather than on the basis of ideology or the internal character of the regime. There are innumerable instances of this in world politics, such as the U.S.-Soviet alliance to defeat Hitler, or the Bush administration's alignment with Syria against Iraq. After the defeat of Napoleon, the anti-French coalition led by the Austrian foreign minister, Prince Metternich, refused to dismember or otherwise extract punitive concessions from France, on the grounds that it would be necessary as a counterweight to future threats to European peace coming from new and unexpected quarters. And indeed, in later years it was not France but Russia and Germany that sought to upset the European status quo. This dispassionate balancing of power, free of considerations of ideology or revenge, was the subject of Kissinger's first book and remains a classic example of realism in practice.[12]

A third and related tenet is that in assessing foreign threats, statesmen should look more closely at military capabilities rather than intentions. Realism holds that the intention is always, in some sense, there; even if today a country looks friendly and non-belligerent, its mood could change tomorrow. Military capabilities—the quantities of tanks, planes, and guns—are not as fickle, but constitute in themselves indicators of intent.

The final precept, or series of precepts, of realist theory, has to do with the need to exclude moralism in foreign policy. Morgenthau attacked the widespread tendency among nations to "identify the moral aspiration of a particular nation with the moral laws that govern the universe," arguing that it led to pride and overreaching, while "the concept of interest defined in terms of power . . . saves us from both that moral excess and that political folly."[13] Kissinger argued along similar lines that there were two kinds of state systems, "legitimate" and "revolutionary" ones. In the former, all member states accepted each other's fundamental legitimacy and did not seek to undermine them or otherwise challenge their right to exist. Revolutionary state systems, on the other hand, were constantly beset by large conflicts because of the unwillingness of certain of their members to accept the status quo.[14] An obvious example of a revolutionary state was the Soviet Union, which since its inception was committed to the struggle for world revolution and the global victory of socialism. But liberal democracies like the United States have at times acted like revolutionary ones as well, when it has sought to promote its form of government in unlikely places from Vietnam to Panama. Revolutionary state systems are inherently more prone to conflict than legitimate ones: their members are not content with co-existence, and regard every conflict as a Manichean struggle over first principles. And since peace, particularly in the nuclear age, is the most important objective, legitimate state systems are vastly to be preferred over revolutionary ones.

What flows from this is a strong opposition to the interjection of moralism into foreign policy. According to Niebuhr,

> the moralist may be as dangerous a guide as the political realist. He usually fails to recognise the elements of injustice and coercion which are present in any contemporary social peace. . . . A too uncritical glorification of co-operation and mutuality therefore results in the acceptance of traditional injustices and the preference of the subtler types of coercion to the more overt types.[15]

This leads to a somewhat paradoxical situation: realists, who are constantly seeking to maintain a balance of power based on military force, are also the most likely to seek accommodation with powerful enemies. The latter flows naturally from the realist position. For if competition between states is in some sense permanent and universal, then changes in the ideology or leadership of hostile states will not fundamentally ameliorate the dilemma of international security. Attempts to seek remedies to the problem of security through revolutionary means—for instance, by attacking the basic legitimacy of rival governments through criticism of human rights abuses—are both misguided and dangerous.

It is therefore no accident that earlier realists like Metternich were diplomats rather than warriors, and that the realist Kissinger, while largely disdaining the United Nations, was the architect of the U.S.-Soviet détente of the early 1970s—that is, a détente between a liberal democracy and a totally unreformed Soviet Union. As Kissinger tried to explain at the time, Soviet communist power was a permanent aspect of international reality, one that could not be wished away or fundamentally reformed, and Americans would have to get used to the idea of accommodation rather than confrontation in dealing with it. The United States and the Soviet Union had a common interest in the avoidance of nuclear war, and Kissinger quite consistently opposed the interjection of human rights considerations, such as Soviet Jewish emigration, into efforts to promote that common interest.

Realism played a large and beneficial role in shaping the way Americans thought about foreign policy after World War II. It did so by saving the United States from its tendency to seek security in a truly naive form of liberal internationalism, such as primary reliance on the United Nations for security. Realism was an appropriate framework for understanding international politics in this period because the world operated according to realist premises. It did so not so much because realist principles reflected timeless truths, but because the world was sharply divided between states of radically differing and mutually hostile ideologies. World politics in the first half of this century was dominated first by aggressive European nationalisms—above all, that of Germany—and then by the clash of fascism, communism, and liberal democracy. Fascism explicitly accepted Morgenthau's contention that all of political life was a ceaseless striving for power, while liberalism and communism shared a universalism in their notions of justice that spread conflict between them into virtually every corner of the globe. The implacable hostility of these ideologies guaranteed that a framework of liberal internationalism, meant to regulate the interactions of a system of *liberal* states, would either be ignored or would be used dishonestly to advance aggressive national aims. Japan, Germany, and Italy flouted resolutions of the League of Nations in the interwar period, just as the Soviet Union's veto in the UN Security Council was sufficient to emasculate that organization after 1946.[16] In such a world, international law was a delusion, and military force was in fact the only remedy to the problem of security. Realism, then, looked like an adequate framework for understanding how the world worked, and provided needed intellectual support for the creation of NATO and other military alliances with Western Europe and Japan after the war.

Realism is a fitting view of international politics for a pessimistic century, and grew quite naturally out of the life histories of many of its major practitioners. Henry Kissinger, for example, had personal experience of seeing civilized life turning to a brutal struggle for power when he had to flee Nazi Germany as a boy. His honors dissertation on Kant, written while he was an undergraduate at Harvard, attacked Kant's view of historical progress and accepted a perspective that at times approaches a kind of nihilism, that there is neither God nor a secular mechanism like Hegel's Universal History that could provide meaning to the flow of events. History was rather a chaotic and ceaseless series of struggles among nations, in which liberalism had no particularly privileged position.[17]

The early contributions of realism to American foreign policy should not, however, blind us to the serious weaknesses of this framework for viewing international relations, both as a description of reality and a prescription for policy. For realism has become something of a fetish among foreign policy "sophisticates," who often accept the premises of realism uncritically, without recognizing the ways in which they no longer fit the world. The persistence of the theoretical framework beyond its appointed time has led to some rather strange proposals for how to think about and act in the post–Cold War world. For example, it was suggested that the West should try to keep the Warsaw Pact alive because the bipolar division of Europe was responsible for peace that has reigned on that continent since 1945;[18] alternatively, it was argued that the end of the division of Europe would lead to a period of greater instability and danger in Europe than was the case during the Cold War, one which could be remedied through the managed proliferation of nuclear weapons to Germany.[19]

Both of these proposals remind one of a doctor who, after treating a cancer patient through a long and agonizing process of chemotherapy that finally forces the cancer into remission, tries desperately to persuade the patient to continue the chemotherapy on the grounds that it has been so successful in the past. Treating a disease that no longer exists, realists now find themselves proposing costly and dangerous cures to healthy patients. To see why the patient is essentially healthy, we need to look again at realist assumptions about the underlying causes of the disease, that is, war among nations.

24

The Power of the Powerless

Realism is a theory that maintains that insecurity, aggression, and war are permanent possibilities in the international state system, and that this condition is a *human* condition, that is, a condition that cannot be altered by the appearance of specific forms and types of human societies because it is ultimately rooted in unchanging human nature. In support of this contention, realists point to the prevalence of war throughout human history, from the first bloody battles recorded in the Bible up to the world wars of this century.

All of this sounds intuitively plausible, but realism rests on two extremely shaky foundations: an impermissible reductionism concerning the motives and behavior of human societies, and failure to address the question of History.

In its purest form, realism tries to banish all considerations of internal politics, and to deduce the possibility of war from the structure of the state system alone. According to one realist, "Conflict is common among states because the international system creates powerful incentives for aggression. . . . States seek to survive under anarchy by maximizing their power relative to other states . . ."[1] But this pure form of realism covertly reintroduces certain highly reductionist assumptions about the nature of the human societies that make up the system, mistakenly attributing them to the "system" rather than to the units that make up the system. There is, for example, absolutely no reason to assume that any state in an anarchic international order should feel threatened by another state, unless one had reason to think that human

254

societies were inherently aggressive. The international order described by realists closely resembles the state of nature of Hobbes, where man is in a state of war of all against all. But Hobbes's state of war does not arise out of the simple desire for self-preservation, but because self-preservation co-exists with vanity or the desire for recognition. Were there not some men who desired to impose their views upon others, particularly those imbued with a spirit of religious fanaticism, then Hobbes himself would argue that the primordial state of war would never arise in the first place. Self-preservation alone is not sufficient to explain the war of all against all.

A peaceful state of nature is precisely what is postulated by Rousseau. Rousseau denies that vanity or *amour-propre* is natural to man, and argues that natural man, fearful and solitary, is essentially peaceful because his few selfish needs are easily satisfied. Fear and insecurity lead not to the perpetual seeking of power after power, but to isolation and quietude: the state of nature is inhabited by cow-like individuals who are content to live and let live, to experience the sentiment of their own existences without dependence on other human beings. The original anarchy therefore produces peace. Or, to put it in different language, a world of slaves seeking the preservation of their own natural existences would be free of conflict, for only masters are driven to the bloody battle. It is perfectly possible to imagine anarchic state systems that are nonetheless peaceful, in which questions of bipolarity and multipolarity are totally irrelevant, *if* one postulated that human societies behaved like Rousseau's man in the state of nature or Hegel's slave, that is, if their *only* interest were in self-preservation. The realist contention that states perceive each other as threats and arm themselves accordingly does not arise from the system so much as from a hidden assumption that human societies in their international behavior tend to resemble Hegel's master seeking recognition, or the vainglorious first man of Hobbes, rather than the timid solitary of Rousseau.

The fact that peace in historical state systems has been so difficult to obtain reflects the fact that certain states seek *more* than self-preservation. Like giant thymotic individuals, they seek acknowledgment of their value or dignity on dynastic, religious, nationalist, or ideological grounds, and in the process force other states either to fight or to submit. The ultimate ground of war among states is therefore *thymos* rather than self-preservation. Just as human history began with the bloody battle for pure prestige, so international conflict begins with a struggle for recognition among states, which is the original source of imperialism. The realist, then, can deduce nothing at all from the bare facts of the distribution of power within the state system. Such information becomes meaningful only if he or she makes certain assumptions about the nature of the societies constituting the system, namely, that at least some of them seek recognition rather than mere self-preservation.

The earlier generation of realists like Morgenthau, Kennan, Niebuhr, and Kissinger allowed some consideration of the internal character of states to enter into their analyses, and could therefore give a better account of the reasons for international conflict than the later academic school of "structural" realists.[2] The former at least recognized that conflict had to be driven by a *human* desire for domination, rather than from the mechanical interaction of a system of billiard balls. Nonetheless, realists of any stripe tend to be driven to highly reductionist explanations of state behavior when talking about internal politics.

It is hard to know, for example, how a realist like Morgenthau can prove empirically that the struggle for power is, as he puts it, "universal in space and time," since there are innumerable instances where both societies and individuals appear to be motivated by something other than the desire to maximize their relative power. The Greek colonels who yielded power to civilians in 1974, or the Argentine junta that stepped down in 1983 to face possible prosecution for crimes committed in office, could not reasonably be portrayed as "power maximizers." Britain in the last quarter of the nineteenth century devoted much of her national energy to the acquisition of new colonies, particularly in Africa, while after World War II it made an almost equal effort sloughing off its empire. Turkey prior to World War I dreamed of a pan-Turkic or pan-Turanian empire stretching from the Adriatic far into Russian Central Asia, but later under the guidance of Ataturk renounced such imperialist objectives and retreated to the borders of a compact nation-state in Anatolia. Are cases of countries seeking to grow *smaller* equally instances of the struggle for power, as those cases where they are seeking to grow larger through conquest and military buildup?

Morgenthau would argue that these cases do illustrate the struggle for power, because there are different forms of power and different ways of accumulating it. Some states seek to preserve what power they have through a policy of status quo; others seek to increase it through a policy of imperialism; while still others seek to demonstrate their power through a policy of prestige. A decolonizing Britain or a Kemalist Turkey are equally power maximizers, because they were forced to consolidate. By growing smaller they guaranteed their power in the long run.[3] A state need not seek to maximize its power through traditional channels of military and territorial expansion: it can do so through economic growth, or by putting itself at the head of the struggle for freedom and democracy.

On further consideration, however, it becomes evident that a definition of "power" so broad that it encompasses the objectives both of states trying to grow smaller, as well as of those using violence and aggression to enlarge their territorial domain, has lost its descriptive or analytical value. Such a definition does not help us understand why nations go to war. For it is clear that some manifestations of the "struggle for power" broadly defined are not only not threatening to others, but positively beneficial. For example, if we interpret the search for export markets by South Korea and Japan as manifestations of a struggle for power on their part, then it is a sort of power struggle that can be pursued indefinitely by both countries to their mutual benefit, and to the benefit of the region as a whole which will have access to ever cheaper products.

It is obviously the case that all states must seek power in order to accomplish their national purposes, even if these go no further than simple survival. The quest for power in this sense is indeed universal, but its meaning becomes trivial. It is quite another thing to say that all states seek to maximize their power, particularly their military power. In what way is it useful to understand contemporary states like Canada, Spain, Holland, or Mexico as power maximizers? Each certainly seeks to become wealthier, but the wealth is desired for the sake of domestic consumption, and not simply to enhance the state's power position relative to that of its neighbors. In fact, these countries would support their neighbors' economic growth because their own prosperity is intimately linked to it.[4]

States therefore do not simply pursue power; they pursue a variety of ends that are dictated by concepts of *legitimacy*.[5] Such concepts act as powerful constraints on the pursuit of power for its own sake, and those states which disregard considerations of legitimacy do so at their own peril. When Britain gave up India and other parts of the empire after World War II, it did so in large measure because of its condition of victorious exhaustion. But it was also the case that many Britons came to believe that colonialism was inconsistent with the Atlantic Charter and the Universal Declaration of Human Rights, on which basis Britain had just concluded the war against Germany. If maximizing its power position was its chief objective, Britain could plausibly have tried to hang on to its colonies as France did after the war, or to win them back when the nation recovered economically. That the latter course was inconceivable was due to the fact that Britain accepted the modern world's verdict that colonialism was an illegitimate form of domination.

The intimate connection that exists between power and concepts of legitimacy is nowhere better illustrated than in Eastern Europe. The years 1989 and 1990 saw one of the most massive shifts in the balance of power that has ever occurred in peacetime, as the Warsaw Pact disintegrated and a unified Germany emerged in the center of Europe. There was no change in the material balance of power: not a single tank in Europe was destroyed in combat, or even displaced because of an arms control agreement. This shift occurred entirely as a result of a change in standards of legitimacy: as communist power was discredited in one Eastern European country after another, and as the Soviets themselves did not have the self-confidence to restore their empire by force, the Warsaw Pact's cohesion melted much more quickly than it would have in the heat of a real war. It does not matter how many tanks and planes a country has if its soldiers and airmen are not willing to get in them and use them against the nation's purported enemies, or if they are not willing to fire upon civilian protesters to protect the regime they ostensibly serve. Legitimacy constituted, in Václav Havel's phrase, "the power of the powerless." Realists who look only at capabilities and not intentions are at a loss when intentions change so radically.

The fact that concepts of legitimacy have changed so dramatically over time suggests a second major weakness of realism: *it does not take account of history.*[6] In sharp distinction to every other aspect of human political and social life, realism portrays international relations as isolated in a timeless vacuum, immune from the evolutionary processes taking place around it. But those apparent continuities in world politics from Thucydides to the Cold War in fact mask significant differences in the manner in which societies seek, control, and relate to power.

Imperialism—the domination by force of one society by another—arises directly out of the aristocratic master's desire to be recognized as superior—his *megalothymia*. The same thymotic drive that led the master to subjugate the slave inevitably leads him to seek recognition from all people by leading his society into a bloody battle with other societies. This process has no logical end point until the master either achieves world empire, or dies. The desire of masters for recognition, and not the structure of the state system, is the original cause of war. Imperialism and war are therefore related to a certain social class, the class of masters, otherwise known as the aristocracy, who derived their social status from their willingness to risk their lives in bygone days. In aristocratic societies (which account for most human societies up until the past couple of hundred years), the striving of princes for universal but *unequal* recognition was widely regarded as legitimate. Wars of territorial conquest for the sake of an ever-expanding dominion were seen as a normal human aspiration, even as their destructive impact might be decried by certain moralists and writers.

The master's thymotic striving for recognition could take other forms, such as religion. The desire for religious mastery—that is, the recognition of one's own gods and idols by other peoples—could accompany the desire for personal mastery, as in the conquests of Cortés or Pizarro, or it could displace secular motives altogether, as in the various religious wars of the sixteenth and seventeenth centuries. It is not an undifferentiated struggle for power, as realists would have it, that is the common ground between dynastic and religious expansionism, but the struggle for recognition.

But these manifestations of *thymos* were to a large extent displaced in the early modern period by increasingly rational forms of recognition whose ultimate expression was the modern liberal state. The bourgeois revolution of which Hobbes and Locke were the prophets sought to morally elevate the slave's fear of death over the aristocratic virtue of the master, and thereby to sublimate irrational manifestations of *thymos* like princely ambition and religious fanaticism into the unlimited accumulation of property. Where once there had been civil conflict over dynastic and religious issues, there were now new zones of peace constituted by the modern liberal European nation-state. Political liberalism in England ended the religious wars between Protestant and Catholic that had nearly destroyed that country during the seventeenth century: with its advent, religion was defanged by being made tolerant.

The civil peace brought about by liberalism should logically have its counterpart in relations between states. Imperialism and war were historically the product of aristocratic societies. If liberal democracy abolished the class distinction between masters and slaves by making the slaves their own masters, then it too should eventually abolish imperialism. This thesis was stated in a slightly different form by the economist Joseph Schumpeter, who argued that democratic capitalist societies were markedly un-warlike and anti-imperialistic because they provided other outlets for the energies that formerly fanned wars:

> The competitive system absorbs the full energies of most of the people at all economic levels. Constant application, attention, and concentration of energy are the conditions of survival within it, primarily in the specifically economic professions, but also in other activities organized on their model. There is much less excess energy to be vented in war and conquest than in any precapitalist society. What excess energy there is flows largely into industry itself, accounts for its shining figures—the type of the captain of industry—and for the rest is applied to art, science, and the social struggle. . . . A purely capitalist world therefore can offer no fertile soil to imperialist impulses. . . . The point is that its people are likely to be essentially of an unwarlike disposition.[7]

Schumpeter defined imperialism as "the objectless disposition on the part of a state to unlimited forcible expansion."[8] This limitless striving for conquest was not a universal characteristic of all human societies, and could not be caused by an abstract quest for security on the part of slave societies. Rather, it sprang up at particular times and places, such as in Egypt after the expulsion of the Hyksos (the Semitic dynasty that ruled Egypt from the eighteenth to the sixteenth centuries B.C.), or after the conversion of the Arabs to Islam, because of the emergence of an aristocratic order whose moral basis was oriented to war.[9]

The genealogy of modern liberal societies in the consciousness

of the slave rather than the master, and the influence on them of
that last great slave ideology, Christianity, is today manifest in the
spread of compassion, and a steadily decreasing tolerance for
violence, death, and suffering. This comes to light, for example,
in the gradual disappearance of capital punishment among developed countries, or in the increasingly low tolerance of developed societies for casualties in war.[10] During the American Civil
War, soldiers were routinely shot for desertion; by World War II,
only one soldier was executed for this crime, and his wife later
sued the U.S. government on his behalf. The British Royal Navy
used to forcibly impress seamen from the lower classes into its
ranks for what amounted to a life of involuntary servitude; it now
must bribe them with pay competitive to civilian-sector jobs, and
provide them with the comforts of home while aboard ship.
Princes in the seventeenth or eighteenth centuries would think
nothing of sending tens of thousands of peasant soldiers to their
death for the sake of their personal glory. Today leaders of democratic countries do not lead their countries to war for other than
serious national causes, and must hesitate before taking such
grave decisions for they know their polities will not permit them
to behave recklessly. When they do, as in the case of America in
Vietnam, they are severely punished.[11] Tocqueville, noting the
rise of compassion already when writing *Democracy in America* in
the 1830s, quotes a letter written in 1675 by Mme. de Sévigné to
her daughter, in which she calmly describes watching a fiddler
broken on a wheel for stealing some paper, and then being quar-
tered after death (i.e., his body cut into four pieces) with " 'his
limbs exposed at the four corners of the city.' "[12] Tocqueville,
amazed that she speaks of this as lightly as she discusses the
weather, attributes the softening of customs that had occurred
since then to the rise of equality. Democracy breaks down the
walls that had earlier divided social classes, walls which prevented
educated and sensitive people like Mme. de Sévigné from even
recognizing the fiddler as a fellow human being. Today, our compassion extends not only to lower classes of human beings, but to
the higher animals as well.[13]

   With the spread of social equality came important changes in
the economics of war as well. Before the Industrial Revolution,
national wealth had to be extracted from the small surpluses eked
out by masses of peasants living at or just above the level of subsistence in what were almost universally agricultural societies. An

ambitious prince could increase his wealth only by grabbing someone else's lands and peasants, or else by conquering certain valuable resources, like the gold and silver of the New World. After
the Industrial Revolution, however, the importance of land, population, and natural resources declined sharply as sources of
wealth in comparison to technology, education, and the rational
organization of labor. The tremendous increases in labor productivity that the latter factors permitted were far more significant
and certain than any economic gains realized through territorial
conquest. Countries like Japan, Singapore, and Hong Kong with
little land, limited populations, and no natural resources found
themselves in an economically enviable position with no need to
resort to imperialism to increase their wealth. As Iraq's attempted
takeover of Kuwait demonstrates, of course, control over certain
natural resources like oil confers potentially great economic benefits. The consequences of this invasion, however, are not likely to
make this method of securing resources seem attractive in the
future. Given the fact that access to those same resources can be
obtained peacefully through a global system of free trade, war
makes much less economic sense than it did two or three hundred
years ago.[14]

At the same time, the economic costs of war, so bemoaned by
Kant, have increased exponentially with advances in technology.
Already by the time of World War I, conventional technology had
made war so costly that entire societies could be undermined by
participation in war, even if they were on the winning side. Nuclear weapons, needless to say, increased the potential social cost
of war many times over that. The role of nuclear weapons in
preserving peace during the Cold War has been widely recognized.[15] It is very hard to disentangle the effects of nuclear weapons from factors like bipolarity in accounting for the absence of
war in Europe after 1945. In retrospect, however, it seems reasonable to speculate that one or another Cold War crisis—over
Berlin, Cuba, or the Middle East—might have escalated into a real
war were the two superpowers not conscious of the horrendous
potential costs of conflict.[16]

The fundamentally un-warlike character of liberal societies is
evident in the extraordinarily peaceful relations they maintain
among one another. There is by now a substantial body of literature noting the fact that there have been few, if any, instances of
one liberal democracy going to war with another.[17] The political

scientist Michael Doyle, for example, maintains that in the two hundred or so years that modern liberal democracies have existed, not one single such instance has occurred.[18] Liberal democracies can, of course, fight states that are not liberal democracies, just as the United States fought in the two world wars, Korea, Vietnam, and most recently the Persian Gulf. The gusto with which they fight such wars may even exceed that of traditional monarchies or despotisms. But among each other, liberal democracies manifest little distrust or interest in mutual domination. They share with one another principles of universal equality and rights, and therefore have no grounds on which to contest each other's legitimacy. In such states *megalothymia* has found other outlets besides war, or else has atrophied to the point that there is little left to provoke a modern version of the bloody battle. The argument then is not so much that liberal democracy constrains man's natural instincts for aggression and violence, but that it has fundamentally transformed the instincts themselves and eliminated the motive for imperialism.

The peaceful influence of liberal ideas on foreign policy can be seen in the changes that have occurred in the Soviet Union and Eastern Europe since the mid-1980s. According to realist theory, democratization of the USSR should make no difference to its strategic position; indeed, many observers schooled in realism predicted quite flatly that Gorbachev would never permit the tearing down of the Berlin Wall or the loss of the Soviet *glacis* in Eastern Europe. And yet, precisely these startling changes occurred in Soviet foreign policy between 1985 and 1989, not as a result of any material change in the Soviet international position, but from what Gorbachev called "new thinking." The Soviet "national interest" was not a given, but was reinterpreted in radically minimal terms by Gorbachev and former foreign minister Eduard Shevardnadze.[19] "New thinking" began with a reassessment of the external threat faced by the Soviet Union. Democratization in the USSR led directly to a belittling of earlier staples of Soviet foreign policy, such as fear of "capitalist encirclement" or NATO as an "aggressive, revanchist" organization. To the contrary, the Soviet Communist party's theoretical journal *Kommunist* explained in early 1988 that "there are no politically influential forces in either Western Europe or the US" that contemplate "military aggression against socialism," and that "bourgeois democracy serves as a definite barrier in the path of unleashing such a war."[20] Perceptions of foreign threat, it would seem, are not determined "objectively" by a state's position in the state system, but are instead heavily influenced by ideology. Changes in threat perception then paved the way for massive unilateral reductions in Soviet conventional forces. The overthrow of communism in Eastern Europe led to similar announcements of unilateral reductions in forces in Czechoslovakia, Hungary, Poland, and other democratizing states. All of this could happen because the new democratic forces in the Soviet Union and Eastern Europe understood better than Western realists that democracies posed little threat to one another.[21]

Some realists have tried to explain away the remarkable empirical evidence concerning the lack of wars between liberal democracies by arguing that liberal democracies have either not been situated next to one another (and therefore not able to fight one another), or have been forced to cooperate out of a strong sense of mutual threat from non-liberal democracies. That is, the state of peaceful relations between such traditional antagonists as Britain, France, and Germany since 1945 is not to be explained by their common commitment to liberal democracy, but rather by their common fear of the Soviet Union which pushed them together into the NATO alliance and the European Community.[22]

This sort of conclusion is possible only if one insists on looking at countries as billiard balls and steadfastly averts one's gaze from what is happening on the inside. There are, in fact, countries whose peaceful relations can be explained primarily as the result of a larger mutual threat, and which will return to hostility as soon as that threat is removed. Syria and Iraq, for example, have lined up with one another during periods of conflict with Israel, but have fought each other tooth and nail at virtually all other times. Even in times of "peace," however, the mutual hostility of such allies is evident for anyone to see. But no such hostility exists between the democracies united against the Soviet Union during the Cold War. Who in contemporary France or Germany is waiting for the opportunity to cross the Rhine to seize new territory or avenge old wrongs? To use John Mueller's phrase, war between contemporary democracies like Holland or Denmark is not even "subrationally thinkable."[23] The United States and Canada have maintained a continent-wide, undefended border for nearly a century, despite the power vacuum represented by Canada. To be consistent, a realist ought to advocate an American takeover of Canada, given the window of opportunity provided by the end of the Cold War—provided, of course, that he is an American. To think that the European order emerging out of the Cold War will return to the competitive great power behavior of the nineteenth century is to be unaware of the thoroughly bourgeois character of life in present-day Europe. The anarchic state system of liberal Europe does not foster distrust and insecurity because most European states understand each other too well. They know that their neighbors are too self-indulgent and consumerist to risk death, full of entrepreneurs and managers but lacking in princes or demagogues whose ambitions alone are sufficient to start wars.

And yet, this same bourgeois Europe was convulsed by war within the lifetime of many people still living. Imperialism and war did not disappear with the advent of bourgeois society; history's most destructive wars have in fact occurred *since* the bourgeois revolution. How do we account for this? Schumpeter's explanation was that imperialism was a kind of atavism, a holdover from an earlier stage in human social evolution: "it is an element that stems from the living conditions, not of the present, but of the past—or, put in terms of the economic interpretation of history, from past rather than present relations of production."[24] While Europe had undergone a series of bourgeois revolutions, its ruling classes through the end of World War I continued to be drawn from the ranks of the aristocracy for whom concepts of national greatness and glory had not been displaced by commerce. The warlike ethos of aristocratic societies could be passed down to their democratic descendants, flaring to the surface in times of crisis or enthusiasm.

To Schumpeter's explanation for the persistence of imperialism and war as an atavistic holdover from aristocratic societies, we should add another drawn directly from the history of *thymos*. Between the older forms of recognition represented by dynastic and religious ambition, and the fully modern resolution it finds in the universal and homogeneous state, *thymos* can take the form of nationalism. Nationalism clearly had much to do with the wars of this century, and its resurgence in Eastern Europe and the Soviet Union is what threatens the peace of post-communist Europe. It is to this question that we now turn.

25

National Interests

Nationalism is a specifically modern phenomenon because it replaces the relationship of lordship and bondage with mutual and equal recognition. But it is not fully rational because it extends recognition only to members of a given national or ethnic group. It is a more democratic and egalitarian form of legitimacy than, say, hereditary monarchy, in which entire peoples could be regarded as part of a patrimonial inheritance. Nationalist movements have therefore not surprisingly been closely associated with democratic ones since the French Revolution. But the dignity nationalists seek to have recognized is not universal human dignity, but dignity for their group. The demand for this kind of recognition leads potentially to conflict with other groups seeking recognition for their particular dignity. Nationalism is therefore fully capable of replacing dynastic and religious ambition as a ground for imperialism, and did precisely that in the case of Germany.

The persistence of imperialism and war after the great bourgeois revolutions of the eighteenth and nineteenth centuries is therefore due not only to the survival of an atavistic warrior ethos, but also to the fact that the master's *megalothymia* was incompletely sublimated into economic activity. The state system over the past couple of centuries has consisted of a mixture of liberal and non-liberal societies. In the latter, irrational forms of *thymos* like nationalism frequently had free play, and all states were affected by nationalism to one degree or another. The nationalities of Europe were closely intertwined with one another, particularly in Eastern and Southeastern Europe, and their disentanglement into sepa-

266

rate nation-states was a great source of conflict—one which continues in many areas. Liberal societies would go to war to defend themselves from attack by non-liberal states, and they would themselves attack and rule over non-European societies. Many ostensibly liberal societies were tarnished by an admixture of intolerant nationalism, failing to universalize their concepts of rights by effectively basing citizenship on race or ethnic origin. "Liberal" England and France in the last decades of the nineteenth century could acquire extensive colonial empires in Africa and Asia, ruling by force rather than by popular consent, because they rated the dignity of Indians, Algerians, Vietnamese, and so on, lower than their own. In the words of the historian William Langer, imperialism "was also a projection of nationalism beyond the boundaries of Europe, a projection on a world scale of the time-honored struggle for power and for a balance of power as it had existed on the Continent for centuries."[1]

The rise of the modern nation-state after the French Revolution had a number of important consequences that changed the nature of international politics in fundamental ways.[2] Dynastic wars, in which a prince led congeries of peasants of different nationalities into battle for the conquest of a city or province, became impossible. The Netherlands could no longer be "owned" by Spain, or Piedmont by the Austrians, simply because of a marriage or conquest in generations past. Under the weight of nationalism, the multinational empires of the Hapsburgs and Ottomans began to collapse. Modern military power, like modern politics, became much more democratic, being passed on the *levée en masse* of entire populations. And with the participation of mass populations in war, war objectives had to satisfy the nation as a whole in some way and not just the ambition of the individual ruler. Alliances and boundaries became much more rigid, because nations and peoples could no longer be traded like so many chess pieces. This was true not just of formal democracies, but of nation-states like Bismarckian Germany which had to be responsive to the dictates of national identity even in the absence of popular sovereignty.[3] Moreover, once mass populations were motivated for war by nationalism they could rise to heights of thymotic anger seldom seen in dynastic conflicts, constraining leaders from dealing with enemies moderately or flexibly. The chief example of this was the Versailles Peace Treaty ending World War I. In contrast to the Congress of Vienna, the Versailles accord could not re-establish a workable balance of power in Europe because of the need to accommodate, on the one hand, the principle of national sovereignty when drawing new boundaries in place of the old German and Austro-Hungarian empires, and because of the demand by the French public for retribution against Germany on the other.

While admitting the very great power of nationalism over the past couple of centuries, however, it is necessary to put this phenomenon in proper perspective. It is very common for journalists, statesmen, and even scholars to treat nationalism as if it reflected a deep and fundamental longing of human nature, and as if the "nations" on which nationalism was based were timeless social entities as old as the state or the family. Common wisdom has it that once awakened, nationalism represents such an elemental force in history that it is unstoppable by other forms of attachment like religion or ideology, and will ultimately vanquish weak reeds like communism or liberalism.[4] Recently, this view has seemingly received empirical support in the resurgence of nationalist feelings throughout Eastern Europe and the Soviet Union, so much so that some observers are predicting that the post–Cold War era will be one of nationalist revival, much like the nineteenth century.[5] Soviet communism maintained that the national question was just an outgrowth of the more fundamental class question, and claimed to have settled the former once and for all by moving toward a classless society. With nationalists turning communists out of office in one Soviet republic after another, and throughout formerly communist Eastern Europe, the evident hollowness of this claim has undercut for many the credibility of the claims of all universalistic ideologies to have superseded nationalism.

Without denying the power of nationalism in large parts of the post–Cold War world, the view of nationalism as permanent and all-conquering is both parochial and untrue. In the first place, this perspective misunderstands how recent and contingent a phenomenon nationalism is. Nationalism does not, in Ernest Gellner's words, "have any very deep roots in the human psyche."[6] Men have felt patriotic attachments to larger social groups for as long as these groups have existed, but it was not until the Industrial Revolution that these groups were defined as linguistically and culturally homogeneous entities. In pre-industrial societies, class differences among people sharing a common nationality were all-pervasive, and stood as impermeable barriers to mutual intercourse. A Russian nobleman would have much more in common with a French nobleman than with a peasant living on his own estate. Not only would his social condition be similar to the Frenchman's, but he would also speak the same language, while often not being able to communicate directly with his own peasant.[7] Political entities took no account of nationality: the Hapsburg emperor Charles V could rule over parts of Germany, Spain, and the Netherlands simultaneously, while the Turkish Ottomans ruled Turks, Arabs, Berbers, and European Christians.

It was the same economic logic of modern natural science discussed in Part Two, however, that forced all societies undergoing it to become radically more egalitarian, homogeneous, and educated. Rulers and ruled had to speak the same language because both were intertwined in a national economy; peasants moving from the countryside had to be made literate in that language and given sufficient education to enable them to work in modern factories and, eventually, offices. Older social divisions of class, kinship, tribe, and sect withered under the pressure of requirements for continual labor mobility, leaving people with only a common language and common linguistic culture as their major form of social relatedness. Nationalism was therefore very much the product of industrialization and the democratic, egalitarian ideologies that accompanied it.[8]

The nations that were created as a result of modern nationalism were largely based on pre-existing "natural" linguistic divisions. But they were also the deliberate fabrications of nationalists, who had a degree of freedom in defining who or what constituted a language or a nation.[9] For example, the currently "re-awakening" nations in Soviet Central Asia did not exist as self-conscious linguistic entities prior to the Bolshevik Revolution; Uzbek and Kazakh nationalists are today going back to libraries to "re-discover" historical languages and cultures that are for many of them entirely new acquisitions. Ernest Gellner points out that there are over eight thousand "natural" languages on earth, of which seven hundred are major, but less than two hundred nations. Many of the older nation-states straddling two or more of these groups, like Spain with its Basque minority, are now under pressure to recognize the separate identity of these new groups.

This indicates that nations are not permanent or "natural" sources of attachment for people throughout the ages. Assimilation or national re-definition are possible and indeed common.[10]

It would appear that nationalisms have a certain life history. At certain stages of historical development, such as in agrarian societies, they don't exist in people's consciousness at all. They grow most intense just at or past the point of transition to industrial society, and become particularly exacerbated when a people, having gone through the first phases of economic modernization, is denied both national identity and political freedom. Thus it is not surprising that the two Western European countries to invent fascist ultranationalism, Italy and Germany, were also the last to industrialize and to unify politically, or that the most powerful nationalisms in the immediate aftermath of World War II were those of Europe's former colonies in the Third World. Given past precedent, it should also not surprise us that the strongest nationalisms of today are found in the Soviet Union or Eastern Europe, where industrialization was relatively late in coming and where national identities were long suppressed by communism.

But for national groups whose identity is more secure and of longer standing, the nation as a source of thymotic identification appears to decline. The passing of the initial, intense period of nationalism is most advanced in the region most damaged by nationalist passions, Europe. On that continent, the two world wars acted as a great spur to redefining nationalism in a more tolerant fashion. Having experienced the horrendous irrationality latent in the nationalist form of recognition, Europe's populations have gradually come to accept universal and equal recognition as an alternative. The result was a deliberate effort on the part of the survivors of those wars to dismantle national borders, and to turn popular passions away from national self-assertion into economic activity. The result, of course, was the European Community, a project that if anything has gained momentum in recent years under the pressure of economic competition from North America and Asia. The EC has obviously not abolished national differences, and the organization has difficulty building attributes of super-sovereignty as its founders hoped. But the sort of nationalism displayed in the EC over questions like agricultural policy and monetary union is already a highly domesticated version, and a far cry from the force that drove two world wars.

Those who say that nationalism is too elemental and powerful a force to be vanquished by a combination of liberalism and economic self-interest should consider the fate of organized religion, the vehicle for recognition that immediately preceded nationalism. There was a time when religion played an all-powerful role in European politics, with Protestants and Catholics organizing themselves into political factions and squandering the wealth of Europe in sectarian wars. English liberalism, as we saw, emerged in direct reaction to the religious fanaticism of the English Civil War. Contrary to those who at the time believed that religion was a necessary and permanent feature of the political landscape, *liberalism vanquished religion in Europe*. After a centuries-long confrontation with liberalism, religion was taught to be tolerant. In the sixteenth century, it would have seemed strange to most Europeans not to use political power to enforce belief in their particular sectarian faith. Today, the idea that the practice of religions other than one's own should injure one's own faith seems bizarre, even to the most pious churchman. Religion has thus been relegated to the sphere of private life—exiled, it would seem, more or less permanently from European political life except on certain narrow issues like abortion.[11]

To the extent that nationalism can be defanged and modernized like religion, where individual nationalisms accept a separate but equal status with their fellows, the nationalistic basis for imperialism and war will weaken.[12] Many people believe that the current move toward European integration is a momentary aberration brought on by the experience of World War II and the Cold War, but that the overall trend of modern European history is toward nationalism. But it may turn out that the two world wars played a role similar to the wars of religion in the sixteenth and seventeenth centuries with respect to religion, affecting the consciousness not just of the generation immediately following but of all subsequent generations.

If nationalism is to fade away as a political force, it must be made tolerant like religion before it. National groups can retain their separate languages and senses of identity, but that identity would be expressed primarily in the realm of culture rather than politics. The French can continue to savor their wines and the Germans their sausages, but this will all be done within the sphere of private life alone. Such an evolution has been taking place in the most advanced liberal democracies of Europe over the past couple of generations. Though the nationalism of contemporary European societies is still quite pronounced, it remains very dif-

ferent in character from the sort that existed in the previous
century when the concept of "peoples" and national identities was
relatively new. Since Hitler's fall, no Western European nationalism has seen the domination of other nationalities as key to its
identity. Just the contrary: the most modern nationalisms have
followed Ataturk's path, seeing their mission as the consolidation
and purification of national identity within a traditional homeland. Indeed, one might say that all mature nationalisms are going through a process of "Turkification." Such nationalisms do
not seem to be capable of creating new empires, they can only
break existing empires apart. The most radical nationalists today
like Schoenhuber's Republican party in Germany or Le Pen's National Front in France have been preoccupied not with ruling
foreigners, but with expelling them and, like the proverbial
greedy burgher, enjoying the good things of life alone and un-
molested. Most surprising and revealing is the fact that Russian
nationalism, usually counted as the most retrograde in Europe,
has been rapidly undergoing the process of Turkification, dis-
carding its former expansionism in favor of a "small Russia" concept.[13] Modern Europe has been moving rapidly to shed
sovereignty and to enjoy national identity in the soft glow of private life. Like religion, nationalism is in no danger of disappear-
ing, but like religion, it appears to have lost much of its ability to
stimulate Europeans to risk their comfortable lives in great acts of
imperialism.[14]

   This does not mean, of course, that Europe will be free from
nationalist conflicts in the future. This will be particularly true for
those newly liberated nationalisms in Eastern Europe and the
Soviet Union that have lain dormant and unfulfilled under communist rule. Indeed, we can expect a higher degree of nationalist
conflict in Europe with the end of the Cold War. Nationalism in
these cases is a necessary concomitant to spreading democratization, as national and ethnic groups long denied a voice express
themselves in favor of sovereignty and independent existence.
The stage was set for civil war in Yugoslavia, for example, by the
free elections held in Slovenia, Croatia, and Serbia in 1990, that
brought to power pro-independence, non-communist governments in the two former republics. The breakup of long-standing
multi-ethnic states promises to be a violent and bloody affair,
moreover, given the degree to which national groups are intertwined. In the Soviet Union, for example, some 60 million people

(half of whom are Russians) live outside their native republics, while one-eighth of Croatia's population is Serbian. Major population transfers have already started to occur in the USSR and will accelerate as different republics move toward independence. Many of the new nationalisms now emerging, particularly in regions of relatively low levels of socio-economic development, are likely to be quite primitive—that is, intolerant, chauvinistic, and externally aggressive.[15]

Moreover, the older existing nation-states are likely to be attacked from below by the claims of smaller linguistic groups demanding separate recognition. Slovaks now want recognition of an identity separate from Czechs. The peace and prosperity of liberal Canada is not enough for many French Canadians of Quebec, who want in addition preservation of their cultural distinctiveness. The potential for new nation-states, in which Kurds, Estonians, Ossetians, Tibetans, Slovenes, and the like each achieve national identity, is endless.

But these new manifestations of nationalism must be put into proper perspective. First, the most intense ones will occur predominantly in the least modernized parts of Europe, particularly in or near the Balkans and the southern parts of the former Russian Empire. They are likely to flare without affecting the long-term evolution of Europe's older nationalisms in the more tolerant direction suggested above. While the peoples of the Soviet Transcaucasus have already been guilty of acts of unspeakable brutality, there is little evidence to date that the nationalisms of the northern half of Eastern Europe—Czechoslovakia, Hungary, Poland, and the Baltic states—will develop in an aggressive direction incompatible with liberalism. This is not to say that existing states like Czechoslovakia may not fracture, or that Poland and Lithuania will not have border disputes. But this need not lead to the maelstrom of political violence characteristic of other areas, and will be counteracted by pressures for economic integration.

Second, the impact of new nationalist conflicts on the broader peace and security of Europe and the world will be much smaller than it was in 1914, when a Serbian nationalist triggered World War I by assassinating the heir to the Austro-Hungarian throne. While Yugoslavia crumbles and newly liberated Hungarians and Romanians torment each other endlessly over the status of the Hungarian minority in Transylvania, there are no great powers left in Europe that would be interested in exploiting such a conflict for the sake of bettering their strategic position. On the contrary, most advanced European states would seek to avoid entanglement in such controversies like a tar baby, intervening only in the face of egregious violations of human rights or threats to their own nationals. Yugoslavia, on whose territory the Great War began, has fallen into civil war and is disintegrating as a national entity. But the rest of Europe has achieved considerable consensus on an approach to settlement of the problem, and on the need to insulate Yugoslavia from larger questions of European security.[16]

Third, it is important to recognize the transitional nature of the new nationalist struggles now occurring in Eastern Europe and the Soviet Union. They are the birth pangs of a new and generally (though not universally) more democratic order in this region, as former communist empires collapse. There is reason to expect that many of the new nation-states that will emerge from this process will be liberal democracies, and that their nationalisms, exacerbated for now by the independence struggle, will mature and ultimately undergo the same process of "Turkification" as Western Europe.

The principle of legitimacy based on national identity took hold in the Third World in a big way after World War II. It came to the Third World later than it did to Europe, because industrialization and national independence came later as well, but when it arrived it had much the same impact. While relatively few countries in the Third World were formal democracies in the years since 1945, almost all of them abandoned dynastic or religious titles to legitimacy in favor of the principle of national self-determination. The newness of these nationalisms meant that they were much more self-assertive than the older, better established, and more confident ones of Europe. Pan-Arab nationalism, for example, was based on the same longings for national unification as the nationalisms of Italy and Germany in the last century, but was never fulfilled through the creation of a single, politically integrated Arab state.

But the rise of Third World nationalism has constrained international conflict in certain ways as well. Broad acceptance of the principle of national self-determination—not necessarily formal self-determination through free elections, but the right of national groups to live independently in their traditional homeland—had made it very hard for anyone to make military intervention or territorial aggrandizement stick. The power of Third World nationalism has been almost universally triumphant, seemingly regardless of relative levels of technology and development: the French were driven out of Vietnam and Algeria, the United States out of Vietnam, the Soviets out of Afghanistan, the Libyans out of Chad, the Vietnamese out of Cambodia, and so forth.[17] The major changes that have occurred in international borders since 1945 have almost all been cases of countries splitting apart along national lines rather than adding to their territory through imperialism—for example, the breakup of Pakistan and Bangladesh in 1971. Many of the factors that make territorial conquest unprofitable for developed countries—the rapidly escalating costs of war, including the cost of ruling a hostile population, the possibility of internal economic development as a more readily available source of wealth, and so on, have applied to conflicts between Third World countries as well.[18]

Nationalism continues to be more intense in the Third World, Eastern Europe, and the Soviet Union, and will persist there for a longer time than in Europe or America. The vividness of these new nationalisms seems to have persuaded many people in developed liberal democracies that nationalism is the hallmark of our age, without noticing its slow decline at home. It is curious why people believe that a phenomenon of such recent historical provenance as nationalism will henceforth be so permanent a feature of the human social landscape. Economic forces encouraged nationalism by replacing class with national barriers and created centralized, linguistically homogeneous entities in the process. Those same economic forces are now encouraging the breakdown of national barriers through the creation of a single, integrated world market. The fact that the final political neutralization of nationalism may not occur in this generation or the next does not affect the prospect of its ultimately taking place.

26

Toward a Pacific Union

Power politics continues to prevail among states that are not liberal democracies. The relatively late arrival of industrialization and nationalism to the Third World will lead to a sharp distinction between the behavior of much of the Third World, on the one hand, and of the industrial democracies on the other. For the foreseeable future, the world will be divided between a post-historical part, and a part that is still stuck in history.[1] Within the post-historical world, the chief axis of interaction between states would be economic, and the old rules of power politics would have decreasing relevance. That is, one could imagine a democratic Europe that was multipolar and dominated by German economic power, in which Germany's neighbors nonetheless felt relatively little sense of military threat and did not take any special efforts to increase their level of military preparedness. There would be considerable economic but little military competition. The post-historical world would still be divided into nation-states, but its separate nationalisms would have made peace with liberalism and would express themselves increasingly in the sphere of private life alone. Economic rationality, in the meantime, will erode many traditional features of sovereignty as it unifies markets and production.

On the other hand, the historical world would still be riven with a variety of religious, national, and ideological conflicts depending on the stage of development of the particular countries concerned, in which the old rules of power politics continue to apply. Countries like Iraq and Libya will continue to invade their

276

neighbors and fight bloody battles. In the historical world, the nation-state will continue to be the chief locus of political identification.

The boundary line between the post-historical and historical worlds is changing rapidly and is therefore hard to draw. The Soviet Union is making a transition from one camp to the other; and its breakup will result in some successor states that successfully make the transition to liberal democracy, and others that will not. China after Tiananmen Square is far from having achieved democracy, but since the beginning of the economic reform its foreign policy has become, so to speak, increasingly *bourgeois*. The current leadership of China seems to understand that it cannot turn the clock back on economic reform, and that China will have to remain open to the international economy. This has discouraged any return to a Maoist foreign policy, despite the attempt to revive aspects of Maoism domestically. The larger states of Latin America—Mexico, Brazil, Argentina—have passed from the historical to the post-historical world in the past generation, and though backsliding is possible in any of them, they are now tightly bound together with the other industrial democracies through economic interdependence.

In many respects, the historical and post-historical worlds will maintain parallel but separate existences, with relatively little interaction between them. There will, however, be several axes along which these worlds will collide. The first is oil, which was the background cause of the crisis caused by the Iraqi invasion of Kuwait. Oil production remains concentrated in the historical world and is crucial for the post-historical world's economic well-being. Despite talk of increasing global interdependence in a variety of commodities at the time of the oil crises of the 1970s, oil remains the only one whose production is sufficiently concentrated that the market in it can be manipulated or disrupted for political reasons, and whose disruption can result in immediately devastating economic consequences for the post-historical world.

The second axis of interaction is less visible than oil presently but in the long run perhaps more troublesome: immigration. There is at present a constant flow of people from countries that are poor and unstable to those that are rich and secure, that has affected virtually all states in the developed world. This flow, constantly increasing in recent years, could be suddenly accelerated by political upheavals in the historical world. Events like the breakup of the Soviet Union, or the outbreak of serious ethnic violence in Eastern Europe, or Hong Kong's absorption by an unreformed communist China, will all be occasions for massive population transfers from the historical to the post-historical worlds. And this flow of people will guarantee that post-historical states will remain interested in the historical world, either to stem the tide, or because these new immigrants have entered the political system and are now pushing their newly adopted hosts toward greater involvement.

It has proven very difficult for post-historical countries to bar immigration for at least two reasons. First, they have had difficulty formulating any just principle of excluding foreigners that does not seem racist or nationalist, thereby violating those universal principles of right to which they as liberal democracies are committed. All developed democracies have imposed limits on immigration at one time or another, but this has usually been done, so to speak, with a bad conscience.

The second reason for growing immigration is economic, since nearly every developed country has experienced shortages of certain kinds of unskilled or semi-skilled labor for which there is an unending supply in the Third World. Not all low-wage jobs can be exported. Economic competition in a single global market will encourage the further integration of regional labor markets, just as early capitalism fostered the growth of unified nation-states with high degrees of internal labor mobility.

The final axis of interaction between the two worlds will be over certain "world order" questions. That is, over and above the particular threat that certain historical countries pose to their neighbors, many post-historical countries will formulate an abstract interest in preventing the spread of certain technologies to the historical world, on the grounds that that world will be most prone to conflict and violence. At the moment, these technologies include nuclear weapons, ballistic missiles, chemical and biological weapons, and the like. But in the future, world order issues could expand to certain types of environmental interests threatened by unregulated technological proliferation. If the post-historical world behaves as differently from the historical world as postulated here, then the post-historical democracies will have a common interest both in protecting themselves from external threats, and in promoting the cause of democracy in countries where it does not now exist.

As a *prescriptive* doctrine, the realist perspective on international relations continues to be quite relevant despite the gains for democracy of the 1970s and 80s. The historical half of the world persists in operating according to realist principles, and the post-historical half must make use of realist methods when dealing with the part still in history. The relationship between democracies and non-democracies will still be characterized by mutual distrust and fear, and despite a growing degree of economic interdependence, force will continue to be the *ultima ratio* in their mutual relations.

On the other hand, as a *descriptive* model for how the world works, realism leaves a great deal to be desired. The insecurity and power-maximizing behavior that realists attribute to all states at all times in human history breaks down under closer examination. The human historical process has engendered a series of concepts of legitimacy—dynastic, religious, nationalistic, and ideological, leading to as many possible bases for imperialism and war. Each of these forms of legitimacy prior to modern liberalism was based on some form of lordship and bondage, so that imperialism was in a sense dictated by the social system. Just as concepts of legitimacy have changed over history, so has international relations; while war and imperialism may have seemed constant throughout history, wars have been fought for very different objectives in each age. There was no "objective" national interest that provided a common thread to the behavior of states in different times and places, but a plurality of national interests defined by the principle of legitimacy in play and the individuals who interpreted it.

And it would seem natural that liberal democracy, which seeks to abolish the distinction between masters and slaves by making men the masters of themselves, should have different foreign policy objectives altogether. What will produce peace in the post-historical world will not be the fact that the major states share a common principle of legitimacy. This state of affairs existed at times in the past, for example, when all the nations of Europe were monarchies or empires. Peace will arise instead out of the specific nature of democratic legitimacy, and its ability to satisfy the human longing for recognition.

The differences between democratic and non-democratic states, and the possibility of a broader historical process leading to the spread of liberal democracy around the world, suggests that the traditional moralism of American foreign policy, with its concern for human rights and "democratic values," is not entirely misplaced.[2] Henry Kissinger argued in the 1970s that revolutionary challenges to communist states like the Soviet Union and China were morally satisfying but practically imprudent, because they blocked the way to "realistic" accommodation on issues like arms control or the settlement of regional disputes. Former President Reagan was sharply criticized for his 1987 call to the Soviets to tear down the Berlin Wall, no more so than in Germany which had long since accommodated itself to the "reality" of Soviet power. But in a world evolving toward democracy, it turned out that these revolutionary challenges to the Soviet Union's legitimacy were both morally satisfying *and* politically prudent, insofar as they accorded with the soon-to-be-expressed aspirations of many of the people living under communism at the time.

No one, of course, would advocate a policy of military challenges to non-democratic states armed with powerful weapons, especially nuclear ones. Revolutions of the sort that occurred in Eastern Europe in 1989 are rare events, even unprecedented ones, and a democracy cannot predicate its foreign policy on the imminent collapse of each dictatorship that it confronts. But in making calculations of power, democracies have to remember that legitimacy is a form of power as well, and that strong states frequently hide grave internal weaknesses. This means that democracies that choose their friends and enemies by ideological considerations—that is, whether they are democratic—are likely to have stronger and more durable allies *in the long run*. And in dealing with enemies, they should not forget the abiding moral differences between their societies or sweep aside questions of human rights in pursuit of the powerful.[3]

The peaceful behavior of democracies further suggests that the United States and other democracies have a long-term interest in preserving the sphere of democracy in the world, and in expanding it where possible and prudent. That is, if democracies do not fight one another, then a steadily expanding post-historical world will be more peaceful and prosperous. The fact that communism has collapsed in Eastern Europe and the Soviet Union and that the immediate military threat from the Warsaw Pact has all but evaporated cannot make us indifferent to what succeeds it. For in the long run the West's chief guarantee against a revival of a threat from that part of the world, or from a reunited Germany,

or from an economically dominant Japan, will be the flourishing
of liberal democracy in those countries.

The need for democratic states to work together to promote
democracy and international peace is an idea almost as old as
liberalism itself. The case for an international league of democracies governed by a rule of law was laid out by Immanuel Kant in
his famous essay, *Perpetual Peace*, as well as in his *Idea for a Universal History*. Kant argued that the gains realized when man
moved from the state of nature to civil society was largely nullified
by the state of war which prevailed between nations: "Through
wasting the powers of the commonwealths in armaments to be
used against each other, through devastation brought on by war,
and even more by the necessity of holding themselves in constant
readiness for war, [states] stunt the full development of human
nature."[4] Kant's writings on international relations subsequently
became the intellectual basis for contemporary liberal internationalism. The Kantian league was the inspiration for American attempts to establish first the League of Nations and then the United
Nations. As noted earlier, postwar realism was in many ways presented as an *antidote* to this strand of liberal internationalism, by
suggesting the real remedy for international security was less international law than the balance of power.

The manifest failure of the League of Nations and the United
Nations to provide collective security against challenges first from
Mussolini, the Japanese, and Hitler, and then against Soviet expansionism, has led to the general discrediting of Kantian internationalism and of international law in general. What many
people have not understood, however, is that the actual incarna-
tions of the Kantian idea have been seriously flawed from the start
by not following Kant's own precepts.[5] Kant's "First Definitive
Article" for perpetual peace states that the constitution of states in
the state system should be republican, that is, they should be
liberal democracies.[6] The "Second Definitive Article" states that
"the law of nations should be founded on a federation of *free*
states,"[7] that is, states sharing republican constitutions. Kant's reasons are straightforward: states based on republican principles
are less likely to fight one another because self-governing peoples
are more reluctant to accept the costs of war than despotisms,
while an international federation, to work, must share common
liberal principles of right. International law is merely domestic
law writ large.

The United Nations did not live up to these conditions from
the beginning. The Charter of the United Nations dropped any
reference to a league of "free nations," in favor of the weaker
principle of the "sovereign equality of all its members."[8] That is,
membership in the United Nations was open to any state possessing certain minimal formal criteria of sovereignty, regardless of
whether they were based on popular sovereignty or not. Thus
Stalin's Soviet Union was from the start a founding member of the
organization, with a seat on the Security Council and the right to
veto resolutions of that body. After decolonization, the General
Assembly came to be populated by a congerie of new Third World
states which shared few of Kant's liberal principles, and who
found the United Nations a useful instrument for pushing illiberal political agendas. With no pre-existing consensus on just principles of political order or the nature of rights, it is not surprising
that the United Nations has not been able to accomplish anything
of real importance since its founding, in the critical area of collective security. It is also not surprising that the UN was always
looked upon with great suspicion by the American people. The
UN's predecessor, the League of Nations, was somewhat more
homogeneous in the political character of its members, though it
came to include the Soviet Union after 1933. But its ability to
enforce principles of collective security was decisively weakened
by the fact that large and important players in the state system—
Japan and Germany—were not democracies, and were not willing
to play by the League's rules.

With the waning of the Cold War and the rise of reform
movements in the Soviet Union and China, the United Nations
has shed some of its former debility. The Security Council's passage of unprecedented economic sanctions against Iraq and an
authorization for the use of force after the invasion of Kuwait
were an indication of the type of international action that may be
possible in the future. The Security Council is still vulnerable,
however, to backsliding on the part of incompletely reformed
powers like Russia and China, while the General Assembly remains populated by nations that are not free. It is reasonable to
question whether the UN will become the basis for a "new world
order" in the next generation.

If one wanted to create a league of nations according to Kant's
own precepts, that did not suffer from the fatal flaws of earlier

international organizations, it is clear that it would have to look much more like NATO than the United Nations—that is, a league of truly free states brought together by their common commitment to liberal principles. Such a league should be much more capable of forceful action to protect its collective security from threats arising from the non-democratic part of the world. The states making it up would be able to live according to the rules of international law in their mutual dealings. In fact, such a Kantian liberal international order has come into being willy-nilly during the Cold War under the protective umbrellas of organizations like NATO, the European Community, the OECD, the Group of Seven, GATT,[9] and others that make liberalism a precondition for membership. The industrial democracies are today effectively linked in a web of binding legal agreements which regulate their mutual economic interactions. While they may engage in political struggles over beef quotas and the nature of the European Monetary Union, or over how to deal with Libya and the Arab-Israeli conflict, the use of force to settle such disputes among the democracies themselves is totally unthinkable.

The United States and other liberal democracies will have to come to grips with the fact that, with the collapse of the communist world, the world in which they live is less and less the old one of geopolitics, and that the rules and methods of the historical world are not appropriate to life in the post-historical one. For the latter, the major issues will be economic ones like promoting competitiveness and innovation, managing internal and external deficits, maintaining full employment, dealing cooperatively with grave environmental problems, and the like. They must, in other words, come to terms with the fact that they are the heirs of the bourgeois revolution started over four hundred years ago. The post-historical world is one in which the desire for comfortable self-preservation has been elevated over the desire to risk one's life in a battle for pure prestige, and in which universal and rational recognition has replaced the struggle for domination.

Contemporary people can argue *ad infinitum* whether they have reached the post-historical world—whether international life will turn up further empires, dictators, unfulfilled nationalisms yearning for recognition, or new religions that will blow in like the whirlwind from the desert. But at a certain point, they must also confront the question of whether the post-historical house which they have built for themselves, a house that served as needed shelter from the desperate storms of the twentieth century, is one that they will be content to live in over the long term. For virtually everybody in the developed world today, it is reasonably clear that liberal democracy is vastly preferable to its major competitors, fascism and communism. But is it worthy of choice in itself? Or does liberal democracy leave us still fundamentally unsatisfied? Are there contradictions that will remain at the heart of our liberal order, even after the last fascist dictator, swaggering colonel, or Communist party boss has been driven from the face of the earth? It is this question to which we will turn in the final section of this book.

Part V
THE LAST MAN

27

In the Realm of Freedom

History properly so-called, in which men ("classes") fight among themselves for recognition and fight against Nature by work, is called by Marx the "realm of necessity" (Reich der Notwendigkeit); beyond (jenseits) *is situated the "realm of freedom"* (Reich der Freiheit), *in which men (mutually recognizing one another without reservation) no longer fight, and work as little as possible.*

—*Alexandre Kojève*, Introduction to the Reading of Hegel[1]

In our earlier discussion of the possibility of writing a Universal History, we said that we would put off, for the time being, the question of whether directional historical change constituted *progress.* If history leads us in one way or another to liberal democracy, this question then becomes one of the goodness of liberal democracy, and of the principles of liberty and equality on which it is based. Common sense would indicate that liberal democracy has many advantages over its major twentieth-century rivals, fascism and communism, while loyalty to our inherited values and traditions would dictate unquestioning commitment to democracy. But the cause of liberal democracy is not necessarily best served by unthinking partisanship, and by the failure to address squarely democracy's failings. And it is obviously impossible to answer the question of whether history has come to an end without looking more deeply at the question of democracy and its discontents.

We have become used to thinking about the question of the survival of democracy in terms of foreign policy. In the eyes of people like Jean-François Revel, democracy's greatest weakness

287

was its inability to defend itself against ruthless and determined tyrannies. The question of whether and for how long the threat from these tyrannies has receded will continue to preoccupy us in a world still full of authoritarianisms, theocracies, intolerant nationalisms, and the like. But let us grant, for the moment, that liberal democracy has vanquished its foreign rivals and for the foreseeable future faces no serious external threats to its survival. Left to themselves, can those stable, long-standing liberal democracies of Europe and America be indefinitely self-sustaining, or will they one day collapse from some kind of internal rot, much as communism has done? Liberal democracies are doubtless plagued by a host of problems like unemployment, pollution, drugs, crime, and the like, but beyond these immediate concerns lies the question of whether there are other deeper sources of discontent within liberal democracy—whether life there is truly *satisfying*. If no such "contradictions" are apparent to us, then we are in a position to say with Hegel and Kojève that we have reached the end of history. But if they are, then we would have to say that History, in the strict sense of the word, will continue.

To answer this question, we said earlier that it would not be sufficient to look around the world for empirical evidence of challenges to democracy, since this evidence would always be ambiguous and potentially deceptive. Certainly, we cannot take the collapse of communism as proof that no future challenges to democracy are possible, or that democracy will not one day suffer the same fate. Rather, we need a trans-historical standard against which to measure democratic society, some concept of "man as *man*" that would allow us to see its potential defects. It was for that reason that we turned to the "first men" of Hobbes, Locke, Rousseau, and Hegel.

Kojève's claim that mankind has already reached the end of history rests on his view that the desire for recognition is the most fundamental human longing. For him, the struggle for recognition drove history from the first bloody battle; history has ended because the universal and homogeneous state embodying reciprocal recognition *fully satisfies* this longing. Kojève's emphasis on the desire for recognition would seem to be quite appropriate as a framework for understanding the future prospects of liberalism, for, as we have seen, the major historical phenomena of the last several centuries—religion, nationalism, and democracy—can be understood in their essence as different manifestations of the struggle for recognition. An analysis of the ways that *thymos* is and is not satisfied in contemporary society is likely to give us greater insight into the adequacy of liberal democracy than would a similar analysis of desire.

The question of the end of history then amounts to a question of the future of *thymos:* whether liberal democracy adequately satisfies the desire for recognition, as Kojève says, or whether it will remain radically unfulfilled and therefore capable of manifesting itself in an entirely different form. Our earlier attempt to construct a Universal History produced two parallel historical processes, one guided by modern natural science and the logic of desire, the other by the struggle for recognition. Both conveniently culminated in the same end point, capitalist liberal democracy. But can desire and *thymos* be so neatly satisfied by the same sorts of social and political institutions? Is it not possible that what satisfies desire is dissatisfying to *thymos*, and vice versa, so that no human society will be satisfying to "man as *man*"?

The possibility that liberal society does not represent the simultaneous satisfaction of desire and *thymos* but instead opens up a grave disjuncture between them is raised by critics of liberalism on both the Left and the Right. The attack from the Left would maintain that the promise of universal, reciprocal recognition remains essentially unfulfilled in liberal societies, for the reasons just indicated: economic inequality brought about by capitalism *ipso facto* implies unequal recognition. The attack from the Right would argue that the problem with liberal society is not the inadequate universality of recognition, but the goal of equal recognition itself. The latter is problematic because human beings are inherently *unequal;* to treat them as equal is not to affirm but to deny their humanity. We will investigate each of these claims in turn.

Of the two, critics of liberal societies on the Left have been far more common over the past century. The problem of inequality will continue to preoccupy liberal societies for generations to come because they are, in a certain sense, unresolvable within the context of liberalism. Even so, they seem to be less fundamental "contradictions" in our present order than those discontents arising from the Right, that is, concerning the desirability of equal recognition as an end in itself.

Social inequality falls into two categories, the sort that is traceable to human convention, and that attributable to nature or nat-

ural necessity. In the first category are legal barriers to equality—
the division of society into closed estates, apartheid, Jim Crow
laws, property qualifications for voting, and the like. In addition,
there are conventional inequalities due to culture, such as the
attitudes of different ethnic and religious groups to economic
activity discussed earlier. The latter do not rise from positive law
or policy, nor are they attributable to nature.

Natural barriers to equality begin with the unequal distribution of natural abilities or attributes within a population. Not everyone can be a concert pianist or a center for the Lakers, nor do
they have, as Madison noted, equal facilities for acquiring property. Handsome boys and beautiful girls will have advantages in
attracting marriage partners over their homelier counterparts.
There are also forms of inequality directly traceable to the workings of the capitalist market: the division of labor within the economy, and the ruthless workings of markets themselves. These
forms of inequality are no more "natural" than capitalism itself,
but they are necessarily implied by the choice of a capitalist economic system. The productivity of a modern economy cannot be
achieved without the rational division of labor, and without creating winners and losers as capital shifts from one industry, region, or country to another.

All truly liberal societies are in principle dedicated to the elimination of conventional sources of inequality. In addition, the dynamism of capitalist economies tends to break down many
conventional and cultural barriers to equality through its continually changing demand for labor. A century of Marxist thought
has accustomed us to think of capitalist societies as highly inegalitarian, but the truth is that they are far more egalitarian in their
social effects than the agricultural societies they replaced.[2] Capitalism is a dynamic force which constantly attacks purely conventional social relationships, replacing inherited privilege with new
stratifications based on skill and education. Without universal literacy and education, without a high degree of social mobility and
occupations open to talent rather than privilege, capitalist societies would not work, or would not work as efficiently as they
could. In addition, virtually all modern democracies regulate business, redistribute income from the rich to the poor, and have
accepted some degree of responsibility for social welfare, from
Social Security and Medicaid in the United States to the more
comprehensive welfare systems of Germany or Sweden. While the

United States remains perhaps the least inclined of Western democracies to take on a paternalistic role, the basic social welfare legislation of the New Deal has been accepted by conservatives, and has proved largely invulnerable to rollback.

What emerges from all of these equalizing processes has been termed "middle-class society." This expression is a misnomer, insofar as the social structure of modern democracies still resembles the classic pyramid, rather than a Christmas ornament bulging in the middle. But the middle of that pyramid remains fairly capacious, and a high degree of social mobility permits almost everyone to identify with the aspirations of the middle class and to think that they are, at least potentially, members of it. Middle-class societies will remain highly inegalitarian in certain respects, but the sources of inequality will increasingly be attributable to the natural inequality of talents, the economically necessary division of labor, and to culture. We may interpret Kojève's remark that postwar America had in effect achieved Marx's "classless society" in these terms: not that all social inequality was eliminated, but that those barriers which remained were in some respect "necessary and ineradicable," due to the nature of things rather than the will of man. Within those limits, such a society could be said to have achieved Marx's "realm of freedom" by effectively abolishing natural need, and by permitting people to appropriate what they wanted in return for a minimum (by any historical standard) amount of work.[3]

Even by this relatively relaxed standard of equality, most existing liberal democracies do not yet fully measure up. Of inequalities due to convention rather than nature or necessity, the hardest to eradicate are those arising from culture. Such is the situation of the so-called black "underclass" in contemporary America. The obstacles confronting a young black growing up in Detroit or the South Bronx only begin with substandard schools, a problem which could in theory be remedied as a matter of public policy. In a society where status is determined almost entirely by education, such an individual is likely to be crippled even before he or she reaches school age. Lacking a home environment capable of transmitting cultural values needed to take advantage of opportunity, such a youngster will feel the constant pull of the "street" that offers a life more familiar and glamorous than that of middle-class America. Under these circumstances, achievement of full legal equality for blacks and the opportunities provided by the

U. S. economy will not make terribly much difference to his or her
life. The solution to such problems of cultural inequality is not
obvious, moreover, since a plausible case has been made that precisely those social policies undertaken to help the black underclass
have hurt them by undercutting the family and increasing their
dependence on the state. No one has solved the problem of "creating culture"—that is, of regenerating internalized moral
values—as a matter of public policy. Thus while the principle of
equality may have been correctly established in America in 1776,
it remains to be implemented fully for many Americans in the
1990s.

Moreover, while capitalism may be capable of creating enormous amounts of wealth, it will continue to fail to satisfy the
human desire for equal recognition, or *isothymia*. With the division
of labor come differences in the dignity of different occupations:
garbage men and busboys will always be treated with less respect
than brain surgeons or football stars, while the unemployed will
have less dignity yet. In prosperous democracies, the problem of
poverty has been transformed from one of natural need, into one
of recognition. The real injury that is done to poor or homeless
people is less to their physical well-being than to their dignity.
Because they have no wealth or property, they are not taken
seriously by the rest of society: they are not courted by politicians
and their rights are not enforced as vigorously by the police and
the judicial system; they cannot find jobs in a society that still
values self-reliance; the jobs they can find they regard as demean-
ing; and they have fewer opportunities to better their situation
through education or to otherwise realize their potential. As long
as the distinction between rich and poor remains, as long as some
occupations are regarded as prestigious while others are seen as
degrading, then no absolute level of material prosperity will ever
correct this situation or overcome the daily damage done to the
dignity of those less well-off. What is satisfying to desire is therefore not simultaneously satisfying to *thymos*.

The fact that major social inequalities will remain even in the
most perfect of liberal societies means that there will be a continuing tension between the twin principles of liberty and equality
upon which such societies are based. This tension, noted clearly
by Tocqueville,[4] will be as "necessary and ineradicable" as the
inequality out of which it grows. Every effort to give the disadvantaged "equal dignity" will mean the abridgment of the free-

dom or rights of other people, all the more so when the sources of disadvantage lie deep within the social structure. Every place granted to a minority candidate for a job or a university education under an affirmative action program means one less place for others; every government dollar spent on national health insurance or welfare means that much less for the private economy; every attempt to protect workers from unemployment or firms from bankruptcy will mean less economic freedom. There is no fixed or natural point at which liberty and equality come into balance, nor any way of optimizing both simultaneously.

At one extreme, the Marxist project sought to promote an extreme form of social equality at the expense of liberty, by eliminating natural inequalities through the reward not of talent but of need, and through the attempt to abolish the division of labor. All future efforts to push social equality beyond the point of a "middle-class society" must contend with the failure of the Marxist project. For in order to eradicate those seemingly "necessary and ineradicable" differences, it was necessary to create a monstrously powerful state. The Chinese communists or the Khmer Rouge in Cambodia could try to eliminate the division between city and countryside, or between physical and intellectual labor, but only at the cost of stripping all people of the most minimal rights. The Soviets could try to reward need rather than work or talent, but only at the cost of a society that lost its interest in working. And these communist societies ultimately ended up accepting a substantial degree of social inequality, what Milovan Djilas labeled the "new class" of party officials and bureaucrats.[5]

With the collapse of communism worldwide, we are now in a remarkable situation where left-wing critics of liberal societies are singularly lacking in *radical* solutions to overcoming the more intractable forms of inequality. For the time being, the thymotic desire for individual recognition has held its own against the thymotic desire for equality. There are today few critics of liberal societies who are willing to advocate the wholesale abandonment of liberal principles, either in the political or economic realm, in order to overcome existing economic inequality.[6] The major arguments concern not the principles of liberal society, but the precise point at which the proper trade-off between liberty and equality should come. Every society will balance liberty and equality differently, from the individualism of Reagan's America or Thatcher's Britain, to the Christian Democracy of the European

continent and the social democracy of Scandinavia. These countries will be very different from one another in their social practices and their quality of life, but the specific trade-offs they choose
can all be made under the broad tent of liberal democracy, without injury to underlying principles. The desire for a greater degree of social democracy need not come at the expense of formal
democracy, and therefore does not in itself refute the possibility
of an end of history.

Despite the present receding of the old economic class issue on
the part of the Left, it is not clear that there will be any end to new
and potentially more radical challenges to liberal democracy based
on other forms of inequality. Already, forms of inequality such as
racism, sexism, and homophobia have displaced the traditional
class issue for the Left on contemporary American college campuses. Once the principle of equal recognition of each person's
human dignity—the satisfaction of their *isothymia*—is established,
there is no guarantee that people will continue to accept the existence of natural or necessary residual forms of inequality. The
fact that nature distributes capabilities unequally is not particularly just. Just because the present generation accepts this kind of
inequality as either natural or necessary does not mean that it will
be accepted as such in the future. A political movement may one
day revive Aristophanes' plan in the *Assembly of Women* to force
handsome boys to marry ugly women and vice versa,[7] or the
future may turn up new technologies for mastering this original
injustice on the part of nature and redistributing the good things
of nature like beauty or intelligence in a "fairer" way.[8]

Consider, for example, what has happened in our treatment
of the handicapped. It used to be that people felt the handicapped had been dealt a bad hand by nature, much as if they had
been born short or cross-eyed, and would simply have to live with
their disability. Contemporary American society, however, has
sought to remedy not only the physical handicap, but the injury to
dignity as well. The way of helping the handicapped that was
actually chosen by many government agencies and universities
was in many respects much more economically costly than it might
have been. Instead of providing the handicapped with special
transportation services, many municipalities changed all public
buses to make them accessible to the handicapped. Instead of
providing discreet entrances to public buildings for wheelchairs,
they mandated ramps at the front door. This expense and effort

was undertaken not so much to ease the physical discomfort of the handicapped, since there were cheaper ways of doing this, but to avoid affronts to their dignity. It was their *thymos* that was to be protected, by overcoming nature and demonstrating that a handicapped person could take a bus or enter the front door of the building as well as anyone else.

The passion for equal recognition—*isothymia*—does not necessarily diminish with the achievement of greater *de facto* equality and material abundance, but may actually be stimulated by it.

Tocqueville explained that when the differences between social classes or groups are great and supported by long-standing tradition, people become resigned or accepting of them. But when society is mobile and groups pull closer to one another, people become more acutely aware and resentful of the remaining differences. In democratic countries, the love of equality was a deeper and more abiding passion than the love of liberty. Freedom could be had without democracy, but equality was the uniquely defining characteristic of democratic ages, and for that reason people clung to it more tenaciously. The excesses of freedom—the arrogant display of a Leona Helmsley or a Donald Trump, the crimes committed by an Ivan Boesky or Michael Milken, the damage done by the *Exxon Valdez* to Prudhoe Bay— are much more visible than the evils of extreme equality like creeping mediocrity or the tyranny of the majority. And while political freedom bestows exalted pleasures on a small number of citizens, equality provides the great mass of people with small enjoyments.[9]

Thus while the liberal project has been largely successful over the past four hundred years in excluding the more visible forms of *megalothymia* from political life, our society will continue to remain preoccupied with questions of equalizing dignity. Today in democratic America there is a host of people who devote their lives to the total and complete elimination of any vestiges of inequality, making sure that no little girl should have to pay more to have her locks cut than a little boy, that no Boy Scout troop be closed to homosexual scoutmasters, that no building be built without a concrete wheelchair ramp going up to the front door. These passions exist in American society because of, and not despite, the smallness of its actual remaining inequalities.

The form that a future left-wing challenge to our present liberalism may take could be considerably different from those with which we are familiar in this century. The threat to liberty posed by communism was so direct and obvious, and the doctrine so discredited at present, that it is hard to see it as anything but totally exhausted throughout the developed world. A future left-wing threat to liberal democracy is much more likely to wear the clothing of liberalism while changing its meaning from within, rather than to stage a frontal attack on basic democratic institutions and principles.

For example, almost all liberal democracies have seen a massive proliferation of new "rights" over the past generation. Not content merely to protect life, liberty, and property, many democracies have also defined rights to privacy, travel, employment, recreation, sexual preference, abortion, childhood, and so on. Needless to say, many of these rights are ambiguous in their social content and mutually contradictory. It is easy to foresee situations in which the basic rights defined by, say, the Declaration of Independence and the Constitution, were seriously abridged by newly minted rights whose aim was a more thoroughgoing equalization of society.

The incoherence in our current discourse on the nature of rights springs from a deeper philosophical crisis concerning the possibility of a rational understanding of man. Rights spring directly from an understanding of what man is, but if there is no agreement on the nature of man, or a belief that such an understanding is in principle impossible, then any attempt to define rights or to prevent the creation of new and possibly spurious ones will be unavailing. As an example of how this could come about, consider the possibility of a future superuniversalization of rights, where the distinction between human and non-human is lost.

Classical political philosophy maintained that man had a dignity somewhere between the beasts and the gods; man's nature was part animal, but he had reason and therefore a specifically human virtue not shared by the other species. For Kant and Hegel, and the Christian tradition on which they built, the distinction between man and non-man was absolutely crucial. Human beings had a dignity superior to anything in nature because they alone were *free:* that is, they were uncaused causes, undetermined by natural instinct and capable of autonomous moral choice.

Today, everybody *talks* about human dignity, but there is no consensus as to why people possess it. Certainly few people believe that man is dignified because he is capable of moral choice. The entire thrust of modern natural science and philosophy since the time of Kant and Hegel has been to deny the possibility of autonomous moral choice, and to understand human behavior entirely in terms of sub-human and sub-rational impulses. What once appeared to Kant as free and rational choice was seen by Marx as the product of economic forces, or by Freud as deeply hidden sexual urges. According to Darwin, man literally evolved from the sub-human; more and more of what he was was understandable in terms of biology and biochemistry. The social sciences in this century have told us that man is a product of his social and environmental conditioning, and that human behavior like animal behavior operates according to certain deterministic laws. Studies of animal behavior indicate that they too can engage in prestige battles and, who knows, can experience pride or feel the desire for recognition. Modern man now sees that there is a continuum from the "living slime," as Nietzsche put it, all the way up to himself; he was different quantitatively but not qualitatively from the animal life out of which he came. Autonomous man, rationally able to follow laws he has created for himself, was reduced to a self-congratulatory myth.

Man's superior dignity entitles him to the conquest of nature, that is, to the manipulation and appropriation of nature for his own purposes, made possible through modern natural science. But modern natural science seems to demonstrate that there is no essential difference between man and nature, that man is simply a more organized and rational form of slime. But if there is no basis for saying that man has a superior dignity to nature, then the justification for man's dominion over nature ends. The egalitarian passion that denies the existence of significant differences between human beings can be extended to a denial of significant differences between man and the higher animals. The animal rights movement argues that monkeys, rats, or sables can suffer just as much as a human being, while dolphins appear to possess a higher form of intelligence; why then is it illegal to kill humans but not these creatures?

But the argument will not stop there. For how does one distinguish between higher and lower animals? Who can determine what in nature suffers? Indeed, why should the ability to experience pain, or the possession of higher intelligence, become a title to superior worth? In the end, why does man have more dignity than any part of the natural world, from the most humble rock to the most distant star? Why should insects, bacteria, intestinal parasites, and HIV viruses not have rights equal to those of human beings?

The fact that most contemporary environmentalists do not believe they do reveals that they still believe in some concept of superior human dignity. That is, they want to protect baby seals and snail darters because *we humans* like having them around. But this is just hypocrisy on their part. If there is no rational basis for saying that human beings have a dignity superior to that of nature, then there is no rational basis for saying that one part of nature, like baby seals, has a dignity superior to another part, like HIV viruses. There is in fact an extremist fringe of the environmental movement that is much more consistent on this score, believing that nature as such—not just sentient or intelligent animals, but all of natural creation—has rights equal to those of man. The consequences of this belief is an indifference to mass starvation in countries like Ethiopia, since this is simply an example of nature paying man back for overreaching, and a conviction that man ought to return to a "natural" global population of a hundred million or so (rather than his current five billion plus) so that he will no longer disturb the ecological balance as he has done since the Industrial Revolution.

The extension of the principle of equality to apply not just to human beings but to non-human creation as well may today sound bizarre, but it is implied in our current impasse in thinking through the question: What is man? If we truly believe that he is not capable of moral choice or the autonomous use of reason, if he can be understood entirely in terms of the sub-human, then it is not only possible but *inevitable* that rights will gradually be extended to animals and other natural beings as well as men. The liberal concept of an equal and universal humanity with a specifically human dignity will be attacked both from above and below: by those who assert that certain group identities are more important than the quality of being human, and by those who believe that being human constitutes nothing distinctive against the non-human. The intellectual impasse in which modern relativism has left us does not permit us to answer either of these attacks definitively, and therefore does not permit defense of liberal rights traditionally understood.

Reciprocal recognition of the sort available in the universal and homogeneous state fails to satisfy many people completely because the rich man will continue, in Adam Smith's words, to glory in his riches, while the poor man will continue to be ashamed of his poverty and feel he is invisible to his fellow men. Despite the current collapse of communism, the imperfect reciprocity of recognition will be the source of future attempts to find alternatives to liberal democracy and to capitalism from the Left.

But while the unequal recognition of equal people is the most familiar charge against liberal democracy, there is reason for thinking that the greater and ultimately more serious threat comes from the Right, that is, from liberal democracy's tendency to grant equal recognition to unequal people. It is that to which we turn now.

28

Men without Chests

*The most universal sign of the modern age: man has lost dignity in his own
eyes to an incredible extent. For a long time the center and tragic hero of
existence in general; then at least intent on proving himself closely related to
the decisive and essentially valuable side of existence—like all metaphysicians
who wish to cling to the dignity of man, with their faith that moral values
are cardinal values. Those who have abandoned God cling that much more
firmly to the faith in morality.*

—*Nietzsche,* The Will to Power[1]

It is impossible to complete our present discussion without referring to the creature who reportedly emerges at the end of history,
the *last man*.

According to Hegel, the universal and homogeneous state
fully reconciles the contradiction that existed in the relationship
of lordship and bondage by making the former slaves their own
masters. No longer is the master recognized only by beings who
are somehow less than human, and no longer are the slaves denied any recognition of their humanity whatsoever. Instead, each
individual, free and cognizant of his own self-worth, recognizes
every other individual for those same qualities. In abolishing the
master-slave contradiction, something was preserved of each of
the terms: both the master's freedom, and the slave's work.

Karl Marx represented one great pole of criticism of Hegel by
denying that recognition was universal; the existence of economic
classes prevented it from becoming so. But the other, and more
profound pole of criticism, was that raised by Nietzsche. For while
Nietzsche's thought was never embodied in mass movements or

political parties as was that of Marx, the questions he raised about
the direction of the human historical process remain unresolved,
and are unlikely to be resolved after the disappearance of the last
Marxist regime from the face of the earth.

For Nietzsche, there was little difference between Hegel and
Marx, because their goal was the same, a society embodying universal recognition. He, in effect, raised the question: Is recognition that can be universalized worth having in the first place? Is
not the *quality* of recognition far more important than its universality? And does not the goal of universalizing recognition inevitably trivialize and de-value it?

Nietzsche's last man was, in essence, the victorious slave. He
agreed fully with Hegel that Christianity was a slave ideology, and
that democracy represented a secularized form of Christianity.
The equality of all men before the law was a realization of the
Christian ideal of the equality of all believers in the Kingdom of
Heaven. But the Christian belief in the equality of men before
God was nothing more than a prejudice, a prejudice born out of
the resentment of the weak against those who were stronger than
they were. The Christian religion originated in the realization that
the weak could overcome the strong when they banded together
in a herd, using the weapons of guilt and conscience. In modern
times this prejudice had become widespread and irresistible, not
because it had been revealed as true, but because of the greater
numbers of weak people.[2]

The liberal democratic state did not constitute a synthesis of
the morality of the master and the morality of the slave, as Hegel
had said. For Nietzsche, it represented an unconditional victory of
the slave.[3] The master's freedom and satisfaction were nowhere
preserved, for no one really *ruled* in a democratic society. The
typical citizen of a liberal democracy was that individual who,
schooled by Hobbes and Locke, gave up prideful belief in his or
her own superior worth in favor of comfortable self-preservation.
For Nietzsche, democratic man was composed entirely of desire
and reason, clever at finding new ways to satisfy a host of petty
wants through the calculation of long-term self-interest. But he
was completely lacking in any *megalothymia,* content with his happiness and unable to feel any sense of shame in himself for being
unable to rise above those wants.

Hegel, of course, maintained that modern man struggled for
recognition as well as the satisfaction of desire, and got it when he

was granted rights by the universal and homogeneous state. Now, it is certainly true that men without rights struggle to achieve them, as they have done in Eastern Europe, China, and the Soviet Union. But it is another matter again whether they are humanly *satisfied* by the mere act of being granted rights. One is reminded of Groucho Marx's joke that he would never want to be a member of a club that would admit him as a member: what is the value of recognition that comes to everyone merely by virtue of being a human being? After a successful liberal revolution, such as the one that occurred in East Germany in 1989, everyone becomes the beneficiary of the new system of rights. This is true whether or not the beneficiaries struggled for freedom, whether they were content with their former slavish existences under the old regime, or instead worked for that regime's secret police. A society that grants such recognition may be the starting point for the satisfaction of *thymos,* and is clearly better than one that denies everyone's humanity. But does the granting of liberal rights by itself constitute the fulfillment of that great desire that led the aristocratic master to risk death? And even if many people were satisfied by this humble sort of recognition, would it be satisfying for the few who had infinitely more ambitious natures? If everyone was *fully content* merely by virtue of having rights in a democratic society, with no further aspirations beyond citizenship, would we not in fact find them worthy of contempt? And on the other hand, if *thymos* remained essentially unfulfilled by universal and reciprocal recognition, would not democratic societies then have exposed a critical weakness?[4]

One can see the inherent contradictions in the concept of universal recognition by observing the "self-esteem" movement in the United States in recent years, exemplified by the commission on self-esteem chartered by the State of California in 1987.[5] This movement begins from the correct psychological observation that successful action in life proceeds from a sense of self-worth, and if people are deprived of it, their belief in their worthlessness will become a self-fulfilling prophecy. Its starting premise, one that is both Kantian and Christian (even if its promoters are unaware of their own intellectual roots), is that everybody is a human being, and therefore possesses a certain dignity. Kant, in the Christian tradition, would have said that all human beings are equally able to decide whether to live by the moral law or not. But this universal dignity depends on man's ability to say that certain acts are contrary to the moral law, and therefore bad. To truly esteem oneself means that one must be capable of feeling shame or self-disgust when one does not live up to a certain standard.

The problem with the present-day self-esteem movement is that its members, living as they do in a democratic and egalitarian society, are seldom willing to make choices concerning what should be esteemed. They want to go out and embrace everybody, telling them that no matter how wretched and degraded their lives, they still have self-worth, that they are *somebody*. They do not want to exclude any person or any act as unworthy. Now, as a tactic, it may be that a person completely down and out in his or her luck can be buoyed at a critical moment by someone express-ing unqualified support for that person's dignity or "personness." But in the end, the mother will know if she has neglected her child, the father will knew if he has gone back to drinking, the daughter will know if she has lied, for "the tricks that work on others count for nothing in that very well-lit back alley where one keeps assignations with oneself." Self-respect must be related to some degree of accomplishment, no matter how humble. And the more difficult the accomplishment, the greater the sense of self-esteem: one takes greater pride in oneself for having gone through basic training as a Marine, than, say, lining up for a soup kitchen. But in a democracy we are fundamentally adverse to saying that a certain person, or way of life, or activity, is better and more worthwhile than another.[6]

There is a further problem with universal recognition, summed up in the question, "Who esteems?" For does not the satisfaction that one derives from recognition depend, in large measure, on the quality of the person doing the esteeming? Is it not much more satisfying to be recognized by someone whose judgment you respect, than by many people without understand-ing? And do not the highest and therefore most satisfying forms of recognition necessarily have to come from ever-smaller groups of people, since the highest degrees of accomplishment can only be judged by people who are similarly accomplished? For exam-ple, if one were a theoretical physicist, it would presumably be much more satisfying for one's work to be recognized by the best among one's fellow physicists, than by *Time* magazine. And even if one is not concerned with such lofty degrees of accomplishment, the question of the quality of recognition remains critical. For example, is the recognition that one receives by virtue of citizenship in a large contemporary democracy necessarily more satisfying than the recognition that people used to receive as members of small, tightly-knit, pre-industrial agricultural communities? For although the latter had no political "rights" in the modern sense, they were members of small and stable social groups, bound by ties of kinship, work, religion, and the like, who mutually "recognized" and respected one another, even if they were often subject to exploitation and abuse by their feudal masters. By contrast, residents of modern cities living in huge apartment blocks may be recognized by the state, but they are strangers to the very people with whom they live and work.

Nietzsche believed that no true human excellence, greatness, or nobility was possible except in aristocratic societies.[7] In other words, true freedom or creativity could arise only out of *megalothymia,* that is, the desire to be recognized as better than others. Even if people were born equal, they would never push themselves to their own limits if they simply wanted to be like everyone else. For the desire to be recognized as superior to others is necessary if one is to be superior to oneself. This desire is not merely the basis of conquest and imperialism, it is also the precondition for the creation of anything else worth having in life, whether great symphonies, paintings, novels, ethical codes, or political systems. Nietzsche pointed out that any form of real excellence must initially arise out of discontent, a division of the self against itself and ultimately a war against the self with all the suffering that entails: "one must still have chaos in oneself to give birth to a dancing star." Good health and self-satisfaction are *liabilities. Thymos* is the side of man that deliberately seeks out struggle and sacrifice, that tries to prove that the self is something better and higher than a fearful, needy, instinctual, physically determined animal. Not all men feel this pull, but for those who do, *thymos* cannot be satisfied by the knowledge that they are merely equal in worth to all other human beings.

Striving to be *unequal* comes to light in all aspects of life, even in events like the Bolshevik Revolution that sought to create a society based on complete human equality. Men like Lenin, Trotsky, and Stalin were not individuals who personally strove to be merely the equals of other people: had this been the case, Lenin would never have left Samara and Stalin might well have remained a seminary student in Tbilisi. To make a revolution and create an entirely new society requires remarkable individuals with greater than usual hardness, vision, ruthlessness, and intelligence, characteristics which all of these early Bolsheviks possessed in abundance. And yet, the type of society they were striving to build sought to abolish the ambitions and characteristics that they themselves possessed. This is perhaps why all leftist movements, from the Bolsheviks and Chinese communists to the German Greens, eventually encounter crises over the "cult of personality" of their leaders, since there is an inevitable tension between the isothymotic ideals of an egalitarian society and the megalothymotic human types needed to create such a society.

Individuals like Lenin or Trotsky, striving for something that is purer and higher, are therefore more likely to arise in societies dedicated to the proposition that all men are *not* created equal. Democratic societies, dedicated to the opposite proposition, tend to promote a belief in the equality of all lifestyles and values. They do not tell their citizens how they should live, or what will make them happy, virtuous, or great.[8] Instead, they cultivate the virtue of toleration, which becomes the *chief* virtue in democratic societies. And if men are unable to affirm that any particular way of life is superior to another, then they will fall back on the affirmation of life itself, that is, the body, its needs, and fears. While not all souls may be equally virtuous or talented, all bodies can suffer; hence democratic societies will tend to be compassionate and raise to the first order of concern the question of preventing the body from suffering. It is not an accident that people in democratic societies are preoccupied with material gain and live in an economic world devoted to the satisfaction of the myriad small needs of the body. According to Nietzsche, the last man has "left the regions where it was hard to live, for one needs warmth."

> One still works, for work is a form of entertainment. But one is careful lest the entertainment be too harrowing. One no longer becomes poor or rich: both require too much exertion. Who still wants to rule? Who obey? Both require too much exertion.
>
> No shepherd and one herd! Everybody wants the same, everybody is the same: whoever feels different goes voluntarily into a madhouse.[9]

It becomes particularly difficult for people in democratic societies to take questions with real moral content seriously in public life. Morality involves a distinction between better and worse, good and bad, which seems to violate the democratic principle of tolerance. It is for this reason that the last man becomes concerned above all for his own personal health and safety, because it is uncontroversial. In America today, we feel entitled to criticize another person's smoking habits, but not his or her religious beliefs or moral behavior. For Americans, the health of their bodies—what they eat and drink, the exercise they get, the shape they are in—has become a far greater obsession than the moral questions that tormented their forebears.

By putting self-preservation first of all things, the last man resembles the slave in Hegel's bloody battle that began history. But the last man's situation is made worse as a result of the entire historical process that has ensued since that time, the complex cumulative evolution of human society toward democracy. For according to Nietzsche, a living thing cannot be healthy, strong, or productive except by living within a certain horizon, that is, a set of values and beliefs that are accepted absolutely and uncritically. "No artist will paint his picture, no general win his victory, no nation gain its freedom," without such a horizon, without loving the work that they do "infinitely more than it deserves to be loved."[10]

But it is precisely our awareness of history that makes this love impossible. For history teaches us that there have been horizons beyond number in the past—civilizations, religions, ethical codes, "value systems." The people who lived under them, lacking our modern awareness of history, believed that their horizon was the only one possible. Those who come late in this process, those who live in the old age of mankind, cannot be so uncritical. Modern education, that universal education that is absolutely crucial in preparing societies for the modern economic world, liberates men from their attachments to tradition and authority. They realize that their horizon is merely a horizon, not solid land but a mirage that disappears as one draws closer, giving way to yet another horizon beyond. That is why modern man is the *last* man: he has been jaded by the experience of history, and disabused of the possibility of direct experience of values.

Modern education, in other words, stimulates a certain tendency toward relativism, that is, the doctrine that all horizons and values systems are relative to their time and place, and that none are true but reflect the prejudices or interests of those who advance them. The doctrine that says that there is no privileged perspective dovetails very nicely with democratic man's desire to believe that his way of life is just as good as any other. Relativism in this context does not lead to the liberation of the great or strong, but of the mediocre, who were now told they had nothing of which to be ashamed.[11] The slave at the beginning of history declined to risk his life in the bloody battle because he was instinctively fearful. The last man at the end of history *knows* better than to risk his life for a cause, because he recognizes that history was full of pointless battles in which men fought over whether they should be Christian or Muslim, Protestant or Catholic, German or French. The loyalties that drove men to desperate acts of courage and sacrifice were proven by subsequent history to be silly prejudices. Men with modern educations are content to sit at home, congratulating themselves on their broadmindedness and lack of fanaticism. As Nietzsche's Zarathustra says of them, "For thus you speak: 'Real are we entirely, and without belief or superstition.' Thus you stick out your chests—but alas, they are hollow!"[12]

There are many people in contemporary democratic societies, particularly among the young, who are not content to merely congratulate themselves on their broadmindedness, but who would like to "live within a horizon." That is, they want to choose a belief and commitment to "values" deeper than mere liberalism itself, such as those offered by traditional religions. But they are faced with an almost insuperable problem. They have more freedom to choose their beliefs than in perhaps any other society in history: they can become Muslims, Buddhists, theosophists, Hare Krishnas, or followers of Lyndon LaRouche, not to speak of more traditional choices like becoming Catholics or Baptists. But the very variety of choice is bewildering, and those who decide on one path or another do so with an awareness of the myriad other paths not taken. They resemble Woody Allen's character Mickey Sachs, who, on learning that he has terminal cancer, engages in a desperate shopping trip in the supermarket of world religions. What finally reconciles him to life is no less arbitrary: he listens to Louis Armstrong's *Potato Head Blues* and decides that there are things of value after all.

When communities were bound together in a single belief handed down from ancestors many generations removed, the authority of that belief was taken for granted and became the constituent element of a person's moral character. Belief bound one to one's family, and to the other members of society as a whole. To make such a choice now in a democratic society involves few costs or consequences, but produces fewer satisfactions. Belief tends to separate rather than bring people together, because there are so many alternatives. One can of course join one of many little communities of believers, but they are unlikely to overlap with the communities of work and neighborhood. And when the belief becomes inconvenient—when one is cut off from the inheritance by one's parents, or when one finds out that one's guru has had his hand in the till—the belief usually just fades away like any other phase of adolescent development

Nietzsche's concern over the last man has been echoed by any number of other modern thinkers who have looked deeply at the character of democratic societies.[13] Tocqueville, for one, anticipated Nietzsche's concern that the master's way of life not pass from the earth with the advent of democracy. The master who gave law to himself and others, rather than passively obeying it, was at once more noble and more satisfied than the slave. Tocqueville therefore saw the intensely private character of life in democratic America as a critical problem, one that might lead to the atrophying of the moral bonds that connected men to one another in pre-democratic communities. Like Nietzsche after him, he was concerned that abolition of the formal relationship between masters and slaves would not make the latter masters of themselves, but would enthrall them to a new kind of slavery.

> I seek to trace the novel features under which despotism may appear in the world. The first thing that strikes the observation is an innumerable multitude of men, all equal and alike, incessantly endeavoring to procure the petty and paltry pleasures with which they glut their lives. Each of them, living apart, is as a stranger to the fate of all the rest; his children and his private friends constitute to him the whole of mankind. As for the rest of his fellow citizens, he is close to them, but does not see them; he touches them, but he does not feel them; he exists only in himself and for himself alone; and if his kindred still remain to him, he may be said at any rate to have lost his country.
>
> Above this race of men stands an immense and tutelary power, which takes upon itself alone to secure their gratifications and to watch over their fate. That power is absolute,

minute, regular, provident, and mild. It would be like the authority of a parent if, like that authority, its object was to prepare men for manhood; but it seeks, on the contrary, to keep them in perpetual childhood; it is well content that the people should rejoice, provided they think of nothing but rejoicing.[14]

In a large country like America, the duties of citizenship are minimal, and the smallness of the individual when compared to the largeness of the country made the former feel not like his own master at all, but weak and impotent in the face of events he cannot control. Except on the most abstract and theoretical level, then, what sense does it make to say that the people have become their own masters?

Tocqueville anticipated Nietzsche in being all too aware of what was lost when societies passed from aristocracy to democracy. The latter, he noted, produced fewer of the beautiful but useless things that are typical of aristocratic societies, from poems and theories of metaphysics to Fabergé eggs; on the other hand, they produced vastly greater quantities of things that are useful but ugly: machine tools, freeways, Toyota Camrys, and prefabricated houses. (Modern-day America has managed to contrive it so that its brightest and most privileged young people produce things that are neither beautiful nor useful, such as the mountains of litigation produced by lawyers every year.) But the loss of fine craftsmanship is a trivial concern when compared to the loss of certain human possibilities in the moral and theoretical sphere, possibilities that were nurtured by the leisured and deliberately anti-utilitarian ethos of aristocratic societies. In a famous passage referring to the mathematician and religious writer Pascal, Tocqueville says:

> If Pascal had nothing in view but some large gain, or even if he had been stimulated by the love of fame alone, I cannot conceive that he would ever have been able to rally all the powers of his mind, as he did, for the better discovery of the most hidden things of the Creator. When I see him, as it were, tear his soul from all the cares of life to devote it wholly to these researches and, prematurely snapping the links that bind the body to life, die of old age before forty, I stand amazed and perceive that no ordinary cause is at work to produce efforts so extraordinary.[15]

Pascal, who as a child had discovered the propositions of Euclid on his own, went into seclusion in a monastery at the age of thirty-one. He had a belt of nails strapped to his chair that he sat on when people came to talk to him to seek advice, and when he felt himself taking any pleasure in the conversation, he would push himself down into this seat in order to mortify his flesh.[16] Pascal, like Nietzsche himself, was sickly throughout his entire adult life, and in his last four years lost completely the ability to communicate with other people. He did not jog or worry about the effects of secondary smoke on his health, and yet he was able to scratch out in the years before his death some of the most profound spiritual meditations in the Western tradition. The fact that so promising a career in a useful field like mathematics could be sacrificed to religious contemplation was particularly infuriating to one American biographer, who suggested that if Pascal had only allowed himself to "cut loose . . . he might have lived out everything that was in him, instead of smothering the better half of it under a mass of meaningless mysticism and platitudinous observations on the misery and dignity of man."[17]

"Formerly, all the world was mad," say the most subtle of the last men.

If Nietzsche's greatest fear was that the "American way of life" should become victorious, Tocqueville was resigned to its inevitability and content that it should spread. Unlike Nietzsche, he was sensitive to the small improvements in the lives of the great mass of people in a democracy. And in any case, he felt that the forward march of democracy was so inexorable that resistance to it was both hopeless and counterproductive: the most one could hope for was to instruct fervent partisans of democracy that there were serious alternatives to democracy, which could be preserved by moderating democracy itself.

Alexandre Kojève shared Tocqueville's belief in the inevitability of modern democracy, even as he too understood its costs in similar terms. For if man is defined by his desire to struggle for recognition, and by his work in dominating nature, and if at the end of history he achieves both recognition of his humanity and material abundance, then "Man properly so-called" will cease to exist because he will have ceased to work and struggle.

> The disappearance of Man at the end of History, therefore, is not a cosmic catastrophe: the natural World remains what it

has been from all eternity. And therefore, it is not a biological catastrophe either: Man remains alive as animal in *harmony* with Nature or given Being. What disappears is Man properly so-called—that is, Action negating the given, and Error, or in general, the Subject *opposed* to the Object . . . [18]

The end of history would mean the end of wars and bloody revolutions. Agreeing on ends, men would have no large causes for which to fight.[19] They would satisfy their needs through economic activity, but they would no longer have to risk their lives in battle. They would, in other words, become animals again, as they were before the bloody battle that began history. A dog is content to sleep in the sun all day provided he is fed, because he is not dissatisfied with what he is. He does not worry that other dogs are doing better than him, or that his career as a dog has stagnated, or that dogs are being oppressed in a distant part of the world. If man reaches a society in which he has succeeded in abolishing injustice, his life will come to resemble that of the dog.[20] Human life, then, involves a curious paradox: it seems to require injustice, for the struggle against injustice is what calls forth what is highest in man.

Unlike Nietzsche, Kojève did not rage at the return to animality at the end of history; rather, he was content to play out the rest of his life working in that bureaucracy meant to supervise construction of the final home for the last man, the European Commission. In a series of ironic footnotes to his lectures on Hegel, he indicated that the end of history meant also the end of both art and philosophy, and therewith, his own life activity. It would no longer be possible to create the great art that was meant to capture the highest aspirations of an era, like Homer's *Iliad*, the Madonnas of da Vinci or Michelangelo, or the giant Buddha of Kamakura, for there would be no new eras and no particular distinction of the human spirit for artists to portray. They could write endless poems on the beauties of springtime or the graceful swell of a young girl's breast, but they could not say anything fundamentally new about the human situation. Philosophy too would become impossible, since with Hegel's system it had achieved the status of truth. "Philosophers" of the future, if they were to say something different from Hegel, could not say anything new, only repeat earlier forms of ignorance.[21] But more than that, "What would disappear . . . is not only philosophy or the search for discursive

Wisdom, but also that Wisdom itself. For in these post-historical animals, there would no longer be any '[discursive] *understanding* of the World and of self.' "[22]

The revolutionaries who battled with Ceaucescu's *Securitate* in Romania, the brave Chinese students who stood up to tanks in Tiananmen Square, the Lithuanians who fought Moscow for their national independence, the Russians who defended their parliament and president, were the most free and therefore the most human of beings. They were former slaves who proved themselves willing to risk their lives in a bloody battle to free themselves. But when they finally succeed, as they eventually must, they will create for themselves a stable democratic society in which struggle and work in the old sense are made unnecessary, and in which the possibility of their ever again being as free and as human as in their revolutionary struggle had been abolished.[23] Today, they imagine that they would be *happy* when they get to this promised land, for many needs and desires which exist in present-day Romania or China would be fulfilled. One day they too will all have dishwashers and VCRs and private automobiles. But would they also be *satisfied* with themselves? Or would it turn out that man's satisfaction, as opposed to his happiness, arose not from the goal itself, but from the struggle and work along the way?

When Nietzsche's Zarathustra told the crowd about the last man, a clamor arose: "Give us this last man, O Zarathustra!" "Turn us into these last men!" they shouted. The life of the last man is one of physical security and material plenty, precisely what Western politicians are fond of promising their electorates. Is this really what the human story has been "all about" these past few millennia? Should we fear that we will be both happy *and* satisfied with our situation, no longer human beings but animals of the genus *homo sapiens*? Or is the danger that we will be happy on one level, but still *dis*-satisfied with ourselves on another, and hence ready to drag the world back into history with all its wars, injustice, and revolution?

29

Free and Unequal

It is difficult for those of us who believe in liberal democracy to
follow Nietzsche very far down the road that he takes. He was an
open opponent of democracy and of the rationality on which it
rested. He hoped for the birth of a new morality that would favor
the strong over the weak, that would heighten social inequality
and even promote a certain kind of cruelty. To be true Nietz-
scheans we would have to harden ourselves in body and in spirit.
Nietzsche—whose fingers turned blue in winter because he refused to heat his room, and who in the years even before the onset
of madness scarcely passed one day in ten without crushing
headaches—points to a way of life softened neither by comfort
nor peace.

On the other hand, we can readily accept many of Nietzsche's
acute psychological observations, even as we reject his morality.
The way in which the desire for justice and punishment is all-too-
frequently anchored in the resentment of the weak against the
strong, the potentially debilitating spiritual effects of compassion
and equality, the fact that certain individuals deliberately do *not*
seek comfort and security and are not satisfied with happiness as
understood by the Anglo-Saxon utilitarian tradition, the way in
which struggle and risk are constituent parts of the human soul,
the relationship between the desire to be greater than others and
the possibility of personal excellence and self-overcoming—all of
these insights may be considered accurate reflections of the human condition, which we can accept without our having to break
with the Christian-liberal traditions in which we live.

313

Indeed, Nietzsche's psychological insights are familiar to us because he is talking about the desire for recognition. Nietzsche's central concern in fact might be said to be the future of *thymos*—man's ability to place value in things, and in himself—which he sees threatened by man's historical sense, and by the spread of democracy. Just as Nietzsche's philosophy may be seen broadly as a radicalization of Hegelian historicism, so his psychology may be seen as a radicalization of Hegel's emphasis on recognition.

While we do not, for now, have to share Nietzsche's hatred of liberal democracy, we can make use of his insights concerning the uneasy relationship between democracy and the desire for recognition. That is, to the extent that liberal democracy is successful at purging *megalothymia* from life and substituting for it rational consumption, we will become last men. But human beings will rebel at this thought. That is, they will rebel at the idea of being undifferentiated members of a universal and homogeneous state, each the same as the other no matter where on the globe one goes. They will want to be citizens rather than *bourgeois*, finding the life of masterless slavery—the life of rational consumption—in the end, *boring*. They will want to have ideals by which to live and die, even if the largest ideals have been substantively realized here on earth, and they will want to risk their lives even if the international state system has succeeded in abolishing the possibility of war. *This* is the "contradiction" that liberal democracy has not yet solved.

Liberal democracy could, in the long run, be subverted internally either by an excess of *megalothymia*, or by an excess of *isothymia*—that is, the fanatical desire for equal recognition. It is my intuition that it is the former that will constitute the greater threat to democracy in the end. A civilization that indulges in unbridled *isothymia,* that fanatically seeks to eliminate every manifestation of unequal recognition, will quickly run into limits imposed by nature itself. We stand at the close of a period in which communism sought to use state power to eliminate economic inequality, and in doing so undercut the basis of modern economic life. If tomorrow's isothymotic passions try to outlaw differences between the ugly and beautiful, or pretend that a person with no legs is not just the spiritual but the physical equal of someone whole in body, then the argument will in the fullness of time become self-refuting, just as communism was. This is not something in which we should take particular comfort, since refutation of the isothymotic premises of Marxism-Leninism took a century and a half to complete. But nature here is an ally, and while one can try to throw nature out with a pitchfork, *tamen usque recurrit*—it will come running back.

Nature, on the other hand, will conspire to preserve a substantial degree of *megalothymia* even in our egalitarian, democratic world. For Nietzsche was absolutely correct in his belief that some degree of *megalothymia* is a necessary precondition for life itself. A civilization devoid of anyone who wanted to be recognized as better than others, and which did not affirm in some way the essential health and goodness of such a desire, would have little art or literature, music or intellectual life. It would be incompetently governed, for few people of quality would choose a life of public service. It would not have much in the way of economic dynamism; its crafts and industries would be pedestrian and unchanging, and its technology second-rate. And perhaps most critically, it would be unable to defend itself from civilizations that were infused with a greater spirit of *megalothymia*, whose citizens were ready to forsake comfort and safety and who were not afraid to risk their lives for the sake of dominion. *Megalothymia* is, as it always was, a morally ambiguous phenomenon: both the good things and the bad things of life flow from it, simultaneously and necessarily. If liberal democracy is ever subverted by *megalothymia*, it will be because liberal democracy needs *megalothymia* and will never survive on the basis of universal and equal recognition alone.

It is therefore not surprising that a contemporary liberal democracy like the United States permits considerable scope for those who desire to be recognized as greater than others. Democracy's effort to banish *megalothymia* or convert it into *isothymia* has been incomplete at best. Indeed, democracy's long-run health and stability can be seen to rest on the quality and number of outlets for *megalothymia* that are available to its citizens. These outlets not only tap the energy latent in *thymos* and turn it to productive uses, but also serve as grounding wires that bleed off excess energy that would otherwise tear the community apart.

The first and most important of these outlets in a liberal society is entrepreneurship and other forms of economic activity. Work is undertaken first and foremost to satisfy the "system of needs"—desire rather than *thymos*. But as we saw earlier, it quickly becomes an arena for thymotic striving as well: the behavior of entrepreneurs and industrialists is difficult to understand simply as a matter of selfish need-satisfaction. Capitalism does not just permit, but positively requires, a form of regulated and sublimated *megalothymia* in the striving of businesses to be better than their rivals. At the level at which entrepreneurs like a Henry Ford, Andrew Carnegie, or Ted Turner operate, consumption is not a meaningful motive; one can only have so many houses and cars and wives before one loses count. Such people of course are "greedy" in wanting ever-larger amounts of money, but the money is more a token or symbol of their ability as entrepreneurs rather than a means to acquire goods for personal consumption. They do not risk their lives, but they stake their fortunes, status, and reputations for the sake of a certain kind of glory; they work extremely hard and put aside small pleasures for the sake of larger and intangible ones; their labor frequently results in products and machines that demonstrate a breathtaking domination of the hardest of masters, nature; and if they are not classically public-spirited, they necessarily participate in the social world constituted by civil society. The classical capitalist entrepreneur described by Joseph Schumpeter is therefore not Nietzsche's last man.

It is in the very design of democratic capitalist countries like the United States that the most talented and ambitious natures should tend to go into business, rather than into politics, the military, universities, or the church. And it would seem not entirely a bad thing for the long-run stability of democratic politics that economic activity can preoccupy such ambitious natures for an entire lifetime. This is not simply because such people create wealth which migrates through the economy as a whole, but because such people are kept out of politics and the military. In those latter occupations, their restlessness would lead them to propose innovations at home or adventures abroad, with potentially disastrous consequences for the polity. This was, of course, precisely the outcome planned by the early founders of liberalism, who hoped to counterpoise the interests against the passions. Ancient republics like Sparta, Athens, and Rome were widely admired for the patriotism and public-spiritedness they engendered: they produced citizens rather than *bourgeois*. But then, prior to the Industrial Revolution, their citizens had little choice: the life of a tradesman involved no glory, dynamism, innovation, or mastery; you just plied the same traditional markets or crafts as your father and grandfather. It is no wonder that the ambitious Alcibiades went into politics where, rejecting the advice of the prudent Nicias, he invaded Sicily and brought destruction on the Athenian state. The founders of modern liberalism understood, in effect, that Alcibiades' desire for recognition might have been better directed toward manufacturing the first steam engine or microprocessor.

The thymotic possibilities of economic life do not need to be conceived narrowly. The project of conquering nature through modern natural science, which has been intimately connected with capitalist economic life, is by its very nature a highly thymotic activity. It involves the desire for mastery over the "nearly worthless materials of nature," and the striving to be recognized as greater than the other scientists and engineers against whom one competes. Science as an activity is hardly risk-free, either for the individual scientist or for society, since nature is fully capable of biting back in the form of nuclear weapons or HIV viruses.

Democratic politics also provides an outlet for ambitious natures. Electoral politics is a thymotic activity, since one is competing with others for public recognition on the basis of conflicting views of right and wrong, just and unjust. But the framers of modern democratic constitutions like Hamilton and Madison understood the potential dangers of *megalothymia* in politics and the way that tyrannical ambition destroyed ancient democracies. They consequently ringed leaders of modern ones around with a plethora of institutional checks on their power. The first and most important is of course popular sovereignty: a modern executive thinks of himself or herself as a *prime minister,* that is, the first among the people's servants, rather than their master.[1] They must appeal to popular passions, whether these are debased or noble, ignorant or informed, and have to do a lot of degrading things in order to get and stay elected. The result is that modern leaders seldom rule: they react and manage and steer, but are institutionally restricted in their field of action so that it is hard for them to leave their personal imprint on the people they govern. Moreover, in most advanced democracies the big issues concerning governance of the community have been settled, reflected in the steady narrowing of the already narrow policy differences between political parties in the United States and elsewhere. It is not clear that those ambitious natures which in earlier ages would have wanted to be *masters* or statesmen would so readily feel the pull of democratic politics.

It is primarily in the realm of foreign policy that democratic politicians can still achieve a degree of recognition unavailable in virtually any other walk of life. For foreign policy has traditionally been the arena for weighty decisions and the clash of big ideas, even if the scope of such clashes is now being restricted by the victory of democracy. Winston Churchill, guiding his country through the Second World War, demonstrated a degree of mastery every bit as great as that of statesmen of pre-democratic ages, and received recognition in return that was worldwide in scope. America's 1991 war in the Persian Gulf indicates that a politician like George Bush, inconsistent and constrained on domestic issues, can nonetheless create new realities on the world stage through the exercise of his constitutionally mandated powers as head of state and commander-in-chief. While the number of failed presidencies in recent decades has taken the luster off the office to a considerable extent, a presidential success like victory in a war results in a degree of public recognition that is completely unavailable to the most successful industrialist or entrepreneur. Democratic politics will thus continue to attract those with the ambition of being recognized as greater.

The fact that a large historical world co-exists with the post-historical one means that the former will hold attractions for certain individuals precisely because it continues to be a realm of struggle, war, injustice, and poverty. Orde Wingate felt himself a malcontent and outsider in interwar Britain, but came into his own helping the Jews of Palestine to organize an army, and assisting the Ethiopians in their struggle for independence against the Italians; he was to die, appropriately, in a plane crash in 1943 deep in the jungles of Burma fighting the Japanese. A Régis Debray could find outlets for his thymotic strivings that were totally absent in prosperous and middle-class France by fighting in the jungles of Bolivia with Che Guevara. It is probably healthy for liberal democracies that the Third World exists to absorb the energies and ambitions of such people; whether it is good for the Third World is a different matter.

Apart from the economic realm and political life, *megalothymia* finds outlets increasingly in purely formal activities like sports, mountain climbing, auto racing, and the like. An athletic competition has no "point" or object other than to make certain people winners and others losers—in other words, to gratify the desire to be recognized as superior. The level or type of competition is completely arbitrary, as are the rules of all sports activities. Consider the sport of Alpine mountain climbing, whose participants are almost invariably from prosperous post-historical countries. To get into physical shape, they must train incessantly; the upper bodies of free solo rock climbers are so highly developed that if they are not careful their muscles can pull tendons from the bone. In the course of their ascents, Himalayan climbers must ride out bouts of dysentery and blizzards in small tents in the Nepalese foothills. The casualty rate for climbing over four thousand meters is significant; every year, as many as a dozen people are killed on peaks like Mont Blanc or the Matterhorn. The Alpinist has, in short, re-created for him or herself all the conditions of historical struggle: danger, disease, hard work, and finally the risk of violent death. But the *object* has ceased to be an historical one, and is now purely formal: for example, being the first American or German to ascend K-2 or Nanga Parbat, and when that has been accomplished, being the first to ascend without oxygen, etc.

For most of post-historical Europe, the World Cup has replaced military competition as the chief outlet for nationalist strivings to be number one. As Kojève once said, his goal was to re-establish the Roman Empire, but this time as a multinational soccer team. It is perhaps no accident that in the most post-historical part of the United States, California, one finds the most obsessive pursuit of high-risk leisure activities that have no purpose but to shake the participant out of the comfort of a bourgeois existence: rock climbing, hang gliding, skydiving, marathon running, ironman and ironwoman races, and so forth. For where traditional forms of struggle like war are not possible, and where widespread material prosperity makes economic struggle unnecessary, thymotic individuals begin to search for other kinds of *contentless* activities that can win them recognition.

In another of his ironic footnotes to his lectures on Hegel, Kojève notes that he was forced to revise his earlier view that man would cease to be human and return to a state of animality as a result of a trip to Japan and a love affair there in 1958. He argued that after the rise of the Shogun Hideyoshi in the fifteenth century, Japan experienced a state of internal and external peace for a period of several hundred years which very much resembled Hegel's postulated end of history. Neither the upper nor lower

classes struggled against each other, and did not have to work
terribly hard. But rather than pursuing love or play instinctively
like young animals—in other words, instead of turning into a
society of last men—the Japanese demonstrated that it is possible
to continue to be human through the invention of a series of
perfectly contentless formal arts, like Noh theater, tea ceremo-
nies, flower arranging, and the like.[2] A tea ceremony does not
serve any explicit political or economic purpose; even its symbolic
significance has been lost over time. And yet, it is an arena for
megalothymia in the form of pure snobbery: there are contending
schools for tea ceremony and flower arrangement, with their own
masters, novices, traditions, and canons of better and worse. It
was the very formalism of this activity—the creation of new rules
and values divorced from any utilitarian purpose, as in sports—
that suggested to Kojève the possibility of specifically *human* activity even after the end of history.

Kojève playfully suggested that instead of Japan becoming
Westernized, the West (including Russia) would become *Japanized*
(a process now well under way, though not in the sense Kojève
intended). In other words, in a world where struggle over all of
the large issues had been largely settled, a purely formal *snobbery*
would become the chief form of expression of *megalothymia*, of
man's desire to be recognized as better than his fellows.[3] In the
United States, our utilitarian traditions make it difficult for even
the fine arts to become purely formal. Artists like to convince
themselves that they are being socially responsible in addition to
being committed to aesthetic values. But the end of history will
mean the end, among other things, of all art that could be considered socially useful, and hence the descent of artistic activity
into the empty formalism of the traditional Japanese arts.

Such are the outlets for *megalothymia* in contemporary liberal
democracies. The striving to be recognized as superior has not
disappeared from human life, but its manifestations and extent
have changed. Rather than seeking recognition for having conquered foreign peoples and lands, megalothymotic individuals try
to conquer Annapurna, or AIDS, or the technology of X-ray li-
thography. In fact, virtually the only forms of *megalothymia* that
are not permitted in contemporary democracies are those leading
to political tyranny. The difference between these societies and
the aristocratic ones that preceded them is not that *megalothymia*
has been banished, but that it has been driven underground, so to

speak. Democratic societies are dedicated to the proposition that all men are created equal, and their predominant ethos is one of equality. While nobody is legally prevented from wanting to be recognized as superior, nobody is encouraged to do so. Thus, those manifestations of *megalothymia* that have survived in modern democracies exist in a certain tension with the publicly stated ideals of society.

30

Perfect Rights
and Defective Duties

While running for president or climbing Mt. Everest may appeal to certain ambitious natures, there is another broad area of contemporary life that provides a more ordinary satisfaction of the desire for recognition. That area is community, that is, associational life below the level of the nation.

Both Tocqueville and Hegel emphasized the importance of associational life as a focus for public-spiritedness in the modern state. In large, modern nation-states, citizenship for the great mass of people is limited to voting for representatives every few years. Government is distant and impersonal in a system where direct participants in the political process are limited to candidates running for office, and perhaps their campaign staffs and those columnists and editorial writers who make politics their profession. This stands in sharp contrast to the small republics of antiquity which demanded the active participation of virtually all citizens in the life of the community, from political decision making to military service.

In modern times, citizenship is best exercised through so-called "mediating institutions"—political parties, private corporations, labor unions, civic associations, professional organizations, churches, parent-teacher associations, school boards, literary societies, and the like. It is through such civic associations that people are drawn outside of themselves and their private selfish concerns. We usually understand Tocqueville to have argued that associational life in civil society was useful because it served as a school for democratic politics at a higher level. But he also felt it was a good thing in itself, because it saved democratic man from being simply *bourgeois*. A private association, no matter how small, constitutes a community, and as such serves as an *ideal* of a larger project toward which an individual can work and sacrifice his own selfish wants. While American associational life does not call forth the great acts of virtue and self-sacrifice celebrated by Plutarch, it results in "daily small acts of self-denial" which are accessible to much larger numbers of people.[1]

Private associational life is much more immediately satisfying than mere citizenship in a large modern democracy. Recognition by the state is necessarily impersonal; community life, by contrast, involves a much more individual sort of recognition from people who share one's interests, and often one's values, religion, ethnicity, and the like. A member of a community is recognized not just on the basis of his or her universal "personness," but for a host of particular qualities that together make up one's being. One can take daily pride in being the member of a militant union, a community church, a temperance league, a women's rights organization, or an anti-cancer association, each of which "recognizes" its members in a personal way.[2]

But if a strong community life is, as Tocqueville implies, democracy's best guarantee that its citizens do not turn into last men, it is constantly threatened in contemporary societies. And what threatens the possibility of meaningful community is not a force external to the community, but those very *principles* of liberty and equality on which they are based, and which now are becoming so universal throughout the world.

According to the Anglo-Saxon version of liberal theory on which the United States was founded, men have perfect rights but no perfect duties to their communities. Their duties are imperfect because they are derived from their rights; the community exists only to protect those rights. Moral obligation is therefore entirely contractual. It is not underwritten by God or fear for one's eternal life or the natural order of the cosmos, but rather by the contractor's self-interest in fulfillment of the contract by others.

The possibility of community is also weakened, in the long term, by the democratic principle of equality. If the strongest communities are bound together by certain moral laws that define wrong and right for its members, these same moral laws also define that community's inside and an outside as well. And if those moral laws are to have any meaning, those excluded from the community by virtue of their unwillingness to accept them must have a different worth or moral status from the community's members. But democratic societies constantly tend to move from simple tolerance of all alternative ways of life, to an assertion of their essential equality. They resist moralisms that impugn the worth or validity of certain alternatives, and therefore oppose the kind of exclusivity engendered by strong and cohesive communities.

It is clear that communities held together only by enlightened self-interest have certain weaknesses with respect to those bound by absolute obligations. The family constitutes the most basic level of associational life, but in many ways the most important. Tocqueville did not appear to regard the family as much of a barrier to the tendency of democratic societies toward social atomization, perhaps because he regarded it as an extension of the self and natural to all societies. But for many Americans, the family, now no longer extended but nuclear, is virtually the only form of associational life or community they know. The much-despised suburban American family of the 1950s was in fact the locus of a certain moral life. For if Americans did not struggle, sacrifice, and endure hardship for their country or great international causes, they frequently did so for the sake of their children.

But families don't really work if they are based on liberal principles, that is, if their members regard them as they would a joint stock company, formed for their utility rather than being based on ties of duty and love. Raising children or making a marriage work through a lifetime requires personal sacrifices that are irrational, if looked at from a cost-benefit calculus. For the true benefits of strong family life frequently do not accrue to those bearing the heaviest obligations, but are transmitted across generations. Many of the problems of the contemporary American family—the high divorce rate, the lack of parental authority, alienation of children, and so on—arise precisely from the fact that it is approached by its members on strictly liberal grounds. That is, when the obligations of family become more than what the contractor bargained for, he or she seeks to abrogate the terms of the contract.

On the level of the largest association, the country itself, liberal principles can be destructive of the highest forms of patriotism which are necessary for the very survival of the community. For it is a widely recognized defect of Anglo-Saxon liberal theory that men would never die for a country based merely on the principle of rational self-preservation. The argument that men would risk their lives to protect their property or their families ultimately fails, for property exists by liberal theory only for the sake of self-preservation, and not the other way around. It would always be possible to leave the country with one's family and money, or to evade the draft. The fact that citizens of liberal countries do not all seek to evade military service reflects the fact that they are motivated by factors like pride and honor. And pride, as we know, was precisely the characteristic that had to be subdued by the mighty Leviathan constituted by the liberal state.

The possibility of strong community life is also attacked by the pressures of the capitalist marketplace. Liberal economic principles provide no support for traditional communities; quite the contrary, they tend to atomize and separate people. The demands of education and labor mobility mean that people in modern societies live to a decreasing extent in the communities where they grew up, or where their families lived before them.[3] Their lives and social connections are more unstable, because the dynamism of capitalist economies means constant shifts in the location and nature of production and therefore work. Under these conditions, it becomes harder for people to put down roots in communities or to establish permanent and lasting ties to fellow workers or neighbors. Individuals must constantly retool for new careers in new cities. The sense of identity provided by regionalism and localism diminishes, and people find themselves retreating into the microscopic world of their families which they carry around with them from place to place like lawn furniture.

In contrast to liberal societies, communities sharing "languages of good and evil" are more likely to be bound together by a stronger glue than those based merely on shared self-interest. Those groups and communities in Asian countries that appear so important to their internal self-discipline and economic success are not based on contracts between self-interested parties. Rather, the community-orientedness of Asian cultures originates in religion, or in doctrines like Confucianism that have acquired the status of religion from being handed down through centuries of tradition. Similarly, the strongest forms of community life in the United States had their origins in shared religious values rather than in rational self-interest. The Pilgrims and other Puritan communities that settled New England were all bound together by a common interest not in their own material well-being, but in the glorification of God. Americans like to trace their love of liberty to these non-conformist sects escaping religious persecution in seventeenth-century Europe. But while these religious communities were highly independent in temper, they were in no way liberal as the generation that made the Revolution understood liberalism. They sought the freedom to practice *their* religion, not freedom of religion *per se*. We could, and often do, regard them today as groups of intolerant and close-minded fanatics.[4] By the time Tocqueville visited the United States in the 1830s, Lockean liberalism had conquered the intellectual life of the country, but a vast majority of the civil associations that he observed remained religious in origin or had religious objectives.

Lockean liberals who made the American Revolution like Jefferson or Franklin, or a passionate believer in liberty and equality like Abraham Lincoln, did not hesitate to assert that liberty required belief in God. The social contract between rational self-interested individuals was not, in other words, self-sustaining; it required a supplementary belief in divine rewards and punishments. Today, we have worked our way toward what is rightly considered a purer form of liberalism: the Supreme Court has decided that even the non-denominational assertion of "belief in God" may offend atheists, and is therefore impermissible in public schools. In a situation in which all moralisms and religious fanaticisms are discouraged in the interest of tolerance, in an intellectual climate that weakens the possibility of belief in any *one* doctrine because of an overriding commitment to be open to *all* the world's beliefs and "value systems," it should not be surprising that the strength of community life has declined in America. This decline has occurred not *despite* liberal principles, but *because* of them. This suggests that no fundamental strengthening of community life will be possible unless individuals give back certain of their rights to communities, and accept the return of certain historical forms of intolerance.[5]

Liberal democracies, in other words, are not self-sufficient: the community life on which they depend must ultimately come from a source different from liberalism itself.[6] The men and women who made up American society at the time of the founding of the United States were not isolated, rational individuals calculating their self-interest. Rather, they were for the most part members of religious communities held together by a common moral code and belief in God. The rational liberalism that they eventually came to embrace was not a projection of that pre-existing culture, but existed in some tension with it. "Self-interest rightly understood" came to be a broadly understandable principle that laid a low but solid ground for public virtue in the United States, in many cases a firmer ground than was possible through appeal to religious or pre-modern values alone. But in the long run those liberal principles had a corrosive effect on the values predating liberalism necessary to sustain strong communities, and thereby on a liberal society's ability to be self-sustaining.

31

Immense Wars of the Spirit

The decline of community life suggests that in the future, we risk becoming secure and self-absorbed last men, devoid of thymotic striving for higher goals in our pursuit of private comforts. But the opposite danger exists as well, namely, that we will return to being first men engaged in bloody and pointless prestige battles, only this time with modern weapons. Indeed, the two problems are related to one another, for the absence of regular and constructive outlets for *megalothymia* may simply lead to its later resurgence in an extreme and pathological form.

It is reasonable to wonder whether all people will believe that the kinds of struggles and sacrifices possible in a self-satisfied and prosperous liberal democracy are sufficient to call forth what is highest in man. For are there not reservoirs of idealism that cannot be exhausted—indeed, that are not even touched—if one becomes a developer like Donald Trump, or a mountain climber like Reinhold Meissner, or politician like George Bush? Difficult as it is, in many ways, to be these individuals, and for all the recognition they receive, their lives are not the most difficult, and the causes they serve are not the most serious or the most just. And as long as they are not, the horizon of human possibilities that they define will not be ultimately satisfying for the most thymotic natures.

In particular, the virtues and ambitions called forth by war are unlikely to find expression in liberal democracies. There will be plenty of metaphorical wars—corporate lawyers specializing in hostile takeovers who will think of themselves as sharks or gunslingers, and bond traders who imagine, as in Tom Wolfe's novel *The Bonfire of the Vanities*, that they are "masters of the universe." (They will believe this, however, only in bull markets.) But as they sink into the soft leather of their BMWs, they will know somewhere in the back of their minds that there have been real gunslingers and masters in the world, who would feel contempt for the petty virtues required to become rich or famous in modern America. How long *megalothymia* will be satisfied with metaphorical wars and symbolic victories is an open question. One suspects that some people will not be satisfied until they prove themselves by that very act that constituted their humanness at the beginning of history: they will want to risk their lives in a violent battle, and thereby prove beyond any shadow of a doubt to themselves and to their fellows that they are free. They will deliberately seek discomfort and sacrifice, because the pain will be the only way they have of proving definitively that they can *think well of themselves*, that they remain *human beings*.

Hegel—as opposed here to his interpreter, Kojève—understood that the need to feel pride in one's humanness would not necessarily be satisfied by the "peace and prosperity" of the end of history.[1] Men would face the constant danger of degenerating from citizens to mere *bourgeois*, and feeling contempt for themselves in the process. The ultimate crucible of citizenship therefore was and would remain the willingness to die for one's country: the state would have to require military service and continue to fight wars.

This aspect of Hegel's thought has led to the charge that he was a militarist. But he never glorified war for its own sake, or saw it as the chief end of man; war was important for its secondary effects on character and community. Hegel believed that without the possibility of war and the sacrifices demanded by it, men would grow soft and self-absorbed; society would degenerate into a morass of selfish hedonism and community would ultimately dissolve. Fear of man's "lord and master, Death" was a force like no other, capable of drawing men outside of themselves and reminding them that they were not isolated atoms, but members of communities built around shared ideals. A liberal democracy that could fight a short and decisive war every generation or so to defend its own liberty and independence would be far healthier and more satisfied than one that experienced nothing but continuous peace.

Hegel's view of war reflects a common experience of combat: for while men suffer horribly and are seldom as frightened and miserable, their experience if they survive has the tendency of putting all other things in a certain perspective. What is commonly called heroism and sacrifice in civilian life seems positively petty, friendship and valor take on new and more vivid meanings, and their lives are henceforth transformed by the memory of having participated in something much greater than themselves. As one writer noted of the end of the American Civil War—surely one of the bloodiest and most terrible conflicts of modern times— "One of Sherman's veterans, going home with all the rest, found that when the armies did melt back into the heart of the people the adjustment was a little difficult. The men had been everywhere and had seen everything, life's greatest experience had ended with most of life still to be lived, to find common purpose in the quiet days of peace would be hard . . ."[2]

But supposing that the world has become "filled up," so to speak, with liberal democracies, such that there exist no tyranny and oppression worthy of the name against which to struggle? Experience suggests that if men cannot struggle on behalf of a just cause because that just cause was victorious in an earlier generation, then they will struggle *against* the just cause. They will struggle for the sake of struggle. They will struggle, in other words, out of a certain boredom: for they cannot imagine living in a world without struggle. And if the greater part of the world in which they live is characterized by peaceful and prosperous liberal democracy, then they will struggle *against* that peace and prosperity, and against democracy.

Such a psychology could be seen at work behind outbreaks like the French *événements* of 1968. Those students who temporarily took over Paris and brought down General de Gaulle had no "rational" reason to rebel, for they were for the most part pampered offspring of one of the freest and most prosperous societies on earth. But it was precisely the *absence* of struggle and sacrifice in their middle-class lives that led them to take to the streets and confront the police. While many were infatuated with unworkable fragments of ideas like Maoism, they had no particularly coherent vision of a better society. The substance of their protest, however, was a matter of indifference; what they rejected was life in a society in which ideals had somehow become impossible.

Boredom with peace and prosperity has had far graver consequences in the past. Take, for example, the First World War. The origins of this conflict remain to this day complex, much-studied, and controversial. Interpretations of the causes of the war, including German militarism and nationalism, the progressive breakdown of the European balance of power, the increasing rigidity of the alliance system, the incentives placed on pre-emption and offense by doctrine and technology, and the stupidity and recklessness of individual leaders, all contain elements of the truth. But in addition, there was another intangible but crucial factor leading to war: many European publics simply wanted war because they were fed up with the dullness and lack of community in civilian life. Most accounts of the decision making leading up to war concentrate on the rational strategic calculus, and fail to take into account the enormous popular enthusiasm which served to push all countries toward mobilization. Austria-Hungary's harsh ultimatum to Serbia following the assassination of Archduke Franz Ferdinand at Sarajevo was greeted in Berlin with frenzied public demonstrations in support of Austria-Hungary, despite the fact that Germany had no direct stake in the quarrel. For seven critical days at the end of July 1914, and the beginning of August, there were huge nationalistic demonstrations before the Foreign Office and the Kaiser's residence; when the latter returned to Berlin from Potsdam on July 31, his motorcade was swamped by crowds clamoring for war. It was in that atmosphere that critical decisions leading to war were taken.[3] These scenes were repeated that week in Paris, Petrograd, London, and Vienna. And much of the exuberance of those crowds reflected the feeling that war meant national unity and citizenship at long last, an overcoming of the divisions between capitalist and proletariat, Protestant and Catholic, farmer and worker, that characterized civil society. As one witness described the feeling among the crowds in Berlin, "No one knows anybody else. But all are seized by one earnest emotion: War, war, and a sense of togetherness."[4]

In 1914, Europe had experienced a hundred years of peace since the last major, continent-wide conflict had been settled by the Congress of Vienna. That century had seen the flowering of modern technological civilization as Europe industrialized, bringing in its train extraordinary material prosperity and the emergence of a middle class society. The pro-war demonstrations that took place in the different capitals of Europe in August 1914 can be seen in some measure as rebellions against that middle-class civilization, with its security, prosperity, and lack of challenge. The growing *isothymia* of everyday life no longer seemed sufficient. On a mass scale, *megalothymia* reappeared: not the *megalothymia* of individual princes, but of entire nations that sought recognition of their worth and dignity.

In Germany, above all, the war was seen by many as a revolt against the materialism of the commercial world created by France and that archetype of *bourgeois* societies, Britain. Germany of course had many specific grievances against the existing order in Europe, from colonial and naval policy to the threat of Russian economic expansion. But in reading German justifications for the war, one is struck by a consistent emphasis on the need for a kind of objectless struggle, a struggle that would have purifying moral effects quite independently of whether Germany gained colonies or won freedom of the seas. The comments of a young German law student on his way to the front in September 1914 were typical: while denouncing war as "dreadful, unworthy of human beings, stupid, outmoded, and in every sense destructive," he nonetheless came to the Nietzschean conclusion that "the decisive issue is surely always one's readiness to sacrifice and not the object of sacrifice."[5] *Pflicht*, or duty, was not understood as a matter of enlightened self-interest or contractual obligation; it was an absolute moral value that demonstrated one's inner strength and superiority to materialism and natural determination. It was the beginning of freedom and creativity.

Modern thought raises no barriers to a future nihilistic war against liberal democracy on the part of those brought up in its bosom. Relativism—the doctrine that maintains that all values are merely relative and which attacks all "privileged perspectives"—must ultimately end up undermining democratic and tolerant values as well. Relativism is not a weapon that can be aimed selectively at the enemies one chooses. It fires indiscriminately, shooting out the legs of not only the "absolutisms," dogmas, and certainties of the Western tradition, but that tradition's emphasis on tolerance, diversity, and freedom of thought as well. If nothing can be true absolutely, if all values are culturally determined, then cherished principles like human equality have to go by the wayside as well.

There is no better example of this than the thought of Nietzsche himself. Nietzsche believed that man's awareness that nothing was true was both a threat and an opportunity. It was a threat because, as noted earlier, it undermined the possibility of life "within a horizon." But it was also an opportunity, because it permitted total human freedom from prior moral constraints. The ultimate form of human creativity for Nietzsche was not art but the creation of what was highest, new values. His project, once he liberated himself from the shackles of earlier philosophy that believed in the possibility of absolute truth or right, was to "re-value all values," beginning with those of Christianity. He deliberately sought to undermine belief in human equality, arguing that this was simply a prejudice instilled in us by Christianity. Nietzsche hoped that the principle of equality would give way one day to a morality justifying the domination of the weak by the strong, and ended up celebrating what amounted to a doctrine of cruelty. He hated societies that were diverse and tolerant, preferring instead those that were intolerant, instinctive, and without remorse—the Indian *Chandala* caste that tried to breed distinct races of men, or the "blond beasts of prey" which "unhesitatingly lay (their) terrible claws upon a populace."[6] Nietzsche's relationship to German fascism has been debated at great length, and while he can be defended from the narrow charges of being the forefather of National Socialism's simpleminded doctrines, the relationship between his thought and nazism is not accidental. Just as in the case of his follower, Martin Heidegger, Nietzsche's relativism shot out all of the philosophical props holding up Western liberal democracy, and replaced it with a doctrine of strength and domination.[7] Nietzsche believed the era of European nihilism, which he was helping to inaugurate, would lead to "immense wars" of the spirit, objectless wars whose only purpose was to affirm war itself.

The modern liberal project attempted to shift the basis of human societies from *thymos* to the more secure ground of desire. Liberal democracy "solved" the problem of *megalothymia* by constraining and sublimating it through a complex series of institutional arrangements—the principle of popular sovereignty, the establishment of rights, the rule of law, separation of powers, and the like. Liberalism also made possible the modern economic world by liberating desire from all constraints on acquisitiveness, and allying it to reason in the form of modern natural science. A new, dynamic, and infinitely rich field of endeavor was suddenly opened up to man. According to the Anglo-Saxon theorists of liberalism, idle masters were to be persuaded to give up their vainglory, and to make their home in this economic world instead.

Thymos was to be subordinated to desire and reason, that is, desire guided by reason.

Hegel too understood that the fundamental transition that had occurred in modern life was the domestication of the master, and his metamorphosis into economic man. But he realized that this did not mean the abolition of *thymos* so much as its transformation into a new and, he believed, higher form. The *megalothymia* of the few would have to give way to the *isothymia* of the many. Men would not cease to have chests, but their chests would no longer inflate with such overbearing pride. Those whom the old, pre-democratic world failed to satisfy were the vast majority of mankind; those left unsatisfied in the modern world of universal recognition are many fewer in number. Hence the remarkable stability and strength of democracy in the contemporary world.

Nietzsche's life work can be seen, in a sense, as an effort to shift the balance back radically in the direction of *megalothymia*. The anger of Plato's guardians no longer had to be constrained by any concept of the common good. There was no common good: all efforts to define such a good simply reflected the strength of those doing the defining. Certainly a common good that protected the self-satisfaction of the last man was impoverished. There were no longer well- or badly-trained guardians, only ones who were more or less angry. They would henceforth be distinguished from one another primarily by the strength of their anger—that is, by their ability to impose their "values" on others. Rather than being one of three parts, as it had been for Plato, *thymos* became the whole of man for Nietzsche.

Looking backward, we who live in the old age of mankind might come to the following conclusion. No regime—no "socioeconomic system"—is able to satisfy all men in all places. This includes liberal democracy. This is not a matter of the incompleteness of the democratic revolution, that is, because the blessings of liberty and equality have not been extended to all people. Rather, the dissatisfaction arises precisely where democracy has triumphed most completely: it is a dissatisfaction *with* liberty and equality. Thus those who remain dissatisfied will always have the potential to restart history.

Moreover, it appears to be the case that rational recognition is not self-sustaining, but must rely on pre-modern, non-universal forms of recognition to function properly. Stable democracy requires a sometimes irrational democratic culture, and a spontaneous civil society growing out of pre-liberal traditions. Capitalist prosperity is best promoted by a strong work ethic, which in turn depends on the ghosts of dead religious beliefs, if not those beliefs themselves, or else an irrational commitment to nation or race. Group rather than universal recognition can be a better support for both economic activity and community life, and even if it is ultimately irrational, that irrationality can take a very long time before it undermines the societies that practice it. Thus, not only is universal recognition not universally satisfying, but the ability of liberal democratic societies to establish and sustain themselves on a rational basis over the long term is open to some doubt.

Aristotle believed that history would be cyclical rather than secular because all regimes were imperfect in some way, and those imperfections would constantly lead people to want to change the regime they lived under into something different. For all of the reasons just enumerated, could we not say the same of modern democracy? Following Aristotle, we might postulate that a society of last men composed entirely of desire and reason would give way to one of bestial first men seeking recognition alone, and vice versa, in an unending oscillation.

And yet, the two legs of this dyad are hardly equal. The Neitzschean alternative forces us to break completely with the desiring part of the soul. This century has taught us the horrendous consequences of the effort to resurrect unbridled *megalothymia*, for in it we have, in a sense, already experienced some of the "immense wars" foretold by Nietzsche. Those pro-war crowds in August 1914 got the sacrifice and danger that they wanted, and much more besides. The subsequent course of the Great War demonstrated that whatever war's beneficial secondary effects in terms of building character or community, they were completely overwhelmed by the destructiveness of its primary consequences. By the twentieth century, the risk of life in a bloody battle had become thoroughly democratized. Rather than the mark of exceptional character, it became an experience forced on masses of men, and ultimately women and children as well. It led not to the satisfaction of recognition, but to anonymous and objectless death. Far from reinforcing virtue or creativity, contemporary war undermined popular faith in the meaning of concepts like courage and heroism, and fostered a deep sense of alienation and *anomie* among those who experienced it. If men of the future become bored with peace and prosperity, and seek new thymotic struggles

and challenges, the consequences threaten to be even more horrendous. For now we have nuclear and other weapons of mass
destruction, which will allow millions to be killed instantly and
anonymously.

Standing as a bulwark against the revival of history and the
return of the first man is the imposing Mechanism of modern
natural science that we described in Part Two of this book, the
Mechanism driven by unlimited desire and guided by reason. A
revival of *megalothymia* in the modern world would mean a break
with this powerful and dynamic economic world, and an attempt
to rupture the logic of technological development. Such ruptures
have proved possible at particular times and places—as when a
country like Germany or Japan immolated itself for the sake of
national recognition—but it is questionable whether the world as
a whole can make such a rupture for any extended length of time.
Germany and Japan were driven by the desire for recognition of
their superiority during the wars of the first half of the twentieth
century, but they also believed that they were securing their economic future as well by conquering for themselves neo-
mercantilist *Lebensraum* or a "co-prosperity sphere." Subsequent
experience demonstrated to both countries that economic security
was much more easily obtained through liberal free trade than
through war, and that the path of military conquest was utterly
destructive of economic values.

Looking around contemporary America, it does not strike me
that we face the problem of an excess of *megalothymia*. Those
earnest young people trooping off to law and business school, who
anxiously fill out their résumés in hopes of maintaining the lifestyles to which they believe themselves entitled, seem to be much
more in danger of becoming last men, rather than reviving the
passions of the first man. For them, the liberal project of filling
one's life with material acquisitions and safe, sanctioned ambitions
appears to have worked all too well. It is hard to detect great,
unfulfilled longings or irrational passions lurking just beneath the
surface of the average first-year law associate.

The same is true in other parts of the post-historical world.
During the 1980s, the leaders of most West European countries
did not display yearnings for great struggle or sacrifice when
confronted with issues like the Cold War, abolition of hunger in
the Third World, or military action against terrorism. There were
fanatics among the young who joined the German Red Army

faction or the Red Brigades in Italy, but they represented a small
lunatic fringe kept alive with Soviet bloc aid. After the great events
of the fall of 1989 in Eastern Europe, a significant number of
Germans had doubts about the wisdom of unification *because it
would cost too much*. These are not the hallmarks of a civilization
wound tight like a spring, ready to immolate itself on the pyre of
new and unforeseen fanaticisms, but rather of one quite satisfied
with what it is and will be.

Plato argued that while *thymos* was the basis of the virtues, in
itself it was neither good nor bad, but had to be trained so that it
would serve the common good. *Thymos*, in other words, had to be
ruled by reason, and made an ally of desire. The just city was one
in which all three parts of the soul were satisfied and brought into
balance under the guidance of reason.[8] The best regime was extremely difficult to realize because it had to satisfy the whole of
man simultaneously, his reason, desire, and *thymos*. But even if it
was not possible for actual regimes to completely satisfy man, the
best regime provided a standard by which one could measure
those regimes that actually existed. That regime was best that best
satisfied all three parts of the soul simultaneously.

By this standard, when compared to the historical alternatives
available to us, it would seem that liberal democracy gives fullest
scope to all three parts. If it would not qualify as the most just
regime "in speech," it might serve as the most just regime "in
reality." For as Hegel teaches us, modern liberalism is not based
on the abolition of the desire for recognition so much as on its
transformation into a more rational form. If *thymos* is not entirely
preserved in its earlier manifestations, neither is it entirely ne-
gated. Moreover, no existing liberal society is based exclusively on
isothymia; all must permit some degree of safe and domesticated
megalothymia, even if this runs contrary to the principles they pro-
fess to believe in.

If it is true that the historical process rests on the twin pillars
of rational desire and rational recognition, and that modern liberal democracy is the political system that best satisfies the two in
some kind of balance, then it would seem that the chief threat to
democracy would be our own confusion about what is really at
stake. For while modern societies have evolved toward democracy, modern thought has arrived at an impasse, unable to come
to a consensus on what constitutes man and his specific dignity,
and consequently unable to define the rights of man. This opens

the way to a hyperintensified demand for the recognition of equal rights, on the one hand, and for the re-liberation of *megalothymia* on the other.[9] This confusion in thought can occur despite the fact that history is being driven in a coherent direction by rational desire and rational recognition, and despite the fact that liberal democracy in reality constitutes the best possible solution to the human problem.

It is possible that if events continue to unfold as they have done over the past few decades, that the idea of a universal and directional history leading up to liberal democracy may become more plausible to people, and that the relativist impasse of modern thought will in a sense solve itself. That is, cultural relativism (a European invention) has seemed plausible to our century because for the first time Europe found itself forced to confront non-European cultures in a serious way through the experience of colonialism and de-colonization. Many of the developments of the past century—the decline of the moral self-confidence of European civilization, the rise of the Third World, and the emergence of new ideologies—tended to reinforce belief in relativism. But if, over time, more and more societies with diverse cultures and histories exhibit similar long-term patterns of development; if there is a continuing convergence in the types of institutions governing most advanced societies; and if the homogenization of mankind continues as a result of economic development, then the idea of relativism may seem much stranger than it does now. For the apparent differences between peoples' "languages of good and evil" will appear to be an artifact of their particular stage of historical development.

Rather than a thousand shoots blossoming into as many different flowering plants, mankind will come to seem like a long wagon train strung out along a road. Some wagons will be pulling into town sharply and crisply, while others will be bivouacked back in the desert, or else stuck in ruts in the final pass over the mountains. Several wagons, attacked by Indians, will have been set aflame and abandoned along the way. There will be a few wagoneers who, stunned by the battle, will have lost their sense of direction and are temporarily heading in the wrong direction, while one or two wagons will get tired of the journey and decide to set up permanent camps at particular points back along the road. Others will have found alternative routes to the main road, though they will discover that to get through the final mountain range they all must use the same pass. But the great majority of wagons will be making the slow journey into town, and most will eventually arrive there. The wagons are all similar to one another: while they are painted different colors and are constructed of varied materials, each has four wheels and is drawn by horses, while inside sits a family hoping and praying that their journey will be a safe one. The apparent differences in the situations of the wagons will not be seen as reflecting permanent and necessary differences between the people riding in the wagons, but simply a product of their different positions along the road.

Alexandre Kojève believed that ultimately history itself would vindicate its own rationality. That is, enough wagons would pull into town such that any reasonable person looking at the situation would be forced to agree that there had been only one journey and one destination. It is doubtful that we are at that point now, for despite the recent worldwide liberal revolution, the evidence available to us now concerning the direction of the wagons' wanderings must remain provisionally inconclusive. Nor can we in the final analysis know, provided a majority of the wagons eventually reach the same town, whether their occupants, having looked around a bit at their new surroundings, will not find them inadequate and set their eyes on a new and more distant journey.

NOTES

By Way of an Introduction

1. "The End of History?" *The National Interest* 16 (Summer 1989): 3–18.
2. For an early effort to respond to some of these criticisms, see my "Reply to My Critics," *The National Interest* 18 (Winter 1989–90): 21–28.
3. Locke and particularly Madison did understand that one of the ends of republican government was the protection of its citizens' prideful self-assertion. See above, pp. 186–188 and footnote 15, pp. 160, 367.

Chapter 1. Our Pessimism

1. Emile Fackenheim, *God's Presence in History: Jewish Affirmations and Philosophical Reflections* (New York: New York University Press, 1970), pp. 5–6.
2. Robert Mackenzie, *The Nineteenth Century—A History*, quoted in R. G. Collingwood, *The Idea of History* (New York: Oxford University Press, 1956), p. 146.
3. *Encyclopaedia Britannica*, eleventh edition (London, 1911), vol. 27, p. 72.
4. Norman Angell, *The Great Illusion: A Study of the Relation of Military Power to National Advantage* (London: Heinemann, 1914).
5. Paul Fussell, *The Great War and Modern Memory* (New York: Oxford University Press, 1975).
6. This point is made in Modris Eksteins, *Rites of Spring: The Great War and the Birth of the Modern Age* (Boston: Houghton Mifflin, 1989), pp. 176–191; see also Fussell (1975), pp. 18–27.
7. Erich Maria Remarque, *All Quiet on the Western Front* (London: G. P. Putnam's Sons, 1929), pp. 19–20.
8. Quoted in Eksteins (1989), p. 291.
9. This point is made in Jean-François Revel, "But We Follow the Worse . . ." *The National Interest* 18 (Winter 1989–90): 99–103.
10. See Gertrude Himmelfarb's response to the original article "The End of History?" *The National Interest* 16 (Summer 1989): 25–26. See also Leszek Kolakowsky, "Uncertainties of a Democratic Age," *Journal of Democracy* 1 no. 1 (1990): 47–50.
11. Emphasis added. Henry Kissinger, "The Permanent Challenge of Peace: US Policy Toward the Soviet Union," in Kissinger, *American Foreign Policy*, third edition (New York: Norton, 1977), p. 302.
12. This includes the present author, who wrote in 1984 that "there has been a fairly consistent pattern among American observers of the Soviet Union to exaggerate the problems of the Soviet system and to underestimate its effi-

ciency and dynamism." Review of Robert Byrnes, ed., *After Brezhnev* in *The American Spectator* 17, no. 4 (April 1984): 35–37.

13. Jean-François Revel, *How Democracies Perish* (New York: Harper and Row, 1983), p. 3.

14. Jeanne Kirkpatrick, "Dictatorships and Double Standards," *Commentary* 68 (November 1979): 34–45.

15. For a good critique of Revel written before *perestroika* and *glasnost'*, see Stephen Sestanovich, "Anxiety and Ideology," *University of Chicago Law Review* 52, no. 2 (Spring 1985): 3–16.

16. Revel (1983), p. 17. It is not entirely clear the degree to which Revel believed his own more extreme formulations about the relative strengths and weaknesses of democracy and totalitarianism. Much of his deriding of democratic failings can be attributed to the rhetorical need of rousing his fellow democrats from their evident torpor and awakening them to the threat of Soviet power. Obviously, if he felt that democracies were as feckless as he sometimes describes them, there would be no point to writing *How Democracies Perish*.

17. Jerry Hough, *The Soviet Union and Social Science Theory* (Cambridge, Mass.: Harvard University Press, 1977), p. 8. Hough goes on to say "There are, of course, scholars who would suggest that political participation in the Soviet Union is somehow not real . . . that the word 'pluralism' can never be used in a qualified sense to describe the Soviet Union . . . such assertions do not seem to me to be worth prolonged and serious discussion."

18. Hough (1977), p. 5. Jerry Hough's rewrite of Merle Fainsod's classic work on Soviet communism, *How the Soviet Union Is Governed*, devotes a long section to the old Brezhnevite Supreme Soviet, which he defends as a forum in which social interests are articulated and defended. This book makes for curious reading in light of the activities of the Congress of People's Deputies and new Supreme Soviet created by Gorbachev after the nineteenth party conference in 1988, and the various republican supreme soviets that have emerged since 1990. See *How the Soviet Union Is Governed* (Cambridge, Mass.: Harvard University Press, 1979), pp. 363–380.

19. James McAdams, "Crisis in the Soviet Empire: Three Ambiguities in Search of a Prediction," *Comparative Politics* 20, no. 1 (October 1987): 107–118.

20. On the Soviet social contract, see Peter Hauslohner, "Gorbachev's Social Contract," *Soviet Economy* 3 (1987): 54–89.

21. See, for example, T. H. Rigby's argument that communist countries achieved legitimacy on the basis of "goal-rationality." "Introduction: Political Legitimacy, Weber and Communist Mono-organizational Systems," in T. H. Rigby and Ferenc Feher, eds., *Political Legitimation in Communist States* (New York: St. Martin's Press, 1982).

22. Samuel Huntington, *Political Order in Changing Societies* (New Haven: Yale University Press, 1968), p. 1. See also the conclusions in Timothy J. Colton, *The Dilemma of Reform in the Soviet Union*, revised and expanded edition (New York: Council on Foreign Relations, 1986), pp. 119–122.

23. For a general description, see Dankwart A. Rustow, "Democracy: A Global Revolution?" *Foreign Affairs* 69, no. 4 (Fall 1990): 75–90.

Chapter 2. The Weakness of Strong States I

1. The concept of legitimation was developed at great length by Max Weber, who devised the famous tripartite division of forms of authority into traditional, rational, and charismatic. There has been considerable debate over which of these Weberian categories best characterized authority in totalitarian states like Nazi Germany or the Soviet Union. See, for example, the various essays in Rigby and Feher (1982). Weber's original discussion of the types of authority is found in *The Theory of Social and Economic Organization*, ed. by Talcott Parsons (New York: Oxford University Press, 1947), pp. 324–423. The difficulty in fitting totalitarian states into Weber's categories suggests the limitations of his rather formal and artificial system of ideal types.

2. This point is made in Kojève's response to Strauss, "Tyranny and Wisdom," in Leo Strauss, *On Tyranny* (Ithaca, N.Y.: Cornell University Press, 1963), pp. 152–153.

3. Internal dissent against Hitler was manifest in the July 1944 plot against his life, and would perhaps have become as pervasive as it did in the Soviet Union had the regime survived a few more decades.

4. On this point, see the Introduction to Guillermo O'Donnell and Philippe Schmitter, eds., *Transitions from Authoritarian Rule: Tentative Conclusions about Uncertain Democracies* (Baltimore: Johns Hopkins University Press, 1986d), p. 15.

5. The classic study of this subject is Juan Linz, ed., *The Breakdown of Democratic Regimes: Crisis, Breakdown, and Reequilibration* (Baltimore: Johns Hopkins University Press, 1978).

6. Quoted from a Swiss journalist in Philippe C. Schmitter, "Liberation by *Golpe*: Retrospective Thoughts on the Demise of Authoritarianism in Portugal," *Armed Forces and Society* 2, no. 1 (November 1975): 5–33.

7. See ibid.; and Thomas C. Bruneau, "Continuity and Change in Portuguese Politics: Ten Years after the Revolution of 25 April 1974," in Geoffrey Pridham, ed., *The New Mediterranean Democracies: Regime Transition in Spain, Greece, and Portugal* (London: Frank Cass, 1984).

8. Kenneth Maxwell, "Regime Overthrow and the Prospects for Democratic Transition in Portugal," in Guillermo O'Donnell, Philippe Schmitter, and Laurence Whitehead, eds., *Transitions from Authoritarian Rule: Southern Europe* (Baltimore: Johns Hopkins University Press, 1986c), p. 136.

9. See Kenneth Medhurst, "Spain's Evolutionary Pathway from Dictatorship to Democracy," in Pridham (1984), pp. 31–32; and Jose Casanova, "Modernization and Democratization: Reflections on Spain's Transition to Democracy," *Social Research* 50 (Winter 1983): 929–973.

10. José Maria Maravall and Julian Santamaria, "Political Change in Spain and the Prospects for Democracy," in O'Donnell and Schmitter (1986c) p. 81. A survey conducted in December 1975 showed 42.2 percent of those polled and 51.7 percent of those expressing an opinion to be in favor of making the changes necessary to bring Spain in line with the democratic countries of Western Europe. John F. Coverdale, *The Political Transformation of Spain after Franco* (New York: Praeger, 1979), p. 17.

11. Despite the opposition of die-hard Francoists, 77.7 percent of eligible

voters voted in the December 1976 referendum and 94.2 percent voted yes. Coverdale (1979), p. 53.

12. P. Nikiforos Diamandouros, "Regime Change and the Prospects for Democracy in Greece: 1974–1983," in O'Donnell, Schmitter, and Whitehead, (1986c), p. 148.

13. Lack of self-confidence within the military was indicated by the reassertion of the traditional hierarchy of command that cut the power base out from under the regime's strong man, Brigadier-General Demetrios Ioannides, backed up by the threat of a coup by the third army. P. Nikiforos Diamandouros, "Transition to, and Consolidation of, Democratic Politics in Greece, 1974–1983: A Tentative Assessment," in Pridham (1984), pp. 53–54.

14. See Carlos Waisman, "Argentina: Autarkic Industrialization and Illegitimacy," in Larry Diamond, Juan Linz, and Seymour Martin Lipset, eds., *Democracy in Developing Countries*, vol. 4, *Latin America* (Boulder, Colo.: Lynne Rienner, 1988b), p. 85.

15. Cynthia McClintock, "Peru: Precarious Regimes, Authoritarian and Democratic," in Diamond et al. (1988b), p. 350. In addition, the sharp polarization between Peru's traditional oligarchy and the country's reformist party, APRA, had by this time softened sufficiently to permit an *Aprista* president to come to power in 1985.

16. On this period in Brazilian history, see Thomas E. Skidmore, *The Politics of Military Rule in Brazil, 1964–1985* (New York: Oxford University Press, 1988), pp. 210–255.

17. Charles Guy Gillespie and Luis Eduardo Gonzalez, "Uruguay: The Survival of Old and Autonomous Institutions," in Diamond et al. (1988b), pp. 223–226.

18. Verwoerd, minister of native affairs after 1950 and prime minister from 1961 to 1966, actually studied in Germany in the 1920s and returned to South Africa bearing a "neo-Fichtean" theory of the *Volk*. See T. R. H. Davenport, *South Africa: A Modern History* (Johannesburg: Macmillan South Africa, 1987), p. 318.

19. Quoted in John Kane-Berman, *South Africa's Silent Revolution* (Johannesburg: South African Institute of Race Relations, 1990), p. 60. The statement was made in the course of the election campaign of 1987.

20. To these cases we can add Saddam Hussein's Iraq. Like many twentieth-century police states, Ba'athist Iraq looked highly formidable, right up to the point its military collapsed under the weight of American bombs. Its imposing military structure, the largest in the Middle East and based on oil reserves second only to Saudi Arabia's, proved hollow because in the end the Iraqi population was not willing to fight for the regime. This strong state displayed a critical weakness by plunging into two destructive and unnecessary wars in less than a decade, wars which a democratic Iraq, responsive to the will of its people, would likely never have fought. While Saddam Hussein has surprised many of his enemies by surviving the war, his future and Iraq's status as a regional power remain in question.

21. Strikes and protests did play a certain role in persuading authoritarian rulers to step down in Greece, Peru, Brazil, South Africa, etc., while in other cases the downfall of the regime was precipitated, as we have seen, by an external crisis. These factors could in no way be said to have *forced* the old regimes from power, however, had the latter been fully determined to hang on.

Chapter 3. The Weakness of Strong States II, or, Eating Pineapples on the Moon

1. In Yu. Afanaseyev, ed., *Inogo ne dano* (Moscow: Progress, 1989), p. 510.

2. The standard definition of totalitarianism was given in Carl J. Friedrich and Zbigniew Brzezinski, *Totalitarian Dictatorship and Autocracy*, second edition (Cambridge, Mass.: Harvard University Press, 1965).

3. Mikhail Heller, *Cogs in the Wheel: The Formation of Soviet Man* (New York: Knopf, 1988), p. 30.

4. The Marquis de Custine, *Journey for Our Time* (New York: Pelegrini and Cudahy, 1951), p. 323.

5. All of these southeastern European countries have experienced a similar evolution since 1989. Parts of the old communist regime succeeded in repackaging themselves as "socialists" and won majorities in reasonably fair elections, but then came under intense attack as their populations became more radical in their demands for democracy. This pressure brought down the Bulgarian regime and seriously weakened all of the other "repackagers" except for Milosevic in Serbia.

6. Ed Hewett, *Reforming the Soviet Economy: Equality versus Efficiency* (Washington, D.C.: Brookings Institution, 1988), p. 38.

7. Anders Aslund, quoting the figures of Selyunin and Khanin and of Abel Aganbegyan, in Aslund, *Gorbachev's Struggle for Economic Reform* (Ithaca, N.Y.: Cornell University Press, 1989), p. 15. Aslund has pointed out that Soviet defense spending as a percentage of GNP, estimated by the CIA at 15–17 percent of net material product for most of the postwar period, was probably more in the range of 25 to 30 percent. Beginning in 1990, Soviet spokesmen like Eduard Shevardnadze began routinely using a figure of 25 percent of GNP as the share of defense spending in the overall Soviet economy.

8. Ibid.

9. For overviews of these different schools of Soviet economists, see Aslund (1989), pp. 3–8; and Hewett (1988), pp. 274–302. For a representative example of Soviet criticism of centralized planning, see Gavril Popov's article "Restructuring of the Economy's Management," in Afanaseyev (1989), pp. 621–633.

10. It is quite clear that both Andropov and Gorbachev were to some degree aware of the magnitude of the economic slowdown when they came into office, and that the early efforts at reform of both leaders were motivated by the perception that they had to act to avert an economic crisis. See Marshall I. Goldman, *Economic Reform in the Age of High Technology* (New York: Norton, 1987), p. 71.

11. Most of the inherent inefficiencies and pathologies of centralized economic management that have been exposed in the course of *perestroika* were documented in the 1950s in books like Joseph Berliner's *Factory and Manager in the USSR* (Cambridge, Mass.: Harvard University Press, 1957), which was based on emigré interviews. Presumably the KGB was fully capable of providing similar analyses to Soviet leaders like Andropov and Gorbachev when they came into office.

12. Gorbachev actually praised the whole of Stalin's record in 1985; by late 1987, he (like Khrushchev) still approved Stalin's acts through the collectiviza-

tion of the 1930s. It was only by 1988 that he was ready to affirm the limited liberalization advocated by Bukharin and Lenin during the period of the "New Economic Policy" in the 1920s. See the reference to Bukharin in Gorbachev's speech on the seventieth anniversary of the Great October Socialist Revolution, November 7, 1987.

13. There are in fact right-wing Russian nationalists like Aleksandr Prokhanov who espouse a reasonably systematic anti-capitalist, anti-democratic ideology that is nonetheless non-Marxist. Aleksandr Solzhenitsyn has been accused of such leanings, but he is in the end a critical supporter of democracy. See his article, "How We Are to Restructure Russia," *Literaturnaya Gazeta* no. 18 (September 18, 1990): 3–6.

14. I fully endorse Jeremy Azrael's view that the Russian people are owed an apology by their numerous Western detractors, who believed them incapable of choosing democracy, and by their own Russophobic intelligentsia.

15. There has been a long-standing debate among academic Sovietologists as to the final success of the totalitarian project, and whether the term "totalitarian" could be accurately used to describe the post-Stalinist USSR or any of the former satellite regimes in Eastern Europe. The present dating of the end of the USSR's totalitarian period is supported by Andranik Migranian in "The Long Road to the European Home," *Novy Mir* 7 (July 1989): 166–184.

16. Václav Havel et al., *The Power of the Powerless* (London: Hutchinson, 1985), p. 27. This term has also been used by Juan Linz to describe Brezhnev-era Communist regimes. It is not correct to say that the Soviet Union under Khrushchev and Brezhnev became just another authoritarian government. Some Sovietologists like Jerry Hough thought they saw the emergence of "interest groups" or "institutional pluralism" in the Soviet Union during the 1960s or 70s. But while a degree of bargaining and compromise took place between, say, the different Soviet economic ministries, or between Moscow and the party's provincial organizations, the interaction occurred according to a very restricted set of rules defined by the state itself. See H. Gordon Skilling and Franklyn Griffiths, eds., *Interest Groups in Soviet Politics*, (Princeton, N.J.: Princeton University Press, 1971), and Hough (1979), pp. 518–529.

17. Hu Yaobang, a former associate of Deng's, was taken by the students as a proponent of reform within the Chinese Communist Party. For a chronology of these events, see Lucian W. Pye, "Tiananmen and Chinese Political Culture," *Asian Survey* 30, no. 4 (April 1990b): 331–347.

18. This was suggested by Henry Kissinger in "The Caricature of Deng as Tyrant Is Unfair," *Washington Post* (August 1, 1989), p. A21.

19. Ian Wilson and You Ji, "Leadership by 'Lines': China's Unresolved Succession," *Problems of Communism* 39, no. 1 (January–February 1990): 28–44.

20. Indeed, these societies were regarded as so different that they were studied by separate disciplines of "Sinology," "Sovietology," or "Kremlinology," that paid attention not to the broad sweep of civil society, but only to politics, its supposed sovereign, and often the politics of a group of ten or twelve powerful men at that.

Chapter 4. The Worldwide Liberal Revolution

1. *Dokumente zu Hegels Entwicklung*, ed. J. Hoffmeister (Stuttgart, 1936), p. 352.

2. An overview of this change is given, *inter alia*, in Sylvia Nasar, "Third World Embracing Reforms to Encourage Economic Growth," *New York Times* (July 8, 1991) p. A1.

3. For an account of the rethinking of the legitimacy of revolutionary dictatorship that has taken place in Latin America over the past decade, see Robert Barros, "The Left and Democracy: Recent Debates in Latin America," *Telos* 68 (1986): 49–70. For an example of the confusion into which events in Eastern Europe have thrown the left, see André Gunder Frank, "Revolution in Eastern Europe: Lessons for Democratic Social Movements (and Socialists?)" *Third World Quarterly* 12, no. 2 (April, 1990): 36–52.

4. James Bryce, *Modern Democracies*, vol. I (New York: Macmillan, 1931), pp. 53–54.

5. Accepting Schumpeter's qualifications of eighteenth-century definitions of democracy, we can say with him that democracy is "free competitions among would-be leaders for the vote of the electorate." Joseph Schumpeter, *Capitalism, Socialism, and Democracy* (New York: Harper Brothers, 1950), p. 284. See also the discussion of definitions of democracy in Samuel Huntington, "Will More Countries Become Democratic?" *Political Science Quarterly* 99, no. 2 (Summer 1984): 193–218.

6. Expansion of the franchise was a gradual process in most democracies including those of England and the United States; many contemporary democracies did not achieve universal adult franchise until fairly late in the twentieth century, and yet could meaningfully have been spoken of as democracies before that point. See Bryce, vol. I (1931), pp. 20–23.

7. There have been pressures for greater democracy in various Middle Eastern countries like Egypt and Jordan, following the Eastern European revolutions of 1989. But in this part of the world, Islam has stood as a major barrier to democratization. As demonstrated by the Algerian municipal elections of 1990, or by Iran a decade earlier, greater democracy may not lead to greater liberalization because it brings to power Islamic fundamentalists hoping to establish some form of popular theocracy.

8. Although Iraq is an Islamic country, Saddam Hussein's Ba'ath party is an explicitly secular Arab nationalist organization. His attempts to wrap himself in the mantle of Islam after his invasion of Kuwait were hypocritical in light of his earlier efforts to portray himself as a defender of secular values against a fanatical Islamic Iran during his war with that country.

9. They can, of course, challenge liberal democracy through terrorist bombs and bullets, a significant but not vital challenge.

10. The suggestion made in my original article "The End of History?" that there were no viable alternatives to liberal democracy drew a number of indignant responses from people who pointed to Islamic fundamentalism, nationalism, fascism, and a number of other possibilities. None of these critics believes that these alternatives are *superior* to liberal democracy, however, and in the course of the entire controversy over the article, no one that I am aware of suggested an alter-

native form of social organization that he or she personally believed was better.

11. Various distinctions of this sort are made in Robert M. Fishman, "Rethinking State and Regime: Southern Europe's Transition to Democracy," *World Politics* 42, no. 3 (April 1990): 422–440.

12. This table is based, with some modifications, on the one in Michael Doyle, "Kant, Liberal Legacies, and Foreign Affairs," *Philosophy and Public Affairs* 12 (Summer 1983a): 205–235. Doyle's qualifications for a country being considered a liberal democracy include a market economy, representative government, external sovereignty, and juridical rights. Excluded are countries that have populations of less than one million.

Inclusion of a number of these states on a list of liberal democracies is likely to be controversial. For example, Bulgaria, Colombia, El Salvador, Nicaragua, Mexico, Peru, the Philippines, Singapore, Sri Lanka, and Turkey are classified by Freedom House as only "partly free," either because the fairness of recent elections was contested, or because of the state's failure to protect individual human rights. There has also been some backsliding: Thailand has ceased to be a democracy since 1990. On the other hand, there are quite a number of states not on this list that as of 1991 became democracies, or have committed themselves to free elections in the near future. See Freedom House Survey, *Freedom at Issue* (January–February 1990).

13. Hence Athenian democracy was able to execute its most famous citizen, Socrates, for in effect exercising his right of free speech and corrupting the young.

14. Howard Wiarda, "Toward a Framework for the Study of Political Change in the Iberio-Latin Tradition," *World Politics* 25 (January 1973): 106–135.

15. Howard Wiarda, "The Ethnocentrism of the Social Science (*sic*): Implications for Research and Policy," *Review of Politics* 43, no. 2 (April 1981): 163–197.

Chapter 5. An Idea for a Universal History

1. Nietzsche, *The Use and Abuse of History* (Indianapolis: Bobbs-Merrill, 1957), p. 55.

2. Herodotus, the so-called "father of history," in fact wrote such an encyclopaedic account of Greek and barbarian societies, but with little by way of a common connecting thread that is apparent to a non-esoteric reader.

3. See *Republic*, Book VII, 543c–569c, and *Politics*, Book VIII, 1301a–1316b.

4. On this point, see Leo Strauss, *Thoughts on Machiavelli* (Glencoe, Ill.: Free Press, 1958), p. 299.

5. For two very different perspectives on past attempts to write Universal Histories, see J. B. Bury, *The Idea of Progress* (New York: Macmillan, 1932); and Robert Nisbet, *Social Change and History* (Oxford: Oxford University Press, 1969).

6. The current practice of numbering years before and after Christ, now adopted by much of the non-Christian world, dates from the work of one such Christian historian of the seventh century, Isidore of Seville. See R. G. Collingwood, *The Idea of History*, (New York: Oxford University Press, 1956), pp. 49, 51.

7. Other early modern efforts to write Universal Histories included those of Jean Bodin, Louis Le Roy's *De la vicissitude ou variété des choses en l'univers*, and, a century later, Bossuet's *Discours sur l'histoire universelle* (Paris: F. Didot, 1852). See Bury, pp. 37–47.

8. Quoted in Nisbet (1969), p. 104. See also Bury (1932), pp. 104–111.

9. See Nisbet (1969), pp. 120–121.

10. For discussion of Kant's essay, see Collingwood, pp. 98–103; and William Galston, *Kant and the Problem of History* (Chicago: University of Chicago Press, 1975), especially pp. 205–268.

11. "An Idea for a Universal History from a Cosmopolitan Point of View," in Immanuel Kant, *On History* (Indianapolis: Bobbs-Merrill, 1963, pp. 11–13.

12. Ibid., p. 16.

13. Kant, "Idea" (1963), pp. 23–26.

14. Superficial misreadings of Hegel in the empiricist or positivist tradition are legion. For example:

> But as far as Hegel is concerned, I do not even think he was talented. He is an indigestible writer. As even his most ardent apologists must admit, his style is "unquestionably scandalous." And as far as the content of his writing is concerned, he is supreme only in his outstanding lack of originality. . . . He devoted these borrowed thoughts and methods with singleness of purpose, though without a trace of brilliance, to one aim: to fight against the open society, and thus to serve his employer, Frederick William of Prussia. . . . And the whole story of Hegel would indeed not be worth relating, were it not for its more sinister consequences, which show how easily a clown may be a "maker of history." (Karl Popper, *The Open Society and Its Enemies* [Princeton, N.J.: Princeton University Press, 1950], p. 227)

> It follows from his metaphysics that true liberty consists in obedience to an arbitrary authority, that free speech is an evil, that absolute monarchy is good, that the Prussian state was the best existing at the time he wrote, that war is good, and that an international organization for the peaceful settlement of disputes would be a misfortune. (Bertrand Russell, *Unpopular Essays* [New York: Simon & Schuster, 1951], p. 22.

The tradition of attacking Hegel's liberal credentials continues with Paul Hirst:

> No attentive reader of Hegel's *Philosophy of Right* could ever confuse the author with a liberal. Hegel's political theory is the view of a Prussian conservative who felt that the reforms after the defeat at Jena in 1806 had gone quite far enough. ("Endism," *London Review of Books* [November 23, 1989])

15. This point is made in Galston (1975), p. 261.

16. This quotation is from the transcription of Hegel's lectures on history that have come down to us as *The Philosophy of History*, trans. Sibree (New York: Dover Publications, 1956), pp. 17–18.

17. Hegel, (1956), p. 19.

18. For a good corrective to conventional views of Hegel as an authoritarian, see Shlomo Avineri, *Hegel's Theory of the Modern State* (Cambridge: Cambridge University Press, 1972), and Steven B. Smith, "What Is Right in Hegel's *Philosophy of Right?*", *American Political Science Review* 83, no. 1 (1989a): 3–18. To take several examples of how Hegel has been misunderstood, while it is true that Hegel supports monarchy, his concept of the monarchy in paras. 275–286 of the *Philosophy of Right* is close to that of a modern head of state and is compatible with existing contemporary constitutional monarchies; far from justifying the Prussian monarchy of his day, it can be read as an esoteric critique of actual practice. It is true that Hegel was opposed to direct elections and favored the organization of society into estates. But this did not arise from opposition to the principle of popular sovereignty *per se*. Hegel's corporatism can be understood as comparable to Tocqueville's "art of association": in a large modern state political participation must be mediated through a series of smaller organizations and associations to be effective and meaningful. Membership in an estate is based not on birth but on occupation, and is open to all. On the question of Hegel's alleged glorification of war, see Part Five, pp. 329–330.

19. For a reading of Hegel that stresses the non-deterministic aspects of his system, see Terry Pinkard, *Hegel's Dialectic: The Explanation of Possibility* (Philadelphia: Temple University Press, 1988).

20. Hegel (1956), pp. 318–323.

21. "Historicism" in this sense should be distinguished from Karl Popper's use of the term in *The Poverty of Historicism* and other works. With his usual lack of insight, Popper identifies historicism as the pretense of being able to predict the future from the historical past, by which account a philosopher like Plato who believes in the existence of an unchanging underlying human nature is as "historicist" as Hegel.

22. That exception was Rousseau, whose *Second Discourse* presents an historical account of man, the nature of whose desires changes radically over time.

23. This meant, among other things, that human beings are not entirely subject to the laws of physics that govern the rest of nature. By contrast, much of modern social science is based on the assumption that the study of man can be assimilated into the study of nature because the essence of man is not different from that of nature. It is perhaps this assumption that is at the root of the inability of social science to establish itself as a widely accepted "science."

24. See Hegel's discussion of the changeable nature of desire in paras. 190–195 of the *Philosophy of Right*.

25. Hegel on consumerism: "What the English call 'comfort' is something inexhaustible and illimitable. [Others can discover to you that what you take to be] comfort at any stage is discomfort, and these discoveries never come to an end. Hence the need for greater comfort does not exactly arise within you directly; it is *suggested to you by those who hope to make a profit from its creation*." Italics added. *Philosophy of Right*, addendum to para. 191.

26. This interpretation of Marx was made fashionable as a result of Georg Lukács's *History and Class Consciousness*.

27. On various of these points, see Shlomo Avineri, *The Social and Political Thought of Karl Marx* (Cambridge: Cambridge University Press, 1971).

28. Kojève's *École Pratique* lectures have been preserved in *Introduction à la lecture de Hegel* (Paris: Gallimard, 1947), translated into English as *Introduction to the Reading of Hegel*, trans. James Nichols (New York: Basic Books, 1969). Kojève's students included many who would become famous in the following generation: Raymond Queneau, Jacques Lacan, Georges Bataille, Raymond Aron, Eric Weil, Georges Fessard, and Maurice Merleau-Ponty. For a complete list, see Michael S. Roth, *Knowing and History* (Ithaca, N.Y.: Cornell University Press, 1988), pp. 225–227. On Kojève, see also Barry Cooper, *The End of History: An Essay on Modern Hegelianism* (Toronto: University of Toronto Press, 1984).

29. Raymond Aron, *Memoirs* (New York and London: Holmes and Meier, 1990), pp. 65–66.

30. Specifically, "Since this date [1806], what has happened? Nothing at all, the *alignment* of the provinces. The Chinese revolution is only the introduction of the Napoleonic Code into China." From an interview in *La quinzaine littéraire*, June 1–15, 1968, cited in Roth (1988), p. 83.

31. Kojève (1947), p. 436.

32. There are certain problems in seeing Kojève himself as a liberal, insofar as he frequently professed an ardent admiration for Stalin and asserted that there was no essential difference between the United States, the Soviet Union, and China of the 1950s: "if the Americans give the appearance of rich Sino-Soviets, it is because the Russians and the Chinese are only Americans who are still poor but are rapidly proceeding to get richer." Nonetheless, this same Kojève was a faithful servant of the European Community and of bourgeois France, and believed that "the United States has already attained the final stage of Marxist 'communism,' seeing that, practically, all the members of a 'classless society' can from now on appropriate for themselves everything that seems good to them, without thereby working any more than their heart desires." Postwar America and Europe certainly implemented "universal recognition" more fully that Stalinist Russia ever did, making the liberal Kojève more plausible than the Stalinist one. Kojève (1947), p. 436.

33. Max Beloff, "Two Historians, Arnold Toynbee and Lewis Namier," *Encounter* 74 (1990): 51–54.

34. There is no single text providing an authoritative definition of modernization theory, and over the years there came to be a number of variations on the original design. Besides in Daniel Lerner, *The Passing of Traditional Society* (Glencoe, Ill.: Free Press, 1958), modernization theory was elaborated in the various works of Talcott Parsons, especially *The Structure of Social Action* (New York: McGraw-Hill, 1937), with Edward Shils, *Toward a General Theory of Action* (Cambridge, Mass.: Harvard University Press, 1951), and *The Social System* (Glencoe, Ill: Free Press, 1951). A short and relatively accessible version of Parson's views is contained in his "Evolutionary Universals in Society," *American Sociological Review* 29 (June 1964): 339–357. In this tradition were the nine volumes sponsored by the American Social Science Research Council between 1963 and 1975, beginning with Lucian Pye's *Communications and Political Development* (Princeton, N.J.: Princeton University Press, 1963), and ending with Raymond Grew's *Crises of Political Development in Europe and the United States* (Princeton, N.J.: Princeton University Press, 1978). For overviews of the history of this literature, see the essays by Samuel Huntington and Gabriel Almond in Myron

Weiner and Samuel Huntington, eds., *Understanding Political Development* (Boston: Little, Brown, 1987), and Leonard Binder "The Natural History of Development Theory," *Comparative Studies in Society and History* 28 (1986): 3–33.

35. *Capital*, vol. 1, trans. S. Moore and E. Aveling (New York: International Publishers, 1967), p. 8.

36. See for example Lerner (1958), p. 46.

37. While the concept of economic development is fairly intuitive, that of "political development" is less so. Implicit in this notion is a hierarchy of historical forms of political organization that, for most American social scientists, culminates in liberal democracy.

38. Thus a standard survey text used by American political science graduate students states: "The literature on political development remains heavily laden with the stability orientations of democratic pluralism and its emphasis on modifying change. . . . Unequipped conceptually to deal with radical change and fundamental system transformation, American social science has been imbued with a normative commitment to order" James A. Bill and Robert L. Hardgrave, Jr., *Comparative Politics: The Quest for Theory* (Lanham, Md.: University Press of America, 1973), p. 75.

39. Mark Kesselman, "Order or Movement? The Literature of Political Development as Ideology," *World Politics* 26, no. 1 (October 1973): 139–154. See also Howard Wiarda, "The Ethnocentrism of the Social Science [*sic*]: Implications for Research and Policy," *Review of Politics* 43, no. 2 (April 1981): 163–197.

40. Other critiques along these lines include Joel Migdal, "Studying the Politics of Development and Change: The State of the Art," in Ada Finifter, ed., *Political Science: The State of the Discipline* (Washington, D.C.: American Political Science Association, 1983), pp. 309–321; and Nisbet (1969).

41. Thus Gabriel Almond, in an overview of modernization theory in which he responds to the charges of ethnocentrism, quotes Lucian Pye's *Communications and Political Development* to the effect that "a generation of instruction in cultural relativism has had its influence, and social thinkers are no longer comfortable with any concept which might suggest a belief in 'progress' or 'stages of civilization.' " Weiner and Huntington (1987), p. 447.

Chapter 6. The Mechanism of Desire

1. This cyclical theory has certain contemporary proponents; see Irving Kristol's response to my original "End of History?" article, *The National Interest* 16 (Summer 1989): 26–28.

2. The cumulative and progressive nature of modern natural science has been challenged by Thomas Kuhn, who has pointed to the discontinuous and revolutionary nature of change in the sciences. In his most radical assertions, he has denied the possibility of a "scientific" knowledge of nature at all, since *all* "paradigms" by which scientists understand nature ultimately fail. That is, the theory of relativity does not simply add a new increment of knowledge to the already established truth of Newtonian mechanics, but renders the whole of Newtonian mechanics wrong in a fundamental sense.

Kuhn's skepticism, however, is not relevant to our present argument, since a scientific paradigm does not have to be "true" in any ultimate epistemological sense for it to have consistent and far-reaching historical consequences. It merely has to be successful at predicting natural phenomena, and in permitting man to manipulate them. The fact that Newtonian mechanics fails at speeds approaching the speed of light and is not an adequate basis for developing atomic power or the hydrogen bomb does not mean that it was inadequate as a means of mastering other aspects of nature, such as global navigation, steam locomotion, or the long-range gun. There is, moreover, a hierarchy among paradigms that is established by nature rather than man: the theory of relativity could not have been discovered *before* having discovered the Newtonian laws of motion. It is this hierarchy among paradigms that ensures a coherence and unidirectionality to the advancement of scientific knowledge.

See Thomas S. Kuhn, *The Structure of Scientific Revolutions*, second edition (Chicago: University of Chicago Press, 1970), particularly pp. 95–110, 139–143, and 170–173. For a review of criticisms of Kuhn, see Terence Ball, "From Paradigms to Research Programs: Toward a Post-Kuhnian Political Science," *American Journal of Political Science* 20, no. 1 (February 1976): 151–177.

3. There are instances of less technologically advanced powers "defeating" more advanced ones, like Vietnam and the United States or Afghanistan and the Soviet Union, but the reasons for these defeats lay in the very different political stakes of the two sides. There is no question that technology provided the capability for military victory in both cases.

4. See Samuel Huntington, *Political Order in Changing Societies* (New Haven, Conn.: Yale University Press, 1968), pp. 154–156. This point is also made in Walt Rostow, *The Stages of Economic Growth: A Non-Communist Manifesto* (Cambridge: Cambridge University Press, 1960), pp. 26–27, 56.

5. Huntington (1968), pp. 122–123.

6. For a comparison of the modernization processes in Turkey and Japan, see Robert Ward and Dankwart Rustow, eds., *Political Development in Japan and Turkey* (Princeton, N.J.: Princeton University Press, 1964).

7. On the Prussian reform, see Gordon A. Craig, *The Politics of the Prussian Army 1640–1945* (Oxford: Oxford University Press, 1955), pp. 35–53; and Hajo Holborn, "Moltke and Schlieffen: The Prussian-German School," in Edward Earle, ed., *The Makers of Modern Strategy* (Princeton, N.J.: Princeton University Press, 1948), pp. 172–173.

8. Alexander Gerschenkron, *Economic Backwardness in Historical Perspective* (Cambridge, Mass.: Harvard University Press, 1962), p. 17. This kind of state-centered reform "from above" is, of course, a two-edged sword; while destroying traditional or feudal institutions it also creates a new, "modern" form of bureaucratic despotism. In the case of Peter the Great, Gerschenkron points out that modernization led to a tightening grip on the Russian peasantry.

9. There are numerous other examples of military-driven modernizations, such as the "One Hundred Days" in China, prompted by China's defeat by Japan in 1895, or the reforms of Reza Shah in the 1920s after the Soviet and British incursions of 1917–18.

10. Senior Soviet military officials like the former chief of the General Staff, Marshal Ogarkov, never accepted radical economic reform and democratization as solutions for the problems of military innovation, however. The need to remain militarily competitive was probably more of a factor in Gorbachev's own

thinking in 1985–86 than in subsequent years. As the aims of *perestroika* became more radical, military preparedness came under stiffer internal challenge. By the early 1990s, the reform process itself had weakened the Soviet economy dramatically and made it less competitive militarily. For an account of the Soviet military's views on the need for economic reform, see Jeremy Azrael, *The Soviet Civilian Leadership and the Military High Command, 1976–1986* (Santa Monica, Calif.: The RAND Corporation, 1987), pp. 15–21.

11. Many of these points are made in V. S. Naipaul, *Among the Believers* (New York: Knopf, 1981).

12. Nathan Rosenberg and L. E. Birdzell, Jr., "Science, Technology, and the Western Miracle," *Scientific American* 263, no. 5 (November 1990): 42–54; on per capita income in the eighteenth century, see David S. Landes, *The Unbound Prometheus: Technological Change and Industrial Development in Western Europe from 1750 to the Present* (New York: Cambridge University Press, 1969), p. 13.

13. Technology and the laws of nature on which it rests provide a certain regularity and coherence to the process of change, but they do not determine the character of economic development in any mechanical way, as Marx and Engels sometimes imply. For example, Michael Piore and Charles Sabel argue that the American form of industrial organization, that since the nineteenth century has emphasized the mass production of standardized goods and highly narrow job specifications at the expense of a craft paradigm of production, was not a necessary one, and has not been adopted to nearly the same extent by other countries with different national traditions like Germany and Japan. See *The Second Industrial Divide* (New York: Basic Books, 1984), pp. 19–48, 133–164.

14. We will use the term "organization of labor" rather than the more familiar "division of labor" because the latter has come to imply the ever-increasing division of manual tasks into ones of mind-numbing simplicity. While the latter has occurred in the course of industrialization, other advances in technology have tended to reverse this process and replace manual tasks with ones of a greater intellectual content and complexity. Marx's vision of an industrial world where workers were mere appendages to their machines has not, by and large, been fulfilled.

15. The proliferation of new, increasingly specialized tasks in turn suggest new applications for technology in the production process. Adam Smith points out in the *Wealth of Nations* how concentration on a single, simple task frequently suggests new possibilities for machine production that would have escaped the attention of a craftsman dissipating his attention on a variety of tasks; hence the division of labor frequently leads to the creation of new technology, as well as the reverse. Adam Smith, *An Inquiry into the Nature and Causes of the Wealth of Nations*, vol. 1 (Oxford: Oxford University Press, 1976), pp. 19–20.

16. Charles Lindblom points out how, as of the late 1970s, half of the American population worked in private-sector bureaucracies, while another thirteen million Americans worked for federal, state, or local government. See his *Politics and Markets: The World's Political-Economic Systems* (New York: Basic Books, 1977), pp. 27–28.

17. Marx agreed that Adam Smith was correct in subordinating machine-

production to the division of labor, but only for the period of manufacturing up to the late eighteenth century, when machines were used only sporadically. See Marx (1967), vol. 1, p. 348.

18. It is hard to believe that this famous vision from *The German Ideology* was meant seriously. Apart from the economic consequences of abolishing the division of labor, it is not clear that a life of such dillettantism could ever be satisfying.

19. In this respect, the Soviets have generally been more sensible, although they too have had their hangups about being both "Red" and "expert." See Maurice Meisner, "Marx, Mao, and Deng on the Division of Labor in History," in Arif Dirlik and Maurice Meisner, eds., *Marxism and the Chinese Experience* (Boulder, Colo.: Westview Press, 1989), pp. 79–116.

20. Durkheim points out that the concept of the division of labor has been employed increasingly in the biological sciences to characterize non-human organisms, and that one of the most basic examples of the phenomenon is the biological division of labor between men and women in the creation of children. See *The Division of Labor in Society* (New York: Free Press, 1964), pp. 39–41, 56–61. See also Karl Marx's discussion of the origins of the division of labor in Marx (1967), vol. 1, pp. 351–352.

21. Large, centralized bureaucracies were characteristic of premodern empires, like those in China and Turkey. These bureaucratic organizations were not organized for the purpose of optimizing economic efficiency, however, and were therefore compatible with stagnant and traditional societies.

22. Of course, these revolutions often benefit from conscious political intervention in the form of land reform.

23. Juan Linz, "Europe's Southern Frontier: Evolving Trends toward What?" *Daedalus* 108, no. 1 (Winter 1979): 175–209.

Chapter 7. No Barbarians at the Gates

1. That is, Rousseau argues that aggression is not, as in Hobbes and Locke, natural to man and part of the original state of nature. Since Rousseau's natural man has few wants, and those that exist are relatively easily satisfied, there is no reason to rob or murder his fellows, no reason, in fact, to live in civil society. See *Discours sur l'Origine, et les Fondemens de l'inégalité parmi les Hommes*, in *Oeuvres Complètes*, vol. 3 (Paris: Éditions Gallimard, 1964), p. 136.

2. For a discussion of the meaning of this natural wholeness and Rousseau's *sentiment de l'existence*, see Arthur Melzer, *The Natural Goodness of Man: On the System of Rousseau's Thought* (Chicago: University of Chicago Press, 1990), particularly pp. 69–85.

3. Bill McKibben's *The End of Nature* (New York: Random House, 1989), argues that for the first time we are on the verge of eliminating a natural domain untouched or unmanipulated by human activity. This observation is of course true, but McKibben is off in the dating of this phenomenon by at least four hundred years. Primitive tribal societies altered their natural habitats; the difference between them and modern technological societies is only one of degree. But the project of conquering nature and manipulating it for the human good was at the core of the early modern scientific revolution; it is a little late for

someone to come along and complain about this manipulation as a matter of principle. What we today see as "nature"—whether a lake in the Angeles National Forest or an Adirondack trail—is in many respects as much a result of human artifice as the Empire State Building or the space shuttle.

4. We must not for now assume the goodness of modern natural science or the economic development it has brought in its train, and therefore ought to defer judgment on how we should regard the possibility of a global cataclysm. If our historical pessimists are correct, if modern technology has not served to make men happier, but has become their master and destroyer, then the prospect of a cataclysm that would, so to speak, wipe the slate clean and force mankind to start over would be a manifestation of the benevolence of nature rather than of nature's cruelty. This was the viewpoint of classical political philosophers like Plato and Aristotle, who believed unsentimentally that all human inventions including their own works would eventually be lost as mankind passed from one cycle to the next. On this point, see Leo Strauss, *Thoughts on Machiavelli* (Glencoe, Ill.: Free Press, 1958), pp. 298–299.

5. According to Strauss, "The difficulty implied in the admission that inventions pertaining to the art of war must be encouraged is the only one which supplies a basis for Machiavelli's criticism of classical political philosophy." Strauss, p. 299.

6. An alternative solution would be to replace the international state system with a world government that would enforce the ban on dangerous technologies, or truly global agreement on the limitation of technology. Apart from the numerous reasons why such an arrangement would be difficult to set up, even in a post-cataclysmic world, the problem of technological innovation would not necessarily be solved. The scientific method would still be available to criminal groups, national liberation organizations, or other dissidents, and would lead to internal technological competition.

Chapter 8. Accumulation without End

1. On Deutscher and other writers who believed that there would be a convergence between East and West on the basis of socialism, see Alfred G. Meyer, "Theories of Convergence," in Chalmers Johnson, ed., *Change in Communist Systems* (Stanford, Calif.: Stanford University Press, 1970), pp. 321ff.

2. The term "high mass consumption" was coined by Walt Rostow (in *The Stages of Economic Growth: A Non-Communist Manifesto* [Cambridge: Cambridge University Press, 1960]), "technetronic era" by Zbigniew Brzezinski (in *Between Two Ages: America's Role in the Technetronic Era*, [New York: Viking Press, 1970)], and "post industrial society" by Daniel Bell. See the latter's "Notes on the Post-Industrial Society" I and II, *The Public Interest* 6–7 (Winter 1967a): 24–35 and (Spring 1967b): 102–118, and his description of the origin of the concept of "post-industrial society" in *The Coming of Post-Industrial Society* (New York: Basic Books, 1973), pp. 33–40.

3. Bell (1967), p. 25.

4. Figure cited in Lucian W. Pye, "Political Science and the Crisis of Authoritarianism," *American Political Science Review* 84, no. 1 (March 1990): 3–17.

5. Even in the case of these older industries, however, socialist economies

have fallen considerably behind their capitalist counterparts in modernizing manufacturing processes.

6. Figures given in Hewett (1988), p. 192.

7. Aron quoted in Jeremy Azrael, *Managerial Power and Soviet Politics* (Cambridge, Mass.: Harvard University Press, 1966), p. 4. Azrael also cites Otto Bauer, Isaac Deutscher, Herbert Marcuse, Walt Rostow, Zbigniew Brzezinski, and Adam Ulam to this effect. See also Allen Kassof, "The Future of Soviet Society," in Kassof, ed., *Prospects for Soviet Society* (New York: Council on Foreign Relations, 1968), p. 501.

8. For a discussion of the ways in which the Soviet system adapted to the demands of increasing industrial maturity, see Richard Lowenthal, "The Ruling Party in a Mature Society," in Mark G. Field, ed., *Social Consequences of Modernization in Communist Societies* (Baltimore: Johns Hopkins University Press, 1976).

9. Azrael (1966), pp. 173–180.

10. This point is made with respect to China in Edward Friedman, "Modernization and Democratization in Leninist States: The Case of China," *Studies in Comparative Communism* 22, nos. 2–3 (Summer–Autumn 1989): 251–264.

Chapter 9. The Victory of the VCR

1. Quoted by Lucian W. Pye in *Asian Power and Politics: The Cultural Dimensions of Authority* (Cambridge, Mass.: Harvard University Press, 1985), p. 4.

2. V. I. Lenin, *Imperialism: The Highest Stage of Capitalism* (New York: International Publishers, 1939).

3. For reviews of this literature, see Ronald Chilcote, *Theories of Comparative Politics: The Search for a Paradigm* (Boulder, Colo.: Westview Press, 1981); James A. Caporaso, "Dependence, Dependency, and Power in the Global System: A Structural and Behavioral Analysis," *International Organization* 32 (1978): 13–43, and idem, "Dependency Theory: Continuities and Discontinuities in Development Studies," *International Organization* 34 (1980): 605–628; and J. Samuel Valenzuela and Arturo Valenzuela, "Modernization and Dependency: Alternative Perspectives in the Study of Latin American Underdevelopment," *Comparative Politics* 10 (July 1978): 535–557.

4. The findings of that commission are reported *inter alia* in *El Segundo Decenio de las Naciones Unidas Para el Desarrollo: Aspectos Basicos del la Estrategia del Desarrollo de America Latina* (Lima, Peru: ECLA, April 14–23, 1969). Prebisch's work was extended by economists like Osvaldo Sunkel and Celso Furtado, and popularized in North America by André Gunder Frank. See Osvaldo Sunkel, "Big Business and 'Dependencia,' " *Foreign Affairs* 50 (April 1972): 517–531; Celso Furtado, *Economic Development of Latin America: A Survey from Colonial Times to the Cuban Revolution* (Cambridge: Cambridge University Press, 1970); André Gunder Frank, *Latin America: Underdevelopment or Revolution* (New York: Monthly Review Press, 1969). Also in this genre is Theotonio Dos Santos, "The Structure of Dependency," *American Economic Review* 40 (May 1980): 231–236.

5. See the description of Prebisch in Walt W. Rostow, *Theorists of Economic Growth from David Hume to the Present* (New York: Oxford University Press, 1990), pp. 403–407.

6. Osvaldo Sunkel and Pedro Paz, quoted in Valenzuela and Valenzuela (1978), p. 544.

7. This point was made originally about German development in the nineteenth century by Thorsten Veblen in his *Imperial Germany and the Industrial Revolution* (New York: Viking Press, 1942). See also Alexander Gerschenkron, *Economic Backwardness in Historical Perspective* (Cambridge, Mass.: Harvard University Press, 1962), p. 8.

8. Some later dependency theorists, recognizing that manufacturing industries were in fact growing in Latin America, made a distinction between a small, isolated "modern" sector tied to Western multinational corporations, and a traditional sector whose possibilities for development were undermined by the former. See Tony Smith, "The Underdevelopment of Development Literature: The Case of Dependency Theory," *World Politics* 31, no. 2 (July 1979): 247–285, and idem, "Requiem or New Agenda for Third World Studies?" *World Politics* 37 (July 1985): 532–561; Peter Evans, *Dependent Development: The Alliance of Multinational, State, and Local Capital in Brazil* (Princeton, N.J.: Princeton University Press, 1979); Fernando H. Cardoso and Enzo Faletto, *Dependency and Development in Latin America* (Berkeley: University of California Press, 1979), and Cardoso, "Dependent Capitalist Development in Latin America," *New Left Review* 74 (July–August 1972): 83–95.

9. Though not all. Fernando Cardoso, for example, admitted that "entrepreneurs seem to have been attracted by 'democratic liberalism' in the same way that other social actors have been," and that "there seem to be structural elements, derived from the formation of a mass, industrialized society, which lead to the search for a social model that values civilian society more highly than the state." "Entrepreneurs and the Transition Process: The Brazilian Case," in O'Donnell and Schmitter (1986b), p. 140.

10. In the United States, the dependency perspective became the basis for a broad-gauged attack on modernization theory and its claims as an empirical social science. In the words of one critic, "the dominant theories employed by American social scientists are by no means universally valid, as their proponents claim them to be; they are very specific to certain American interests in Latin America, and thus are more accurately characterized as expression of an ideology than as solid foundations of scientific knowledge." The notion that either the political or economic liberalism of the developed world should be the end point of historical development was attacked as a form of "cultural imperialism" which "superimposes American, or more broadly, Western cultural choices upon other societies . . ." See Susanne J. Bodenheimer, "The Ideology of Developmentalism: American Political Science's Paradigm-Surrogate for Latin American Studies," *Berkeley Journal of Sociology* 15 (1970): 95–137; Dean C. Tipps, "Modernization Theory and the Comparative Study of Society: A Critical Perspective," *Comparative Studies of Society and History* 15 (March 1973): 199–226. A small industry grew up around the effort to project dependency theory backward in a highly tendentious reading of history, such that the world of the sixteenth century was already seen as a capitalist "world system" divided into a "center" and an exploited "periphery." This is represented by the work of Immanuel Wallerstein, including his *The Modern World-System*, 3 volumes (New York: Academic Press, 1974 and 1980). For critiques,

not entirely unsympathetic, which expose his reading of the historical record, see Theda Skocpol, "Wallerstein's World Capitalist System: A Theoretical and Historical Critique," *American Journal of Sociology* 82 (March 1977): 1075–1090; and Aristide Zolberg, "Origins of the Modern World System: A Missing Link," *World Politics* 33 (January 1981): 253–281.

11. This argument is made in Pye (1985), p. 4.

12. Quote in ibid., p. 5.

13. Ibid.

14. Figures taken from "Taiwan and Korea: Two Paths to Prosperity," *Economist* 316, no. 7663 (July 14, 1990): 19–22.

15. One measure of the growth of a broad, educated middle class is regular newspaper readership, the act which according to Hegel would replace the daily prayer for those middle-class societies at the end of history. Newspaper readership is now as high in Taiwan and South Korea as in the United States. Pye (1990a), p. 9.

16. Ibid. Taiwan by the early 1980s had the lowest "Gini coefficient" (a measure of even income distribution) of any developing country. See Gary S. Fields, "Employment, Income Distribution and Economic Growth in Seven Small Open Economies," *Economic Journal* 94 (March 1984): 74–83.

17. On other attempts to defend *dependencia* theory from Asian evidence, see Peter Evans, "Class, State, and Dependence in East Asia: Lessons for Latin Americanists," and Bruce Cumings, "The Origins and Development of the Northeast Asian Political Economy: Industrial Sectors, Product Cycles, and Political Consequences," both in Frederic C. Deyo, ed., *The Political Economy of the New Asian Industrialism* (Ithaca, N.Y.: Cornell University Press, 1989), pp. 45–83, 203–226.

18. On the competitive nature of successful Japanese industrial sectors, see Michael Porter, *The Competitive Advantage of Nations* (New York: Free Press, 1990), pp. 117–122.

19. This argument is made by Lawrence Harrison in *Underdevelopment Is a State of Mind: The Latin American Case* (New York: Madison Books, 1985).

20. Werner Baer, *The Brazilian Economy: Growth and Development*, third edition (New York: Praeger, 1989), pp. 238–239.

21. Figure quoted from a study by Baranson in Werner Baer, "Import Substitution and Industrialization in Latin America: Experiences and Interpretations," *Latin American Research Review* 7, no. 1 (Spring 1972): 95–122. Many formerly underdeveloped European and Asian countries protected infant industries, but it is not clear that this was the source of their early economic growth. In any case, import substitution was particularly indiscriminate in Latin America, and was continued long after it could be justified for the protection of new industries.

22. On this point, see Albert O. Hirschman, "The Turn to Authoritarianism in Latin America and the Search for Its Economic Determinants," in David Collier, ed., *The New Authoritarianism in Latin America* (Princeton, N.J.: Princeton University Press, 1979), p. 85.

23. On the public sector in Brazil, see Baer (1989), pp. 238–273.

24. Hernando de Soto, *The Other Path: The Invisible Revolution in the Third World* (New York: Harper and Row, 1989), p. 134.

25. In the Foreword to ibid., p. xiv.

26. Quoted in Hirschman (1979), p. 65.

27. See Sylvia Nasar, "Third World Embracing Reforms to Encourage Economic Growth," *New York Times* (July 8, 1990), pp. A1, D3.

Chapter 10. In the Land of Education

1. Nietzsche, *The Portable Nietzsche* (New York: Viking, 1954), p. 231.

2. Seymour Martin Lipset, "Some Social Requisites of Democracy: Economic Development and Political Legitimacy," *American Political Science Review* 53 (1959): 69–105. See also the chapter "Economic Development and Democracy" in S. M. Lipset, *Political Man: Where, How, and Why Democracy Works in the Modern World* (New York: Doubleday, 1960), pp. 45–76; Phillips Cutright, "National Political Development: Its Measurements and Social Correlate," *American Sociology Review* 28 (1963): 253–264; and Deane E. Neubauer, "Some Conditions of Democracy," *American Political Science Review* 61 (1967): 1002–1009.

3. R. Hudson and J. R. Lewis, "Capital Accumulation: The Industrialization of Southern Europe?" in Allan Williams, ed., *Southern Europe Transformed* (London: Harper and Row, 1984), p. 182. See also Linz (1979), p. 176. These were higher growth rates than either the six original members of the EC, or the nine members, after the community underwent its initial expansion, in a comparable period.

4. John F. Coverdale, *The Political Transformation of Spain after Franco* (New York: Praeger, 1979), p. 3.

5. Linz (1979), p. 176.

6. Coverdale (1979), p. 1.

7. "Taiwan and Korea: Two Paths to Prosperity," *Economist* 316: 7663 (July 14, 1990), p. 19.

8. Pye (1990a), p. 8.

9. According to one source, a fifth of the Afrikaner population at the time could be classified as "poor whites," defined as "a person who has become dependent to such an extent, whether from moral, economic or physical causes, that he is unfit, without help from others, to find proper means of livelihood for himself . . ." Davenport (1987), p. 319.

10. In 1936, 41 percent of Afrikaners were rural; this figure had dropped to 8 percent by 1977, while 27 percent were blue-collar workers and 65 percent had become white-collar managers and professionals. Figures from Hermann Giliomee and Laurence Schlemmer, *From Apartheid to Nation-Building* (Johannesburg: Oxford University Press, 1990), p. 120.

11. In the early 1960s Peter Wiles pointed out that the Soviet Union was beginning to educate its technocratic elite according to functional rather than ideological criteria, and that this would eventually make them understand the irrationality of other aspects of their economic system. See *The Political Economy of Communism* (Cambridge, Mass.: Harvard University Press, 1962), p. 329. Moshe Lewin has made a great deal of urbanization and education as the ground for *perestroika*. See *The Gorbachev Phenomenon: A Historical Interpretation* (Berkeley, Calif.: University of California Press, 1987).

12. As noted in Part One above, a number of African countries including

Botzwana and Namibia became democracies in the 1980s, and many more are scheduled to hold elections in the 1990s.

13. Parsons (1964), pp. 355–356.

14. A variant of the functional argument is that liberal democracy is necessary to ensure the correct working of the market. That is, authoritarian regimes overseeing market economies are seldom content simply to leave them alone, but rather are constantly tempted to use the authority of the state to tamper with them in the interests of growth, justice, national power, or any of a myriad of other political goals. Only the existence of a political "marketplace," it can be argued, can prevent undue state interference in the economy by providing feedback and resistance to unwise government policies. This argument is made by Mario Vargas Llosa in de Soto (1989), pp. xviii–xix.

15. Something like this occurred in the Soviet Union in the 1960s and 70s, when the party to some extent became less a ruler directing the course of economic development from above than an adjudicator mediating between the interests of different sectors, ministries, and enterprises. The party might dictate, on ideological grounds, that agriculture be collectivized and ministries operate according to a central plan; but ideology provides little guidance in resolving a struggle between, say, two branches of the chemical industry for investment resources. To say that the Soviet party-state played this sort of mediating role among institutional interests is not to imply that true democracy existed, or that it did not *rule* with a firm hand in other areas of society.

16. For views blaming environmental damage on capitalism, see Marshall Goldman, *The Spoils of Progress: Environmental Pollution in the Soviet Union* (Cambridge, Mass.: MIT Press, 1972). For overviews of environmental problems in the Soviet Union and Eastern Europe, see Joan Debardleben, *The Environment and Marxism-Leninism: The Soviet and East German Experiences* (Boulder, Colo.: Westview, 1985); and B. Komarov, *The Destruction of Nature in the USSR* (London: M. E. Sharpe, 1980).

17. See "Eastern Europe Faces Vast Environmental Blight," *Washington Post* (March 30, 1990), p. A1; "Czechoslovakia Tackles the Environment, Government Says a Third of the Country is 'Ecologically Devastated,' " *Christian Science Monitor* (June 21, 1990), p. 5.

18. On this general line of argument, see Richard Lowenthal "The Ruling Party in a Mature Society," in Field (1976), p. 107.

19. This point of view is contained in much of the analysis in the contributions by O'Donnell, Schmitter, and Przeworski to the *Transitions from Authoritarian Rule* volumes, O'Donnell and Schmitter, eds. (1986a, 1986b, 1986c, 1986d).

20. Most of this literature, however, discusses how education qualifies people for democracy and aids in its consolidation, rather than explaining why education should predispose people toward democracy. See for example Bryce (1931), pp. 70–79.

21. In developed countries one obviously finds under-employed Ph.D.s who earn less than real-estate developers with high-school diplomas, but by and large there remains a high correlation between income and education.

22. This argument is presented by David Apter in *The Politics of Modernization* (Chicago: University of Chicago Press, 1965).

23. This argument is made in Huntington (1968), pp. 134–137. On the

social consequences of Americans being "born equal," see Louis Hartz, *The Liberal Tradition in America* (New York: Harcourt Brace, 1955).

24. An exception to this generalization is the emergence of a large Spanish-speaking population in the American Southwest, which differs from earlier ethnic groups by virtue of its size and relatively lower degree of linguistic assimilation.

25. An analogous situation exists in the Soviet Union; but instead of old social classes left over from feudalism, there exists a "new class" of party bureaucrats and *nomenklatura* managers with entrenched privileges and authority. Like Latin American *latifundia*, they can use their traditional authority to subvert electoral processes in their favor. This class constitutes a tenacious social obstacle to the emergence of either capitalism or democracy, and its power must be broken if either is to emerge.

26. Dictatorship in itself is obviously not sufficient to bring about egalitarian social reform. Ferdinand Marcos used the power of the state to reward his personal friends, thereby exacerbating existing social inequalities. But a modernizing dictatorship dedicated to economic efficiency could in theory achieve a thoroughgoing transformation of Philippine society in a much shorter period of time than a democracy.

27. Cynthia McClintock, "Peru: Precarious Regimes, Authoritarian and Democratic," in Larry Diamond, Juan Linz, and Seymour Martin Lipset, *Democracy in Developing Countries*, vol. 4, *Latin America* (Boulder, Colo.: Lynne Rienner, 1988b), pp. 353–358.

28. Part of the reason for this was that much of what was expropriated from the old oligarchs was transferred into the hands of an inefficient state sector, which grew from 13 to 23 percent of GDP while the military was in power.

29. Interview with Andranik Migranian and Igor Klyamkin in *Literaturnaya Gazeta* (August 16, 1989), translated in *Détente*, November 1989; and "The Long Road to the European Home," *Novy Mir*, no. 7 (July 1989): 166–184.

30. A similar point is made by Daniel H. Levine in his criticism of the O'Donnell and Schmitter volumes on transitions from authoritarianism. It is very hard to imagine democracy emerging in any form, much less its becoming consolidated and stable, where no one believes in democratic legitimacy for its own sake. See "Paradigm Lost: Dependence to Democracy," *World Politics* 40, no. 3 (April 1988): 377–394.

31. A broad argument for the superiority of authoritarian regimes as promoters of early industrialization is given in Gerschenkron (1962). The link between absolutism and Japan's post-1868 economic growth is made in Koji Taira, "Japan's Modern Economic Growth: Capitalist Development under Absolutism," in Harry Wray and Hilary Conroy, eds., *Japan Examined: Perspectives on Modern Japanese History* (Honolulu: University of Hawaii Press, 1983), pp. 34–41.

32. Figures given in Samuel P. Huntington and Jorge I. Dominguez, "Political Development," in Fred I. Greenstein and Nelson Polsby, eds., *Handbook of Political Science*, vol. 3 (Reading, Mass.: Addison-Wesley, 1975), p. 61.

Chapter 11. The Former Question Answered

1. Both Syria and Iraq claim to be socialist in some way, though this reflects the international fashion at the time these regimes came to power more

than the reality of their governments. Many people will object to trying to classify various of these countries as "totalitarian," given the limitations of state control in each one of them; a better term would perhaps be "failed" or "incompetent" totalitarianisms, which nonetheless fails to capture their brutality.

2. It has been commonly noted that communism first became victorious not in a developed country with a large industrial proletariat like Germany, as Marx predicted it would, but in semi-industrialized, semi-Western Russia, and then in a China that was overwhelmingly peasant and agricultural. For an account of communist attempts to come to grips with this reality, see Stuart Schram and Hélène Carrère-d'Encausse, *Marxism and Asia* (London: Allen Lane, 1969).

3. See Walt Rostow, *The Stages of Economic Growth* (Cambridge: Cambridge University Press, 1960), pp. 162–163.

4. This point is made by Tsvetan Todorov in his review of Zygmunt Bauman's *Modernity and the Holocaust* in *The New Republic* (March 19, 1990): 30–33. Todorov correctly points out that Nazi Germany cannot be taken as an exemplar of modernity; rather, it contained modern and anti-modern elements, the latter of which go some distance in explaining why the Holocaust was possible.

5. See, for example, classic works like Ralf Dahrendorf's *Society and Democracy in Germany* (Garden City, N.Y.: Doubleday, 1969); and Fritz Stern's *The Politics of Cultural Despair* (Berkeley: University of California Press, 1961). The latter traces a number of Nazi themes to a nostalgia for an organic, pre-industrial society, and a broad unhappiness with the atomizing and alienating characteristics of economic modernity. Khomeini's Iran can be seen as a parallel case: Iran after World War II underwent a period of extremely rapid economic growth which completely disrupted traditional social relationships and cultural norms. Fundamentalist Shi'ism, like fascism, can be seen as a nostalgic effort to recover a form of pre-industrial society through new and radically different means.

6. Revel (1989–90), pp. 99–103.

Chapter 12. No Democracy without Democrats

1. *Capital*, vol. 3 (New York: International Publishers, 1967), p. 820.

2. The two exceptions are the Asian market-oriented authoritarian state, to which we will return in Part Four, and Islamic fundamentalism.

3. From an historicist standpoint, one cannot assert the superiority of one form of "refutation" over another; in particular, there are no grounds for saying that a society that survives on the basis of its superior economic competitiveness is somehow more "legitimate" than one that survives on the basis of its military power.

4. This argument, and the comparison of world history to a dialogue, is made by Kojève in Strauss (1963), pp. 178–179.

5. On this point, see Steven B. Smith, *Hegel's Critique of Liberalism: Rights in Context* (Chicago: University of Chicago Press, 1989), p. 225.

6. It has been argued that matriarchal societies once existed in the Mediterranean region but were overwhelmed by patriarchal ones at a certain historical era. See for example Maija Gimbutas, *Language of the Goddess* (New York: Harper and Row, 1989).

7. Such an approach is not without its own problems, however. First and foremost is the question of where the trans-historical understanding of man comes from. If we are not to accept religious revelation as a guide, that standard must be based on some form of private philosophical reflection. Socrates did this by observing other men and engaging in a dialogue with them. We, who come after Socrates, can engage in a similar dialogue with the great thinkers of previous times, who have had the deepest understanding of the possibilities of human nature. Or we can look deeply into our own souls to understand the true sources of human motivation, as Rousseau and countless writers and artists have done. Now, in the sphere of mathematics and to a lesser degree in the natural sciences, private reflection can yield inter-subjective agreement on the nature of the truth, in the form of Descartes' "clear and distinct ideas." No one would think of going to the marketplace to find the solution to a difficult partial differential equation; one would go to a mathematician, whose correct solution would find approbation from other mathematicians. But in the realm of human things, there are no "clear and distinct ideas," no general consensus concerning the nature of man, or on the questions of justice or of human satisfaction or the best regime that are derived from it. Individuals may believe that they have "clear and distinct ideas" concerning these topics, but so do lunatics and madmen, and the distinction between the two is not always clear-cut. The fact that an individual philosopher may have persuaded a circle of followers of the "evidentness" of his views may guarantee that the philosopher is not a lunatic, but it does not protect the group from being subject to a kind of aristocratic prejudice. See Alexandre Kojève, "Tyranny and Wisdom," in Strauss (1963), pp. 164–165.

8. In a letter to Kojève of August 22, 1948, Leo Strauss notes that even within Kojève's Hegelian system, a philosophy of nature is still "indispensable." He asks: "How else can the uniqueness of the historical process . . . be accounted for? It can only be necessarily unique if there *can* be only *one* 'earth' of finite duration in infinite time. . . . Besides, why should the one, temporal, finite earth not be subject to cataclysms (every 100,000,000 years), with total or partial repetitions of the historical process? Only a teleological concept of nature can help out there." Quoted in Leo Strauss, *On Tyranny*, Revised and Expanded Edition, Victor Gourevitch and Michael S. Roth, eds (New York: Free Press, 1991), p. 237. See also Michael Roth, *Knowing and History: Appropriations of Hegel in Twentieth Century France* (Ithaca, N.Y.: Cornell University Press, 1988), pp. 126–127.

9. Kant (1963), pp. 13–17. Kant describes Nature as a volitional agent standing outside of human beings; we may however understand this as a metaphor for an aspect of human nature existing potentially in all people, but realized only in the course of their social and historical interaction.

Chapter 13. In The Beginning, a Battle to the Death for Pure Prestige

1. Hegel, *The Phenomenology of Mind*, trans. J. B. Baillie (New York: Harper and Row, 1967), p. 233.

2. Kojève (1947), p. 14.

3. On the question of Kojève's relationship to the real Hegel, see Michael S. Roth, "A Problem of Recognition: Alexandre Kojève and the End of History,"

History and Theory 24, no. 3 (1985): 293–306; and Patrick Riley, "Introduction to the Reading of Alexandre Kojève," *Political Theory* 9, no. 1 (1981). pp. 5–48.

4. For accounts of Kojève's interpretation of Hegel on the struggle for recognition, see Roth (1988), pp. 98–99; and Smith (1989), pp. 116–117.

5. This point is made by Smith (1989a), p. 115. See also Steven Smith, "Hegel's Critique of Liberalism," *American Political Science Review* 80, no. 1 (March 1986): 121–139.

6. David Riesman in *The Lonely Crowd* (New Haven: Yale University Press, 1950) used the term "other-directed" to refer to what he saw as a creeping conformism in postwar American society, which he contrasted to the "inner-directedness" of Americans in the nineteenth century. For Hegel, no human being can be truly "inner-directed"; man cannot even become a human being without interacting with other human beings and being recognized by them. What Riesman describes as "inner-directedness" would actually be a form of covert "other-directedness." For example, the apparent self-sufficiency of strongly religious people is in fact based on a once-removed "other-directedness," since man himself creates religious standards and the objects of his devotion.

7. See also Friedrich Nietzsche, *On the Genealogy of Morals*, 2:16 (New York: Vintage Books, 1967), p. 86.

8. For an example of the contemporary lack of comprehension of the human motive that lies behind dueling, see John Mueller, *Retreat from Doomsday: The Obsolescence of Major War* (New York: Basic Books, 1989), pp. 9–11.

9. Hobbes, *Leviathan* (Bobbs-Merrill, 1958), p. 170.

10. This formulation comes from Rousseau in the *Social Contract*, who says "l'impulsion du seul appetit est esclavage." *Oeuvres complètes*, vol. 3 (Paris: Gallimard, 1964), p. 365. Rousseau himself uses the word "freedom" in both the Hobbesian and Hegelian senses. On the one hand, he speaks in the *Second Discourse* of man in the state of nature being free to follow his own natural instincts, such as the need for nourishment, a female, and rest; on the other hand, the passage just quoted indicates his sense that "metaphysical" freedom requires liberation from the passions and needs. His account of human perfectibility is quite similar to Hegel's understanding of the historical process as one of free human self-creation.

11. More precisely, in the first version of the *Social Contract* Rousseau says "dans la constitution de l'homme l'action de l'âme sur le corps est l'abyme de la philosophie." Rousseau (1964), vol. 3, p. 296.

Chapter 14. The First Man

1. Hobbes (1958), p. 106.

2. In contrast to Hobbes's state of nature, the bloody battle was intended to be in some sense a characterization of the state of affairs at an actual historical moment (or, more precisely, at the starting point of history).

3. Emphasis added. Hobbes (1958), p. 106.

4. Hobbes, *De Cive* Preface 100–101. See also Melzer (1990), p. 121.

5. See the Kojève letter to Leo Strauss, November 2, 1936, where he concludes: "Hobbes fails to appreciate the value of work and therefore underesti-

mates the value of struggle ('vanity.') According to Hegel, the working slave realizes 1. The *idea* of freedom, 2. The *actualization* of this idea in struggle. Thus: initially 'man' is always master or slave; the 'full human being' at the 'end' of history is master and slave (that is to say both and neither). Only this can *satisfy* his 'vanity.' " Emphasis in original. Quoted in Leo Strauss, *On Tyranny*, Revised and Expanded Edition, Victor Gourevitch and Michael Roth, eds. (New York: Free Press, 1991), p. 233.

6. The comparison of Hobbes and Hegel is made in Leo Strauss, *The Political Philosophy of Hobbes* (Chicago: University of Chicago Press, 1952), pp. 57–58. In a note, Strauss explains that "M. Alexandre Kojevnikoff and the writer intend to undertake a detailed investigation of the connection between Hegel and Hobbes," a project which was, unfortunately, never completed.

7. According to Hobbes, "*Joy* arising from imagination of a man's own power and ability is that exultation of the mind which is called GLORYING, which, if grounded upon the experience of his own former actions, is the same with *confidence*, but if grounded on the flattery of others, or only supposed by himself for delight in the consequences of it, is called VAINGLORY, which name is properly given because a well-grounded *confidence* begets attempt, whereas the supposing of power does not and is therefore rightly called *vain*." Emphasis in the original. Hobbes (1958), p. 57.

8. See Leo Strauss, *Natural Right and History* (Chicago: University of Chicago Press, 1953), pp. 187–188.

9. Hobbes was one of the first philosophers to postulate the principle of universal human equality on a non-Christian basis. For according to him, men were fundamentally equal in their ability to kill one another; if one was physically weaker, then he could still get the better of his opponent through cunning or by ganging up with other men. The universalism of the modern liberal state and of liberal human rights was therefore built initially on the postulated universality of the fear of violent death.

10. Strauss notes that Hobbes initially praised aristocratic virtue and that his replacement of aristocratic pride with the fear of violent death as the primary moral fact occurred only later in his career. See Strauss (1952), chap. 4.

11. Emphasis in original. On this point, see Strauss (1952), p. 13.

12. The concept of tacit consent is not as preposterous as it looks at first glance. Citizens of old and established liberal democracies, for example, may vote in elections for leaders, but they are usually never called upon to approve the country's basic constitutional arrangements. How do we then know that they approve of them? Evidently through the fact that they remain in the country of their own volition, and participate in (or at least do not protest) the existing political process.

13. To Hobbes's right of self-preservation, Locke adds another fundamental human right, the right to property. The right to property is derivative from the right to self-preservation: if one has the right to life, one has the right to the means to life, such as food, clothing, a house, land, and the like. The establishment of civil society not only prevents the proud from killing each other, it permits men to protect the natural property which they possessed in the state of nature and to increase it peacefully.

The conversion of natural property into conventional property, that is, into property sanctioned by a social contract among property owners, leads to a very fundamental change in human life. For prior to civil society, human acquisitiveness was limited, according to Locke, to what a man could accumulate through his own labors for his own consumption, provided it did not spoil. But civil society is the precondition for a liberation of human acquisitiveness: man can accumulate not just what he needs, but whatever he wants without limit. For Locke explains that the origin of all value (we would now say, all "economic" value) is human labor that multiplies the value of the "almost worthless materials" of nature more than a hundredfold. Unlike the state of nature, where the accumulation of wealth might come at the expense of another, in civil society the pursuit of unlimited wealth is possible and permitted because the unprecedented productivity of labor leads to the enrichment of all. It is possible and permitted, that is, provided that civil society protects the interests of the "industrious and rational" over against the "quarrelsome and contentious." See Locke, *Second Treatise of Government* (Indianapolis: Bobbs-Merrill, 1952), pp. 16–30; Abram N. Shulsky, "The Concept of Property in the History of Political Economy," in James Nichols and Colin Wright, eds., *From Political Economy to Economics . . . and Back?* (San Francisco: Institute for Contemporary Studies Press, 1990), pp. 15–34; and Strauss (1953), pp. 235–246.

14. For a review and critique of the literature on classical republicanism and the American founding, see Thomas Pangle, *The Spirit of Modern Republicanism* (Chicago: University of Chicago Press, 1988), pp. 28–39.

15. A number of serious American scholars have noted that Locke gives considerably more scope to pride and spiritedness than is often thought. Locke without question tries to deflate the pride of the domineering and aggressive, and tries to get them to follow their rational self-interest. But Nathan Tarcov has pointed out that in *Some Thoughts Concerning Education*, Locke encourages people to take pride in their liberty and to disdain slavery: life and liberty become ends in themselves, worthy potentially even of the sacrifice of life, rather than means to the protection of property. Thus the patriotism of a free man in a free country can coexist with the desire for comfortable self-preservation, as in fact they seem to have done historically in the United States.

While there is clearly a frequently unrecognized side to Locke that emphasizes recognition, just as there is to Madison and Hamilton, it seems to me that Locke remains firmly on the other side of the great ethical divide in his preference for self-preservation over pride. Even if a prideful Locke emerges from a careful reading of his work on education, it is not clear that this qualifies in a major way the primacy that he places on self-preservation in the *Second Treatise*. See Nathan Tarcov, *Locke's Education for Liberty* (Chicago: University of Chicago Press, 1984), particularly pp. 5–8 and 209–211; Tarcov, "The Spirit of Liberty and Early American Foreign Policy," in Zuckert (1988), pp. 136–148. See also Pangle (1988), pp. 194, 227; and Harvey C. Mansfield, *Taming the Prince: The Ambivalence of Modern Executive Power* (New York: Free Press, 1989), pp. 204–211.

16. The potential incompatibility of capitalism and family life is discussed in Joseph Schumpeter's *Capitalism, Socialism, and Democracy* (New York: Harper Brothers, 1950), pp. 157–160.

Chapter 15. A Vacation in Bulgaria

1. *Republic* 386c, quoting Homer's *Odyssey*, XI, 489–491.

2. There have been very few systematic studies of the phenomenon of *thymos* or recognition in the Western philosophical tradition, despite its importance to that tradition. One attempt to do so is Catherine Zuckert, ed., *Understanding the Political Spirit: Philosophical Investigations from Socrates to Nietzsche* (New Haven, Conn.: Yale University Press, 1988). See also Allan Bloom's discussion of *thymos* in the commentary to his translation of Plato's *Republic* (New York: Basic Books, 1968), pp. 355–357, 375–379.

3. *Thymos* could also be translated as "heart" or "heartiness."

4. For a further discussion of the role of *thymos* in Plato, see Catherine Zuckert, "On the Role of Spiritedness in Politics," and Mary P. Nicholas, "Spiritedness and Philosophy in Plato's *Republic*" in Zuckert (1988).

5. The discussion of the three parts of the soul occurs in *Republic* 435c–441c. The initial discussion of *thymos* occurs in Book II, 375a–375e and 376c. See also 411a–411e, 441e, 442e, 456a, 465a, 467e, 536c, 547e, 548c, 550b, 553e–553d, 572a, 580d, 581a, 586c–586d, 590b, 606d. This multi-partite characterization of human nature had a long history after Plato, and was disputed seriously for the first time by Rousseau. See Melzer (1990), pp. 65–68; 69.

6. *Republic* 439e–440a.

7. The relative undervaluing of *thymos* or pride in Hobbes is evident in his less than satisfactory definition of anger. Anger, he says, is "sudden *courage*," while courage is "the same with hope of avoiding that hurt by resistance," which in turn refers to fear, which is "*Aversion* with opinion of HURT from the object." Contrary to Hobbes, one would think that courage is *derived from* anger, and that anger itself is a completely independent passion that has nothing to do with the mechanism of hope and fear.

8. Anger with oneself is the equivalent of shame, and Leontius could equally well have been described as feeling ashamed.

9. *Republic* 440c–440d.

10. Emphasis added. Havel et al. (1985), pp. 27–28.

11. Havel et al. (1985), p. 38.

12. See for example not only the frequent references to dignity and humiliation scattered throughout "The Power of the Powerless," but also Havel's first New Year's address to the nation, in which he stated that "The state, which calls itself a state of the working people, is *humiliating* workers. . . . The previous regime, armed with its arrogant and intolerant ideology, *denigrated* man into a production force and nature into a production tool. . . . Throughout the world, people are surprised that the acquiescent, *humiliated*, skeptical Czechoslovak people who apparently no longer believed in anything suddenly managed to find the enormous strength in the space of a few weeks to shake off the totalitarian system in a completely decent and peaceful way." Emphasis added. Quoted in *Foreign Broadcast Information Service* FBIS-EEU-90-001, 2 January 1990, pp. 9–10.

13. The well-known, American-accented Soviet television journalist Vladimir Posner has written a self-exculpatory biography in which he tries to justify his own moral choices as he rose to the top of the Soviet journalistic profession under Brezhnev. He is less than honest with his readers (and per-

haps, with himself) in explaining the degree to which he was forced to compromise himself, and then asks rhetorically who could condemn him for having made such choices, given the evil nature of the Soviet system. This routine acceptance of moral degradation is itself part of the degradation of thymotic life that Havel sees as an inevitable consequence of post-totalitarian communism. See Posner, *Parting with Illusions* (New York: Atlantic Monthly Press, 1989).

Chapter 16. The Beast with Red Cheeks

1. Quoted in Abraham Lincoln, *The Life and Writings of Abraham Lincoln* (New York: Modern Library, 1940), p. 842.

2. Strictly speaking, the desire for recognition can be considered a form of desire like hunger or thirst, only one whose object is not material but ideal. The close relationship between *thymos* and desire is evident in the Greek word for desire, *epithymia*.

3. Emphasis added. Adam Smith, *The Theory of Moral Sentiments* (Indianapolis: Liberty Classics, 1982), pp. 50–51. I am grateful to Abram Shulsky and Charles Griswold, Jr., for this and other insights on Adam Smith. See also Albert O. Hirschman, *The Passions and the Interests* (Princeton, N.J.: Princeton University Press, 1977), pp. 107–108.

4. Rousseau would agree here with Smith that the natural needs are relatively few, and that the desire for private property arises entirely out of man's *amour-propre* or vanity, that is, his tendency to compare himself with other men. Where they differ, of course, is in their assessment of the moral acceptability of what Smith calls "bettering one's condition."

5. Alexis de Tocqueville, *The Old Regime and the French Revolution* (Garden City, N.Y.: Doubleday Anchor Books, 1955). See particularly part 3, chapters 4–6.

6. For empirical documentation of this phenomenon, see Huntington (1968), pp. 40–47.

7. Lincoln's reference to his belief in a just God, however, raises the question of whether the greatest acts of thymotic self-overcoming need to be supported by belief in God.

8. There is an economic or sociological context to the abortion issue insofar as the proponents and opponents tend to be grouped according to education, income level, whether they are urban or rural, etc., but the substance of the debate concerns rights, not economics.

9. The Romanian case is a complicated one because there is evidence that the Timisoara demonstrations were not entirely spontaneous, and that the uprising had been planned in advance by the military.

10. See, for example, "East German VIPs Now under Attack for Living High Off Party Privileges," *Wall Street Journal* (November 22, 1989), p. A6.

Chapter 17. The Rise and Fall of *Thymos*

1. Nietzsche, *Twilight of the Idols and the Antichrist* (London: Penguin Books, 1968a), p. 23.

2. See Joan Didion's short but brilliant essay on this subject, "On Self-

Respect," in Didion, *Slouching Towards Bethlehem* (New York: Dell, 1968), pp. 142–148.

3. Aristotle discusses *thymos* under the rubric of "greatness of soul" (*megalopsychia*) or magnanimity, which for him is the central human virtue. The great souled man "claims much and deserves much" with respect to honor, the greatest of all external goods, and in doing so observes a mean between vanity on the one hand (claiming much and deserving little) and smallness of soul (claiming little and deserving much). Greatness of soul subsumes all the other virtues (i.e., courage, justice, moderation, truthfulness, etc.) and requires *kalokagathia* (translated as "gentlemanliness" or "moral nobility."). The great-souled man, in other words, demands the greatest recognition for possessing the greatest virtue. It is interesting to note that according to Aristotle, the great-souled man likes to own "beautiful but useless" things, because it is better to be independent (*autarkous gar mallon*). The desire for useless things on the part of the thymotic soul arises out of the same impulse that leads it to risk its physical life. Aristotle, *Nichomachean Ethics* II 7–9; IV 3. The acceptability of the desire for recognition or honor is one of the chief differences between Greek and Christian morality.

4. According to Socrates, *thymos* is not sufficient to complete a just city; it must be complemented by the third part of the soul, reason or wisdom, in the form of the philosopher-king.

5. See for example *Republic* 375b–376b. Socrates in fact misleads Adeimantus considerably when he suggests that *thymos* is most frequently the ally of reason, rather than being reason's enemy.

6. As a reminder of the very different ethical connotations once possessed by *megalothymia*, consider the following passage from Clausewitz:

> Of all the passions that inspire man in battle, none, we have to admit, is so powerful and so constant as the longing for honor and renown. The German language unjustly tarnishes this by associating it with two ignoble meanings in the terms "greed for honor" (*Ehrgeiz*) and "hankering after glory" (*Ruhmsucht*). The abuse of these noble ambitions has certainly inflicted the most disgusting outrages on the human race; nevertheless their origins entitle them to be ranked among the most elevated in human nature. In war they act as the essential breath of life that animates the inert mass. Other emotions may be more common and more venerated—patriotism, idealism, vengeance, enthusiasm of every kind—but they are no substitute for a thirst for fame and honor.

From Carl von Clausewitz, *On War*, edited and translated by Michael Howard and Peter Paret (Princeton: Princeton University Press, 1976), p. 105. I am grateful to Alvin Bernstein for this reference.

7. The desire for glory is, of course, incompatible with the Christian virtue of humility. Albert O. Hirschman *The Passions and the Interests* (Princeton, N.J.: Princeton University Press, 1977), pp. 9–11.

8. Note particularly chapter 15 of *The Prince*. On this general interpretation of Machiavelli, "the greater Columbus," see Strauss (1953), pp. 177–179, and also Strauss's chapter on Machiavelli in Leo Strauss and Joseph Cropsey, eds.,

History of Political Philosophy, second edition (Chicago: Rand McNally, 1972), pp. 271–292.

9. See Book I, chapter 43 of the *Discourses*, entitled "Those only who combat for their own glory are good and loyal soldiers." Niccoló Machiavelli, *The Prince and the Discourses* (New York: Modern Library, 1950), pp. 226–227. See also Michael Doyle, "Liberalism and World Politics," *American Political Science Review* 80, no. 4 (December 1986): 1151–1169; and Mansfield (1989), pp. 137, 239.

10. Mansfield (1989), pp. 129, 146.

11. See Harvey C. Mansfield, Jr., "Machiavelli and the Modern Executive," in Zuckert (1988), p. 107.

12. This is the theme of Hirschman (1977), who cogently traces the deliberate downplaying of *thymos* in early modern thought.

13. The desire for recognition was also central to the thought of Jean-Jacques Rousseau, whose work constituted the first major attack on the liberalism of Hobbes and Locke. While disagreeing sharply with the vision of civil society put forward by Hobbes and Locke, Rousseau agreed with them that the desire for recognition was the fundamental cause of evil in man's social life. The term Rousseau used for the desire for recognition was "*amour-propre*," or vanity ("self-love"), which he contrasted with "*amour de soi*" (or "love of self") that he believed characterized natural man before he was corrupted by civilization. *Amour de soi* was related to the fulfilling of man's natural needs for food, rest, and sex; it was a selfish passion, but essentially harmless because Rousseau believed that man in the state of nature lived a solitary and unaggressive life. *Amour-propre*, on the other hand, arose in the course of human historical development when men first entered society and begin to compare themselves to each other. This process of comparing of one's worth with that of another was for Rousseau the fundamental source of human inequality, and of civilized man's wickedness and unhappiness; it was the source of private property and of all the social inequities that arise from it.

Rousseau's solution was not, like that of Hobbes and Locke, to banish man's willful self-esteem altogether. Following Plato, Rousseau sought to make *thymos* in a way the basis for public-spirited citizenship in a democratic and egalitarian republic. The purpose of legitimate government as described in the *Social Contract* was not to protect property rights and private economic interests, but the creation of a social analogue of natural freedom, the *volonté générale* or general will. Man re-acquired his natural freedom not, as Locke would have it, by being left alone by the state so that he could make money or acquire property, but rather by actively participating in the public life of a small and cohesive democracy. The general will, made up of the individual wills of the citizens of the republic, could be thought of as a single, giant thymotic individual who found satisfaction in his own freedom to be self-determining and self-assertive. See Jean-Jacques Rousseau *Oeuvres complètes*, vol. 3 (Paris: Gallimard, 1964), pp. 364–365; see also the discussion in Arthur Melzer, *The Natural Goodness of Man* (Chicago: University of Chicago Press, 1990), of the disunity in the soul caused by man's entry into society and his consequent dependence on other men, pp. 70–71.

14. Of course, the ethical trade did not go all that smoothly in Japan, where the aristocratic ethos was preserved in the military. Japan's burst of imperialism

that ultimately led to the Pacific War with the United States can be understood as the last gasp of the traditional thymotic class.

15. *The Federalist Papers* (New York: New American Library, 1961), p. 78.

16. *Federalist* (1961), pp. 78–79.

17. This interpretation of the *Federdalist* is presented by David Epstein in *The Political Theory of the Federalist* (Chicago: University of Chicago Press, 1984), pp. 6, 68–81, 136–141, 183–184, and 193–197. I am grateful to David Epstein for pointing out the importance of *thymos* not only in the *Federalist*, but in a variety of other political philosophers.

18. *Federalist* (1961), p. 437.

19. See the first chapter of C. S. Lewis, *The Abolition of Man, or, Reflections on education with special reference to the teaching of English in the upper forms of schools* (London: Collins, 1978), pp. 7–20.

20. From "On the Thousand and One Goals," in *Thus Spoke Zarathustra*, Book I (in *The Portable Nietzsche* (New York: Viking, 1954), pp. 170–171.

21. See also Nietzsche, *On the Genealogy of Morals*, 2:8 (New York: Vintage Books, 1967), p. 70.

Chapter 18. Lordship and Bondage

1. Kojève (1947), p. 26.

2. The "long-term" here is *very* long, measured in the thousands of years since the first appearance of master-slave social relations virtually up until the French Revolution. When Kojève (or Hegel) refers to slaves, he is not speaking narrowly of people with the legal status of chattel, but of all people whose dignity is not "recognized," including, for example, the legally free peasantry in pre-revolutionary France.

3. The following rather sketchy account of the historical process in Hegel's *Phenomenology* again follows the interpretation of Kojève, and ought again to be thought of as the work of the synthetic philosopher Hegel-Kojève. On this subject, see Roth (1988), pp. 110–115; and Smith (1989a), pp. 119–121.

4. Masters, of course, seek recognition from other masters, but in the process they seek to convert those masters into slaves in a series of subsequent prestige battles. Prior to rational, reciprocal recognition one can only be recognized by slaves.

5. Kojève argues that the fear of death is metaphysically necessary to the slave's subsequent development, not because he flees it, but because it reveals to him his essential *nothingness*, the fact that he is a being who has no permanent identity or whose identity is to negate (that is, to change the being of) over time. Kojève (1947), p. 175.

6. Kojève distinguishes the slave from the *bourgeois*, who works for himself.

7. At this point, we might note a certain convergence between Hegel and Locke on the question of work. For Locke, as for Hegel, work was the primary source of *value*: it was human labor, and not the "almost worthless materials" of nature, that was the greatest source of wealth. For Locke, as for Hegel, there was no positive natural end that was served by work. Men's natural needs were relatively few and easily satisfied; the Lockean man of property who accumulated unlimited amounts of gold and silver did not work for the sake of those

needs, but was working to satisfy a constantly changing horizon of new needs. Man's labor was in that sense creative, for it involved the endless setting of newer and more ambitious tasks. Man's creativity also extended to himself, as he invented new needs for himself. Finally, Locke like Hegel had a certain anti-natural bent insofar as he believed that human beings found satisfaction in their ability to manipulate nature and turn it to their own purposes. The doctrines of both Locke and Hegel, then, could equally well serve as justifications for capitalism, the economic world created by the progressive unfolding of modern natural science.

Locke and Hegel differed, however, on a seemingly minor but nonetheless important point. The purpose of labor, for Locke, was to satisfy desire. These desires were not fixed, they grew and changed constantly, but their constant characteristic was their demand to be satisfied. For Locke, labor was an essentially unpleasant activity undertaken for the sake of the objects of value it created. And while the specific purposes of labor could not be defined in advance on the basis of natural principles—that is, Locke's law of nature was silent on the question of whether one should work as a shoe salesman or a microchip designer—there was nonetheless a natural basis for work. Work and the unlimited accumulation of property were undertaken as a means of escaping from the terror of death. The fear of death remained a negative pole away from which all human labor sought to move. Even if a rich man had far more than his natural needs demanded, his obsessive accumulation of wealth was driven in the end by the desire to hedge against bad times and the possible return of the poverty that was his natural condition.

8. On these points, see Smith (1989a), p. 120; and Avineri (1972), pp. 88–89.

9. See Kojève in Strauss (1963), p. 183.

Chapter 19. The Universal and Homogeneous State

1. This phrase has been rendered variously as "The march of God in the world, that is what the state is," or "It is the way of God in the world, that there should be the state." From the addition to paragraph 258 of the *Philosophy of Right*.

2. Compare this to the definition of nationalism by Ernest Gellner: "Nationalism as a sentiment or as a movement, can best be defined in terms of this principle [that the political and national unit should be congruent]. Nationalist *sentiment* is the feeling of anger aroused by the violation of the principle, or the feeling of satisfaction aroused by its fulfillment. A nationalist *movement* is one actuated by a sentiment of this kind." From *Nations and Nationalism* (Ithaca, N.Y.: Cornell University Press, 1983), p. 1.

3. This point is also made by Gellner (1983), p. 7.

Chapter 20. The Coldest of All Cold Monsters

1. *The Portable Nietzsche* (New York: Viking, 1954), pp. 160–161.

2. Of course, as Kojève points out, there is a certain element of desire in the Christian's belief in an eternal life. A Christian's desire for grace may have no higher motive than his natural instinct for self-preservation. Life everlasting

is the ultimate fulfillment of the man who is driven by the fear of violent death.

3. As noted earlier, of course, a good deal of conflict ostensibly over material objects like a province or a national treasury in fact masks a struggle for recognition on the part of the conqueror.

4. These terms all come from modern social science, seeking to define the "values" that make modern liberal democracies possible. According to Daniel Lerner, for example, "It is a major hypothesis of this study that high empathic capacity is the predominant personal style only in modern society, which is distinctively industrial, urban, literate, and *participant*." (Lerner 1958, p. 50.) The term "civic culture," first used by Edward Shils, was defined as "a third culture, neither traditional nor modern but partaking of both: a pluralistic culture based on communication and persuasion, a culture of consensus and diversity, a culture that permitted change but moderated it." Gabriel A. Almond and Sidney Verba, *The Civic Culture* (Boston: Little, Brown, 1963), p. 8.

5. The centrality of the virtue of tolerance in modern America has been ably described by Allan Bloom in *The Closing of the American Mind* (New York: Simon and Schuster, 1988), particularly chapter 1. Its corresponding vice, intolerance, is today considered much more unacceptable that most of the traditional vices of ambition, lust, greed, etc.

6. See the general discussion of prerequisites for democracy that precedes each of the volumes of the Diamond-Linz-Lipset series *Democracy in Developing Countries* (Boulder, Colo.: Lynne Rienner, 1988a); specifically, the discussion in volume 4 on Latin America (1988b), pp. 2–52. See also the discussion of preconditions for democracy in Huntington (1984), pp. 198–209.

7. National unity is the only true precondition for democracy listed by Dankwart Rustow in "Transitions to Democracy," *Comparative Politics* 2 (April 1970): 337–363.

8. Samuel Huntington suggests that the large number of Catholic countries participating in the current "third wave" of democratization makes the latter in some sense a Catholic phenomenon, related to the change in Catholic consciousness in a more democratic and egalitarian direction in the 1960s. While there is clearly something to this line of argument, it would seem to beg the question of why Catholic consciousness changed when it did. Certainly, there is nothing inherent in Catholic doctrine that should predispose it toward democratic politics, or falsify the traditional argument that the authoritarian and hierarchical structure of the Catholic Church predisposed the latter to favor authoritarian politics. The prior causes of change in Catholic consciousness would seem to be (1) the general legitimacy of democratic ideas that infected Catholic thought (rather than arising out of the latter): (2) rising levels of socioeconomic development that had taken place in most Catholic countries by the 1960s; and (3) the long-term "secularization" of the Catholic Church, following in the steps of Martin Luther 400 years later. See Samuel Huntington, "Religion and the Third Wave," *The National Interest* no. 24 (Summer 1991) 29–42.

9. And even Turkey has had problems sustaining democracy since the secularization of the state. Of the thirty-six countries with Muslim majorities, Freedom House in 1984 rated twenty-one as "not free," fifteen as "partially free," and none as "free." From Huntington (1984), p. 208.

10. See the discussion of Costa Rica in Harrison (1985), pp. 48–54.

11. This argument was made most notably by Barrington Moore in *Social Origins of Dictatorship and Democracy* (Boston: Beacon Press, 1966).

12. There are numerous problems with this thesis which limit its explanatory power. For example, a number of centralizing monarchies such as that of Sweden later developed into highly stable liberal democracies. Feudalism is seen by some authors to be as much an obstacle to subsequent democratic development as its opposite, constituting the chief difference in the experiences of North and South America. See Huntington (1984), p. 203.

13. The French have, over time, engaged in many efforts to break themselves of the habit of centralism, including attempts to devolve authority in certain areas like education to locally elected bodies. This has occurred under both conservative and socialist governments in the recent past. The ultimate success of these efforts at decentralization remains to be seen.

14. A similar argument about sequencing, beginning with national identity, then moving to effective democratic institutions, and then to expanded participation, is made by Robert A. Dahl, *Polyarchy: Participation and Opposition* (New Haven: Yale University Press, 1971), p. 36. See also Eric Nordlinger, "Political Development: Time Sequences and Rates of Change," *World Politics* 20 (1968): 494–530; and Leonard Binder, et al. *Crises and Sequences in Political Development* (Princeton: Princeton University Press, 1971).

15. The breakdown of Chilean democracy in the 1970s, for example, might have been averted had Chile possessed a parliamentary system rather than a presidential one, which would have permitted the resignation of a government and the realignment of coalitions without wrecking the country's entire institutional structure. On the question of parliamentary versus presidential democracy, see Juan Linz, "The Perils of Presidentialism," *Journal of Democracy* 1, no. 1 (Winter 1990): 51–69.

16. This is the theme of Juan Linz's *The Breakdown of Democratic Regimes: Crisis, Breakdown, and Reequilibriation* (Baltimore: Johns Hopkins University Press, 1978).

17. On this general question, see again Diamond et al. (1988b), pp. 19–27. The academic study of comparative politics up through the end of World War II focused on constitutional law and legal doctrines. Under the influence of continental sociology, postwar "modernization theory" ignored law and politics and focused almost exclusively on underlying economic, cultural, and social factors in explaining the origins and success of democracy. Over the past couple of decades, there has been something of a return to the former perspective, associated with the scholarship of Juan Linz of Yale University. While not denying the importance of economic and cultural factors, Linz and his associates have properly emphasized the autonomy and dignity of politics, and put it into much better balance with the realm of the sub-political.

18. By Weber's account, Western freedom exists because the Western city was based on a self-defense organization of independent warriors, and because Western religions (Judaism and then Christianity) purged the class relations of magic and superstition. Several specifically medieval innovations, such as the guild system, are needed to explain the emergence of the free and relatively egalitarian social relations of the medieval city. See Weber's *General Economic History* (New Brunswick, N.J.: Transaction Books, 1981, pp. 315–337).

19. While it is by no means evident that durable democratic institutions will be established in the USSR as a result of the initial Gorbachevean round of reform, there are no absolute cultural obstacles to its taking root over the next generation. In terms of factors like educational levels, urbanization, economic development, and the like, the Russians actually have many advantages over Third World countries like India and Costa Rica that have democratized successfully. Indeed, the belief that a certain people cannot democratize for deep cultural reasons becomes in itself a significant obstacle to democratization. A certain Russophobia among the Russian elite itself, a deep pessimism in the ability of Soviet citizens to take control of their own lives, and a fatalism about the inevitability of strong state authority, at a certain point become self-fulfilling prophecies.

Chapter 21. The Thymotic Origins of Work

1. Quoted in Kojève (1947), p. 9.
2. See Part Two, "The Victory of the VCR," above.
3. See Thomas Sowell, *The Economics and Politics of Race: An International Perspective* (New York: Quill, 1983); and Sowell, "Three Black Histories," *Wilson Quarterly* (Winter 1979): 96–106.
4. R. V. Jones, *The Wizard War: British Scientific Intelligence, 1939–1945* (New York: Coward, McCann, and Geoghan, 1978), pp. 199, 229–230.
5. The notion that work is essentially unpleasant has deep roots in the Judeo-Christian tradition. In the story of Creation in the Hebrew Bible, work is done in the image of God who labored to create the world, but it is also a curse laid upon man as a result of his fall from Grace. The content of "life everlasting" is not said to be work, but "eternal rest." See Jaroslav Pelikan, "Commandment or Curse: The Paradox of Work in the Judeo-Christian Tradition," in Pelikan et al., *Comparative Work Ethics: Judeo-Christian, Islamic, and Eastern* (Washington, D.C.: Library of Congress, 1985), pp. 9, 19.
6. This view would also be supported by Locke, who sees labor only as a means of producing things useful for consumption.
7. A modern economist would try to explain the behavior of such an individual by using a purely formal definition of "utility," which would encompass any end actually pursued by human beings. That is to say, the modern workaholic would be said to derive a "psychic utility" from his labor, just as Weber's ascetic Protestant entrepreneur would be said to derive a "psychic utility" from his hope for eternal salvation. The fact that the desire for money, leisure, recognition, or for eternal salvation can all be lumped together under a formal rubric of utility indicates the disutility of such formal definitions in economics to explain anything truly interesting about human behavior. While saving the theory, such an all-inclusive definition of utility robs it of any real explanatory power.

It would be more sensible to part company with the conventional economic definition of "utility," and restrict its use to a more limited but commonsensical meaning: utility is anything that satisfies human desire or relieves human pain, primarily through the acquisition of property or other material possessions. Hence the ascetic who daily mortifies his flesh for a purely thymotic satisfaction could not be spoken of as a "utility maximizer."

8. Among the writers mentioned by Weber himself as having noted the relationship between Protestantism and capitalism was the Belgian writer Émile de Laveleye, who wrote a widely used textbook on economics in the 1880s, and the British critic Matthew Arnold. Others include the Russian author Nikolay Mel'gunov, John Keats, and H. T. Buckle. On precedents for Weber's thesis, see Reinhold Bendix, "The Protestant Ethic—Revisited," *Comparative Studies in Society and History* 9, no. 3 (April 1967): 266–273.

9. Many of Weber's critics pointed to the emergence of capitalism prior to the Reformation, for example in Jewish or Italian Catholic communities. Others pointed out that the Puritanism discussed by Weber was a decayed Puritanism that only emerged *after* the spread of capitalism, and which therefore could serve as capitalism's carrier but not its originator. Finally, the argument has been made that the relative performance of Protestant and Catholic communities is better explained by the obstacles to economic rationalism created by the Counterreformation, rather than any positive contribution of Protestantism.

Some of the critical literature on Weber's thesis includes: R. H. Tawney, *Religion and the Rise of Capitalism* (New York: Harcourt, Brace and World, 1962); Kemper Fullerton, "Calvinism and Capitalism," *Harvard Theological Review* 21 (1929) 163–191; Ernst Troeltsch, *The Social Teaching of the Christian Churches* (New York: Macmillan, 1950); Werner Sombart, *The Quintessence of Capitalism* (New York: Dutton, 1915); and H. H. Robertson, *Aspects of the Rise of Economic Individualism* (Cambridge: Cambridge University Press, 1933). See also the discussion of Weber in Strauss (1953), footnote 22, pp. 60–61. Strauss points out that the Reformation was preceded by a revolution in rational philosophical thought that also justified the endless accumulation of material wealth, which shared responsibility for spreading the legitimacy of capitalism.

10. See Emilio Willems, "Culture Change and the Rise of Protestantism in Brazil and Chile," in S. N. Eisenstadt, ed., *The Protestant Ethic and Modernization: A Comparative View* (New York: Basic Books, 1968), pp. 184–208; Lawrence E. Harrison's book on the impact of culture on progress, forthcoming from Basic Books in 1992; and David Martin, *Tongues of Fire: The Explosion of Protestantism in Latin America* (Oxford: Basil Blackwell, 1990). Contemporary "Liberation Theology" in Latin America is a worthy heir to the Counterreformation insofar as it has served to de-legitimize rational, unlimited capitalist accumulation.

11. Weber himself wrote books on the religions of China and India to explain why the spirit of capitalism did not arise in those cultures. This is a slightly different point from the question of why these cultures encouraged or inhibited capitalism imported from the outside. On the latter point, see David Gellner, "Max Weber, Capitalism and the Religion of India," *Sociology* 16, no. 4 (November 1982): 526–543.

12. Robert Bellah, *Tokugawa Religion* (Boston: Beacon Press, 1957), pp. 117–126.

13. Ibid., pp. 133–161.

14. *India: A Wounded Civilization* (New York: Vintage Books, 1978), pp. 187–188.

15. Apart from the spiritual torpor induced by Hinduism, Myrdal noted that the Hindu prohibition on killing cows was itself a major impediment to economic growth in a country where the population of unproductive cows was

half as large as its large human population. Gunnar Mydal, *Asian Drama: An Inquiry into the Poverty of Nations* (New York: Twentieth Century Fund, 1968), vol. 1, pp. 89–91, 95–96, 103.

16. This argument is made by Daniel Bell in *The Cultural Contradictions of Capitalism* (New York: Basic Books, 1976), p. 21. See also Michael Rose, *Reworking the Worth Ethic: Economic Values and Socio-Cultural Politics* (New York: Schocken Books, 1985), pp. 53–68.

17. See Rose (1985), p. 66; also David Cherrington, *The Work Ethic: Working Values and Values that Work* (New York: Amacom, 1980), pp. 12–15, 73.

18. Nearly 24 percent of the American work force employed full time worked 49 hours per week or more in 1989, compared with only 18 percent ten years earlier, according to the Bureau of Labor Statistics. According to a Louis Harris survey, the median number of leisure hours per week for American adults fell to 16.6 hours in 1987 from 26.2 in 1973. Statistics cited in Peter T. Kilborn, "Tales from the Digital Treadmill," *New York Times* (June 3, 1990), Section 4, pp. 1, 3. See also Leslie Berkman, "40-Hour Week Is Part Time for Those on the Fast Track," *Los Angeles Times* (March 22, 1990), part T, p. 8. I am thankful to Doyle McManus for these references.

19. On the difference between British and Japanese workers, see Rose (1985), pp. 84–85.

Chapter 22. Empires of Resentment, Empires of Deference

1. For a longer discussion of this topic, see Roderick McFarquhar, "The Post-Confucian Challenge," *Economist* (February 9, 1980): 67–72; Lucian Pye, "The New Asian Capitalism: A Political Portrait," in Peter Berger and Hsin-Huang Michael Hsiao, eds., *In Search of an East Asian Development Model* (New Brunswick, N.J.: Transaction Books, 1988), pp. 81–98; and Pye (1985), pp. 25–27, 33–34, and 325–326.

2. In Japan, the primary social relationships are not with one's contemporaries, but vertical ones between *sempai* and *kohai*, superior and inferior. This is true in the family, in a university, or in a company, where one's primary attachment is to an elder patron. See Chie Nakane, *Japanese Society* (Berkeley: University of California Press, 1970), pp. 26ff.

3. For example, Locke's first treatise on government begins with an attack on Robert Filmer, who sought to justify patriarchal political authority on the model of the family. For a discussion, see Tarcov (1984), pp. 9–22.

4. This is not accidental; Locke defends the rights of children against certain forms of parental authority in the *Second Treatise*.

5. Pye (1985, p. 72), points out that the Japanese family differed from the Chinese family by placing a stress on personal honor as well as family loyalty, thus enabling it to be more outward-looking and adaptable.

6. The family *per se* would not seem to be a particular asset to economic rationality. In Pakistan and parts of the Middle East, family ties are every bit as strong as in East Asia, and yet this frequently constitutes an obstacle to economic rationalization because it encourages nepotism and tribally based preferment. In East Asia, the family consists not just of the presently living members of the extended family, but a long line of dead ancestors who expect certain standards

of behavior from the individual. Strong families thus tend to promote a sense of internal discipline and rectitude, rather than requiring nepotism.

7. The Recruit scandal of 1989 and other scandals that brought down two LDP prime ministers in a year, as well as the LDP's loss of its majority in the Diet's upper house, are evidence of Western-style accountability in the Japanese political system. Nonetheless, the LDP managed to contain the damage successfully and retain its hegemony over the political system, without having to engage in any structural reforms either of itself or of the way Japanese politicians and bureaucrats do business.

8. The South Koreans, for example, have sought to imitate not the American Democratic or Republican parties, but the Japanese LDP in setting up their own governing party.

9. In recent years, certain Japanese management practices emphasizing group loyalty and cohesion have been exported to the United States and Britain with some success, packaged together with Japanese direct investment in plant and equipment. Whether other Asian social institutions with a greater moral content such as the family or sense of nation could be similarly exported is questionable, given their rootedness in the particular cultural experiences of the countries from which they came.

10. It is not clear whether Kojève believed that the end of history required the creation of a literally universal and homogeneous state. On the one hand, he spoke of history having ended in 1806, when the state system was obviously still intact; on the other, it is hard to conceive of a state being fully rational prior the elimination of all morally meaningful national differences. His own work on behalf of the European Community indicates that he regarded the withering away of existing national borders as an historically meaningful task.

Chapter 23. The Unreality of "Realism"

1. III 105.2. Contrast this to I 37, 40–41.

2. Thus Kenneth Waltz's book, *Theory of International Politics* (New York: Random House, 1979), pp. 65–66, contains the following passage:

> Although changes abound, continuities are as impressive, or more so, a proposition that can be illustrated in a number of ways. One who reads the apocryphal book of First Maccabees with events in and after World War I in mind will gain a sense of the continuity that characterizes international politics. Whether in the second century before Christ or in the twentieth century after, Arabs and Jews fought among themselves and over the residues of northern empire, while states outside of the arena warily watched or actively intervened. To illustrate the point more generally, one may cite the famous case of Hobbes experiencing the contemporaneity of Thucydides. Less famous, but equally striking, is the realization by Louis J. Halle of the relevance of Thucydides in the era of nuclear weapons and superpowers.

3. Reinhold Niebuhr's most succinct formulation of his views on interna-

tional relations is perhaps contained in *Moral Man in Immoral Society: A Study in Ethics and Politics* (New York: Scribner's, 1932). Morgenthau's textbook is *Politics among Nations: The Struggle for Power and Peace* (New York: Knopf, 1985), which saw six editions, the last edited by Kenneth Thompson after Morgenthau's death.

4. Waltz originally distinguishes between causes at the level of states, and causes at the level of the state system, in *Man, the State, and War* (New York: Columbia University Press, 1959).

5. Realists show their kinship with liberal internationalists by stressing the lack of a common sovereign and international law as the root of war. In fact, as we will see, lack of a common sovereign would not appear to be the critical factor in preventing war.

6. For a variation of this argument, see Thrasymachus's definition of justice as "the advantage of the stronger" in Plato's *Republic*, Book I, 338c–347a.

7. In contrast to many other early postwar realists, George Kennan did not believe that expansion was necessarily inherent to Russia, but was the product of Soviet Russia's nationalism combined with a militarized Marxism. His original strategy of containment was predicated on the eventual breakdown of a Soviet communism forced inward on itself.

8. For a version of this argument, see Samuel Huntington, "No Exit: The Errors of Endism," *The National Interest* 17 (Fall 1989): 3–11.

9. Kenneth Waltz has criticized realists like Morgenthau, Kissinger, Raymond Aron, and Stanley Hoffmann for permitting the admixture of the impurity of domestic politics into their theories of conflict, e.g., by making distinctions between "revolutionary" and "status quo" states. He, by contrast, seeks to explain international politics purely on the basis of the system's structure without any consideration whatsoever of the domestic character of its component nations. In an astonishing reversal of customary linguistic usage, he calls theories that take account of domestic politics "reductionist," in contrast to his theory, which reduces the entire complexity of world politics to the "system," of which one can know essentially one fact: whether it is bipolar or multipolar. See Waltz (1979), pp. 18–78.

10. On this point, see Waltz (1979), pp. 70–71, 161–193. In theory, a multipolar system like the classical European concert of nations should have some advantages over a bipolar one because a challenger to the system can be balanced through a quick shifting of allies; moreover, since power is more generally distributed, shifts in the balance at the margin make less of a difference. This works best in a dynastic world, however, in which states are perfectly free to make and break alliances with one another, and can physically adjust power balances by adding or subtracting provinces. In a world where nationalism and ideology constrain a state's freedom to make allies, however, multipolarity becomes a disadvantage. It is not at all clear that World War I was the result of multipolarity so much as a *decayed* multipolarity that increasingly resembled bipolarity. Germany and Austria-Hungary, for a combination of nationalistic and ideological reasons, become locked in a more or less permanent alliance, forcing the rest of Europe into a equally inflexible alliance against them. The threat to Austria's integrity represented by Serbian nationalism then pushed a delicately tipped bipolar system into war.

11. Niebuhr (1932), p. 110.

12. Henry A. Kissinger, *A World Restored: Metternich, Castlereagh and the Problems of Peace 1812–1822* (Boston: Houghton Mifflin, 1973), particularly pp. 312–332.

13. Morgenthau (1985), p. 13.

14. Ibid., pp. 1–3.

15. Niebuhr (1932), p. 233.

16. The only exception being, of course, the response to the North Korean attack in 1950, which came about only because of the Soviet Union's boycott of the UN.

17. On Kissinger's dissertation, see Peter Dickson, *Kissinger and the Meaning of History* (Cambridge: Cambridge University Press, 1978).

18. John Gaddis, "One Germany—In Both Alliances," *New York Times* (March 21, 1990), p. A27.

19. John J. Mearsheimer, "Back to the Future: Instability in Europe after the Cold War," *International Security* 15, no. 1 (Summer 1990): 5–56.

Chapter 24. The Power of the Powerless

1. Mearsheimer (1990), p. 12.

2. Waltz's attempt to purge consideration of internal politics from his theory of international relations stems from his desire to make that theory rigorous and scientific—in his terms, to keep distinct the "unit" and "structural" levels of analysis. The great intellectual edifice he constructs in his efforts to find regular and universal laws of human behavior in international politics results, in the end, in a series of banal observations about state behavior which could be summarized in the observation that "balances of power count."

3. See the response of the Athenians following the Corinthian appeal to the Lacedaemonians in Thucydides, *History of the Peloponnesian War*, I 76, where they argue the equivalence of Athens and Sparta despite the latter's support for the status quo; and their argument in the Melian dialogue, III 105. (see epigraph to chapter 23).

4. Problems arise, of course, when neighbors grow disproportionately fast, a situation that frequently gives rise to resentment. Facing such a situation, however, modern capitalist states generally do not bend their efforts to undermining their neighbor's success, but to duplicating it.

5. For a statement on the interrelationship of power and legitimacy, and a critique of simplistic notions of "power politics," see Max Weber (1946), "Politics as a Vocation," pp. 78–79; and "The Prestige and Power of the 'Great Powers,' " pp. 159–160.

6. A similar objection to the ahistorical perspective of Kenneth Waltz's realist theory, but from a Marxist perspective, is made in Robert W. Cox, "Social Forces, States, and World Orders," in Robert O. Keohane, ed., *Neorealism and Its Critics* (New York: Columbia University Press, 1986), pp. 213–216. See also George Modelski, "Is World Politics Evolutionary Learning?" *International Organization* 44, no. 1 (Winter 1990): 1–24.

7. Joseph A. Schumpeter, *Imperialism and Social Classes* (New York: Meridian Books, 1955), p. 69.

8. Ibid., p. 5.

9. Schumpeter did not make use of the concept of *thymos*, giving instead a rather functional or economic account of the limitless striving for conquest as a holdover from a time when it was a required survival skill.

10. This turned out to be true even in the Soviet Union, where casualties arising from the Afghan war proved to be much more politically salient, even under the Brezhnev regime, than outside observers were inclined to think.

11. None of these trends is contradicted by the high level of violence in contemporary American cities, or by the increasingly common portrayal of violence in popular culture. For mainstream middle-class societies in North America, Europe, and Asia, personal experience of violence or death is much lower than two or three centuries ago, if for no other reason than improvements in health care which have decreased infant mortality and raised life expectancies. The graphic portrayal of violence on film is probably a reflection of how unusual it is in the lives of the people who attend those films.

12. Tocqueville (1945), vol. 2, pp. 174–175.

13. Some of these points have been made by John Mueller in his book *Retreat from Doomsday: The Obsolescence of Major War* (New York: Basic Books, 1989). Mueller points to the disappearance of slavery and dueling as examples of long-standing social practices that have been abolished in the modern world, and suggests that major war between developed countries may be heading in the same direction. Mueller is correct to point out these changes but, as Carl Kaysen (1990) notes, they are presented as isolated phenomena taking place outside of the general context of human social evolution over the past few hundred years. The abolition of slavery and dueling have a common root in the abolition of the relationship of lordship and bondage brought about by the French Revolution, and the conversion of the master's desire for recognition into the rational recognition of the universal and homogeneous state. Dueling in the modern world is an artifact of the master's morality, demonstrating his willingness to risk his life in a bloody battle. The root cause for the secular decline of slavery, dueling, and war is the same, i.e., the advent of rational recognition.

14. Many of these general points are made by Carl Kaysen in his excellent review essay of John Mueller, "Is War Obsolete?" *International Security* 14, no. 4 (Spring 1990): 42–64.

15. See for example John Gaddis, "The Long Peace: Elements of Stability in the Postwar International System," *International Security* 10, no. 4 (Spring 1986): 99–142.

16. Of course, nuclear weapons were themselves responsible for the most serious U.S.-Soviet confrontation of the Cold war, the Cuban missile crisis, but even here the prospect of nuclear war prevented the conflict from moving to actual armed conflict.

17. See for example Dean V. Babst, "A Force for Peace," *Industrial Research* 14 (April 1972): 55–58; Ze'ev Maoz and Nasrin Abdolali, "Regime Types and International Conflict, 1816–1976," *Journal of Conflict Resolution* 33 (March 1989): 3–35; and R. J. Rummel, "Libertarianism and International Violence," *Journal of Conflict Resolution* 27 (March 1983): 27–71.

18. This conclusion depends, to some extent, on Doyle's definition of a liberal democracy. England and the United States went to war in 1812, at a time when the British Constitution had already acquired many liberal features. Doyle

avoids this problem by dating Britain's transformation into a liberal democracy from the passage of the Reform Bill of 1831. This date is somewhat arbitrary—the franchise in Britain remained limited until well into the twentieth century, and Britain certainly did not extend its liberal rights to its colonies in 1831. Nonetheless, Doyle's conclusions are both correct and striking. Doyle (1983d), pp. 205–235; and Doyle (1983b), pp. 323–353. See also his "Liberalism and World Politics," *American Political Science Review* 80, no. 4 (December 1986): 1151–1169.

19. For elucidation of changing Soviet definitions of "national interest," see Stephen Sestanovich, "Inventing the Soviet National Interest," *The National Interest* no. 20 (Summer 1990): 3–16.

20. V. Khurkin, S. Karaganov, and A. Kortunov, "The Challenge of Security: Old and New," *Kommunist* (January 1, 1988), p. 45.

21. Waltz has suggested that the internal reforms in the Soviet Union were brought about by changes in the international environment, and that *perestroika* itself should be thought of as a confirmation of realist theory. As noted earlier, it is certainly the case that external pressures and competition did much to promote reform in the Soviet Union, and realist theory might be vindicated if it were taking a step back in order to take two steps forward at a later date. But this misses entirely the fundamental changes in national objectives that have occurred in the Soviet Union, and in the basis for Soviet power, since 1985. See his comments in the *United States Institute of Peace Journal* 3, no. 2 (June 1990): pp. 6–7.

22. Mearsheimer (1990), p. 47. In a remarkable feat of reduction, Mearsheimer compresses the two hundred-year record of peace among liberal democracies to just three cases, Britain and the United States, Britain and France, and the Western democracies after 1945. Beginning with the U.S.-Canadian example, there were, needless to say, many more cases than these. See also Huntington (1989), pp. 6–7.

23. There is a minority in contemporary Germany that advocates return of former German territories now in Poland, Czechoslovakia, and the Soviet Union. This group consists largely of those expelled from those regions after World War II, or their descendants. The parliaments of the former West and East Germanies and of the new united Germany have all renounced these claims. The re-emergence of a politically significant degree of revanchism in a democratic Germany against a democratic Poland will be an important test of the thesis that liberal democracies don't fight one another. See also Mueller (1990), p. 240.

24. Schumpeter (1955), p. 65.

Chapter 25. National Interests

1. William L. Langer, "A Critique of Imperialism," in Harrison M. Wright, ed., *The New Imperialism: Analysis of Late Nineteenth-Century Expansion*, second edition (Lexington, Mass.: D. C. Heath, 1976), p. 98.

2. On this point, see Kaysen (1990), p. 52.

3. It was this rigidity and not an inherent defect in multipolarity that explains the breakdown of the nineteenth-century concert of Europe and the ultimate outbreak of World War I. Had states continued to be organized by dynastic principles of legitimacy in the nineteenth century, it would have been much easier for the concert of Europe to adjust to growing German power

through a series of alliance shifts. Indeed, without the national principle, Germany itself would never have united.

4. Many of these points are made by Ernest Gallner in *Nations and Nationalism* (Ithaca, N.Y.: Cornell University Press, 1983).

5. See, for example, John Gray, "The End of History—or of Liberalism?" *The National Review* (October 27, 1989): 33–35.

6. Gellner (1983), p. 34.

7. The Francophilism of the Russian aristocracy is perhaps an extreme case, but in virtually all countries there were pronounced dialectical differences in the language spoken by the aristocracy and by the peasantry.

8. One should be careful not to apply this kind of economic explanation for nationalism too mechanically. While nationalism can broadly be seen as an outgrowth of industrialization, nationalist ideologies can take on a life of their own, independent of the level of economic development of a country. How else can one explain nationalist movements in essentially pre-industrial countries like Cambodia or Laos after World War II?

9. Thus, for example, Ataturk spent a great deal of time toward the end of his career in historical and linguistic "researches" that in effect invented a basis for the kind of modern Turkish national consciousness that he desired.

10. Gellner (1983), pp. 44–45.

11. I am of course aware of the existence of powerful Christian Democratic parties throughout Europe, but the fact that they are democratic before they are Christian, and the secular nature of their interpretation of Christianity, is simply a measure of liberalism's triumph over religion. Intolerant, anti-democratic religion disappeared from European politics with the death of Franco.

12. This future direction in the evolution of nationalism is supported by Gellner (1983), p. 113.

13. There is of course a wing of the Russian nationalist movement that remains chauvinist and imperial, heavily represented in the high command of the former Soviet Union. As one would expect, the major old-style imperialist nationalisms are to be found in the less developed parts of Eurasia. One example is the chauvinistic Serbian nationalism of Slobodan Milosevic.

14. Mearsheimer takes note of nationalism as virtually the only aspect of internal politics he finds relevant to the prospects for peace or war. He identifies "hypernationalism" as a source of conflict, and suggests that "hypernationalism" is itself caused by the external environment or, alternatively, that it is caused by the improper teaching of national histories in schools. Mearsheimer does not seem to recognize that nationalism and "hypernationalism" do not appear randomly, but arise out of a specific historical, social, and economic context, and like all such historical phenomena are subject to internal laws of evolution. Mearsheimer (1990), pp. 20–21, 25, 55–56.

15. When Zviad Gamsakhurdia's pro-independence Round Table emerged victorious in elections in Georgia in 1991, one of the first things it did was to pick a fight with Georgia's Ossetian minority, denying that the latter had any rights to recognition as a separate national minority. This contrasted sharply with Boris Yeltsin's performance as Russian president. Yeltsin in 1990 toured the Russian republic's constituent nationalities and assured them that association with Russia would be purely voluntary.

16. It is interesting that many new national groups are seeking sovereignty despite the fact that their size and geographical position make them unviable militarily as independent entities, at least according to realist premises. This suggests that the state system is not perceived to be as threatening as it once was, and that the traditional argument for large states—national defense—is not as salient.

17. There are, of course, several important exceptions to that rule, such as the Chinese occupation of Tibet, the Israeli occupation of the West Bank and Gaza, and the Indian absorption of Goa.

18. It has been frequently noted that despite the irrationality of existing national borders in Africa which cut across tribal and ethnic lines, not a single one has been successfully changed since independence. See Yehoshafat Harkabi, "Directions of Change in the World Strategic Order: Comments on the Address by Professor Kaiser," in *The Changing Strategic Landscape: IISS Conference Papers, 1988*, Part II, Adelphi Paper No. 237 (London: International Institute for Strategic Studies, 1989), pp. 21–25.

Chapter 26. Toward a Pacific Union

1. This distinction corresponds to a large extent to the old distinction between North and South, or between the developed and underdeveloped worlds. The correspondence is not complete, however, because there are underdeveloped states like Costa Rica or India that are functioning liberal democracies, while certain developed states like Nazi Germany have been tyrannies.

2. For a description of a nonrealist foreign policy, see Stanley Kober, "*Idealpolitik*," *Foreign Policy* no. 79 (Summer, 1990): 3–24.

3. One of the chief weapons for waging the ideological struggle were organizations like Radio Free Europe, Radio Liberty, and Voice of America, which broadcast continuously into the Soviet bloc throughout the Cold War. Frequently slighted or neglected by realists who believed the Cold War was entirely a matter of tank divisions and nuclear warheads, the U.S.-sponsored radios turned out to play a major role in keeping alive the idea of democracy in Eastern Europe and the Soviet Union.

4. From the Seventh Thesis of *An Idea for a Universal History*. Kant (1963), p. 20. Kant was particularly concerned that the moral improvement of mankind could not occur until the problem of international relations had been solved, because this required "a long internal working of each political body toward the education of its citizens" (ibid., p. 21).

5. For a view that Kant himself did not regard perpetual peace as a practical project, see Kenneth Waltz, "Kant, Liberalism, and War," *American Political Science Review* 56 (June 1962): 331–340.

6. Kant defines a republican constitution as established "firstly by principles of the freedom of the members of a society (as men); secondly, by principles of dependence of all upon a single common legislation (as subjects); and, thirdly, by the law of their equality (as citizens)." From *Perpetual Peace*, in Kant (1963), p. 94.

7. Ibid., p. 98.

8. See Carl J. Friedrich, *Inevitable Peace* (Cambridge, Mass.: Harvard University Press, 1948), p. 45.

9. GATT of course does not require its members to be democracies, but has strict criteria with regard to the liberalism of their economic policies.

Chapter 27. In the Realm of Freedom

1. Kojève (1947), p. 435 (footnote).

2. On this point, see Gellner (1983), pp. 32–34, 36.

3. Kojève's use of the term "classless society" to describe postwar America, sensible as it may be in some respects, is manifestly not Marxist.

4. Tocqueville (1945), vol. 2, pp. 99–103.

5. See Milovan Djilas, *The New Class: An Analysis of the Communist System* (New York: Praeger, 1957).

6. Virtually all of those who criticized my original "End of History?" article from the Left pointed to the numerous existing economic and social problems of contemporary liberal societies, but not one of these critics was willing to advocate openly the abandonment of liberal principles in order to solve them, as Marx and Lenin had done in an earlier era. See for example Marion Dönhoff, "Am Ende aller Geschichte?" *Die Zeit* (September 22, 1989), p. 1; and André Fontaine, "Après l'histoire, l'ennui?" *Le Monde* (September 27, 1989), p. 1.

7. For those that think this is a remote prospect, consider Smith College's list of "Specific Manifestations of Oppression," which includes something called "lookism," which is "the belief that appearance is an indicator of a person's value." Quoted in the *Wall Street Journal* (November 26, 1990), p. A10.

8. On this point with regard to John Rawls's theory of justice, see Allan Bloom, "Justice: John Rawls versus the Tradition of Political Philosophy," in Bloom, *Giants and Dwarfs: Essays 1960–1960* (New York: Simon and Schuster, 1990), p. 329.

9. Tocqueville (1945), vol. 2, pp. 100–101.

Chapter 28. Men without Chests

1. Nietzsche, *The Will to Power* I:18 (New York: Vintage Books, 1968b), p. 16.

2. See Nietzsche, *On the Genealogy of Morals* 2:11, (New York: Vintage Books, 1967), pp. 73–74; 2:20, pp. 90–91; 3:18, pp. 135–136; *Beyond Good and Evil* (New York: Vintage Books, 1966), aphorisms 46, 50, 51, 199, 201, 202, 203, 229.

3. See *Beyond Good and Evil*, aphorism 260; also aphorism 260 on vanity and recognition of the "common man" in democratic societies.

4. See the discussion of recognition in Leo Strauss's reply to Kojève in Strauss, *On Tyranny* (1963), p. 222. See also his letter to Kojève of August 22, 1948, where he suggests that Hegel himself believed that wisdom and not merely recognition was necessary to satisfy man, and that therefore "the end state owes its privilege to wisdom, to the rule of wisdom, to the popularization of wisdom . . . and not to its universality and homogeneity as such." Quoted in Strauss (1991), p. 238.

5. The California Task Force to Promote Self-Esteem and Personal and Social Responsibility was the brainchild of Assemblyman John Vasconcellos, and

issued its final report in mid-1990. See "Courts, Parents Called Too Soft on Delinquents," *Los Angeles Times* (December 1, 1989), p. A3.

6. The California self-esteem task force defined self-esteem as "Appreciating my own worth and importance and having the character to be accountable for myself and to act responsibly towards others." Much rests on the second half of that definition. As one critic noted, "When the self-esteem movement takes over a school, teachers are under pressure to accept every child as is. To keep children feeling good about themselves, you must avoid all criticism and almost any challenge that could conceivably end in failure." See Beth Ann Krier, "California's Newest Export," *Los Angeles Times* (June 5, 1990), p. E1.

7. See for example *Beyond Good and Evil*, aphorisms 257, 259.

8. See Plato, *Republic*, Book VIII, 561c–d.

9. Nietzsche, *The Portable Nietzsche* (1954), p. 130.

10. Nietzsche, *The Use and Abuse of History* (1957), p. 9.

11. The way in which Nietzschean relativism became part of our general culture, and how the nihilism that once filled Nietzsche with dread is now worn with a happy face in contemporary America, has been brilliantly documented in Allan Bloom's *The Closing of the American Mind* (New York: Simon and Schuster, 1988), particularly pp. 141–240.

12. Nietzsche, *The Portable Nietzsche*, p. 232.

13. Another example is Max Weber, whose bemoaning of the "disenchantment" of the world in the face of growing bureaucratization and rationalization, and whose fear that spirituality will give way to " 'specialists without spirit and sensualists without heart' " is well known. He dismisses our contemporary civilization in the following paragraph: "After Nietzsche's devastating criticism of those 'last men' who 'invented happiness,' I may leave aside altogether the naive optimism in which science—that is, the technique of mastering life which rests upon science—has been celebrated as the way to happiness. Who believes in this?—aside from a few big children in university chairs or editorial offices." "Science as a Vocation," in *From Max Weber: Essays in Sociology* (New York: Oxford University Press, 1946), p. 143.

14. Tocqueville, (1945), vol. 2, p. 336.

15. Ibid., p. 45.

16. See Mme. Périer, "La vie de M. Pascal," in Blaise Pascal, *Pensées* (Paris: Garnier, 1964), pp. 12–13.

17. Eric Temple Bell, *Men of Mathematics* (New York: Simon & Schuster, 1937), pp. 73, 82.

18. Kojève (1947), pp. 434–435 (footnote).

19. See the chapters on international relations in Part Four above.

20. Kojève asserted that: "If Man becomes an animal again, his arts, his loves, his play must also become purely natural again. Hence it would have to be admitted that after the end of history, men would construct their edifices and works of art as birds build their nests and spiders spin their webs, would perform musical concerts after the fashion of frogs and cicadas, would play like young animals, and would indulge in love like adult beasts." Kojève (1947), p. 436 (footnote).

21. Kojève's last project was the writing of a work entitled *Essai d'une histoire raisonnée de la philosophie païenne* (Paris: Gallimard, 1968) in which he hoped to

record the entire cycle of rational human discourse. Within that circle, beginning with the pre-Socratics and ending with Hegel, all possible philosophies of the past, and any possible philosophies of the future, could be located. See Roth (1985), pp. 300–301.

22. Emphasis in original. Kojève (1947), p. 436.

23. Strauss (1963, p. 223) says "The state through which man is said to become reasonably satisfied is, then, the state in which the basis of man's humanity withers away, or in which man loses his humanity. It is the state of Nietzsche's 'last man.' "

Chapter 29. Free and Unequal

1. This point is made by Harvey Mansfield in *Taming the Prince* (1989), pp. 1–20.

2. Kojève (1947), p. 437 (footnote).

3. See John Adams Wettergreen, Jr., "Is Snobbery a Formal Value? Considering Life at the End of Modernity," *Western Political Quarterly* 26, no. 1 (March 1973): 109–129.

Chapter 30. Perfect Rights and Defective Duties

1. Tocqueville (1945), vol. 2, p. 131.

2. While Tocqueville is the most well-known proponent of associational life in modern society, Hegel makes rather similar arguments for such "mediating institutions" in the *Philosophy of Right*. Hegel as well thought that the modern state was too large and impersonal to serve as a meaningful source of identity, and therefore argued that society ought to be organized into *Stände*—classes or estates—like the peasantry, the middle class, and the bureaucracy. The "corporations" favored by Hegel were neither closed medieval guilds nor the mobilizational tools of the fascist state, but rather associations organized spontaneously by civil society that served as a focus for community and virtue. In this respect, Hegel himself is quite different from Kojève's interpretation of him. Kojève's universal and homogeneous state makes no room for "mediating" bodies like corporations or *Stände*; the very adjectives Kojève uses to describe his end state suggests a more Marxist vision of a society where there is nothing between free, equal, and atomized individuals and the state. See also Smith (1989), pp. 140–145.

3. These effects are offset to some extent by improvements in communications, which permit new kinds of associations to emerge of physically disparate people linked by common interests and objectives.

4. For a discussion of this point, see Thomas Pangle, "The Constitution's Human Vision," *The Public Interest* 86 (Winter 1987): 77–90.

5. As noted earlier, strong communities in Asia come at the expense of individual rights and tolerance: strong family life is supported by a degree of social ostracism of people who don't have children; social conformity in areas like dress, education, sexual preference, employment, and the like, is stressed rather than disdained.

The degree to which defense of individual rights and community cohesion are at cross purposes is illustrated by the case of a community in Inkster, Michigan, which sought to push back the drug trade by establishing a traffic checkpoint. The constitutionality of doing so was challenged by the ACLU on Fourth Amendment grounds, and the checkpoint had to be removed pending a review by the courts. The drug trade, which had made life in the neighborhood virtually unlivable, returned. Cited in Amitai Etzioni, "The New Rugged Communitarianism," *Washington Post*, Outlook Section, January 20, 1991, p. B1.

6. Pangle (1987), pp. 88–90.

Chapter 31. Immense Wars of the Spirit

1. Hegel in the *Philosophy of Right* states very clearly that there will still be wars at the end of history. On the other hand, Kojève suggests that the end of history will mean the end of all large disputes, and hence the elimination of the need for struggle. Why Kojève chooses to take this very un-Hegelian position is not at all clear. See Smith (1989a), p. 164.

2. Bruce Catton, *Grant Takes Command* (Boston: Little, Brown, 1968), pp. 491–492.

3. On the public mood in Europe on the eve of the Great War, see Modris Eksteins, *Rites of Spring* (Boston: Houghton Mifflin, 1989), pp. 55–64.

4. Ibid., p. 57.

5. Ibid., p. 196.

6. See *Twilight of the Idols* (1968a), pp. 56–58; *Beyond Good and Evil* (1966) p. 86; and *Thus Spoke Zarathustra* in *The Portable Nietzsche* (1954), pp. 149–151.

7. See the discussion of Nietzsche's relationship to German fascism in the introductory chapter of Werner Dannhauser, *Nietzsche's View of Socrates* (Ithaca, N.Y.: Cornell University Press, 1974).

8. See *Republic*, Book IV, 440b, 440e.

9. I am grateful to Henry Higuera for providing this formulation of the problem.

BIBLIOGRAPHY

Afanaseyev, Yury, ed. 1989. *Inogo ne dano*. Progress, Moscow.

Almond, Gabriel A., and Sidney Verba. 1963. *The Civic Culture*. Little, Brown, Boston.

Angell, Norman. 1914. *The Great Illusion: A Study of the Relation of Military Power to National Advantage*. Heinemann, London.

Apter, David. 1965. *The Politics of Modernization*. University of Chicago Press, Chicago.

Aron, Raymond. 1990. *Memoirs: Fifty Years of Political Reflection*. Holmes & Meier, New York and London.

Aslund, Anders. 1989. *Gorbachev's Struggle for Economic Reform: The Soviet Reform Process, 1985–88*. Cornell University Press, Ithaca, N.Y.

Avineri, Shlomo. 1968. *The Social and Political Thought of Karl Marx*. Cambridge University Press, Cambridge.

Avineri, Shlomo. 1972. *Hegel's Theory of the Modern State*. Cambridge University Press, Cambridge.

Azrael, Jeremy. 1987. *The Soviet Civilian Leadership and the High Command, 1976–1986*. RAND Corporation, Santa Monica, Calif.

Azrael, Jeremy. 1966. *Managerial Power and Soviet Policy*. Harvard University Press, Cambridge, Mass.

Babst, Dean V. 1972. "A Force for Peace." *Industrial Research* 14 (April): 55–58.

Baer, Werner. 1989. *The Brazilian Economy: Growth and Development*, third edition. Praeger, New York.

Baer, Werner. 1972. "Import Substitution and Industrialization in Latin America: Experiences and Interpretation." *Latin American Research Review* 7, no. 1 (Spring): 95–122.

Ball, Terence. 1976. "From Paradigms to Research Programs: Toward a Post-Kuhnian Political Science." *American Journal of Political Science* 20, no. 1 (February): 151–177.

Barros, Robert. 1986. "The Left and Democracy: Recent Debates in Latin America." *Telos* 68: 49–70.

Bell, Daniel. 1967a. "Notes on the Post-Industrial Society I." *The Public Interest* no. 6: 24–35.

Bell, Daniel. 1967b. "Notes on the Post-Industrial Society II." *The Public Interest* no. 7: 102–118.

Bell, Daniel. 1973. *The Coming of Post-Industrial Society: A Venture in Social Forecasting*. Basic Books, New York.

Bell, Daniel. 1976. *The Cultural Contradictions of Capitalism*. Basic Books, New York.

Bell, Eric Temple. 1937. *Men of Mathematics*. Simon & Schuster, New York.

Bellah, Robert N. 1957. *Tokugawa Religion*. Beacon Press, Boston.

Beloff, Max. 1990. "Two Historians, Arnold Toynbee and Lewis Namier." *Encounter* 74: 51–54.

Bendix, Reinhard. 1967. "The Protestant Ethic–Revisited." *Comparative Studies in Society and History* 9, no. 3 (April): 266–273.

Berger, Peter, and Hsin-Huang Michael Hsiao. 1988. *In Search of an East Asian Development Model*. Transaction Books, New Brunswick, N.J.

Berliner, Joseph S. 1957. *Factory and Manager in the USSR*. Harvard University Press, Cambridge, Mass.

Bill, James A., and Robert L. Hardgrave. 1973. *Comparative Politics: The Quest for a Theory*. University Press of America, Lanham, Md.

Binder, Leonard. 1986. "The Natural History of Development Theory." *Comparative Studies in Society and History* 28: 3–33.

Binder, Leonard, et al. 1971. *Crises and Sequences in Political Development*. Princeton University Press, Princeton, N.J.

Bloom, Allan. 1987. *The Closing of the American Mind: How Higher Education Has Failed Democracy and Impoverished the Souls of Today's Students*. Simon & Schuster, New York.

Bloom, Allan. 1990. *Giants and Dwarfs: Essays 1960–1990*. Simon & Schuster, New York.

Bodenheimer, Susanne J. 1970. "The Ideology of Developmentalism." *Berkeley Journal of Sociology*: 95–137.

Breslauer, George W. 1982. *Khrushchev and Brezhnev as Leaders: Building Authority in Soviet Politics*. Allen & Unwin, London.

Bryce, James. 1931. *Modern Democracies*, 2 volumes. Macmillan, New York.

Brzezinski, Zbigniew. 1970. *Between Two Ages: America's Role in the Technetronic Era*. Viking Press, New York.

Bury, J. B. 1932. *The Idea of Progress*. Macmillan, New York.

Caporaso, James. 1978. "Dependence, Dependency, and Power in the Global System: A Structural and Behavioral Analysis." *International Organization* 32: 13–43.

Cardoso, Fernando H., and Enzo Faletto. 1969. *Dependency and Development in Latin America*. University of California Press, Berkeley.

Cardoso, Fernando Henrique. 1972. "Dependent Capitalist Development in Latin America." *New Left Review* 74 (July–August).

Casanova, Jose. 1983. "Modernization and Democratization: Reflections on Spain's Transition to Democracy." *Social Research* 50: 929–973.

Catton, Bruce. 1968. *Grant Takes Command*. Little, Brown, Boston.

Cherrington, David J. 1980. *The Work Ethic: Working Values and Values that Work*. Amacom, New York.

Chilcote, Ronald. 1981. *Theories of Comparative Politics: The Search for a Paradigm*. Westview Press, Boulder, Colo.

Clausewitz, Carl von. 1976. *On War*, edited and translated by Michael Howard and Peter Paret. Princeton University Press, Princeton.

Collier, David, ed. 1979. *The New Authoritarianism in Latin America*. Princeton University Press, Princeton, N.J.

Collingwood, R. G. 1956. *The Idea of History*. Oxford University Press, New York.

Colton, Timothy. 1986. *The Dilemma of Reform in the Soviet Union*. Council on Foreign Relations, New York.

Cooper, Barry. 1984. *The End of History: An Essay on Modern Hegelianism.* University of Toronto Press, Toronto.

Coverdale, John F. 1979. *The Political Transformation of Spain after Franco.* Praeger, New York.

Craig, Gordon A. 1964. *The Politics of the Prussian Army, 1640–1945.* Oxford University Press, Oxford.

Custine, The Marquis de. 1951. *Journey for Our Time.* Pelegrini and Cudahy, New York.

Cutright, Phillips. 1963. "National Political Development: Its Measurements and Social Correlates." *American Sociology Review* 28: 253–264.

Dahl, Robert A. 1971. *Polyarchy: Participation and Opposition.* Yale University Press, New Haven, Conn.

Dahrendorf, Ralf. 1969. *Society and Democracy in Germany.* Doubleday, Garden City, N.Y.

Dannhauser, Werner J. 1974. *Nietzsche's View of Socrates.* Cornell University Press, Ithaca and London.

Davenport, T. R. H. 1987. *South Africa: A Modern History.* Macmillan South Africa, Johannesburg.

de Soto, Hernando. 1989. *The Other Path: The Invisible Revolution in the Third World.* Harper and Row, New York.

Debardleben, Joan. 1985. *The Environment and Marxism-Leninism: The Soviet and East German Experience.* Westview, Boulder, Colo.

Deyo, Frederic C., ed. 1987. *The Political Economy of the New Asian Industrialism.* Cornell University Press, Ithaca, N.Y.

Diamond, Larry, J. Linz, and S. M. Lipset, eds. 1988a. *Democracy in Developing Countries.* Lynne Rienner, Boulder, Colo.

Diamond, Larry, J. Linz, and S. M. Lipset, eds. 1988b. *Democracy in Developing Countries,* vol. 4, *Latin America.* Lynne Rienner, Boulder, Colo.

Dickson, Peter. 1978. *Kissinger and the Meaning of History.* Cambridge University Press, Cambridge.

Didion, Joan. 1968. *Slouching Towards Bethlehem.* Dell, New York.

Dirlik, Arif, and Maurice Meisner, eds. 1989. *Marxism and the Chinese Experience: Issues in Contemporary Chinese Socialism.* Westview Press, Boulder, Colo.

Djilas, Milovan. 1957. *The New Class: An Analysis of the Communist System.* Praeger, New York.

Dos Santos, Theotonio. 1980. "The Structure of Dependency." *American Economic Review* 40 (May): 231–236.

Doyle, Michael. 1983a. "Kant, Liberal Legacies, and Foreign Affairs I." *Philosophy and Public Affairs* 12 (Summer): 205–235.

Doyle, Michael. 1983b. "Kant, Liberal Legacies, and Foreign Affairs II." *Philosophy and Public Affairs* 12 (Fall): 323–353.

Doyle, Michael. 1986. "Liberalism and World Politics." *American Political Science Review* 80, no. 4 (December): 1151–1169.

Durkheim, Emile. 1964. *The Division of Labor in Society.* Free Press, New York.

Earle, Edward Meade, ed. 1948. *Makers of Modern Strategy: Military Thought from Machiavelli to Hitler.* Princeton University Press, Princeton.

Eisenstadt, S. N., ed. 1968. *The Protestant Ethic and Modernization: A Comparative View.* Basic Books, New York.

Eksteins, Modris. 1989. *Rites of Spring: The Great War and the Birth of the Modern Age*. Houghton Mifflin, Boston.

Epstein, David F. 1984. *The Political Theory of the Federalist*. University of Chicago Press, Chicago.

Evans, Peter. 1979. *Dependent Development: The Alliance of Multinational, State, and Local Capital in Brazil*. Princeton University Press, Princeton, N.J.

Fackenheim, Emile. 1970. *God's Presence in History: Jewish Affirmations and Philosophical Reflections*. New York University Press, New York.

Field, Mark G., ed. 1976. *Social Consequences of Modernization in Communist Societies*. Johns Hopkins University Press, Baltimore.

Fields, Gary S. 1984. "Employment, Income Distribution and Economic Growth in Seven Small Open Economies." *Economic Journal* 94 (March): 74–83.

Finifter, Ada. 1983. *Political Science: The State of the Discipline*. American Political Science Association, Washington, D.C.

Fishman, Robert M. 1990. "Rethinking State and Regime: Southern Europe's Transition to Democracy." *World Politics* 42, no. 3 (April): 422–440.

Frank, André Gunder. 1969. *Latin America: Underdevelopment or Revolution?* Monthly Review Press, New York.

Frank, André Gunder. 1990. "Revolution in Eastern Europe: Lessons for Democratic Social Movements (and Socialists?)." *Third World Quarterly* 12, no. 2 (April): 36–52.

Friedman, Edward. 1989. "Modernization and Democratization in Leninist States: The Case of China." *Studies in Comparative Communism* 22, nos. 2–3 (Summer–Autumn): 251–264.

Friedrich, Carl J. 1948. *Inevitable Peace*. Harvard University Press, Cambridge, Mass.

Friedrich, Carl J., and Zbigniew Brzezinski. 1965. *Totalitarian Dictatorship and Autocracy*, second edition. Harvard University Press, Cambridge, Mass.

Fukuyama, Francis. 1989. "The End of History?" *The National Interest* no. 16 (Summer): 3–18.

Fukuyama, Francis. 1989. "A Reply to My Critics." *The National Interest* no. 18 (Winter): 21–28.

Fullerton, Kemper. 1924. "Calvinism and Capitalism." *Harvard Theological Review* 21: 163–191.

Furtado, Celso. 1970. *Economic Development of Latin America: A Survey from Colonial Times to the Cuban Revolution*. Cambridge University Press, Cambridge.

Fussell, Paul. 1975. *The Great War and Modern Memory*. Oxford University Press, New York.

Gaddis, John Lewis. 1986. "The Long Peace: Elements of Stability in the Postwar International Situation." *International Security* 10, no. 4 (Spring): 99–142.

Galston, William. 1975. *Kant and the Problem of History*. University of Chicago Press, Chicago.

Gellner, David. 1982. "Max Weber: Capitalism and the Religion of India." *Sociology* 16, no. 4 (November): 526–543.

Gellner, Ernest. 1983. *Nations and Nationalism*. Cornell University Press, Ithaca, N.Y.

Gerschenkron, Alexander. 1962. *Economic Backwardness in Historical Perspective*. Harvard University Press, Cambridge, Mass.

Giliomee, Hermann, and Laurence Schlemmer. 1990. *From Apartheid to Nation-Building* (Johannesburg: Oxford University Press).

Gimbutas, Maija. 1989. *Language of the Goddess*. Harper and Row, New York.

Goldman, Marshall I. 1972. *The Spoils of Progress: Environmental Pollution in the Soviet Union*. MIT Press, Cambridge, Mass.

Goldman, Marshall I. 1987. *Gorbachev's Challenge: Economic Reform in the Age of High Technology*. Norton, New York.

Gray, John. 1989. "The End of History—Or the End of Liberalism?" *National Review* (October): 33–35.

Greenstein, Fred I., and Nelson Polsby. 1975. *Handbook of Political Science*, volume 3. Addison-Wesley, Reading, Mass.

Grew, Raymond, ed. 1978. *Crises of Political Development in Europe and the United States*. Princeton University Press, Princeton, N.J.

Hamilton, Alexander, J. Madison, and J. Jay. 1961. *The Federalist Papers*. New American Library, New York.

Harkabi, Yehoshafat. 1988. "Directions of Change in the World Strategic Order: Comments on an Address by Professor Kaiser," in *The Changing Strategic Landscape: IISS Conference Papers, 1988*, Part II, Adelphi Paper No. 237. International Institute for Strategic Studies, London.

Harrison, Lawrence E. 1985. *Underdevelopment Is a State of Mind: The Latin American Case*. Madison Books, New York.

Hartz, Louis. 1955. *The Liberal Tradition in America*. Harcourt Brace, New York.

Hauslohner, Peter. 1987. "Gorbachev's Social Contract." *Soviet Economy* 3, no. 1: 54–89.

Havel, Václav, et al. 1985. *The Power of the Powerless*. Hutchinson, London.

Hegel, Georg W. F. 1936. *Dokumente zu Hegels Entwicklung*. Stuttgart.

Hegel, Georg W. F. 1956. *The Philosophy of History*, trans. J. Sibree. Dover Publications, Inc., New York.

Hegel, Georg W. F. 1967a. *The Phenomenology of Mind*, trans. J. B. Baillie. Harper and Row, New York.

Hegel, Georg W. F. 1967b. *Hegel's Philosophy of Right*, trans. T. M. Knox. Oxford University Press, London.

Heller, Mikhail. 1988. *Cogs in the Wheel: The Formation of Soviet Man*. Knopf, New York.

Hewett, Ed A. 1988. *Reforming the Soviet Economy: Equality versus Efficiency*. Brookings Institution, Washington, D.C.

Himmelfarb, Gertrude. 1989. "Response to Fukuyama." *The National Interest* no. 16 (Summer): 24–26.

Hirst, Paul. 1989. "Endism." *London Review of Books* no. 23.

Hobbes, Thomas. 1958. *Leviathan, Parts I and II*. Bobbs-Merrill, Indianapolis.

Hoffman, Stanley. 1965. *The State of War*. Praeger, New York.

Hough, Jerry. 1977. *The Soviet Union and Social Science Theory*. Harvard University Press, Cambridge, Mass.

Hough, Jerry, with Merle Fainsod. 1979. *How the Soviet Union Is Governed*. Harvard University Press, Cambridge, Mass.

Huntington, Samuel P. 1968. *Political Order in Changing Societies*. Yale University Press, New Haven, Conn.

Huntington, Samuel P. 1984. "Will More Countries Become Democratic?" *Political Science Quarterly* 99, no. 2 (Summer): 193–218.

Huntington, Samuel P. 1989. "No Exit: The Errors of Endism." *The National Interest* no. 17 (Fall): 3–11.

Huntington, Samuel P. 1991. "Religion and the Third Wave." *The National Interest* no. 24 (Summer): 29–42.

Huntington, Samuel P., and Myron Weiner. 1987. *Understanding Political Development.* Little, Brown, Boston.

Johnson, Chalmers, ed. 1970. *Change in Communist Systems.* Stanford University Press, Stanford, Calif.

Kane-Berman, John. 1990. *South Africa's Silent Revolution.* Southern Book Publishers, Johannesburg.

Kant, Immanuel. 1963. *On History.* Bobbs-Merrill, Indianapolis.

Kassof, Allen, ed. 1968. *Prospects for Soviet Society.* Council on Foreign Relations, New York.

Kober, Stanley. 1990. *"Idealpolitik."* *Foreign Policy* no. 79 (Summer): 3–24.

Landes, David S. 1969. *The Unbound Prometheus: Technological Change and Industrial Development in Western Europe from 1750 to the Present.* Cambridge University Press, New York.

Marx, Karl. 1967. *Capital: A Critique of Political Economy,* 3 volumes, trans. S. Moore and E. Aveling. International Publishers, New York.

McAdams, A. James. 1987. "Crisis in the Soviet Empire: Three Ambiguities in Search of a Prediction." *Comparative Politics* 20, no. 1 (October): 107–118.

McFarquhar, Roderick. 1980. "The Post-Confucian Challenge." *Economist* (February 9): 67–72.

McKibben, Bill. 1989. *The End of Nature.* Random House, New York.

Mearsheimer, John J. 1990. "Back to the Future: Instability in Europe after the Cold War." *International Security* 15, no. 1 (Summer): 5–56.

Melzer, Arthur M. 1990. *The Natural Goodness of Man: On the System of Rousseau's Thought.* University of Chicago Press, Chicago.

Migranian, Andranik. 1989. "The Long Road to the European Home." *Novy Mir* no. 7 (July): 166–184.

Modelski, George. 1990. "Is World Politics Evolutionary Learning?" *International Organization* 44, no. 1 (Winter): 1–24.

Moore, Barrington, Jr. 1966. *Social Origins of Dictatorship and Democracy.* Beacon Press, Boston.

Morgenthau, Hans J., and Kenneth Thompson. 1985. *Politics Among Nations: The Struggle for Power and Peace,* sixth edition. Knopf, New York.

Mueller, John. 1989. *Retreat from Doomsday: The Obsolescence of Major War.* Basic Books, New York.

Myrdal, Gunnar. 1968. *Asian Drama. An Inquiry into the Poverty of Nations,* 3 vols. Twentieth Century Fund, New York.

Naipaul, V. S. 1978. *India: A Wounded Civilization.* Vintage Books, New York.

Naipaul, V. S. 1981. *Among the Believers.* Knopf, New York.

Nakane, Chie. 1970. *Japanese Society.* University of California Press, Berkeley, Calif.

Neubauer, Deane E. 1967. "Some Conditions of Democracy." *American Political Science Review* 61: 1002–1009.

Nichols, James, and Colin Wright, eds. 1990. *From Political Economy to Economics . . . and Back?* Institute for Contemporary Studies, San Francisco, Calif.

Niebuhr, Reinhold. 1932. *Moral Man and Immoral Society: A Study in Ethics and Politics.* Scribner's, New York.

Nietzsche, Friedrich. 1954. *The Portable Nietzsche,* ed. W. Kaufmann. Viking Press, New York.

Nietzsche, Friedrich. 1957. *The Use and Abuse of History,* trans. A. Collins. Bobbs-Merrill, Indianapolis.

Nietzsche, Friedrich. 1966. *Beyond Good and Evil. Prelude to a Philosophy of the Future,* trans. W. Kaufmann. Vintage Books, New York.

Nietzsche, Friedrich. 1967. *On the Genealogy of Morals and Ecce Homo,* trans. W. Kaufmann. Vintage Books, New York.

Nietzsche, Friedrich. 1968a. *Twilight of the Idols and The Anti-Christ,* trans. R. J. Hollingdale. Penguin Books, London.

Nietzsche, Friedrich. 1968b. *The Will to Power,* trans. W. Kaufmann and R. J. Hollingdale. Vintage Books, New York.

Nisbet, Robert. 1969. *Social Change and History.* Oxford University Press, Oxford.

Nordlinger, Eric A. 1968. "Political Development: Time Sequences and Rates of Change." *World Politics* 20: 494–530.

O'Donnell, Guillermo, Philippe Schmitter, and Laurence Whitehead, eds. 1986a. *Transitions from Authoritarian Rule: Comparative Perspectives.* Johns Hopkins University Press, Baltimore.

O'Donnell, Guillermo, Philippe Schmitter, and Laurence Whitehead, eds. 1986b. *Transitions from Authoritarian Rule: Latin America.* Johns Hopkins University Press, Baltimore.

O'Donnell, Guillermo, Philippe Schmitter, and Laurence Whitehead, eds. 1986c. *Transitions from Authoritarian Rule: Southern Europe.* Johns Hopkins University Press, Baltimore.

O'Donnell, Guillermo, and Philippe Schmitter, eds. 1986d. *Transitions from Authoritarian Rule: Tentative Conclusions About Uncertain Democracies.* Johns Hopkins University Press, Baltimore.

Pangle, Thomas. 1987. "The Constitution's Human Vision." *The Public Interest* no. 86 (Winter): 77–90.

Pangle, Thomas. 1988. *The Spirit of Modern Republicanism: The Moral Vision of the American Founding.* University of Chicago Press, Chicago.

Parsons, Talcott. 1937. *The Structure of Social Action.* McGraw-Hill, New York.

Parsons, Talcott. 1951. *The Social System.* Free Press, Glencoe, Ill.

Parsons, Talcott. 1964. "Evolutionary Universals in Society." *American Sociological Review* 29 (June): 339–357.

Parsons, Talcott. 1967. *Sociological Theory and Modern Society.* Free Press, New York.

Parsons, Talcott, and Edward Shils, eds. 1951. *Toward a General Theory of Action.* Harvard University Press, Cambridge, Mass.

Pascal, Blaise. 1964. *Pensées.* Garnier, Paris.

Pelikan, Jaroslav, J. Kitagawa, and S. Nasr. 1985. *Comparative Work Ethics: Judeo-Christian, Islamic, and Eastern.* Library of Congress, Washington, D.C.

Pinkard, Terry. 1988. *Hegel's Dialectic: The Explanation of Possibility.* Temple University Press, Philadelphia.

Plato. 1968. *The Republic of Plato,* trans. A. Bloom. Basic Books, New York.
Popper, Karl. 1950. *The Open Society and Its Enemies.* Princeton University Press, Princeton, N.J.
Porter, Michael E. 1990. *The Competitive Advantage of Nations.* Free Press, New York.
Posner, Vladimir. 1989. *Parting with Illusions.* Atlantic Monthly Press, New York.
Pridham, Geoffrey, ed. 1984. *The New Mediterranean Democracies: Regime Transition in Spain, Greece, and Portugal.* Frank Cass, London.
Pye, Lucian W. 1985. *Asian Power and Politics: The Cultural Dimensions of Authority.* Harvard University Press, Cambridge, Mass.
Pye, Lucian W. 1990a. "Political Science and the Crisis of Authoritarianism." *American Political Science Review* 84, no. 1 (March): 3–17.
Pye, Lucian W. 1990b. "Tiananmen and Chinese Political Culture: The Escalation of Confrontation." *Asian Survey* 30, no. 4 (April): 331–347.
Pye, Lucian W., ed. 1963. *Communications and Political Development.* Princeton University Press, Princeton, N.J.
Remarque, Erich Maria. 1929. *All Quiet on the Western Front.* G. P. Putnam's, London.
Revel, Jean-François. 1983. *How Democracies Perish.* Harper and Row, New York.
Revel, Jean-François. 1989. "But We Follow the Worse . . ." *The National Interest* no. 18 (Winter): 99–103.
Riesman, David, with Reuel Denney and Nathan Glazer. 1950. *The Lonely Crowd: A Study of the Changing American Character.* Yale University Press, New Haven, Conn.
Rigby, T. H., and Ferenc Feher, eds. 1982. *Political Legitimation in Communist States.* St. Martin's Press, New York.
Riley, Patrick, "Introduction to the Reading of Alexandre Kojève," *Political Theory* 9, no. 1 (1981): 5–48.
Robertson, H. H. 1933. *Aspects of the Rise of Economic Individualism.* Cambridge University Press, Cambridge.
Rose, Michael. 1985. *Re-working the Work Ethic: Economic Values and Socio-Cultural Politics.* Schocken Books, New York.
Rosenberg, Nathan, and L. E. Birdzell, Jr. 1990. "Science, Technology, and the Western Miracle." *Scientific American* 263, no. 5 (November): 42–54.
Rostow, Walt Whitman. 1960. *The Stages of Economic Growth: A Non-Communist Manifesto.* Cambridge University Press, Cambridge.
Rostow, Walt Whitman. 1990. *Theorists of Economic Growth from David Hume to the Present.* Oxford University Press, New York.
Roth, Michael S. 1985. "A Problem of Recognition: Alexandre Kojève and the End of History." *History and Theory* 24, no. 3: 293–306.
Roth, Michael S. 1988. *Knowing and History: Appropriations of Hegel in Twentieth Century France.* Cornell University Press, Ithaca, N.Y.
Rousseau, Jean-Jacques. 1964. *Oeuvres complètes.* 4 vols. Éditions Gallimard, Paris.
Rummel, R. J. 1983. "Libertarianism and International Violence." *Journal of Conflict Resolution* 27 (March): 27–71.
Russell, Bertrand. 1951. *Unpopular Essays.* Simon & Schuster, New York.
Rustow, Dankwart A. 1970. "Transitions to Democracy: Toward a Dynamic Model." *Comparative Politics* 2 (April): 337–363.

Rustow, Dankwart A. 1990. "Democracy: A Global Revolution?" *Foreign Affairs* 69, no. 4 (Fall): 75–91.

Sabel, Charles, and Michael J. Piore. 1984. *The Second Industrial Divide.* Basic Books, New York.

Schmitter, Philippe C. 1975. "Liberation by *Golpe*: Retrospective Thoughts on the Demise of Authoritarianism in Portugal." *Armed Forces and Society* 2, no. 1 (November): 5–33.

Schumpeter, Joseph A. 1950. *Capitalism, Socialism and Democracy.* Harper Brothers, New York.

Schumpeter, Joseph A. 1955. *Imperialism and Social Classes.* Meridian Books, New York.

Sestanovich, Stephen. 1985. "Anxiety and Ideology." *University of Chicago Law Review* 52, no. 2 (Spring): 3–16.

Sestanovich, Stephen. 1990. "Inventing the Soviet National Interest." *The National Interest* no. 20 (Summer): 3–16.

Skidmore, Thomas E. 1988. *The Politics of Military Rule in Brazil, 1964–1985.* Oxford University Press, New York.

Skilling, H. Gordon, and Franklyn Griffiths. 1971. *Interest Groups in Soviet Politics.* Princeton University Press, Princeton, N.J.

Skocpol, Theda. 1977. "Wallerstein's World Capitalist System: A Theoretical and Historical Critique." *American Journal of Sociology* 82 (March): 1075–1090.

Smith, Adam. 1976. *An Inquiry into the Nature and Causes of the Wealth of Nations,* 2 vols., Oxford University Press, Oxford.

Smith, Adam. 1982. *The Theory of Moral Sentiments.* Liberty Classics, Indianapolis.

Smith, Steven B. 1983. "Hegel's Views on War, the State, and International Relations." *American Political Science Review* 77, no. 3 (September): 624–632.

Smith, Steven B. 1989a. *Hegel's Critique of Liberalism: Rights in Context.* University of Chicago Press, Chicago.

Smith, Steven B. 1989b. "What is 'Right' in Hegel's Philosophy of Right?" *American Political Science Review* 83, no. 1 (March): 4–17.

Smith, Tony. 1979. "The Underdevelopment of Development Literature: The Case of Dependency Theory." *World Politics* 31, no. 2 (July): 247–285.

Sombart, Werner. 1915. *The Quintessence of Capitalism.* Dutton, New York.

Sowell, Thomas. 1983. *The Economics and Politics of Race: An International Perspective.* Quill, New York.

Sowell, Thomas. 1979. "Three Black Histories." *Wilson Quarterly* (Winter): 96–106.

Stern, Fritz. 1974. *The Politics of Cultural Despair: A Study in the Rise of German Ideology.* University of California Press, Berkeley.

Strauss, Leo. 1952. *The Political Philosophy of Hobbes: Its Basis and Genesis,* trans. E. Sinclair. University of Chicago Press, Chicago.

Strauss, Leo. 1953. *Natural Right and History.* University of Chicago Press, Chicago.

Strauss, Leo. 1958. *Thoughts on Machiavelli.* Free Press, Glencoe, Ill.

Strauss, Leo. 1963. *On Tyranny.* Cornell University Press, Ithaca, N.Y.

Strauss, Leo. 1991. *On Tyranny. Including the Strauss-Kojève Correspondence,* revised and expanded edition, ed. V. Gourevitch and M. Roth. Free Press, New York.

Strauss, Leo, and Joseph Cropsey, eds. 1972. *History of Political Philosophy*, second edition. Rand McNally, Chicago.

Sunkel, Osvaldo. 1972. "Big Business and 'Dependencia.'" *Foreign Affairs* 50 (April): 517–531.

Tarcov, Nathan. 1984. *Locke's Education for Liberty*. University of Chicago Press, Chicago.

Tawney, R. H. 1962. *Religion and the Rise of Capitalism*. Harcourt, Brace and World, New York.

Tipps, Dean C. 1973. "Modernization Theory and the Comparative Study of Societies: A Critical Perspective." *Comparative Studies in Society and History* 15 (March): 199–226.

Tocqueville, Alexis de. 1945. *Democracy in America*, 2 vols. Vintage Books, New York.

Tocqueville, Alexis de. 1955. *The Old Regime and the French Revolution*. Doubleday Anchor, New York.

Troeltsch, Ernst. 1950. *The Social Teaching of the Christian Churches*. Macmillan, New York.

Valenzuela, Samuel, and Arturo Valenzuela. 1978. "Modernization and Dependency: Alternative Perspectives in the Study of Latin American Underdevelopment." *Comparative Politics* (July): 535–557.

Veblen, Thorsten. 1942. *Imperial Germany and the Industrial Revolution*. Viking Press, New York.

Wallerstein, Immanuel. 1974. *The Modern World-System*, 3 vols. Academic Press, New York.

Waltz, Kenneth. 1959. *Man, the State, and War: A Theoretical Analysis*. Columbia University Press, New York.

Waltz, Kenneth. 1962. "Kant, Liberalism, and War." *American Political Science Review* 56 (June): 331–340.

Waltz, Kenneth. 1979. *Theory of International Politics*. Random House, New York.

Ward, Robert, and Dankwart Rustow, eds. 1964. *Political Development in Japan and Turkey*. Princeton University Press, Princeton, N.J.

Weber, Max. 1930. *The Protestant Ethic and the Spirit of Capitalism*. Allen & Unwin, London. First published 1904–1905.

Weber, Max. 1946. *From Max Weber: Essays in Sociology*. Oxford University Press, New York.

Weber, Max. 1947. *Max Weber: The Theory of Social and Economic Organization*, ed. Talcott Parsons. Oxford University Press, New York.

Weber, Max. 1981. *General Economic History*. Transaction Books, New Brunswick, N.J.

Wettergreen, John Adams, Jr. 1973. "Is Snobbery a Formal Value? Considering Life at the End of Modernity." *Western Political Quarterly* 26, no. 1 (March): 109–129.

Wiarda, Howard. 1973. "Toward a Framework for the Study of Political Change in the Iberio-Latin Tradition." *World Politics* 25 (January): 106–135.

Wiarda, Howard. 1981. "The Ethnocentrism of the Social Science [*sic*]: Implications for Research and Policy." *Review of Politics* 43, no. 2 (April): 163–197.

Wiles, Peter. 1962. *The Political Economy of Communism*. Harvard University Press, Cambridge, Mass.

Williams, Allan, ed. 1984. *Southern Europe Transformed: Political and Economic Change in Greece, Italy, Spain, and Portugal.* Harper and Row, New York.

Wilson, Ian, and You Ji. 1990. "Leadership by 'Lines': China's Unresolved Succession." *Problems of Communism* 39, no. 1 (January–February): 28–44.

Wray, Harry, and Hilary Conroy, eds. 1983. *Japan Examined: Perspectives on Modern Japanese History.* University of Hawaii Press, Honolulu, Hawaii.

Wright, Harrison M., ed. 1961. *The "New Imperialism": Analysis of Late Nineteenth Century Expansion,* second edition. D. C. Heath, Boston.

Zolberg, Aristide. 1981. "Origins of the Modern World System: A Missing Link." *World Politics* 33 (January): 253–281.

Zuckert, Catherine H. 1988. *Understanding the Political Spirit: Philosophical Investigations from Socrates to Nietzsche.* Yale University Press, New Haven, Conn.

INDEX